D0398794

Enemies

The Culture of Conspiracy in

Within

Modern America

ROBERT ALAN GOLDBERG

YALE UNIVERSITY PRESS

NEW HAVEN & LONDON

Designed by James Johnson and set in Swift Roman, Gill Sans,
and Crackhouse types by Achorn Graphic Services, Inc.
Printed in the United States of America by R. R. Donnelley & Sons.

Library of Congress Cataloging-in-Publication Data

Goldberg, Robert Alan, 1949–
Enemies within : the culture of conspiracy in modern America / Robert A. Goldberg
p. cm.
Includes bibliographical references and index.
ISBN 0-300-09000-5 (cloth : alk. paper)

1. Conspiracies—United States—History. 2. United States—Social conditions.
3. United States—Politics and government.   I. Title.
HV6285 .G65 2001
973—dc21
200100008

A catalogue record for this book is available from the British Library.

The paper in this book meets the guidelines for permanence and durability
of the Committee on Production Guidelines for Book Longevity
of the Council on Library Resources.

1   2   3   4   5   6   7   8   9   10

For Annie

Contents

Preface

An examination of history reveals a persistent thread of
convenient tragedy linked to the turning points of the
fates of nations. And, in the smoke of the funeral pyre,
not all the faces are crying.
OLIVER STONE

—Humpty Dumpty Was Pushed
BUMPER STICKER, 1980s

We live, writes *Newsweek* columnist Jonathan Alter, in an "age of
conspiracism."[1] Other observers of the American scene, like Michael
Kelly, William Safire, and Garry Wills, have similarly recognized
that conspiratorial themes permeate mainstream thinking and
color the discourse on current events. The script has become familiar: Individuals and groups, acting in secret, move and shape recent
American history. Driven by a lust for power and wealth, they practice deceit, subterfuge, and even assassination, sometimes brazenly
executed. Nothing is random or the matter of coincidence. Institutional process, miscalculation, and chance bend to the conspirators'
single-minded will. The cry of conspiracy is not easily silenced. Not
only is conspiracy thinking dramatic and rigorously integrated, but
it finds occasional grounding in historical evidence.[2]

There is a hunger for conspiracy news in the United States. Fifteen monthly magazines, more than two dozen newsletters, six publishing houses, and hundreds of internet websites inform the initiated and net novices in the workings of the diverse hidden hands
of subversion and cover-up. The tabloid *Weekly World News,* available
at the supermarket check-out counter, repeatedly conjures up stories about the Kennedy assassination, the government capture of
alien spacecraft, and the evolving plot of the Antichrist. Mishaps are
no longer accidents, and websites quickly disseminate conspiracy

beliefs about such events as the crashes of TWA Flight 800 and Princess Diana's automobile. Left joins right in sounding the alarm against the Council on Foreign Relations and the Trilateral Commission and other carriers of the New World Order. Paralleling these suspicions are survey results that indicate that more than three-quarters of Americans have concluded that President John Kennedy was the victim of a conspiracy. In fact, more Americans are certain that extraterrestrials have visited Earth than believe that "feminist" is a compliment. How many conspiratorial layers can you peel away from recent U.S. history? Marilyn Monroe, Malcolm X, Martin Luther King, Vietnam POWs, Karen Silkwood, and even the "man shortage" of the 1980s have become conspiratorial puzzle pieces. The grassy knoll, the New World Order, Area 51, and Roswell are conspiracy's shorthand terms now incorporated into the national lexicon. They are no longer litmus tests of paranoia but the symbols of enlightened skepticism.[3]

Our age flows in continuity with the past. These recent examples are part of a long and central tradition in our nation's history. For generations, Americans have entertained visions of vast conspiracies that target their religion, race, and nation. Salem witches, British ministers, Catholic priests, slaveholders, Wall Street bankers, Jews, Bolsheviks, and black militants, all in their turn and among many other suspects, have been cast in the plotter's role. The enemy appears chameleon-like, pervasive, and opportunistic. The legal definition of conspiracy, which is straightforward if not rigorous, is conducive to such diverse perceptions of plots and plotters. The crime of conspiracy requires "an agreement between two or more persons" that results in "either an unlawful act or a lawful act by unlawful means."[4] Those within the anticonspiracy core, activists and entrepreneurs who spin theories that are strenuously logical and crammed with facts, find foundation here and then move to a more expansive view of crimes and misdemeanors. Secret dealings of all sorts are within their range, from presidential murder to threats against American institutions to the cover-up of classified information. Intensity of belief and knowledge of plot details are greatest in this core. With increasing emotional and intellectual distance from the nucleus, suspiciousness lessens along with commitment to the specifics of the plot. At the periphery, where the subculture joins the mainstream, receptivity and only a vague, seamless account of conspiracy remains. The meaning of conspiracy has now slipped its legal moorings and lost even the little precision it once had. Thus conspiracy thinking is not only a tight belief system but a habit, a perception, a posture.

While conspiracy imaging may be mainstream and flourish in a climate of tolerance, scholarly analysis has principally emphasized psychological explanations rather than historical and social context. Thus the activities of authorities, perceptions fostered by the media, and political and technological change factor little into an equation that spotlights the mental health of the counterconspiracy entrepreneur. The catalyst for this conceptual framework was a brief essay written in 1964 by historian Richard Hofstadter, "The Paranoid Style in American Politics." Hofstadter's highly influential essay fixed scholarly attention for a generation, and in the hands of journalists helped fashion popular stereotypes of the conspiracy theorist. Focusing on the "distorted style" of "heated exaggeration, suspiciousness, and conspiratorial fantasy," Hofstadter donned the white coat of a clinician.[5] Conspiracy theorists were marginal men and women whose personality disorders caused them to project their problems, status grievances, and wounds into public affairs. In creating demons, forsaking compromise, and portraying their struggle in apocalyptic terms, they ignored the real issues of wealth and power in a doomed quest for a cure. Paranoia became contagious in times of stress and anxiety occasioned by war, rapid growth, or economic depression. Visions of the counterconspiracy communities would infect large numbers of alienated and frightened Americans bewildered by change. Once the crisis had passed, the fever would break and conspiracy thinking would revert to the extremist fringes.[6]

Richard Hofstadter's influence is still apparent at the start of the twenty-first century. Daniel Pipes recently observed in his book *Conspiracy: How the Paranoid Style Flourishes and Where It Comes From,* that while "political paranoids need not suffer from personal paranoia . . . often the two go together." It was the "dregs" and "nuts," he argued, who fashioned a discourse that was a "form of pornography."[7] Working with the descriptions of paranoid personality disorder found in the *Diagnostic and Statistical Manual of Mental Disorders,*

Robert Robins and Jerold Post similarly maintained that conspiracy thinkers are "frustrated, angry individuals" with "fragile self-esteem" who have "lost their moorings." In counterconspiracy they find "an antidote for the poisonous feeling of powerlessness."[8] If flaws are internal and personal, a study of conspiracy thinking offers a means to defend, rather than examine the status quo. This sheds little light on the society that creates and nurtures countersubversives.

My book builds on the work of such scholars as Paul Boyer, Mark Fenster, Steven Goldzwig, Leo Ribuffo, Michael Rogin, and Gordon Wood. Rather than reducing public fears to the sum of individual disorders, I seek to consider conspiracy imaging in its historical, social, and political environment. My attention is less on the mental maladies of the countersubversives than on their rhetorical strategies, their business acumen, and the interplay within conspiracy-minded communities. The conspiracy theorist does not operate in a vacuum. Actors outside countersubversive subcultures are critical to the success or failure of conspiracy explanations. What roles do the media play in mainstreaming conspiracy imaging? How do the targets of conspiracy thinkers affect the plausibility of the plot? My focus will be on the United States in the decades since World War II. This period departs from the past in the regularity of the drumbeat, the multiplicity of messages and carriers, the number of believers, and the depth of immersion of popular culture in conspiracy thinking. A plethora of cases are available for close analysis. For reasons of centrality, popularity, viability over time, range, and accessibility and variety of sources I have chosen five: the "master" conspiracy (the Communist fifth column to the New World Order), the rise of the Antichrist, the assassination of President John Kennedy, the plot against black America, and the Roswell incident. Although I will consider them separately, their scenarios entwine, making them mutually reinforcing. Those who believe wage a struggle not simply for symbolic gain. This is a contest for authority and a struggle for legitimacy. The stakes are high. Control of past and present delivers the future.

In the course of researching and writing, an author encounters a spectrum of reactions, ranging from indifference to robust enthusiasm. So it has been with this book, with the response predominantly supportive. At times, after being asked my topic, I would see the questioner's eyes glaze over and the smile freeze. I could read the thoughts: another conspiracy nut expounding his pet theory. The author had become the subject. Far more representative were those who urged me to tell them the "truth." Who really shot JFK? What did the Air Force cover up at Roswell? Often, listeners volunteered puzzle pieces—a personal experience about seeing a UFO or a friend's report on happenings in the New World Order. The average American's awareness of conspiracy theories did not surprise me. The extent of skepticism about official explanations did.

The heavier the debts accumulated, the richer is the writer's reward. From the first this project has been dependent upon others for support, critique, and encouragement. The Research Committee, the College of Humanities, and the Undergraduate Research Opportunities Program of the University of Utah have been generous in granting funds and time away from teaching. The Interlibrary Loan department at the Marriott Library under the direction of Linda Burns was indispensable to my research. Other helpful hands and hearts were offered by Lindsay Adams, Peggy Adams Alexander, Ben Alivio, Susan Anderson, Megan Armstrong, Carrie Baird, Jim Baughman, Debby Berdan, Johna Burke, Lara Deisley, Linda Dubrow, Kirse Granat-May, Tom Harvey, Andrew Hunt, Ray and Leslie Johnson, Janet Kaufman, Greg Kite, Scott Kramer, Rachel Larson, Isabel Moreira, Lonnie Norton, Rafi Schwartz, Dwayne and Jody Shrontz, Darla Staley, and Fred and Irene Tannenbaum. Elisa Della Piana was the perfect research assistant. She not only worked long hours without complaint but helped mold the research process. Brent Herridge of Herridge and Associates did an excellent job reproducing the book's illustrations. Few editors are as supportive as Chuck Grench and Larisa Heimert. Beyond the campus, Rocky, Mike, and Gabe at Chuck's Chevron; Steve, Leslie, Tammie, Denise, Sherie, and Jared at the Dodo Restaurant; and the old warriors who play at John and Craig Bennett's Squashworks kept up spirits while bringing me down to earth.

Reading all or part of the manuscript and thus saving me from error and embarrassment were colleagues Jim Clayton, Ron Coleman, Ann Darling, Ray Gunn, Jim Keener, and Dick Tompson. A special thanks goes to an inner circle of critical but loving friends. The brothers Mack, David and Michael, were the utility infielders of conspiracy research. David found a calling by rummaging through bins of discards in secondhand stores for relevant research materials. Michael traveled with me to Roswell for the 1997 encounter, demanding that we rent a red convertible both to make a statement and to enhance the ambience. Jeff Walker made an excellent sounding board, eager to believe the best and the worst about everyone. Paul Allen diligently reviewed the manuscript, repeatedly complaining that the genius of conspiracism had eluded me. Dean May, who has read every word I have ever published, again demonstrated his uncanny ability to render high praise while delivering insightful criticism that shook me to my core. Chris Lino, so acutely aware of my sensitivities, ignored them all to insist that his ideas guide the book. His partner Colleen Lindstrom has my undying gratitude for gentling him down and making him the mensch that he is. All authors should have Mike Zuhl as a friend and first reader. His enthusiasm ensured the completion of this work.

Family is my foundation. My father, brothers, and sister gave their love and support unconditionally. My sons are the lights of my life and their imprint is evident throughout this work. Discussions with David, who rejects the logic of all conspiracy theories, forced me to tighten my argument and mine the primary materials more intensively. Josh, who accepts all claims of government deception and championed conspiracism in every instance, offered the counterargument frequently and with little solicitation. Stephen and Peter, with their secret machinations and carefully drawn plots, provided practical experience in the conspiracy art.

This book is dedicated to Annie. She deserves it. Watching hundreds of films and television shows, reading countless manuscript drafts, and absorbing endless hours of soul searching, she has helped shape every part of this project. Her love, as well, has shaped me.

An American Tradition

> . . . a series of oppressions, begun at a distinguished period and pursued unalterably through every change of ministers, too plainly prove a deliberate and systematic plan of reducing us to slavery.
> —THOMAS JEFFERSON

> And it shall come in a day when the blood of saints shall cry unto the Lord, because of secret combinations and the works of darkness.
> —MORMON 8:27, Book of Mormon

> To assume that the [Japanese] enemy has not planned fifth column activities for us in a wave of sabotage is simply to live in a fool's paradise.
> —EARL WARREN, 1942

Conspiracy thinking is not American born. The Latin word *conspirare*—to breathe together—suggests both drama and a deeply rooted past. The fear of conspiracy was a prominent feature on the mental maps of the first English settlers in the New World. Early colonists suspected both neighbors and strangers of secret alliances and dangerous plots. Subsequent waves of immigrants not only invigorated traditional beliefs but expanded the pool of potential conspirators. Well into the twentieth century, Europeans would cue their American kin about the means and ends of conspiracy and its perpetrators.

Yet conspiracy imaging has also adapted and developed traits reflective of the American environment. It drew life from a sense of mission that convinced Americans of their special role in history. The Reverend Jonathan Edwards explained: "When God is about to turn the earth into a paradise, he does not begin his work where there is some growth already, but in the wilderness." President Woodrow Wilson was similarly mindful of the holy mandate. Presenting his League of Nations treaty to the Senate in 1919, he announced: "The stage is set, the destiny disclosed. It has come about by no plan of our conceiving, but by the hand of God who led us into this way. We cannot turn back. We can only go forward, with lifted eyes and freshened spirit, to follow the vision."[1] God's people, particularly Protestants, had to be on guard to realize their calling. Revolutionary success would raise aspirations of America's purpose. It would also awaken new conspirators eager to undermine the workings of the republic at home and abroad. American diversity contributed energy to the national dynamic. At the same time, it deepened suspicions of unfamiliar identities and gnawed at the sense of internal security. Resonating with core values and fueled by ethnic, racial, and religious differences, conspiracy thinking became an American tradition.

When Puritans disembarked from the *Arbella* in 1630, they knew that the Massachusetts colony would soon be a battleground. Their errand into the wilderness was to raise a Bible commonwealth devoted to God's commandments. "The God of Israel is among us," Governor John Winthrop announced, and "we shall be as a city upon a hill," offering the model of holiness that would surely regenerate the world.[2] The Puritans were just as certain that the enemies of the Lord were close at hand. Indian peoples, whether Pequots, Narragansetts, or Wampanoags, became actors in the supernatural drama, the minions of Satan who would wage savage war against the visible saints. Battling for the Lord against the Satanic conspiracy justified cruelty, and atrocities were common. Even the converted "praying" Indians could expect little quarter. Contested spaces and tribal names changed, but the cry of conspiracy, real and imagined, remained constant and echoed throughout the history of the westward movement.[3]

If Indian peoples stood outside the walls, Satan also counted allies within. During the seventeenth century, New Englanders repeatedly heard and believed the accusation of witchcraft, a reminder of the importance of their holy work. Magistrates presided over more than 240 cases, reviewing evidence that the Devil was "loose" in Massachusetts. He had, the Boston minister Cotton Mather reported after consulting the Book of Revelation, "decoyed a fearful knot of proud, forward, ignorant, envious, and malicious creatures, to list themselves in his service." In making their "Diabolical Compact" with Satan, members of the "witch gang" were granted supernatural powers to torment God's anointed and agitate their communities. Now they gathered at "prodigious *witch meetings,*" to "concert and consult" about "the methods of rooting out the Christian religion from the country."[4] In all, Puritan courts condemned thirty-six women and men to death. Those who confessed to escape the gallows only fueled the fire of conspiracy thinking.[5]

Events in Salem village in 1691 and 1692 accounted for most of the victims. Over a period of ten months, forty-eight young girls denounced mainly isolated, middle-aged women of low social and economic status for "entertaining" Satan and attempting to lure them into a conspiracy. Proof of the plot was abundant. Repeatedly, townspeople witnessed the torment of the accusers, who shrieked and writhed, tortured by invisible hands. Salem minister Samuel Parris drew the line sharply: "Here are but two parties in the world: the Lamb and his followers, and the dragon and his followers. . . . Here are no neuters. Everyone is on one side or the other."[6] Of the approximately two hundred women and men charged in Salem, twenty were executed. This was a small number, Cotton Mather declared, for "It is not *one Devil* alone, that has Cunning or Power enough to apply the Multitudes of *Temptations,* whereby Mankind is daily diverted from the Service of God; No, the *High Places* of our Air, are Swarming full of those *Wicked Spirits.*"[7]

Historians have mined the records for generations and have broached diverse scenarios to explain the happenings in Salem: personal animosities, local conflicts, population pressures on exhausted land, and the imperial challenge to the Puritan theocracy. Against this backdrop, they naturally mount a defense of the innocent and carefully note the counterconspiracy—the collusion among the accusers, who were abetted by politically ambitious officials and clergy eager to defend their authority. The playwright Arthur Miller, tuned to the conspiratorial atmosphere of Salem, made it a metaphor for his own times, the witch hunt of the 1950s known as McCarthyism. There were, Miller wrote of Salem, "wheels within wheels in this village, and fires within fires!"[8]

Witches troubled Americans less in the eighteenth century. New foes were not long in appearing. The citizens of New York City found that the enemy within the gate was a Trojan horse of their own making. In 1712 slaves rose in a "bloody conspiracy" to avenge "some hard usage" at the hands of their masters. Bound by a blood oath and armed with guns, knives, and hatchets, they set a fire to lure their white masters into a killing field. For the nine whites who died, twenty-one blacks were condemned to death: "Some were burnt," wrote Governor Robert Hunter, "others hanged, one broke on the wheel, and one hung alive in chains."[9] Events three decades later reflect the dance between the real and the imagined. In 1741, the rumor of black conspiracy was sufficient cause to hang proactively eighteen blacks and burn another eleven at the stake. The fear of slave conspiracies fired white imaginations for more than a century, with actual plots swelling the power of countersubversives.[10]

The chant of conspiracy offered the Revolutionary generation both explanation and a spur to action. Why had the British violated the peace that so long had characterized imperial-colonial relations? What design could be divined from the diverse parliamentary measures and taxes passed in the 1760s and 1770s? American newspaper editors, politicians, and clergymen searching for a rationale quickly rejected as groundless the Empire's avowed defense needs and requirements of administrative efficiency. More consistent with experience, they discerned a diabolical and willful pattern to events. In this, the colonists had learned their lessons well from England's opposition leaders and a recent history scarred with Jacobite uprisings and French conspiracies. Liberty was in danger. Corrupt government ministers, arrogant in their power, were plotting to destroy the rights of Englishmen and women. Thomas Jefferson spoke for many: "A series of oppressions, begun at a distinguished period and pursued unalterably through every change of ministers, too plainly prove a deliberate and systematic plan of reducing us to slavery." When combined with the sense of American exceptionalism and traditional distrust of government, the image of conspiracy became vivid. In linking events, conspiracy thinking accelerated the rush to revolution.[11]

The articulate shared their vision of conspiracy, and a broad co-lonial consensus organized against the threat. In 1765 widespread resistance confronted the collectors of the Stamp Tax, and a boycott of British goods pressured repeal. Jonathan Mayhew warned fellow Americans not to relax their guard against "evil-minded individuals . . . who spared no wicked arts, no deceitful, no dishonorable, no dishonest means. . . . Power aims at extending itself, and operating according to mere *will*. . . . While men *sleep, then the enemy cometh and soweth tares*."[12] Committees of correspondence circulated a con-spiracy interpretation that made the writs of assistance, a standing army, restrictions on trade, and taxes into shackles of slavery forged to weaken the will and ability to resist tyranny. Declared the Boston town meeting in 1770, "many recent events . . . afford great reason to believe that a deep-laid and desperate plan of imperial despotism has been laid, and partially executed, for the extinction of all civil liberty."[13] When Protestants perceived a link between legislation granting Canadian Catholics religious toleration and the Coercive Acts that punished Boston for its Tea Party and restricted the power of town meetings throughout Massachusetts, the mask was off the conspiracy. The pope stood behind the English throne. The revolu-tionary cause had become holy, a crusade against not only tyranny but papal power.[14]

Still, Americans would cross the last bridge to independence only when they convinced themselves that their king was not only aware of the plot but a coconspirator. In sealing the connection, Thomas Jefferson enshrined conspiracy in the Declaration of Inde-pendence, proclaiming the people's right to revolution "when a long train of abuses and usurpations, pursuing invariably the same object, evinces a design to reduce them under absolute despotism." Americans more steeped in the biblical Book of Revelation would go farther, identifying King George III as the Antichrist. They had discovered that the numerical conversion of the Hebrew and Greek translations of "royal supremacy in Great Britain" totaled 666. Across the Atlantic Ocean, British ministers similarly talked con-spiracy to explain the changing fortunes of empire. Even the king was convinced that he had been the victim of a "desperate con-spiracy."[15]

Conspiracy thinking did not abate when the British threat was turned aside. In the 1780s and 1790s, a struggle for control of the new republic played out in conspiratorial charge and counter-charge. Political activists who curried favor by imagining their op-ponents as aristocratic counterrevolutionaries were tarred in reply as demagogic proponents of "mobocracy." Shays's Rebellion, the conflict over the ratification of the Constitution, and the Whiskey Rebellion provided abundant grist for countersubversives in an age flush with conspiracy explanations.[16]

Nor was America immune to new foreign contagions. Particu-larly insidious to New England Federalists was the Order of the Illu-minati, a secret society of freethinkers that preached resistance to state authority and vowed to destroy ecclesiastical power.[17] Birthed in Bavaria in 1776 by professor of law Adam Weishaupt, the Illumi-nati was said to have penetrated France by means of the secret Free-mason fraternal order and then to have engineered the Revolution. The Order sighted the United States as the next target. The Reverend Jedediah Morse was among the first to sound the alarm, warning that "the world was in the grip of a secret revolutionary conspir-acy."[18] In words that were echoed during the Red Scare of the 1950s, Morse convinced listeners: "I now have in my possession complete and indubitable proof . . . an official, authenticated list of the names, ages, places of nativity, [and] professions of the officers and members of a society of *Illuminati*."[19]

Congress acted in the wake of the Illuminati scare and amid concerns that French intrigues in national politics had, in President John Adams's words, placed America "in a hazardous and afflictive position."[20] In summer 1798 it passed the Alien Act, which autho-rized the president to arrest and expel foreign nationals involved "in any treasonable or secret machinations against the govern-ment." The Sedition Act followed, limiting the freedoms of speech and press and setting fines and terms of imprisonment for those who "unlawfully combine or conspire together with intent to op-pose any measure or measures of the government."[21] The threat did not match the response; the new republic proved less fragile than its creators assumed. Somewhat more substantive was the abortive plot of Vice President Aaron Burr to split the western territories from the United States. This scheme, too, hardly broke the surface of American history.[22]

Concerns about the Freemasons reappeared in the 1820s. In the "age of the common man," a rapidly growing, exclusive, secret society ran counter to a prevailing ideology that rejected privilege and pretensions of superior status. The republic must be saved, proclaimed the Vermont anti-Mason Edward Barber, from a "haughty aristocracy," a "monster" that has sunk its "fangs into the bosom of the Constitution."[23] Suspicion ignited activism in 1826 when a New York Mason who threatened to expose the secrets of his order was kidnaped and murdered. Authorities were unable to solve the crime, sparking rumors that fraternal discipline had held them in check and allowed the guilty to escape justice. This touched off a mass movement that spread to New England and the Midwest and launched a third party, the first in U.S. history. The future was in the balance. Freemasonry, General William Wadsworth revealed, was the master plot: "Every religion and conspiracy which had agitated Europe for the last fifty years may be distinctly traced [to it], and the secret workings of this all pervading order can be clearly seen."[24] The Reverend Nathaniel Emmons of Massachusetts concurred: it was the "darkest and deepest plot that ever was formed in this wicked world against the true God, the true religion, and the temporal and eternal interests of mankind." Among the prominent Americans supporting the anti-Masonic movement were John Quincy Adams, William Lloyd Garrison, and Thurlow Weed.[25]

Concurrent with the anti-Masonic furor, Americans added Mormons to the company of plotters. Missouri Governor Lilburn Boggs was blunt: "The Mormons must be treated as enemies, and must be exterminated . . . if necessary, for the public peace."[26] The Church of Jesus Christ of Latter-day Saints was one of several American-born sects that emerged from a region of New York burned over by repeating waves of religious enthusiasm. It was not the preaching of communitarianism and end-times prophecy that differentiated Mormons in American eyes nor their claim as the one true church. Rather, it was the vengeance of Mormon enterprise in building their city of God. Americans imagined Mormons as soldiers who moved in lockstep to the command of their prophet Joseph Smith. Converts to Mormonism seemed to have escaped from freedom, obeying orders to vote as a bloc and pooling financial resources for the church's good. The prophet's revival of the practice of polygamy affronted moral sensibilities and made the situation more urgent. A broad coalition of religious, political, and economic opponents forced the saints to flee New York, Ohio, Missouri, and Illinois, with haven finally found in Utah. Fear of the "Mormon Power" and its "ecclesiastical despotism" was not quieted for decades and could still be felt at the end of the nineteenth century.[27] Perhaps a reflection of the true Americanism of the church, the index of the Book of Mormon contains one-half page of citations for "secret combinations," with appended supplementary references.[28]

Even more appalling to Protestant Americans was the papist plot that flared in the decades before the Civil War. The "tyrant of the Tiber" had for centuries proven a tenacious adversary. Now he renewed the assault, and "the cloven foot of this subtle foreign heresy," warned Samuel F. B. Morse, inventor of the telegraph and son of the Reverend Jedediah Morse, was pressing upon the neck of Protestant America.[29] Nativists accused Catholics of placing their allegiance to the pope above their loyalty to the United States. Catholics, enslaved by the secrets they had disclosed in the confessional, were herded to the polls and voted as commanded. Once the Catholic hierarchy had control of government, it would end the separation of church and state, ban the Bible, and destroy the freedoms of press, speech, and religion. The Irish immigration was an essential component of the papal conspiracy. Here were the foot soldiers of the pope's crusade, ready to bully Protestants into submission while voting Catholics to power. The sins of the Catholic Church were not merely political. "Its whole energy," insisted Presbyterian minister Lyman Beecher, "has been put forth to corrupt the principles and debauch the morals of mankind; . . . it has been the great teacher of fraud, perfidy, perjury, and murder; . . . it has deluged the nations with the blood of the saints."[30]

A brisk market developed for anti-Catholic conspiracy theories. Books like "ex-nun" Maria Monk's *Confessions,* purportedly exposing the sexual secrets of the nunnery, satisfied readers with more prurient appetites. Fears degenerated into violence in 1834 when a Protestant mob in Charleston, Massachusetts, burned the Ursuline Convent; ten years later in Philadelphia rioting left twenty dead and scores wounded. During the 1850s, the American Party, more popularly known as the Know-Nothings, championed nativist concerns in politics and showed significant strength in New York, Massachusetts, Pennsylvania, and Maryland. Protestants did not find relief from their fears of popish plotting for another century.[31]

Fears of Masons, Mormons, and Catholics faded as the North and South drifted apart and toward civil war. In making sense of decades of sectional conflict rooted in economic difference and ideological divergence, leaders on both sides of the Mason-Dixon line found comfort in conspiracy thinking. Their newspapers, sermons, and stump speeches cut subversive images in bold relief, recasting the unintentional and coincidental as malevolent premeditation. Both northerners and southerners, finding these signals consistent with traditional beliefs and fears, were receptive and used them to assert sectional identities and mobilize energies for struggle. In a cycle of action and reaction, conspiracy charges frayed and eventually tore the bonds of union.[32]

In the late 1830s abolitionists, opposing slavery as an immoral institution that robbed blacks of their humanity, initiated an attack on the slave-power conspiracy. Large plantation owners and slaveholders, the "slaveocracy," were leveraging their wealth and power to intimidate the federal government and advance the slavery evil. These "Lords of the Lash," in league with the northern moneyed "Lords of the Loom," cried Wendell Phillips, had plotted slavery's expansion by annexing Texas, provoking the Mexican War, and organizing filibustering expeditions to secure new lands in Latin America.[33] In the 1850s, the abolitionists were joined in countersubversion by the more numerous antislavery activists. Unlike abolitionists who opposed slavery because of its consequences for black people, they focused on the slave power's conspiracy against white northerners. If not conspiracy, how could a long history of abuse of constitutional rights be explained? The House of Representatives' gag rule restricting the right of petition, mob attacks on the freedoms of speech and press, the banning of antislavery literature from the mails, and unwarranted searches in southern cities revealed the hidden hand raised against antislavery advocates. "Incidents are no longer incidents," concluded antislavery proponent Stephen Embro. "They are links in the chain of demonstration, infallible, plain, conclusive."[34]

The slave power also posed an economic threat. Western land

beckoned to white yeomen farmers, offering a ladder of mobility. Yet without territorial curbs on the plantation system, the promise of economic opportunity was empty; northern farmers knew that they could not compete against slave labor. The slaveocracy, however, would not accept restraints, for it demanded virgin soil for cotton production and new markets for a surplus slave population. New slave states also maintained southern parity in the U.S. Senate and balanced the northern-dominated House of Representatives. Cunningly, slaveholders concealed their territorial ambitions behind a plan to build a transcontinental railroad and with northern confederates passed the Kansas-Nebraska Act in 1854. This legislation repealed the Missouri Compromise, which had restricted slavery's domain for thirty years. Land long closed to the advance of slavery had now opened. A sense of betrayal ignited indignation in meetings across the North. From them emerged the Republican Party, which stood on a platform of free soil, free labor, free men. Three years later, the Supreme Court's Dred Scott decision prohibited Congress and its agents from restricting slavery in the territories. Many, including Abraham Lincoln, were convinced that the conspiracy had reached the highest levels of government. Powerful foes had besieged the Constitution and the northern economic future. Northerners would surrender neither without a fight. The bloody war that followed would confirm them in conspiracy thinking. Surely, Abraham Lincoln's death by conspiracy in the final act of the Civil War was their irrefutable proof.[35]

White southerners took pride in a distinctive way of life; Dixie was the land of the large mansion houses where cotton was king. Slavery was their foundation, and whites were convinced that it was God-given, scientifically sanctioned, and uniquely productive. The antislavery movement thus challenged the core of their community. Whether they owned slaves or not, the majority of southerners were determined to resist the threat to law, property, and racial order. South Carolina Congressman James Hammond expressed a shared opinion: "I warn the abolitionists, ignorant and infatuated barbarians as they are, that if chance shall throw any of them into our hands, they may expect a felon's death."[36] But the danger of "incendiary" abolitionist literature touched deeper fears. While they persuaded themselves that slaves were happy and docile, southerners armed for their lives in preparation for black insurrection. Those who spoke in countersubversive tones did not lack for examples. In spinning the incidents of conspiracy into a tight web, the South built solidarity and resolve. At the same time, it lost perspective and created a menace out of scale and more cohesive than the evidence allowed.

Southern newspapers were heavy with news of the conspiracy against slavery. North of the divide, men and women appeared to move collectively in disobedience to the fugitive slave laws and protection of the underground railroad conspiracy. Who promoted the publication of Uncle Tom's Cabin and then financed its stage production? How could the Republican Party advance so quickly? John Brown's attempt to seize the government arsenal at Harper's Ferry and incite slave insurrection could not have been planned and executed without an extended family of plotters. Southerners were certain that the wave of support for Brown that swept the North and raised him to heroic rank was manufactured and clear evidence of collusion. The danger was home-grown as well. In 1822 South Carolina authorities uncovered Denmark Vesey's conspiracy and executed thirty-seven slaves. At least three slaves were convicted and hung for the Charleston, South Carolina, fire scare of 1825–26, during which a number of the city's wooden buildings were torched. The bloodiest uprising occurred in Virginia in 1831. Sixty whites perished in Nat Turner's rebellion and seventy slaves were summarily executed. A traumatized South subsequently flinched at the very hint of black unrest. More frequent acts of passive or less violent resistance on the plantations also constantly reminded slave owners of their vulnerability. By 1861 the South had become an armed camp prepared to defend itself from enemies within and without.[37]

Countersubversion continued to permeate national debate as the United States industrialized in the second half of the nineteenth century. Although the Civil War did much to douse conspiracy thinking rooted in section, the rise of the Ku Klux Klan in the South reflected the persistence of prewar patterns. Klansmen recast Reconstruction legislation into a Radical Republican intrigue to turn slaves into masters and "Africanize" the South. The Klan conspiracy against federal policy was to claim almost one thousand black and white lives. A tough federal response smothered Klan terror in a wave of prosecutions. Martial law and the suspension of habeas corpus were necessary to remove the threat from South Carolina. In 1915 the Hollywood spectacular *Birth of a Nation* reframed historical events to give credence to the Klan's conspiratorial interpretation.[38]

As the economic order changed, different visions of the future battled for power. Conspiracy was a prominent theme in the competition. Capitalists denounced radicals for scheming to overthrow the government and cited as proof events like the 1886 Haymarket Square bombing that left seven policemen dead. The radical response counted strikebreakers, Pinkerton detectives, and blacklists, among other union-busting tactics, on the roll of robber baron sins. Novelists like Ignatius Donnerly painted the conflict more vividly. In his book *Caesar's Column,* published in 1890, Donnerly described the Brotherhood of Destruction, a secret society that rises to destroy the "abominable despotism" of the Hebrew-dominated aristocracy that has brought "the universal misery and wretchedness of the working class."[39] More prosaic currency wars pitted inflation-minded silverites against deflationary gold bugs and unleashed a barrage of literature uncovering their respective subversive activities. The Populist Party platform of 1892 put American economic problems in perspective, charging that "a vast conspiracy against mankind has been organized on two continents, and it is rapidly taking possession of the world."[40] The intrigue between Wall Street and European banking houses awaited more explicit description in the twentieth century.[41]

Economic plots did not replace traditional intrigues. Indian rebellions in the West, culminating in the Ghost Dance Movement of the 1890s, nourished white conspiracy thinking. Americans implicated Mormons in these uprising while continuing to rail at the theocracy on the Salt Lake. Claims that the extermination of the buffalo was a conspiracy between the U.S. Army and hide hunters to end Indian resistance appeared only in the late twentieth century. Catholics' allegiance to the pope still exposed them to Protestant charges of dual loyalty. A rising tide of immigration from southern and eastern Europe brought fresh troops to papist forces and raised new fears. In the 1890s the American Protective Association would draw over one half-million Americans to its anti-Catholic banner with promises to curb immigration and fight papal power in politics.[42] Nativists discerned the new immigrants' complicity in other nefarious undertakings. Their drinking habits fed the arrogant "liquor power," which prohibitionists charged with fixing prices, bribing judges, and controlling the "ballot box via the rum hole."[43] Meanwhile, corrupt political machines, in league with the saloon menace, tightened their hold on city government with immigrant votes.[44]

Conspiracy thinking spilled over into the new century. Progressive-era muckraking journalists, seeking to spur reform and sell magazines, published sensational and lurid exposés of a diversity of ills plaguing the United States. They targeted the white slave trade, corrupt labor unions, sweatshop abuses, child-labor horrors, cover-ups of foul practices in the beef industry, and patent medicine scams. Their pens revealed that business conspiracies in restraint of trade barely scratched the surface of corporate treachery. Corruption even tainted the Senate. Certainly, the insinuation or discovery of secret deals and hidden cabals that gave their stories a conspiratorial spin enhanced the muckrakers' appeal.[45]

The entry of the United States into World War I doubled the guard against conspiracy. Hyphenated Americans were suspect, and Germans in particular were the focus of national fears. Former President Theodore Roosevelt worried about German-Americans but had a more expansive view of the danger, refusing to define the menace by ethnicity. Thus he netted U.S. senators who opposed intervention, dissenting native-born Americans, and the Hearst newspapers, which he accused of "play[ing] the Kaiser's game." Roosevelt wrote: "The Hun within our gates is the worst of the foes of our own household. . . . Whether he is pro-German, or poses as a pacifist, or a peace at-any-price-man, matters little. He is the enemy of the United States."[46] Disfranchisement and the establishment of internment camps were his solutions to the domestic threat. Some dismissed this response as too lenient.

The radical Industrial Workers of the World was considered even more dangerous. Already suspect for its rhetoric of sabotage and class struggle, the IWW's opposition to a war for capitalists' profits drew the fire of government authorities, opinion makers, and local vigilantes. "Why wait," asked the Wall Street Journal, "until grain or elevators be burned, . . . factories dismantled, or even these utilities temporarily held up? The nation is at war, and treason must be met with preventive as well as punitive measures. . . . The price of delay must be paid on the field of France."[47] The Department of Justice quickly confronted "Imperial Wilhelm's Warriors," staging nationwide raids on iww branches in September 1917 and arresting Wobblies for conspiracy to disrupt the war effort and for antidraft agitation. On trial in Chicago, 101 iww leaders faced 17,500 charges; guilty verdicts sent thirty-five Wobblies to Leavenworth Penitentiary for five years, thirty-three for ten years, and fifteen for twenty years. Later trials brought seventy-three more convictions. In all, more than two thousand Wobblies, Socialists, and pacifists were trapped in the World War I witch hunt that transformed dissent into subversion.[48]

The pressure on dissidents did not ease during the Red Scare that followed the war. Bolshevik pleas to the workers of the world to throw off their chains and uproot the capitalist system had spurred American resistance to the coming revolution. Prominent among those fanning the fears of conspiracy was Attorney General A. Mitchell Palmer, who hoped to ride the antiradical wave into the White House. The danger, claimed Palmer, was extreme: "Like a prairie-fire, the blaze of revolution was sweeping over every American institution of law and order. . . . It was eating its way into the homes of the American workman, its sharp tongues of revolutionary heat were licking the altars of the churches, leaping into the belfry of the school bell, crawling into the secret corners of American homes." Palmer found the nucleus of the conspiracy in a "small clique of outcasts from the East Side of New York" who were "under the criminal spell of Trotzky and Lenin."[49] In response, he created within the Justice Department a Bureau of Investigation charged with gathering information on all domestic radicals. Under J. Edgar Hoover's direction, a file index of sixty thousand names was compiled. In November and December 1919 agents without arrest warrants organized coast-to-coast raids and jailed alleged radicals. In January 1920 more than four thousand suspected Communists were seized in coordinated raids in thirty-three cities. Those arrested, if citizens, were tried in state courts under antisyndicalist laws; if immigrants, they were held for deportation hearings. Attorney

General Palmer underscored their deviousness: "Out of the sly and crafty eyes of many of them leaps cupidity, cruelty, insanity, and crime; from their lopsided faces, sloping brows, and misshapen features may be recognized the unmistakable criminal type."[50]

A revived Ku Klux Klan waved the banner of countersubversion in the 1920s. Unlike the Klan of the post–Civil War years, this hooded movement was not primarily southern or terrorist. Preaching a multifaceted program based upon law and order, "100 Percent Americanism," and militant Protestantism, it enlisted nationally perhaps as many as six million men and women, with the most powerful klaverns organized in Indiana, Colorado, Ohio, Texas, Illinois, Pennsylvania, and California. In recruiting members, the Klan resurrected the specter of the Catholic conspiracy. The word again went out that the pope's puppets were preparing to advance their holy cause. The Boulder, Colorado, klavern newspaper admonished Protestants to awaken to the danger. Fifteen million Catholics were "organizing and working as a unit through many societies that are military and are drilled and equipped with arms and ammunition." Their aim was obvious: "to make America Catholic."[51] On another front, the papists schemed to ruin the quality of the public schools and Romanize students by placing Catholics on school boards and employing them as teachers. "In the event of their success," wrote Klan sympathizer Alma White, "there would be a string of beads around every Protestant child's neck and a Roman Catholic catechism in his hand. 'Hail Mary, Mother of God,' would be on every child's lips and the idolatrous worship of dead saints a part of the daily program."[52]

The Klan recruiters exploited anti-Semitism, long a tradition in Europe and kindled in America by the immigration of two million Jews from Russia and Eastern Europe. Numbers alone heightened suspicion, but most provocative to Americans was an expanding Jewish economic and political sphere. In the Klan litany the Jews were "Jonah[s] on the Ship of State," incapable of assimilation because of their conceited religious and social exclusiveness.[53] Scornful of American values, the Jews planned to undermine Protestant hegemony. Well-organized "Hebrew syndicates" forced Protestants from positions of economic power. The motion picture industry, an early casualty of Jewish influence, produced debauching films, commercialized the Sabbath, and lured Protestants from churches. Protestant women were warned of the lascivious Jews, "men in whose characters animal passions and greed are the predominant forces."[54] Some even believed that Jewish financiers were aiding the pope in the scheme to disinherit Protestant Americans.[55]

Automobile manufacturer and American folk hero Henry Ford corroborated the Klan's charges against the Jews. Ford based his ideas on *The Protocols of the Elders of Zion,* an account—fabricated by the Czarist secret police at the turn of the century—of an alleged Jewish conspiracy against Christianity. To spread the word, Ford published *The Protocols'* claims in his newspaper the *Dearborn Independent* for ninety-one consecutive weeks and then compiled them in book form. He also Americanized the Jewish "program" for his readers: Darwinism, Bolshevism, control of the liquor traffic and prostitution, political machines, the spread of jazz, and the corruption of baseball. Jews were also guilty of dominating the slave trade, Ford declared, and of manipulating the South into secession in 1861. Ford detected the Jewish hand in the recent world war: "International financiers are behind all wars. They are what is called the international Jew: German Jews, French Jews, English Jews, American Jews. I believe that in all those countries except our own the Jewish financier is supreme. . . . Here the Jew is a threat."[56] Jews were thus especially cunning, for they not only ruled the world's economy, but with communism had mastered the proletariat. He even discovered that the traitor Benedict Arnold had Jewish associates and that the Rothschilds had financed the Hessians.[57]

Conspiracy theories in the 1920s were not always complex and expansive. The sudden death of President Warren Harding and the subsequent revelations of scandals in his administration begged for a secret plot. Gaston Means provided it in his book, *The Strange Death of President Harding,* which alleged that the president's wife and personal physician had conspired to poison Harding to prevent his impeachment and plans for divorce. The proof was in Mrs. Harding's suspicious decision not to allow an autopsy of the body to determine cause of death. Although Means's book is out of print, curious readers may still find in the catalogue of the American Opinion Book Services (an arm of the John Birch Society) Attorney General Harry Daugherty's version, *The Inside Story of the Harding Tragedy.*

The catalogue describes Harding as an "honest and dedicated patriot and fighter against communist subversion whose reputation was smeared and vilified after his death by 'Insiders' of the Conspiracy."[58]

The Great Depression gave conspiracy thinking an economic twist but involved the usual suspects. At first, conspiracy theorists like radio priest Father Charles Coughlin blamed "plutocrats" and "money-changers" and other members of the economic elite for planning the crash: "The sands of intrigue and of evil machinations have filtered through the hour glass of their control."[59] Soon they borrowed from Henry Ford and Adolf Hitler. As outlined in *The Protocols of the Elders of Zion,* the Jews had brought economic ruin and were a step closer to world domination. The "Jew Deal" of President Franklin Roosevelt, born Rosenfeld, was not America's salvation but a continuation of the plot. With the support of mainstream business and political leaders, William Pelley of the Silver Shirts and Gerald L. K. Smith joined Coughlin in bringing charges of Jewish perfidy.[60]

Domestic plotters did double duty in foreign intrigues. Revisionists reexamined the origins of U.S. involvement in World War I and replaced Wilsonian idealism with cynical manipulation. Isolationists in the 1930s alleged that the public had been tricked into war by munitions makers and bankers anxious to protect their investments and to profit from the carnage. Not surprisingly, North Dakota Senator Gerald Nye's committee charged with reviewing the arms business found that the "merchants of death" had grown wealthy on war. The popular impression, however, took no note of obvious consequences but instead confirmed conspiracy. Only a small leap in logic would be necessary to find Jewish fingerprints on the plot and revise it to fit current events. The most influential of those who made that leap was the famed aviator Col. Charles Lindbergh. In a nationally broadcast radio address in 1941, he admonished members of the "Jewish race" to abandon their "pro-war policy." Their motivation for advocating intervention Lindbergh found understandable, but as he reminded listeners, the "reasons . . . are not American." Moreover, he warned darkly, in time of war "they will be among the first to feel its consequences." Lindbergh continued: "Their greatest danger to this country lies in their large ownership and influence in our motion pictures, our press, our radio, and our Government." He concluded, "We cannot allow the natural passions and prejudices of other peoples to lead our country to destruction."[61]

The Japanese bombing of Pearl Harbor closed the debate on intervention but released new fears of conspiracy. Did President Roosevelt back-door the United States into the war against Germany by manipulating the Japanese into firing the first shot in the Pacific? Why did Washington delay in warning Pearl Harbor of the impending attack? Were Hawaii commanders Adm. Husband Kimmel and Gen. Walter Short dismissed to cover up the plot? Charles Beard, who spiced his book on the constitutional convention with suggestions of elite intrigue, waded into the controversy early. Avoiding words like *conspiracy* and *plot*, Beard nevertheless exposed presidential calculation. Roosevelt and Secretary of State Cordell Hull, he wrote, "were expecting if not actively seeking war; and having this expectation, they continued to 'maneuver' the Japanese and awaited the denouement."[62] The prestige of Beard's prior work and the Yale University Press imprint gave his charges weight. Military comrades of Kimmel and Short came to their defense and blamed Washington for withholding vital information from Pearl Harbor despite having broken the Japanese diplomatic code. They also found it curious that American aircraft carriers were conveniently away on maneuvers and out of harm's way on the day of the attack. Suspicious to other revisionists was the delay in opening the official investigation, the suppression of its findings for ten months, and then the final release of the report in 1945 with fifty-two pages withheld. During the Cold War, critics who accused Roosevelt of being soft on communism alleged that Pearl Harbor was sacrificed to ensure U.S. involvement in Europe and to save his Russian pals. Most recently, John Toland has claimed that "the comedy of errors on the sixth and seventh [of December 1941] appears incredible. It only makes sense if it was a charade, and Roosevelt and the inner circle had known about the attack."[63] Japanese intentions, surprisingly, are insignificant in these conspiracy scenarios, and the Empire's burden of guilt has shifted to American shoulders. The U.S. Senate offered conspiracy theorists some consolation in 1999. It voted to overrule military authorities and clear Kimmel and Short of all charges of dereliction of duty.[64]

Leftists were similarly prone to conspiracy imaging. American Communists, like their counterparts in Moscow, repeatedly decried the international capitalist plot to destroy the Soviet Union and the proletariat's vanguard. The subsequent Soviet alliance with the United States and Great Britain during World War II did little to ease concerns. Communists questioned Allied strategy which delayed the opening of a second front against the Nazis in France until 1944 while the Soviets bore the brunt of the fighting. Asked party leaders: was this a capitalist trick to bleed Russia white and leave her too weak to resist postwar imperialism?[65]

Among the most vocal in crying conspiracy were federal authorities. Franklin Roosevelt set the administration's tone, denouncing opponents of his foreign policy as "appeaser fifth columnists" in the service of a totalitarian world conspiracy.[66] He summoned J. Edgar Hoover of the Federal Bureau of Investigation and charged him with gathering information on the activities of American fascists and Communists. Zealous FBI agents, on cue from their director and Justice Department prosecutors, fashioned a dragnet to trap prominent anti-Semites and right-wingers like Gerald Winrod, William Pelley, Lawrence Dennis, and Elizabeth Dilling. They and twenty-six others were indicted and tried for conspiracy to encourage insubordination in the armed forces and violation of the Smith Act, which made it illegal for anyone to advocate or even belong to an organization that advocated the overthrow of the U.S. government by force. The conspiracy charge repeatedly proved a favorite of prosecutors. Its vagueness, the assumed collective responsibility of the accused, and the courts' customary flexibility in the admission of circumstantial evidence gave the government the advantage. This case ended in mistrial and the defendants were freed, but the government had exacted punishment in lost time and resources. Only Pelley, who in a previous trial had been found guilty of conspiracy to impair the war effort, served time in prison.[67]

The federal government was more successful in its countersubversive action against Japanese-Americans. In February 1942 President Franklin Roosevelt issued Executive Order 9066, removing all

Japanese-Americans living on the West Coast to relocation camps in the interior. Guilty only by reason of ancestry, 112,000 men, women, and children saw their liberties sacrificed to regional and national fears, both latent and current. California Attorney General Earl Warren, who later served as chief justice of the U.S. Supreme Court, made the case for evacuation. "I believe," he testified, "that . . . the greatest danger to continental United States is that from well-organized sabotage and fifth-column activity." He reported that a review of California land ownership maps revealed "that it is more than just accident" that Japanese-Americans had settled near airplane factories, manufacturing plants, dams, railroads, power lines, sugar refineries, and air bases. The absence of evidence of disloyalty or sabotage was, in fact, proof of their treachery: "I believe we are just being lulled into a false sense of security. . . . When, nobody knows of course, but we are approaching an invisible deadline."[68] The presidential order was challenged, but the Supreme Court upheld it and the countersubversive reasoning on which it was based.

This brief survey spotlights the centrality and persistence of conspiracy imaging in U.S. history. Since their arrival, Americans have positioned themselves defensively to repel subversives, both supernatural and mundane. Though repeatedly under siege, the perimeter holds fast, and dangerous outsiders remain at bay. Only rarely, as in the 1850s and 1930s, do the conspirators seem even temporarily to have penetrated key institutions. Conspiracy imaging draws power by merging with and reinforcing traditional American values and beliefs: a sense of mission, Protestant supremacy, concern about encroachments on liberty, anti-elitism, maintenance of the racial order, and the sanctity of private property. In the midst of diversity, conspiracy thinking nurtures a sense of peoplehood while discovering the enemies of the American dream. The exposure of real plotters, meanwhile, acts to energize these beliefs and validate the images they birthed. Moreover, in focusing on culprits and combinations, countersubversion personalizes problems and insulates institutions from popular discontent. Critical to the tenacity and flexibility of countersubversive interpretations are their articulate champions. Politicians, religious leaders, journalists, government officials, and leading industrialists, along with other role models, have cleared a path for ordinary men and women. If the eccentrics among the conspiracy-minded have received a disproportionate share of attention, it is necessary to remember that their mates inhabit all social and political groups.

With the ground prepared, Americans entered the second half of the twentieth century haunted by, yet attached to, their conspiracy fears. The past continued to exert its hold, conjuring up familiar demons while changing circumstances advanced new dangers. As before, conspiracy theorists sounded the alarm against threats to the nation in the loud and exaggerated style that so distracted the "conspiracy as paranoia" school of scholars. Now their cries were especially urgent, for the enemy was not only within but in charge. Competition and cooperation within the conspiracy-minded subcultures shaped their cases while new means of communication offered the message unmediated and without hostile decoding. Peppered with simultaneous and diverse conspiracy accusations, the public softened to fresh revelations. Individually and collectively, charges of plot making became more credible. They were even more convincing when the conspiracist streams converged. Other influential voices raised in countersubversion verified these claims to create an atmosphere charged with conspiracy.

The Master Conspiracy

> Today Moscow and Washington are, and for many years
> have been, but two hands of one body controlled by one
> brain.
> —ROBERT WELCH, 1966

Americans in the postwar world were well prepared for global conspiracy thinking. Protestants had been suspicious of Catholics and
Jews for centuries. Witches in league with the Devil were also
known to have global ambitions. The threat now was more mundane, but clearly recognizable. It began in 1919 when the Bolshevist
call for world revolution and a seemingly responsive wave of strikes
had startled Americans into a red panic. Radicals, already castigated
for their opposition to World War I, saw their activism tarred as
un-American during the subsequent Red Scare. Concerns resurfaced
during the 1930s with the growing influence of Communist Party
members in labor unions, civil rights groups, and Hollywood. Soviet
spies had, in fact, infiltrated the federal government. The menace
appeared even more insidious because of the work of "red fronts,"
organizations of non-Communist "fellow travelers" who had been
duped into following the party line. The fragile coalition of capitalism and communism against the Axis powers during the 1940s
quickly shattered in wartime suspicions and postwar incidents. As
the peace chilled, Americans demanded explanations. Conspiracy
became a popular one, with liberals and conservatives competing
to rally the nation and avenge the betrayal at home and abroad.

The Red Scare of the 1950s was for most Americans a sudden
fright, and they soon moved on to other, more mundane concerns.
Some were not so easily reassured, and they kept their faith in conspiracy, convinced that communism had been confronted but not

defeated. In the front ranks of the suspicious were Robert Welch and the members of his John Birch Society. To understand and thus master the enemy, Welch studied history for secret patterns and intrigues. He found what he was looking for in a centuries-old master conspiracy of "Insiders," for whom communism was but one means to world domination. Evolving over decades, his work and that of like-minded countersubversives broke their subcultural confines to raise mainstream consciousness of the real menace—the conspiracy to create a New World Order. As in the immediate postwar years, events appeared to validate the conspiracy-minded while opinion makers absorbed their fears. Core values and beliefs again underwrote conspiracy thinking and promoted its patriotism and apparent truth.

In August 1936 President Franklin Roosevelt summoned FBI director J. Edgar Hoover to the White House to share his concerns about domestic subversion. He had lost patience with the harshest critics of the New Deal, and congressional investigations of American fascism and communism had caught his attention. With enemies to his right and left, the president directed Hoover to get a "broad picture" and authorized "that investigations be made."[1] Hoover, always sensitive to enemies within, was eager to accommodate and seized the opportunity to increase his and the Bureau's power. Taking an expansive view of this vague verbal order, he launched a full-scale surveillance operation that involved informers, wiretaps, bugs, mail openings, and break-ins. Agents spread their nets widely, and the president was fed information about his opponents in Congress and the media. The mission expanded further when the Bureau went beyond intelligence gathering to discredit dissidents and influence public opinion. Using Roosevelt's authorization as precedent, Hoover was to fashion a surveillance apparatus on his own initiative and with the compliance of future presidents. The fear of real and imagined conspiracies energized this internal security system and justified secrecy, deceit, and the violation of civil liberties in defense of the nation. Though mainly undercover, government activism did not occur in a vacuum, and it cultivated public fears about internal threats.[2]

The president worried about his critics on both ends of the political spectrum, but Hoover and fellow anticommunists were convinced that the greatest threat came from the far Left. Events of the 1930s heightened their vigilance. Isolated and unable to expand its base despite the Great Depression, the American Communist Party followed the new line from Moscow and discarded radicalism to pursue power. Party leaders obediently turned away from confrontation and advocated the "popular front," an alliance with progressive groups to confront fascism. Softening its image would enable the movement to enter the American mainstream, reach sympathizers, and increase membership. Claiming that they were the true heirs of the American Revolution, Communists linked Washington, Jefferson, and Lincoln to Marx, Lenin, and Stalin in the movement's pantheon. The watchwords of the party became "Communism is twentieth-century Americanism." In accord with the new agenda, Communists supported New Deal efforts at reform and applauded Roosevelt's anti-Nazi foreign policies. In 1938 the Communist movement even embraced Democratic Party candidates and sought a place in the New Deal coalition. The Soviets could boast, as well, that Communist cells had infiltrated the federal bureaucracy in preparation for espionage activities. Complementing these efforts were gains in the labor movement, with Communist organizers proving critical to the growth and success of the Congress of Industrial Organizations (CIO). By the end of the 1930s, Communists or party sympathizers led from one-fourth to one-third of the CIO's forty international unions. Under the popular-front arch the Communists formed and led a network of organizations that addressed real concerns. Antifascism, civil rights, intellectual freedom, and peace were causes around which targeted groups could be mobilized for their own ends, as well as those of the Communists. Between 1936 and 1938, recruiting drives doubled the rolls of the party to eighty-two thousand men and women, with another five hundred thousand organized in affiliated groups.[3]

For conspiracy theorist Elizabeth Dilling, Franklin Roosevelt's New Deal was an integral piece of this ominous pattern. In two self-published books, she denounced the New Deal as "a deliberate, comprehensive plan to change the American form of government to a Red dictatorship." She believed that relief programs gutted self-reliance and individual initiative. An expanding bureaucracy and new federal regulations foreshadowed collectivism and ignited her fears for liberty. To Dilling, Roosevelt was merely a puppet of the "red ruling clique," ordered to ignore congressional authority and constitutional checks and balances.[4] The federal government was lost, and now the heartland was under attack. The conspiracy, Dilling wrote, "is boring within our churches [and] schools . . . and is undermining America like a cancerous growth."[5]

More credible than Dilling, who was later prosecuted for conspiracy to overthrow the government, was Texas Congressman Martin Dies, who chaired the House of Representatives' Special Committee on Un-American Activities. Created in 1938 and supplied with information by the FBI, the Dies Committee investigated charges of Communist influence in the federal government and denounced more than a thousand officials as party members or sympathizers. "Fifth columnists," warned Dies, "are not always garbed in the uniform of foreign troops nor do they always speak with a foreign accent. They may be native-born American citizens. Such figurative parachutists have already landed in the federal government. They await the 'zero hour' when Stalin gives the command to attack."[6] It was the Dies Committee that pioneered the strategy of guilt by association and first hurled such accusations as "soft on communism" and "coddling Communists" at government leaders. While the pain of the Great Depression focused American attention, most gave little credence to such attacks. By 1939 economic recovery had brought sufficient relief and a Gallup poll recorded that three-quarters of the respondents were suspicious enough to favor continuation of the work of the Dies Committee. Meanwhile, federal authorities had created an employee loyalty program and compiled a list of subversive organizations, membership in which was cause for dismissal.[7]

Fears of subversion eased during World War II and the American alliance with the Soviet Union against the Axis powers. But in the postwar world anticommunists found new opportunity to hawk their charges of conspiracy. Many began to listen. Russian resistance to U.S. objectives brought frustration and checked the sense of omnipotence that had mushroomed dramatically in the clouds over Hiroshima and Nagasaki. Alarmed and uncertain, Americans watched victory become retreat before an enemy seemingly bent upon world conquest. The Communists curtained off

Eastern Europe and now embroiled China in civil war. France, Italy, Greece, Turkey, the Middle East, and Southeast Asia appeared to totter, vulnerable to military assault from the outside and subversion from within. Containing the threat meant drawing a political, economic, and military line dividing the free world from the slave world, friend from foe, and patriot from traitor.

Still, the Communists grew bolder. In 1948 Russian troops sealed road and rail approaches to Berlin. In 1949 the Soviet Union ended the United States' atomic monopoly by exploding its own bomb, and China was "lost" to the Communists. The following year, North Korean tanks and infantry crossed the thirty-eighth parallel and invaded South Korea. By early 1951, American and United Nations troops confronted 850,000 Chinese "volunteers" in bloody and indecisive combat.

In just five years the world had been transformed. America was on the defensive, its mission denied and security threatened. Explanations that stressed ideological competition, the passing of colonial empires, nationalism, or long-standing animosities gave little solace and found few advocates. More attractive was a spin compatible with tradition that offered a guide to counterattack. America reeled before the international Communist onslaught because of enemies within. Traitors had infiltrated government, the schools, the media, and the churches, betraying secrets and weakening the national will to resist. If Americans did not awaken to the danger, the red tide would not only lap at their shores but submerge the homeland. As in the past, opinion leaders mentored ordinary Americans in countersubversion. Members of the Republican Party, long out of power and hungry for a lever to reclaim it, dusted off New Deal conspiracy theories to accuse Democrats of intrigue. Eagerly they ferreted out new evidence of the continuing plot. Democrats understood the power of conspiracy thinking and tried to turn it to their advantage. Liberals in the Truman administration became willing participants in the postwar witch hunt. In the attempt, they only enhanced the credibility of their conservative critics. In defensive reflex, Hollywood entered the conspiracy wars and made anti-communism entertaining.

World War II had barely ended when the Republicans opened up their barrage. In the congressional election year of 1946, they capitalized on Cold War friction and hammered the Democrats for being "soft" on communism. At the same time, Republicans pleaded with voters not to let foreign communists distract them from the more insidious danger at home. Liberals had betrayed the nation, serving as willing dupes of the Soviet Union in its international intrigues and undermining the Constitution on the domestic front. They traced the conspiracy to the New Deal; reform and government regulations amounted to "creeping socialism," and America was far along on the road to collectivism. The choice was clear to House Republican leader Joseph Martin: "The people will vote tomorrow between chaos, confusion, bankruptcy, state socialism and communism, and the preservation of American life."[8] As Republican candidates asked voters: "Got enough inflation? . . . got enough debt? . . . got enough strikes? . . . got enough communism?"[9] The November elections testified to the efficacy of the Republican strategy. For the first time since 1928, voters delivered both houses of Congress into their hands.[10]

Control of Congress enabled Republicans to tighten the perception of conspiracy between liberals and Communists. The 80th Congress launched twenty-two investigations of communist subversion in government and American life, with the House Committee on Un-American Activities in the forefront. Its members scrutinized red influence in Hollywood and listened to actor Ronald Reagan describe "the Communist plan . . . to take over the motion picture business."[11] While discovering some Communists and much progressive sentiment in the industry, the committee discerned little trace of propaganda on film. It left the impression, nevertheless, that Hollywood was a hotbed of radicalism, and committee chairmen scheduled investigation sequels. Studio moguls quickly moved to protect profits, doing penance through blacklists and the dissemination of the anticommunist message. Television and radio executives took a cue from the film industry and similarly cleansed themselves of suspicious characters. More disturbing, committee members unearthed information that Alger Hiss and other officials in the State Department had spied for the Soviet Union during the 1930s. When President Harry Truman dismissed the accusation as a "red herring," Republicans condemned him not only for blindness but for the far worse sin of complicity in appearing to cover up the affair. The Hiss case, California Congressman Richard Nixon ominously declared, was only "a small part of the shocking story of Communist espionage in the United States."[12] The later arrest of spies at home and abroad gave further credence to his and Republican accusations that Communists and their Democratic fellow travelers had subverted the nation and left it exposed.[13]

Countersubversion became a Republican staple. Earl Warren, running on the national ticket with Thomas Dewey in 1948, declared: "While we spend billions to halt the spread of the communist conspiracy abroad, we find this same conspiracy reaching its stealthy fingers to grab the framework of our own free institutions and tear them down."[14] In January 1950 Richard Nixon condemned the "master plot" and observed that "This conspiracy would have come to light long since had there not been a definite . . . effort on the part of certain high officials in two administrations to keep the public from knowing the facts."[15] Indiana Senator William Jenner asserted that "this country today is in the hands of a secret inner coterie . . . which is directed by agents of the Soviet Union. . . . Our only choice is to impeach President Truman to find out who is the secret invisible government."[16] Asked Senator Homer Capehart: "How much more are we going to have to take? . . . Hydrogen bombs threatening outside and New Dealism eating away the vitals of the nation. In the name of Heaven, is this the best America can do?"[17]

In conceding the existence of a conspiracy, Democrats shielded Republicans from charges of opportunism. President Harry Truman realized that containing the Russians demanded a long-term mobilization of resources that war-weary Americans seeking normalcy were reluctant to commit. To rally the nation to its world responsibilities he conjured up a monolithic menace and "scare[d] hell out of the American people." His Truman Doctrine in 1947 thus framed the Cold War in absolute and moralistic terms as a crusade for freedom against terrorism, atheism, and communist dictatorship. Awakened to the global threat, Americans returned to a war footing and supported their president and the continuation of a military-industrial machine that poured men and resources into a defense of the anticommunist world.[18]

Logically, Communists at home were at least as dangerous as those abroad and just nine days after his Truman Doctrine speech, the president acted. Disturbed by the arrest of Soviet spies in Canada and bridling at charges that he was soft on communism, Truman signed an executive order that created FBI-assisted screening boards to investigate the loyalty of federal employees. Reasonable grounds for dismissal went beyond overt acts of sabotage and espionage to include advocacy and "sympathetic association" with members of groups on the attorney general's list of subversive organizations.[19] Dissent had become synonymous with treason, and guilt by association a proper gauge of subversion. In 1948 during his uphill battle for reelection, Truman attempted to appease the public by moving against what he privately considered a negligible threat. Without evidence of an actual plot or any incidents of violence, the Justice Department arrested the twelve members of the American Communist Party's national board for conspiracy to teach and advocate the violent overthrow of the U.S. government. Eleven of the defendants were convicted, with the Supreme Court upholding the verdict. In 1951 federal authorities targeted the party's second echelon, arresting more than fifty Communist leaders.[20]

Defense and Justice Department officials, meanwhile, formulated plans to arrest Communist Party members in the event of war. Warned Attorney General J. Howard McGrath: "There are today many Communists in America. They are everywhere—in factories, offices, butcher shops, on street corners, in private business—and each carries in himself germs of death for society."[21] Hoping to panic the membership, the FBI leaked information to the press that it was prepared to detain more than twenty-six thousand people. These contingency plans, while modified, became law in 1950 when liberals and conservatives voted in lopsided majorities to pass the McCarran Internal Security Act and later override Truman's veto. Alert to the "world-wide conspiracy" and anxious "to prevent it from accomplishing its purpose in the United States," Congress mandated the arrest of communist subversives and their confinement, without trial, in detention centers.[22] The danger was extreme, said Minnesota's liberal Senator Hubert Humphrey, and demanded such measures. He reminded his colleagues: "We are not living in a peaceful world. . . . When there is a real menace to our internal security we must be able to act with speed and certainty."[23]

Truman's attempt to seize the initiative backfired. His actions seemed belated and reluctant, forced only by the prompting of his opponents. At the same time, administration red-baiting mimicked Republican accusations, validated them, and heightened suspicion. Even Truman's anticommunist measures brought him no relief. The loyalty boards' dismissal of more than twelve hundred federal employees, with another six thousand tendering their resignations, gave quantitative measure to an internal security problem. Yet even these breaches were muted in the uproar over the arrests in 1950 of Julius and Ethel Rosenberg for disclosing atomic secrets to their Soviet handlers. The Truman administration either was lax, incompetent, or, said its sharpest critics, a part of the conspiracy.[24]

Style, not substance, separated Wisconsin Senator Joseph McCarthy from the anti-Truman pack. McCarthy was a brawler, abrasive and crude, lacking even the facade of senatorial civility. Propped up with briefcases stuffed with lists of names, affidavits, files, and secret memos, he appeared to have the facts that proved conspiracy. McCarthy's dramatics drew attention, but real power came from his base. Sure of the firm support of his party and with important allies like the Hearst, McCormick, Gannett, and Scripps-Howard newspaper chains, he made the Red Scare his own, as commentators acknowledged by affixing his name to the era. In February 1950 he told the Women's Republican Club of Wheeling, West Virginia: "Today we are engaged in a final, all-out battle between communist atheism and Christianity." America was losing the struggle, McCarthy contended, "not because our only powerful potential enemy has sent men to invade our shores, but rather because of the traitorous actions of those who have been treated so well by this Nation." Here stood the people's champion, the defender of their birthright against the red-tainted elite "born high with silver spoons in their mouths."[25] McCarthy then raised his hand and claimed to hold a list of names "that were made known to the Secretary of State as being members of the Communist party and who nevertheless are still working and shaping policy in the State Department."[26]

Neither rebuttal nor demands for evidence daunted McCarthy, who answered critics with more sensational charges. How, asked McCarthy, could America's "carefully planned retreat from victory" be explained? President Harry Truman, General George C. Marshall, and Secretary of State Dean Acheson had organized "a conspiracy on a scale so immense as to dwarf any previous venture in the history of man." McCarthy revealed not only the plotters but their aim: "To the end that we shall be contained and frustrated and finally fall victim to Soviet intrigue from within and Russian military might from without."[27] Those who denounced McCarthy were "Commiecrats," "dupes of the Kremlin," or "egg-sucking phony liberals."[28] McCarthy's hyperbole grabbed the headlines; in personifying the abstract and simplifying the complex it made good newspaper copy. The American people were impressed; a Gallup poll showed McCarthy's favorable rating climbing to 50 percent in December 1953. Even after his censure by the Senate, one-third of Americans still had a positive impression. This should not be surprising in light of other survey results during the 1950s indicating that 70 percent of Americans believed that the Soviet Union sought to "rule the world," and that in case of war, 40 percent proposed interning or imprisoning members of the Communist Party and 13 percent favored "shooting or hanging" them.[29]

Americans became even more receptive to conspiracy thinking when opinion makers not marked by obvious partisanship joined their voices in countersubversion. Francis Cardinal Spellman of New York bluntly rejected Democratic reassurances and announced a state of emergency in 1946: "Only the bat blind can fail to be aware of the Communist invasion of our country."[30] In spite of years of counterattack by the Truman administration, FBI Director J. Edgar Hoover claimed in 1950 that the United States still harbored more than half-a-million Communists and fellow travelers. "Something utterly new," he later wrote in his best-seller *Masters of Deceit,* "has taken root in America during the past generation, a communist mentality representing a systematic, purposive, and conscious attempt to destroy Western civilization and roll history back to the ages of barbaric cruelty and despotism."[31] Judge Irving R. Kaufman, in sentencing the Rosenbergs to death in 1951, declared: "It is so difficult to make the people realize that this country is engaged in a life and death struggle with a completely different system. This struggle is not only manifested externally between these two forces but this case indicates quite clearly that it also involves the employment by the enemy of secret as well as overt, outspoken forces among our own people."[32] General Mark Clark, commander of the United Nations forces in Korea, had a "nagging fear" that "perhaps Communists had wormed their way so deep into our government . . . that they were able to exercise an inordinate degree of power in shaping the course of America in the dangerous postwar era."[33] In a 1952 publication the Chamber of Commerce censured federal officials for the "whitewashing of espionage cases" and "a dangerous penetration of our military arm by Communists." The subversive threat had not abated, and "Communists and their followers have achieved positions in our government where they can do immense harm to national welfare and security."[34] According to the evangelist Billy Graham, communism was "master-minded by Satan. . . . I think there is no other explanation for the tremendous gains of Communism in which they seem to outwit us at every turn."[35]

Motion pictures offer other clues to the mainstreaming of conspiracy thinking. Film presents an opening to the past, for it reflects the attitudes, anxieties, and values of a people and their times. Its messages expose a society's dreams and myths while nurturing identities. But motion pictures are more than mirrors. Disguised as entertainment, film plays an opinion-shaping role. It engages events and debates ideas. It praises and condemns, instructs us on what is right and wrong, and helps us distinguish friend from foe. When their images are as large as the silver screen, the power of filmmakers to reflect and mold perceptions cannot be underestimated.

Hollywood made amends for its flirtation with the Left by enlisting in the countersubversive campaign. Between 1947 and 1954, movie makers churned out fifty anticommunist films, with one-fourth produced in 1952 alone. These films bombed at the box office in their initial screenings but found a large audience when rerun as second features on double bills. Not comfortable with heavy ideological messages, Hollywood proved adept at recasting the familiar gangster genre to fit the Communist conspiracy. Communists were shadowy figures, regimented strong-armed goons, cruel to animals, hard faced, and humorless. *The Conspirator* (1949) had them spitting out pithy one-liners like "One never questions," "It is forbidden," and "This is a serious breach of discipline." Propaganda, blackmail, murder, and, according to *Red Menace* (1949), other "corkscrew tactics" were their chosen means to power. In *Invasion USA* (1952) Nazis were recycled into communist soldiers who methodically A-bombed San Francisco and New York City into submission. The films worked as primers about communist sabotage and espionage techniques, with full disclosure about disguises, special knocks, cover stories, and hidden microfilm. Typical American dupes were members of minorities, or effete intellectuals, or guys with "plenty of gripes" enticed into the party by women and whiskey. Authorities explained why we fight: "The Communists don't give nobody a second chance. That's where the United States is different. We give folks just as many chances as they deserve."[36] The movies also gave blunt warning. Communism's rueful victim in *My Son John* (1952) cautioned the vulnerable: "As the seller of habit-forming drugs gives the innocent their first inoculations with the cunning worthy of a serpent, there are other snakes lying in wait. . . . Even now the eyes of the Soviet agents are on some of you. . . . It is too late to save me. It is not too late to save yourself." At film's end, hope prevails and the lessons are learned—trust authority, shore up military defenses, return to church, and stay on guard.[37]

Representative of the message but atypical in its profitability was the 1952 production *Big Jim McClain*. The film opens in documentary fashion in the hearing room of the House Committee on Un-American Activities, with the congressmen playing themselves. The voice-over solemnly declares: "Undaunted by the vicious campaign of slander launched against them as a whole and as individuals, they have staunchly continued their investigation, pursuing their stated beliefs that anyone who continued to be a Communist after 1945 is guilty of high treason." (Clearly, Hollywood knew how to take direction.) Enter stars John Wayne and James Arness, who play the roles of committee investigators assigned the task of ferreting out reds. They grow disgusted by the antics of the witnesses who hide their disloyalty behind the Constitution. In spite of the evidence, these "agents of the Kremlin . . . walk out free . . . to contaminate more kids." The audience, agitated by the miscarriage of justice, empathizes with a frustrated Arness, who grits his teeth and declares: "I shouldn't have handed him that subpoena. I should have stuffed it down his throat with my hand still around it."

These traitors escape, but Wayne and Arness are back on the case the next day with Operation Pineapple, an investigation of Communists in Hawaii. After a brief but significant stop at Pearl Harbor and the memorial to the *U.S.S. Arizona,* they begin surveillance work. Sinister music identifies the reds, whose arrogance, stuffy accents, "country-club set" ways, and passwords betray them to an audience well-schooled in subversive manners. Wayne has no patience for apologists or ideological fencing. "Look baby," he says, "I don't know the why. I've heard all the jive. This one's a Commie because momma won't tuck him in at night. That one because girls wouldn't welcome him with open arms. I don't know the why. The what I do know. Was like when I was wearing the uniform. I shot at the guy on the other side of the perimeter because he was the enemy." As Wayne and Arness piece together the conspiracy, a parade of repentant ex-Communists open up to them, while informers are congratulated for doing their patriotic duty. Neither love, nor scenic Hawaii, nor the murder of Arness keeps Wayne from cracking the sabotage ring that plotted to paralyze the islands' communications and trade. Again, the Communists manipulate constitutional protections to elude punishment, but the strength of the nation is revealed. With the Marine Corps Hymn playing in the background, the faces of the American melting pot appear, arrayed in battle gear, united in defense of the homeland.

As the Red Scare lost its intensity, studio executives had little incentive to continue making anticommunist films. Yet audiences still reacted to the message, which was retold for the rest of the decade in the seemingly unrelated science fiction genre. *It Came from Outer Space* (1953), *Invasion of the Saucer Men* (1957), and *Invisible Invaders* (1959) suggest a displacement of the conspiracy from the Soviet Union to the far reaches of the galaxy. In *Invaders from Mars* (1953) aliens are truly enemies within. Using brain implants, they take control of parents and neighbors and plot to infiltrate America's military and scientific defenses. The possessed lose their will, becoming zombielike, just as Americans imagined the brainwashed who joined the Communist Party. More disquieting was *Invasion of the Body Snatchers* (1956). Seed pods from outer space duplicate and replace humans one by one as they sleep. Other than a lingering flat affect, the transformation is undetectable. Appearances deceive and no one's allegiance is certain. The danger grows palpable as the invaded are regimented into a hive of activity and mechanically follow orders to spread the contagion. All seems lost when the protagonist's romantic interest falls asleep. Yet, as in the anticommunist films, salvation appears in the form of federal authorities who can be trusted to know what to do.[38]

The emerging medium of television did its part to shore up morale. Weekly episodes of *Biff Baker, USA* (1952–53), *Passport to Danger* (1951–52), *Foreign Intrigue* (1951–55), and *Secret File* (1954–55) brought communist and assorted threats into the living room. The popular *I Led Three Lives,* which aired between 1953 and 1956, recounted the exploits of FBI "counterspy" Herbert Philbrick as he posed as a member of the Communist Party. Television offered quick relief, for the plotters repeatedly suffered defeat within a half-hour. Like the movies, television not only exposed the secrets of the Communist conspiracy but testified to the inherent goodness of American institutions and values.[39]

Countersubversion blanketed the United States, with local leaders confirming national messages. State governments and corporations instituted loyalty programs to weed out "security risks." By 1955 laws had been passed in forty-five states to punish sedition, criminal anarchy, and advocacy of the violent overthrow of the U.S. government. Civil rights groups and labor union locals purged anyone suspected of disloyalty. Universities required loyalty oaths from professors and barred controversial speakers from campus. In New York, the state Medical Society and the Association of Architects demanded that members swear allegiance to America. Indiana even expected professional wrestlers to take the pledge. Meanwhile, grassroots patriots were kept busy pulling subversive books from library shelves and hunting public school classrooms for freethinkers.[40]

By the mid-1950s domestic and international events had robbed conspiracy thinking of its urgency. Confidence in the federal government was restored when General Dwight Eisenhower, hero of World War II and holder of strong anticommunist credentials, won election as president in 1952. He initiated a new internal security program that tightened requirements, making federal employees subject to discharge not only for disloyalty but as "risks" because of personal misconduct or "perversion."[41] Eisenhower later authorized J. Edgar Hoover to escalate the war on the reeling Communist Party, and the FBI launched its Counter Intelligence Program (COINTELPRO). This operation went beyond surveillance to infiltrate, discredit, and disrupt. In the 1960s Hoover widened his aim and moved against targets on both the Left and Right. Internal security was further enhanced when the Internal Revenue Service and the Central Intelligence Agency added their resources to the war on dissidents. With Republicans now on guard in Washington, the subversion issue had lost its allure and become expendable. It was time to get on with the business of governing, a task made easier when Senator Joseph McCarthy embarrassed himself and gave his party the opportunity to discard him. Americans relaxed and Gallup polls recorded that those who believed that Communist infiltration of the government was the nation's most important issue declined from 17 percent in March 1954 to 4 percent by the end of the year. The world crisis had eased as well. America's apparent retreat before the red peril had ended; a truce quieted the fighting in Korea, and communist penetration in Latin America and Southeast Asia had been temporarily blunted. With Stalin dead and denounced, Soviet and U.S. leaders could ease Cold War tensions at a summit in Geneva.[42]

Countersubversion was respectable and compelling in the decade after World War II. Republicans and Democrats, locked in political combat, had incited public paranoia to gain advantage. In scripting events at home and abroad to fit the plot, they found willing allies in Hollywood and among other opinion shapers. Their conspiracism proved more slogan than theory. In building the case, they submerged the principles of formal logic in a casual sequencing of events and association of individuals. Frequent repetition, sensationalism, and the status of the advocates sustained its power. Although conspiracy thinking was a response to real dangers, it also bloated the evidence out of proportion to the threat. The Truman and Eisenhower security programs dismissed only thirty-nine hundred federal employees, with a small minority fired on loyalty grounds. Senator Joseph McCarthy did not find a single Communist in either the State Department or the U.S. Army. No instances of sabotage were recorded in the postwar era. The espionage activities of Hiss and the Rosenbergs also predate the period. Grains of truth had thus nurtured suspicion. Manipulation then created design and quickened the national pulse. Wrapped in the flag, conspiracy thinking absorbed and absolved the sins of false reasoning, opportunism, and character assassination.[43]

If there was a consensus about subversion, it was conditional. With distance from the dedicated anticommunists who composed the conspiracy-minded core, recognition of the nuances and faith in the nature of the plot faltered. Fears about spies and communist intrigue did not challenge mainstream acceptance of the New Deal. Business, the middle class, labor, and the elderly had gained too much from the welfare state to seek a rollback of programs or to imagine it a communist inspiration. The conspiracy explanation was thus comfortable as long as its assumptions were not probed too deeply. With provocative stimuli gone, most Americans could break their conditioning to accusations of red subversion.

Conspiracy thinking retreated to its core by the end of the 1950s. Although confined it did not grow moribund, for the conspiracy-minded sensed that the threat had actually become more dangerous. The rise of Eisenhower and the fall of McCarthy only confirmed in their minds the facts of betrayal and the power of the conspirators. Rather than suffering defeat, Communists still burrowed into the federal government, the judiciary, churches, news agencies, school boards, professional associations, and civil rights organizations. The intrigue continued, now hidden and unimpeded. Deception fostered complacency, and Americans no longer heeded the warnings of conspiracy. The vigilant few knew what needed to be done. And they knew that time was running out.

The most determined member of the countersubversive core was Robert H. W. Welch, Jr. The oldest of six children, Welch was born on a farm in North Carolina in 1899. He was a precocious child who impressed his parents by reading before his third birthday, mastering the multiplication tables by age four, and translating Latin when he was seven. In 1912 Welch enrolled at the University of North Carolina and graduated four years later at age sixteen in the top one-third of his class. Welch then entered Annapolis, but he lost interest in a naval career after two years and transferred to Harvard Law School. Studying was a low priority, and his first two years there were undistinguished and uneventful. Crisis attended his third year. He took an immediate dislike to the liberal professor and later Supreme Court justice Felix Frankfurter, who he believed was "teaching the Marxist class concept of labor." Welch's hagiographer wrote: "Every single lecture found Robert jumping to his feet for rebuttal against some fallacy in logic or error in premise." Soon Welch "could stomach Frankfurter no more" and left law school to begin a candy-making business. After ten years and "shattered credit and a business reputation that is a liability," he joined his brother's candy company in charge of sales and advertising. The business prospered despite the hard times of the 1930s, and Welch achieved a measure of financial stability. Welch, like other conservatives, condemned the New Deal as a "cancer of state socialism" and lamented: "My America is being made over into a carbon copy of thousands of despotisms that have gone before."[44] Wartime found him serving the nation in the Office of Price Administration and on the War Production Board.[45]

His business reputation grew after the war, and he held positions on the board of directors of the conservative National Association of Manufacturers and as a regional vice president. He also became more active in Republican circles and followed the party line in denouncing the Truman administration's timidity before the Communists in China, rejecting welfare and big government, and championing Joseph McCarthy. Similarly, in book-length letters to his friends he outlined the conspiracy against America. Lenin had initiated the plot and now Stalin pushed it to completion, his hand visible in the betrayal at the wartime Yalta Conference, treachery against the freedom fighters of China, the firing of General Douglas MacArthur, and Hollywood propaganda. Harry Truman, George Marshall, and Dean Acheson were merely puppets who jumped at the Communists' bidding. In mouthing these charges, Welch was well within the mainstream of his party.[46]

Welch soon lost patience with his fellow Republicans who understood conspiracy primarily as a political weapon to be used against Democrats. Few were tempted to believe that it alone unlocked the secrets of history and current events. Even more upsetting to Welch was the conviction that the Communists had converted Republican leaders and that his erstwhile allies were now subverting the nation. If fellow Republicans had worked hard to clear the path to conspiracy, only a small minority could follow Welch to its end.

Welch presented his case in 1956 in a sixty-thousand-word letter, packed with source notes, to a few close friends. Seeking a wider audience, he later published the manuscript as *The Politician*. After careful study, Welch confirmed that General George Marshall was "a conscious, deliberate, dedicated agent of the Soviet conspiracy" who "used" Presidents Franklin Roosevelt and Harry Truman to fashion "a world-wide police state, absolutely and brutally governed from the Kremlin." More startling was the revelation that Marshall's "protégé" Dwight Eisenhower was either "a mere stooge" or "a Communist"; the evidence "would fit just as well into one theory or the other." Welch had compiled an abundance of incriminating material. As general, Eisenhower had speeded the opening of the second front to benefit the Soviets. As president, he not only failed to roll back communism in Korea but had stifled uprisings behind the Iron Curtain and leashed Chiang Kai-shek to prevent him from liberating China. Eisenhower then advanced the plot domestically by engineering the censure of Senator McCarthy and refusing to dismantle New Deal programs. Welch's conclusion, so dependent on images of American omnipotence, ruled out miscalculation, "chance," and "stupidity" as explanations. "There is but one word to describe his purposes and actions. That word is treason."[47]

In spite of the odds, Welch was convinced that he could awaken Americans and rally them to the cause. To initiate the counterattack, Welch invited eleven friends to a meeting in Indianapolis in December 1959. The men included President Eisenhower's first commissioner of internal revenue, a former personal aide of Gen. Douglas MacArthur, two past presidents of the National Association of Manufacturers, a banker, and a University of Illinois professor. Well-to-do businessmen filled out the rest of the group. All the men were sympathizers and felt the same fears that haunted Welch.[48]

For two days the men listened patiently as Welch outlined the problem and the task ahead. In a style reminiscent of the Truman

Doctrine speech, Welch pitted America against communism "in a *world-wide* battle, the first in history, between light and darkness, between freedom and slavery; between the spirit of Christianity and the spirit of the anti-Christ for the souls and bodies of men." The communist assault had begun in 1917, Welch maintained, with the formation of the Soviet Union. With his base secured, Lenin dispatched "gangsters" first to subvert Eastern Europe and then to subjugate the "masses of Asia." All went according to plan, and by 1945, the Communists prepared to encircle Western Europe. Welch prophesied that by the early 1960s, "the Communists will be able to take Western Europe by telephone." Gradually, the net was closing on the United States, but external pressure alone would not force surrender. More critical was the treasonous "fifth column" that deceived its way to power, strangled the Constitution with socialism, and now promised to surrender national sovereignty to international conspirators. Borrowing from Elizabeth Dilling and Martin Dies, Welch ticked off the signs of subversion: welfare programs, a growing federal bureaucracy, high taxes, an unbalanced budget, and government regulations. Communist "Trojan horses" had already entered the schools, media, and churches, preaching permissiveness and immorality to sap American strength. The conspirator was ahead of schedule, and the last domino was beginning to totter.[49]

Nothing Welch said surprised his listeners. He blended traditional fears of government power with militant anticommunism, economic orthodoxy, and concerns about the loss of America's moral fiber. What distinguished Welch from other conservatives was his continuing insistence on the existence of an international conspiracy. For Welch, all events moved toward a predetermined end. Acquaintance connoted collusion, and association became guilt. Inconsistency and ambiguity were, in themselves, marks of a clever plot and intended to disguise and deceive. In fact, a "principle of reversal" or "double think" governed communist strategy.[50] Seemingly anticommunist actions like the war in Vietnam or an expanding military budget covered and deliberately accelerated the plot to bring regimentation and collectivism at home. Only those well-versed in the means and ends of conspiracy could master the sinister pattern; no fact then escaped understanding; no detail lacked purpose. Also apparent to the group was the power of conspiracy fears in giving men and women a cause and mobilizing them for action.

Robert Welch's manner was in sharp contrast to his dramatic message. Sixty years of age in 1959, bald and paunchy, Welch projected the image of a middle-aged college professor. His delivery was flat and monotonic. He spoke as he wrote: a string of declarative sentences, shorn of any adornment, that numbingly piled detail upon detail. Films of his speeches show him reading mechanically from his notes and making little eye contact with listeners. Nervous before an audience of any size, he was constantly adjusting his tie or watch and repeatedly clearing his throat and wiping perspiration from his brow and upper lip. Sinus drainage produced periodic snorts, and a dry throat made him gulp audibly. Rather than diminishing his supporters' enthusiasm, these mannerisms actually enhanced their admiration. Welch's lack of flash and intensity suggested solid, detached scholarship and testified to the truth of his accusations. His motives appeared above reproach, and he was respected as a dedicated and sincere man who had sacrificed a successful business career for his country. Welch associate E. Merrill Root explained: "You feel a power. It is not what we would call today 'charisma.' . . . It is a quiet power. It affirms and insists, through conviction, through an amazing knowledge, through a goodness and integrity that seems almost tangible."[51]

Welch proposed to defeat the conspiracy with an organization modeled on the communist enemy. To withstand factionalism, he proposed a "monolithic body" that was "under completely authoritative control at all levels." He named the group after John Birch, a forgotten Baptist missionary killed by Chinese Communists just ten days after victory over Japan. As the first casualty of the Cold War and the victim of a government cover-up, Birch was a martyr to American freedom. Welch followed up his Indianapolis seminar with twenty-eight similar presentations, and by the end of 1960 the society had succeeded in securing eighteen thousand members and organizing active chapters in thirty-four states. At the society's height in 1965, an estimated eighty thousand to one hundred thousand Birchers carried the message to the grassroots.[52]

The Birch Society's campaign was primarily educational. Welch expected Birchers to know their enemy and assigned them to read one hundred books—"One Hundred Steps to the Truth"—along with the movement's weekly newsletter and monthly bulletin. Meetings became study groups as members watched Welch on film or discussed current reading assignments. To reach prospective members, chapters opened book stores, sponsored anticommunist speakers, and erected billboards trumpeting society positions: "Support your Local Police," "Get the US out of the UN," and "No to Gun Control." Welch also created single-issue front groups like the Movement to Restore Decency (MOTOREDE) and the Committee Against Summit Entanglements (CASE) to educate sympathizers about the organization's program and to expand membership rolls. Coordinated letter-writing campaigns and the exposure of local conspirators filled members' time. Basking in their secret knowledge and relishing anointment as freedom fighters, Birchers eagerly took up a proselytizing mission to convert the nation.[53]

The movement's indoctrination program and authoritarian structure never shaped a single mind of the community of believers. Birchers, many of whom were wealthy and highly educated, did not surrender their wills or follow their leader blindly. No one was disciplined for disagreeing with the official line, and Welch repeatedly reminded members not to participate in any activities with which they disagreed. Large numbers had not read *The Politician* and dissented when informed of Welch's contention that Eisenhower was a communist conspirator. Others were never fully convinced by his description of the extent of the conspiracy or by the equation of liberalism with treason. Highly suspicious, but not obsessed, they enjoyed the company of like-minded women and men and joined in a modest campaign against changes that threatened to disrupt their lives. A poll of Birchers found that nearly two-thirds joined for such amorphous goals as "protecting" the United States and "preserving" capitalism. One in five sought fellowship; nearly half of the recruits joined relatives and personal friends already belonging to local chapters. Trust fostered commitment. As volunteers they retained freedom of action and remained in the movement only as long as it met their needs. For some, Welch's means proved too restrained, and the society became a way station on a journey farther right. Even within the core of the countersubversive subculture there were gradations of belief and commitment.[54]

Current events gave the organization momentum. The launching of Sputnik, communist revolution in Cuba, war in Laos and Vietnam, and the walling of Berlin signaled the renewal of an international offensive. The Soviet Union now targeted America with thermonuclear warheads and, with a Cuban launch pad on the doorstep, posed a credible threat. John Kennedy's election in 1960 and his New Frontier programs promised more government programs and regulations. Meanwhile, civil rights activists confronted segregation, bringing not only domestic turmoil but the danger of federal encroachment on states' rights. The signs were familiar to Robert Welch and his followers. Pressure from without and intrigue within were neither coincidental nor random events. Breaking cover, the communists had clearly accelerated the timetable of subversion.

Birch Society allies within the subculture like businessmen J. Howard Pew and Arthur Kohlberg, Billy James Hargis of the Christian Crusade, Dr. Fred C. Schwarz of the Christian Anti-Communist Crusade, and former FBI agent Dan Smoot validated this interpretation. So, too, did influential conservatives. Arizona Senator Barry Goldwater, in *The Conscience of a Conservative,* warned: "Our defenses against the accumulation of unlimited power in Washington are in poorer shape, I fear, than our defenses against the aggressive designs of Moscow. Like so many other nations before us, we may succumb through internal weakness rather than before a foreign foe." In *Why Not Victory,* Goldwater asked Americans to "realize once and for all that our enemy is not a nation but a political movement made up of ideologically possessed people who have organized themselves as an armed force and secured control over entire countries. They have a cadre in every country and use Moscow as their command post."[55] According to FBI Director J. Edgar Hoover, the communists had "infiltrated every conceivable sphere of activity; youth groups; radio, television, and motion picture industries; church, school and education groups; the press; nationality minority groups and political units."[56] It was Robert Welch whom Ronald Reagan had in mind when he declared in 1961: "One of the foremost authorities on communism in the world today has said that we have ten years. Not ten years to make up our minds, but ten years to win or lose—by 1970 the world will be all slave or all free."[57]

As the Birch message slipped the confines of the anticonspiracy subculture and touched the right bank of the American mainstream, opinion makers closed ranks and moved to douse its appeal. Editor and publisher Thomas Storke fired the opening gun in January 1961 in his *Santa Barbara News-Press*. In front-page editorials, he charged the society with creating turmoil in the California community and isolated the Birchers as a "tiny, fanatical, highly vocal minority."[58] The *New York Times Magazine* took up the challenge with three articles appearing in 1961. Drawing parallels with Nazis, the *Magazine* rejected Birchers as "authoritarian" and "crackpots."[59] *Time* magazine followed that lead, describing *The Politician* as Robert Welch's *Mein Kampf.* The Birch Society, *Time* concluded, was "a goose step away from the formation of goon squads."[60] Other national magazines, like *Christian Century, Look, Newsweek,* and the *Saturday Evening Post* delegitimized the society as extremist by repeating Welch's charge that Eisenhower was a communist coconspirator. Because many Birchers were Roman Catholic, condemnation from the Jesuit weekly *America* was telling. So, too, was the stand of the *Pilot,* the official organ of the Boston archdiocese, which denounced the John Birch Society as "unbalanced, excited, and definitely out of focus."[61] The conservative *National Review* rendered a final judgment in 1962 and found the society "damaging [to] the cause of anti-Communism." As columnist Russell Kirk noted: "Cry wolf often enough and everyone takes you for an imbecile or a knave, when after all there *are* wolves in this world."[62]

National political figures joined in the hunt. Former Vice President Richard Nixon and Senators Mike Mansfield, Frank Church, Thomas Dodd, and Milton Young spoke out on the floor of Congress. Senator Thomas Kuchel of California called for a congressional investigation. Most conservatives listened to Senator Goldwater, who accused Robert Welch of being "far removed from reality and common sense" and called for his resignation.[63] Attorney General Robert Kennedy also dismissed the movement: "I think that they are ridiculous, and I don't think that anybody should pay much attention to them."[64] J. Edgar Hoover was of a different mind, and his agency added Robert Welch and the John Birch Society to its surveillance list. The Internal Revenue Service similarly targeted the movement. Many Americans listened to the influential and rejected Birch-style conspiracy thinking. A Gallup poll conducted in April 1961 found that only 8 percent of those who had heard about the Birch Society had a favorable impression, compared with 43 percent who were unfavorable. Fifty-nine percent were negative by July 1964.[65]

Birch leaders firmed morale and kept cognitions consistent by dismissing the "smear campaign" as part of the global conspiracy launched "on directives issued from Moscow." In spite of these reassurances, the media barrage had effect. It forced the movement into retreat in 1961 and 1962; recruiting slowed, defections increased, and Birchers assumed a lower profile. While remaining active in the emerging conservative movement, they were forced to conceal their affiliation to assert influence. The society did regain momentum when hostile opinion makers relaxed. Chapter membership expanded as Birchers took advantage of the enthusiasm aroused by the Goldwater presidential campaign and then the disappointment that followed its defeat. They complained that a "curtain of silence" muffled their voices.[66] Without mainstream political or media support, their reach was restricted. The Gallup organization, in response to the society's waning influence, dropped questions about it from surveys taken during the second half of the decade.

Internal changes further intensified Birchers' isolation and tested their resolve. Robert Welch, engaged in continual study of the enemy, revealed to members in 1964 that his focus on communist intrigue was misplaced; communism was merely a subplot of the master conspiracy. Welch moved to a higher level of understanding with the works of Scottish professor John Robison and ex-Jesuit Augustin de Barruel. Writing in the aftermath of the French Revolution, these monarchists had created a counterhistory in defense of the aristocracy. Winning the hearts and minds of present and future readers would assuage some of the pain of recent defeat and mobilize defenses. The Revolution, they argued, was not rooted in poverty and despotism. Rather than a rising of the masses, it was the work of Adam Weishaupt's Illuminati, a secret society that plotted to destroy all civil and religious authority and abolish marriage, the family, and private property. It was the Illuminati who schemed to turn contented peasants "from Religion to Atheism, from decency to dissoluteness, from loyalty to rebellion."[67] Welch was persuaded: "The French people under Louis XVI had as little cause to let themselves be led by conspiratorial destructivists into insane horrors and a murderous clamor for 'liberty' as the Negroes in America have today in demand for 'freedom.'"[68]

The fall of France, Robison continued, had not satisfied Weishaupt, and he planned to use Masonic lodges to sow intrigue across national borders. Although authorities later exposed and disbanded the secret society, Welch learned from the British conspiracist Nesta Webster and the American evangelist Gerald Winrod (whose anti-Semitism he rejected) that the Illuminati had gone underground only to reemerge as the masterminds of the revolutions of 1848. Now, discarding the Masonic organization as their vehicle, they chose new means to world power. With tentacles in international banking and trade, national political parties, and influential newspapers, the plotters engineered revolution, assassination, war, and depression to speed them to global dictatorship. To create an "activist arm" they employed Karl Marx to write the *Communist Manifesto* and thereby bring the working class under control.[69] Later, they bankrolled Lenin and Stalin to enlist the Russian masses in conspiratorial adventures. Welch's vision had cleared: financiers, government leaders, socialists, liberals, and communists were merely pawns of a "clique of international gangsters" whose "sole objective" was global "tyrannical rule." Concealed behind their puppets, the identities of these "INSIDERS" were unknown even to Welch.[70]

Welch made the conspiracy his own when he pressed American events into the pattern. He uncovered the work of the Insiders in Progressive-Era legislation. The income tax and the Federal Reserve System concentrated power in Washington and allowed the conspirators to control government revenues and credit, as well as the money supply. The direct election of senators was specifically designed to reduce the authority of the states. Meanwhile, programmed financial panics and depressions tightened the Insiders' grip on economic resources. After plotting the sinking of the *Lusitania*, they then pulled the lever of war in 1917 to secure the revolution in Russia and accelerate collectivization of the American society and economy. Peace, Welch continued, brought new peril when

President Woodrow Wilson, a dupe of his confidant Col. Edward House, tried to shackle the United States to the League of Nations. Franklin Roosevelt's New Deal savaged individual freedoms and brought the intrigue closer to its goal of submerging states' rights under federal authority. Roosevelt also heeded conspirators' demands in foreign policy. Diplomatic recognition of the Soviet Union in 1933 bailed the Communists out of financial disaster and prevented their certain overthrow. American generals conducted World War II as directed, with the salvation of the Insiders' base in Russia the major priority. On the home front, the emergency enabled conspirators to gain experience with rationing, wage and price controls, and other forms of regimentation.[71]

The end of World War II quickened the Insiders' pace. Welch accused Presidents Truman and Eisenhower of treason for surrendering national sovereignty to the United Nations and in regional defense pacts creating the North Atlantic Treaty Organization (NATO) and the Southeast Asia Treaty Organization (SEATO). The Vietnam conflict was a "completely phony war" to distract Americans from the advance of domestic socialism and federal power toward a "totalitarian police state."[72] The war, deliberately prolonged to erode patriotism and foment generational skirmishing, weakened the nation from within. Other manifestations of the plot were the drug epidemic, a rising divorce rate, birth control, pornography, civil rights agitation, Medicare, Medicaid, federal control of the public schools, and fluoridation of water supplies. The Insiders' hands were everywhere, and loyalty to God, nation, and family were in rapid decline. America was in the Insiders' grasp, claimed Welch in 1966, with "60 to 80 percent" already lost.[73] The conspirators had reached their endgame, with the United States about to become a province of what Welch called in 1972 the "New World Order."[74]

Welch realized that his new thesis would startle members, so he broached it "little by little" and led them "along to where they would be interested."[75] His caution was perceptive, for only the steadfast could cling to the shifting line. Men and women who enlisted to fight a familiar enemy were confused by Welch's claim that the greater peril was posed by exotic Illuminati or secretive Insiders who cleverly disguised themselves as both communists and capitalists. Although anticommunism and fear of encroaching government control were acceptable traditions in U.S. history, the new crusade raised questions about Welch's judgment. Moreover, Welch's revelation was less a detailed proof than a listing of names and events loosely bound by the accusation of collusion. Mere chronology became the evidence of conspiracy; all history was suspect. Conservative critics took the opportunity to pry members from the movement. Ronald Reagan, preparing for the California governor's race, disavowed the John Birch Society and suggested that it had been infiltrated by a "kind of lunatic fringe."[76] Barry Goldwater reiterated his opposition to Welch and the Birch organization. Once more under siege and now without conviction to sustain them, members reconsidered their allegiance to the movement. Perhaps as many as thirty thousand women and men, or one-third of the membership, deserted in 1967 and 1968.[77]

Though bypassed and shorn of members, the Birch Society persisted in its educational mission and waited for Americans to awaken. Robert Welch continued to unfold the Insiders' plot, and the faithful dutifully read and distributed his message. Particularly encouraging to Birchers was research that replicated Welch's findings and further flushed out the "facts" of the conspiracy. Society sympathizer Dan Smoot identified the members of the Council on Foreign Relations as the "sinister people" at "the top of the pyramid in the invisible government."[78] Kent and Phoebe Courtney of the Conservative Society of America also made the council their prime mover in "subjecting the United States to the control of a socialist world order."[79] The council was an obvious suspect. Organized in the 1920s, the CFR was a bipartisan research and discussion group that promoted international cooperation and interdependence. It rose to prominence during World War II, operating as a think tank for the State Department and aided in planning America's global strategy during the Cold War. Its goals alone would have drawn the attention of the suspicious. Funds from the Rockefeller, Ford, and Carnegie Foundations and a roster filled with members of the eastern establishment made the council the Insiders' den.[80] Focused more narrowly on Republican Party politics, Phyllis Schlafly's book *A Choice Not an Echo* similarly singled out members of the elite as America's "secret kingmakers." It was these men who selected presidential candidates, controlled the news media, and fostered an

"America Last pro-Communist foreign policy." She reminded her readers: "Most of what is ascribed to 'accident' or 'coincidence' is really the result of human plans."[81]

Conspiracy thinkers expanded on Welch's theory. Gary Allen, writing in the Birch Society's *American Opinion* magazine, discovered that the Council on Foreign Relations was planning the merger of the United States and the Soviet Union to serve as "the base for a dictatorial government of the world."[82] International bankers, he argued, directed the plot, knowing that a new world order would deliver global trade, transportation, and communication into their hands. He continued his analysis in the widely circulated *None Dare Call It Conspiracy*, published in 1971. Relying on information from retired army officers formerly "high in military intelligence," he revealed that the Illuminati used capitalism as "the anvil" and communism as "the hammer" to "conquer the world." Americans remained unknowing because "the elite of the academic world and mass communications media" had been instructed to camouflage the sinister operation. Allen could name names: Rockefeller, Rothschild, Baruch, Morgan, Schiff, and Warburg were the ringleaders who dominated the "world supra-government."[83] A subsequent book exhaustively delineated the Rockefeller family's role in the undertaking. Of particular interest was the contrived ploy of Watergate, a "coup d'etat" intended to deliver the White House to the unelectable Nelson Rockefeller.[84] The Utah conservative Cleon Skousen discovered "Force X" or the "control center," and exposed London bankers and Wall Street financiers as the "master planners" for "a global, socialist, dictatorial-oriented society."[85] Updating and detailing Welch's script were Des Griffin's *Fourth Reich of the Rich* (1976), A. Ralph Epperson's *The Unseen Hand* (1985) and *The New World Order* (1990), and James Perloff's *The Shadows of Power* (1988). Welch's disciples had increased the conspiracy cast severalfold: the internationalist Bilderbergers and Trilateral Commission, New Age Religionists, Presidents Lyndon Johnson and Richard Nixon; Cecil Rhodes, John Wilkes Booth, Jews, Masons, and the printers at the U.S. mint, whose dollar bill carried the phrase *Novus Ordo Seclorum*—poorly translated as "New World Order." Perloff and Epperson had even identified the Insiders' fingerprints on the assassination of John F. Kennedy.[86]

Each of these authors meticulously borrowed from those who came before, by repetition transforming allegations into facts and building a database that contained only self-reinforcing information. The accumulation of details, relevant and extraneous, was shaped to convict and to guarantee that acquittal was impossible. In reprinted, revised, and new editions, the story became homogenized and predictable. Meanwhile, duplication moderated perceptions of recklessness, and longevity enhanced acceptability. Long before journeys through the linked websites of cyberspace, readers could close their minds to ambiguity and find comfort and security in the mutually referenced and familiar.

Birchers circulated the news in pamphlet, book, and filmstrip versions, with hundreds of thousands of copies distributed. Searching for a national audience, they waited for events to give credence to fears. Their patience was rewarded and optimism renewed when setbacks in the 1970s rattled America's sense of omnipotence and stroked conspiracy fears. The nation reeled before a series of international defeats: failure in Vietnam, falling dominoes in Cambodia and Laos, and communist gains in Africa and the Middle East. As the Soviets reached nuclear parity, tight defense budgets and a demoralized military establishment raised doubts about national security. The final frustration occurred in 1979, with the seizure of the U.S. embassy in Teheran. Nightly, Americans watched the drama, their television screens filled with demonstrators taunting the hostages and their adversary's crisis of will.[87]

As the countersubversives knew, the domestic flank was also vulnerable. The conspiracy brought high taxes that bled Americans and supported a bloated federal bureaucracy bent upon amassing more power. "Social engineers" initiated affirmative action programs to lift minority over majority. Conspiracists scorned Supreme Court decisions that "coddled" criminals, legalized abortion, and eased restrictions on pornography. Sexual freedom, shifting gender roles, and experimentation with drugs, they were convinced, did not rise from changing lifestyles and values but revealed the depravity and ruthlessness of the conspirators. Meanwhile, Watergate exposed the immorality of the nation's leaders and shrouded politics for a decade. The Arab oil embargo, shortages, recession, and double-digit inflation revealed that the assault was economic as well as spiritual.

Shamed by their impotence, Americans sought explanation for the retreat and culprits to punish.

Conspiracy theorists were eager to expose the enemy. From 1945 to 1972, almost one-half of the government's key foreign policy decision makers had ties to the Council on Foreign Relations. In the State Department the figure was even higher. President Richard Nixon was a member of the council and had appointed more than one hundred CFR and Trilateral Commission colleagues to posts in his administration. Both organizations had recruited President Jimmy Carter. Others on the membership roster during the Carter administration were Vice President Walter Mondale, Secretary of State Cyrus Vance, and Secretary of Defense Harold Brown. Carter's national security adviser, Zbigniew Brzezinski, had been the director of the Trilateral Commission. The reasons for America's decline were now obvious. The evidence of infiltration could not be denied. The enemy had penetrated the highest circles of power and was executing its globalist agenda. Even for Americans less sensitive to intrigue than John Birchers, the circumstances were suspicious.[88]

The Left joined the Right in targeting the CFR and the Trilateral Commission. While shying away from an explicit accusation of conspiracy, leftists nevertheless drafted an indictment that John Birchers would have found acceptable. Laurence Shoup and William Minter, writing in 1977, characterized the CFR as the vehicle of "the New York financial oligarchy" that sought "world hegemony" through "a conscious attempt to organize and control a global empire." In a foreword to Shoup and Minter's book *Imperial Brain Trust,* G. William Domhoff invited readers to understand how monopoly capitalists in the CFR "carefully and secretively planned the politics of modern-day imperialism and then introduced them into government."[89] Holly Sklar also took aim from the Left, defining trilateralism as "the creed of an international ruling class whose locus of power is the global corporation. The owners and managers of global corporations view the *entire world as their factory, farm, supermarket, and playground.*" Behind a facade of aid programs and employing the rhetoric of reform, the internationalists engage in "sinister" and "insidious" repressive practices to pacify the Third World and shape it to corporate needs. Trilateralists, she discovered, also "manage" American affairs, suppressing dissent with the FBI's Counter Intelligence Program and controlling the national media.[90] "In sum, trilateralism is not a computerized dictatorship, but a dynamic alliance among powerful individuals and power blocs."[91] Not all readers were so sophisticated as to catch the nuances of her argument. Countersubversives added such books to their list of recommended readings.

More important were the echoes from the mainstream. In the mid-1970s, highly publicized congressional probes into the assassinations of President John F. Kennedy and the Reverend Martin Luther King, Jr., exposed the covert operations of the CIA and FBI and thickened the conspiratorial atmosphere. In the 1977 and 1978 *Congressional Record* and in his memoirs, *With No Apologies,* published in 1979, Barry Goldwater railed at the overweening influence of the Council on Foreign Relations and the Trilateral Commission. He followed the standard account, conjuring up the old demons of Rothschild, Rockefeller, and Morgan and linking them to the CFR. The organization's internationalist policies, he barked, "have been damaging to the cause of freedom and particularly to the United States." It was the CFR, the Arizonan remembered, that sponsored Cold War subversives like Alger Hiss, Owen Lattimore, and Harry Dexter White. Now the battleground was the Panama Canal, and America was once more surrendering to "unknown influence."[92] Turning to the Trilateral Commission, Goldwater denounced the banker David Rockefeller's "newest international cabal" as "a skillful, coordinated effort to seize control and consolidate the four centers of power—political, monetary, intellectual, and ecclesiastic." Goldwater looked for the hidden operators controlling events and discovered Rockefeller and Brzezinski, who had recruited Carter while he was still governor of Georgia and "immediately commenced grooming him for the presidency." In words no countersubversives could misunderstand, Goldwater resolved: "The outsider had been co-opted by the insiders."[93] Presidential contender Ronald Reagan made the Trilateral Commission a campaign issue in 1980. He censured Carter for his ties and the appointment of nineteen fellow members to top posts, thus creating a secret government within. The American Legion convention that year unanimously adopted a resolution that called for a congressional investigation of the "disproportionate number of elitist members" of the CFR and Trilateral

Commission in the Carter administration.[94] Meanwhile, radio talk show hosts found that the CFR and the Trilateralists were call-in favorites. They have remained favorites for decades.[95]

Ronald Reagan's election in 1980 broke the stride of the counter-subversives just as Dwight Eisenhower's victory had in 1952. Like the Birchers, Reagan preached the creed of "less government and more responsibility," condemned permissiveness, and rejected compromise with the Soviet "evil empire." The conspiracy-minded, however, immediately saw through the deception. Reagan made George Bush his vice president and appointed William Casey, Donald Regan, and Alexander Haig; all bore the mark of the CFR. More than 250 other members of the organization were to take administration positions. Deficit spending and a ballooning national debt continued to sap American resources, and Reagan's rhetoric did not disguise his failure to dismantle the federal bureaucracy. These policies, combined with aid to Poland, friendly relations with the Communist Chinese, and trust in the glasnost policies of Soviet Premier Mikhail Gorbachev, convinced Robert Welch that Reagan was a "lackey" of the globalists. It was clear to the society's director of public relations John McManus that "someone other than the President is in control."[96] But to McManus's consternation, no one was listening: "Ronald Reagan's effect on the movement has been devastating. Everybody went to sleep."[97] A coordinated blackout of news was under way, charged countersubversive James Perloff, and authors who sought to spread the truth were "blacklisted by the publishing world."[98] Americans were even less responsive to countersubversives farther to the right. Members of the Christian Identity movement, who advocated the creation of whites-only enclaves and prophesied a coming race war, were not only isolated but brought to trial for conspiracy to overthrow the government.[99]

Even those closer to the center of American politics could not upset the calm. Though hardly a conspiracist, columnist Jack Anderson warned in 1984 of "standby" legislation that would grant the Federal Emergency Management Agency (FEMA) emergency power to "suspend the Constitution and the Bill of Rights, effectively eliminat[ing] private property [and] abolish[ing] free enterprise."[100] In 1987 North Carolina Senator Jesse Helms rose in the Senate to deliver a jeremiad warning of the "campaign against the American people" by the "insiders' club." Banks, multinational corporations, foundations, and the media were "working in concert with the masters of the Kremlin in order to create what some refer to as a new world order."[101] Few were convinced. Outside the anticonspiracy core, few challenged the president's patriotism, and opinion makers proclaimed the Reagan Revolution.[102]

The decline of the John Birch Society defused the opposition as well. Robert Welch suffered a crippling stroke in early 1984 and died a year later. Georgia Congressman Larry McDonald, who had taken Welch's place at the helm, was killed when a Soviet jet fighter downed the South Korean commercial airliner that carried him and 268 other persons. This new evidence of the master conspiracy did not revive Birchers demoralized by the death of the founder, and many withdrew from the organization. In 1986 an emergency transfusion of $1.5 million raised from donations and property sales "prevented literally the shutting down of our operation" and appeased creditors owed more than $9 million. Restructuring, staff reductions, and vigorous cost cutting brought stability, but the movement at the end of the 1980s was reduced by more than two-thirds to eighteen thousand members. It was so weak that it could raise only a feeble protest as the CFR member George Bush captured the presidency. Birchers protested his "phonily fomented" war against Iraq, which they perceived as a ploy to advance the United Nations and reduce American independence.[103] Seeming to taunt his prey, the president declared a "new world order" in the wake of the Gulf War victory.[104]

The 1992 election brought no better news. The conspiracy-minded reviewed Bill Clinton's résumé and found that the one-worlders had "bought" him as a young man with a Rhodes scholarship to Great Britain and that his mentor at Georgetown University was a New World Order sycophant.[105] They had indoctrinated Clinton for leadership, as they had Carter, with the globalist tenets of the CFR and Trilateral Commission. With the presidency the goal, his "handlers" marshaled media resources to protect their protégé from charges of drug use, draft dodging, sexual indiscretions, and Whitewater financial misconduct.[106] These efforts bore fruit as President Clinton advanced such New World Order building blocks as the North American Free Trade Agreement (NAFTA) and General

Agreement on Tariffs and Trade (GATT), which evolved into the World Trade Organization (WTO). American cooperation with the International Monetary Fund (IMF) accelerated the conspiracy's aims of controlling the world's credit and draining the economic sovereignty of nations. At the same time, Clinton consigned U.S. power and interests to the United Nations by sending troops to Somalia and the Balkans to serve under foreign command. He coordinated these efforts with plans to enable gays to serve in the military and with gun control legislation that defied constitutional rights. His national health care initiative proposed a computer code for each American and the creation of a national database to track medical histories. The real purpose of the scheme, countersubversives contended, was to regiment the nation and repress dissidents, thus laying "a cornerstone of totalitarianism" and accelerating the incorporation of the United States into the New World Order.[107] Conspiracists scanned news reports throughout the 1990s trying to divine the final act in the American drama—the "emergency" that would serve Clinton as a pretext for declaring martial law and completing the subversion of the Constitution. Among the possibilities were racial rioting, gang violence, drug abuse, urban or biological terrorism, a contrived financial panic, global warming, or the Y2K crisis. The Republican Party offered no alternative. Its leader, Georgia Congressman Newt Gingrich, was also a member of the CFR.[108]

The globalists' vehicle to American power was already operational. Created in 1979, the Federal Emergency Management Agency spearheaded the national response to disasters by allocating resources and coordinating relief efforts. In pursuit of this mission, Presidents Carter, Reagan, Bush, and now Clinton had in a series of executive orders granted FEMA officials the authority to relocate populations, seize property, commandeer communications and transportation networks, and regulate fuel and food supplies. The potential for abuse of power was sufficient to agitate countersubversives. Reports of financial malfeasance and the mismanagement of relief efforts after Hurricane Andrew and the Los Angeles riots in 1992 convinced them that the agency's public role was a cover for a more sinister assignment. Was a national disaster the trigger for totalitarian rule? Did evacuation plans really mean relocation and internment? Were public shelters a euphemism for concentration camps? Remembering the fate of Japanese-Americans during World War II and FBI plans for Communists during the 1950s, the conspiracy-minded surmised the real purpose of FEMA and its budget of almost $2 billion. Under the guise of relief efforts, FEMA was in the process of building a gulag of detention camps across the United States. When the word was given, officials would confiscate all weapons and confine tax protesters, gun owners, and other dissidents. Conspiracists were also convinced that it was FEMA, under U.N. direction, that operated the fleet of black helicopters that patrolled American skies in training for the "black operation."[109]

As such ideas incubated in the countersubversive core, two events gave them credence in a wider community. In 1992 war broke out at Ruby Ridge in the Idaho back country when U.S. marshals attempted to bring the former Green Beret Randy Weaver to trial for selling an illegally sawed-off shotgun to a government informant. Weaver was a longtime conspiracist who accepted the Christian Identity movement gospel that Jews were Satan's spawn and blacks and Hispanics were inferior "mud people." In the coming apocalypse, Aryan warriors would do battle with ZOG, the Zionist Occupation Government that ran America for the New World Order. When the marshals moved in, shots were exchanged, leaving a federal officer and Weaver's fourteen-year-old son dead. The next day an FBI sniper accidentally shot and killed Weaver's wife while she cradled her infant. One hundred FBI agents and assorted National Guardsmen, U.S. marshals, and state and local police deployed helicopters and armored vehicles in an eleven-day siege of Weaver's shack. His surrender came in the media glare and before scores of cheering sympathizers who had gathered in support. The public clamor over the standoff was intensified during the trial when Weaver's attorney put the federal government on the defensive with charges that the FBI tampered with evidence and covered up misconduct. Judge Edward Long agreed: FBI behavior during the proceedings had "served to obstruct the administration of justice" and had showed a "callous disregard for the rights of the defendant." Nor did the uproar end with Weaver's acquittal in the death of the marshal. Countersubversives felt full vindication in 1997 when the former head of the FBI's violent-crime section was sentenced to prison for obstructing justice by destroying an internal after-action report critical of the Bureau's conduct.[110]

The following year the federal government found itself pitted against the self-proclaimed prophet David Koresh and his Branch Davidian disciples in the outskirts of Waco, Texas. Studying the Book of Revelation, Koresh became convinced that the end of days had arrived and war with the Antichrist was imminent. An attempt to search the compound for illegal firearms set off a gun battle that killed six Davidians and four federal officers. Floating additional charges of child abuse and illegal drug making against Koresh, an army of FBI and Alcohol, Tobacco, and Firearms agents laid siege. Federal patience lasted fifty-one days and ended when the FBI and ATF attacked the compound with armored vehicles, helicopters, and a barrage of tear gas grenades. The assault left eighty-one men, women, and children dead, with most killed in the fire that consumed the compound's wooden buildings. Again conspiracists raised questions that challenged the official account of the incident. Was there evidence that the Davidians had committed a crime? Was the response excessive and provocative? Had the means guaranteed the end? Once more the federal government's credibility was compromised when information later surfaced to cast doubt on its version of events.[111]

These incidents gave new life to conspiracy thinking. No longer content to operate covertly, the plotters had come out into the open in deadly confrontation. Moreover, federal aggression against conspiracists served to energize mobilization among their comrades. At gun shows and survivalist seminars, countersubversives made personal contact with gun rights advocates, tax protesters, and Christians preparing for the millennium. The John Birch Society, maintaining its role as the conspiracist think tank, experienced a surge in membership and funding. Other groups borrowed ideas while putting their own spin on the conspiracy. Casting for recruits, members of Aryan Nations, Ku Klux Klan organizations, neo-Nazi units, and skinhead brotherhoods added racism and anti-Semitism to the critique of the New World Order. They found their gospel of action in *The Turner Diaries*. Written in 1978 in novel form, this book told the tale of a rising of white Christians against the race-mixing, gun-confiscating Zionist Occupation Government. With assassinations, bombings, and finally nuclear weapons, the rebels released America from ZOG's yoke and reclaimed the nation's Christian birthright. Sales of The Turner Diaries remained brisk the entire decade. For those steeped in conspiracy thinking as well as the less suspicious, Oliver Stone's JFK, released in 1991, offered big-screen validation of secret plots and government intrigue.[112]

Feeding off of these fears and drawing much media coverage was a new addition to the countersubversive core, the militia movement. The movement was a diverse collection of latter-day minutemen united by their belief in the right to bear arms and their distrust of the federal government. Chapters were autonomous, with the first units organizing in Montana and Michigan in early 1994. By 1997 the movement had spread to all fifty states and counted an estimated fifty thousand members and one hundred thousand sympathizers. Of the approximately four hundred paramilitary groups that composed the movement, one-fourth were anti-Semitic or white supremacist.[113]

Countersubversives were eager to sound the alert. Opening booths in preparedness expos and gun shows, they distributed thick catalogues of recommended readings covering such topics as "History and Conspiracy," the "Jewish Issue," "Masonry," and "Globalism." The Militia of Montana sold videotapes titled "A Call to Arms/Equipping for the New World Order," "Battle Preparations Now," "The Illuminati Today," and "Bio-Chip Mark of the Beast." It also advertised Underground Bases and Tunnels and America Under Siege, which "documents the location of possible concentration camps, UN troop locations."[114] In addition, countersubversives could subscribe to magazines like the Militia of Montana Intelligence Report, The Patriot Report, and Contact, which carried news of black helicopters, detention camps, and other NWO machinations. Shortwave radio broadcasts supplemented the conspiracist press, and listeners were invited to tune in to such programs as "Unraveling the NWO," "Minuteman's Corner," and "End Day Prophecy." The information was certainly available, but only a minority was well-versed in conspiracy. Theory, even when diluted, did not make exciting reading. Instructional videotapes and less abstract magazine articles allowed easier access and were more satisfying. With distance from the countersubversive center, slogans replaced concepts, yet still proved sufficient to spur commitment and activism.[115]

The conspiracy-minded were quick to capitalize on new technologies. The internet provided grassroots activists with the means to reach a wide audience and disperse their ideas without delay or restraint. Here was participatory democracy in pure form. Without supervising authority, cyberspace privileged no interpretation. Moreover, access was easy and anonymous, with only a computer and modem necessary to make the link. On-screen membership forms thus revolutionized recruiting by transforming curiosity into commitment with the click of a mouse. The web page had replaced the storefront as the headquarters and enlistment center for social protest. Also heightening a sense of community were news groups like alt.conspiracy and misc.activism.militia, which made conspiracy thinking interactive. The John Birch Society took advantage early and went online to showcase its positions and sell products. The Society's "E-mail Alert Network" gave instant access to supporters and prepared them for action. More sophisticated was Aryan Nation's LibertyNet. Like PatriotNet and PaulRevereNet, it allowed users with the proper password to dial into a computerized bulletin board and post messages, send e-mail, and link to supplementary websites. In browsing the sites, the suspicious burrowed into a community that confirmed itself with replicating information while filtering out contradictions. With repeated hits, cyberopinions became dogma, and the marketplace closed to competitors.[116]

As the militias and the message spread, new evidence of the plot emerged and heightened vigilance. Storage depots for Russian tanks were sighted in Oregon and Texas, probably close to FEMA detention camps. Observers also spotted forty thousand U.N. troops in San Diego County, California, and fourteen thousand in Anchorage, Alaska. A Nepalese Gurkha detachment was reported to have crossed the Canadian border and taken up positions in Montana. Secret codes were discovered on the backs of interstate highway signs giving travel directions for the invading armies. The government, meanwhile, was cleverly disguising the flight of New World Order aircraft in American skies by encouraging reports of UFO sightings.[117]

Distrust became so intense that the April 19, 1995, bombing of the Alfred P. Murrah Federal Building in Oklahoma City, which killed 168 persons and injured hundreds more, became another instance of government treachery. Conspiracists hatched theories accusing federal agents of planting bombs to destroy evidence critical of their role at Waco, or to justify the imposition of martial law, or to frame countersubversives. Like Lee Harvey Oswald, convicted bomber, Timothy McVeigh, was innocent, or a "patsy," or had a double.[118] Both prosecution and defense attorneys in the McVeigh trial were clearly in step with the times, as they made their respective cases with conspiracy accusations. The fear spread to a wider public. A few days after the Oklahoma City bombing the Gallup organization found that 39 percent of conservatives and 42 percent of liberals believed that "the federal government has become so large and powerful that it poses an immediate threat to the rights and freedom of ordinary citizens."[119] Surveys later in the decade replicated these findings, with three-quarters of Americans convinced that federal officials were involved in conspiracy and cover-up.[120]

The conspiracists had certainly been successful in raising the level of concern in America during the 1990s. More important, however, was the cooperation of mainstream leaders in relaying these fears and shaping suspicions. Women and men were more likely to credit the influential, whose credentials acted to ease skepticism. Often, these credentials alone distinguished the opinion makers of American society from members of the conspiracy core. Thus the former chair of the Atomic Energy Commission and Washington State Governor Dixie Lee Ray condemned the 1992 U.N. Earth Summit for its attempt "to bring about a change in the present system of independent nations. . . . Fear of environmental crisis, whether real or not, is expected to lead to compliance. If force is needed, it will be provided by a UN green-helmeted police force, already authorized by the Security Council."[121] Phyllis Schlafly's Eagle Forum also warned against U.N. treaties "designed to control human behavior, energy consumption, private property, and natural resources. . . . [The Clinton administration] is steadily putting American trade and prosperity under the control of international organizations."[122] In 1994 the Oklahoma state legislature passed a resolution that asked the U.S. Congress "to cease any support of the establishment of a 'new world order' or to any form of global government."[123] The Utah House of Representatives passed a similar resolution two years later. The National Rifle Association, always tuned to its members' views, denounced the "Jack-booted government thugs" who participated in the Ruby Ridge and Waco sieges.[124] Convinced that the brew of tragedy and conspiracy still had appeal two years later, TLC television network executives offered an episode on the Oklahoma City bombing in its 1997 "Conspiracy Week" series. Ads tantalizingly asked: "Did they really catch the man behind the Oklahoma City bombing? Or was there a conspiracy? . . . Who bombed Oklahoma City?"[125] The mainstream press occasionally gave comfort to countersubversives. A *New York Times* editorial, if scrambling the chronological sequence, partially validated their concerns: "The F.B.I. had been justly criticized in recent years for erratic and furtive behavior, first with the Branch Davidians in Waco and then at the Ruby Ridge standoff."[126] The *Houston Chronicle* agreed, calling the Bureau of Alcohol, Tobacco, and Firearms "the worst disaster in law enforcement history."[127]

In 1999 new revelations about federal conduct at Waco led mainstream commentators to confirm charges of whitewash and cover-up. The FBI, after years of "unqualified denials," conceded that it had used pyrotechnic teargas canisters in the assault on the Branch Davidian compound.[128] Although the Bureau rejected this as the cause of the fires that killed most of the Branch Davidians, the retreat cast doubt on its account of a Koresh-ordered mass suicide. Chief counsel Robert Charles of the 1995 congressional committee assigned to investigate Waco fumed: "It boggles the mind that they would have withheld that from us. If you put it together with the other pieces of evidence that have come to light . . . it suggests to me that there was a concerted effort on the part of the FBI or the Justice Department or both to cover up damning facts."[129]

Attorney General Janet Reno was shaken by the news. With her eye on the conspiracy thinkers and grasping for credibility, she ordered an internal investigation to control the damage. When that failed to halt the uproar, Reno, having lost confidence in the FBI, sent U.S. marshals into the J. Edgar Hoover Building to seize pertinent evidence. The *New York Times* put the news on the front page for days while praising the "tenacity" of the conspiracy theorists who discredited the official report.[130] *Newsweek* magazine, meanwhile, made it a cover story and printed another conspiracist accusation, "that elite units from the Army's secretive Delta Force may have played a larger role than was previously acknowledged." Reno's call for an internal investigation did not dispel distrust. Henry Ruth, Jr., a former Watergate prosecutor, called for an independent inquiry: "If they don't reopen the whole thing now and actually use outside investigators, this will be like the Kennedy assassination for the next fifty years."[131] Newspaper editors and opinion makers across the country took up his call. Gloating in the Birch Society's *New American*, Charles Key could not resist asking the obvious question: "If officials in the Justice Department lied to us about Waco, what else has the government lied to us about?"[132]

Broadening the context were the doses of conspiracism that Americans received at the flick of their television remotes. *The X-Files*, a Chris Carter production on the Fox Network, began its run in 1993 and built a devoted following, with some episodes picking up a market share of 22, or almost twenty million viewers. By the end of the decade, viewers could watch *The X-Files*, which the more zealous consider a documentary, every day of the week and compare notes in hundreds of related web sites and chat rooms. Merchandisers also enable X-filers to find community through purchase of a host of such products as books, coffee mugs, lunch boxes, key chains, watches, screensavers, and Christmas ornaments, among many other items.[133]

Framed by the watchwords "The truth is out there," each installment follows intrepid and plucky FBI agents Dana Scully and Fox Mulder, whose computer logon is "Trust NO1," in their efforts to solve the unexplained and bring perpetrators to justice. They operate in an atmosphere tense with suspicion, unable at times to distinguish friend from foe. As the critic Charles Taylor observed, "They're watching their backs as much as they're watching the skies."[134] In the central theme, the plot thickens in the hands of insiders, usually cast in dim light; without conscience, they converse in hushed, foreign accents. This sinister cabal not only controls America but rules the world. Its resources and reach are unlimited; all events are manipulated under thick layers of secrecy. The character pointedly named Deep Throat observed in one episode, "There are limits to my knowledge, Mr. Mulder. Inside the intelligence community there are so-called black organizations, groups within groups conducting covert activities unknown even to the highest levels of power."[135] One episode detailed how the conspirators engineered the assassinations of John Kennedy, Martin Luther King, and an extraterrestrial; the Anita Hill–Clarence Thomas confrontation; and the repeated failure of the Buffalo Bills football team to win a Super Bowl. As Mulder explained, it is "a conspiracy, wrapped in a plot, inside a government agenda."[136] In the X-Files motion picture spinoff (1998), art imitated conspiracy theory. The secret syndicate orders the bombing of a federal building in Dallas to destroy incriminating evidence of extraterrestrial contact. FEMA plays a starring role, with its large budget funding black helicopters, alien containment and removal, and the dissemination of a virus to create hosts for the new body snatchers.[137]

The X-Files not only portrays a familiar enemy but is the classic countersubversive quest. Against great odds, individuals wage an unrelenting battle to unveil the plot and force the wider society to confront the truth. Each episode brings the heroes a step closer, with the conspirators beating a retreat as the hour draws to a close. Yet the structure of the television narrative demands that the beast repeatedly escape and rise more threatening than before. Optimism nevertheless prevails, and fans look hopefully to the series' eventual end for full disclosure and thus the ultimate victory.[138]

Americans had attained a high level of fluency with New World Order images by the end of the twentieth century. Hollywood films feasted on the conspiracy. Shadow Conspiracy (1996) discovered the plot in the highest circles of the federal government. Enemy of the State (1998) depicted the National Security Agency's zealous efforts to search for and destroy anyone who stood in its path to power. The machinery of the "surveillance state" awed viewers who may have agreed with the protagonist that "the only privacy left is inside your head."[139] A John Birch Society movie critic gave thumbs up to The Siege (1998), in which the federal government declares martial law in Brooklyn, New York, to cope with terrorism. With the Clinton administration "hardwired into Hollywood" and the scenario "chillingly possible," the reviewer asked whether the film should "be regarded as a cautionary tale or a trial balloon?"[140] Those more inclined to games could purchase "The Illuminati," in card and board versions. The object of both was "to take control of the world."[141] Fans of professional wrestling could love or hate the NWO, a gang of muscled brutes eager to savage opponents. An assortment of NWO hats, T-shirts, and action figures are available online, at the arena, on in the local toy store. Financial adviser Larry Abraham assured men and women who purchased his newsletter that it would protect them from the Insiders' latest project, "the collapse of the U.S. stock market." Having spent his career tracking this "powerful group of billionaires, politicians, and financiers," he would show investors "how to profit in any market by mimicking their steps, move by move."[142] Those who subscribed would receive his book *Call It Conspiracy* as a bonus gift. Pat Buchanan ended the century by announcing his conversion from the Republican to the Reform Party, a more effective platform to campaign against "the godless New World Order."[143]

The master conspiracy has proven a flexible weapon in the struggle for power in recent American history. Beginning in the 1930s, politicians focused voters on Communists, charging that traitors had infiltrated the federal government in service to foreign enemies. Capitalizing on legitimate concerns in the changing postwar world, they fabricated an interpretation premised on malevolence. Not even presidents and the members of their inner circle were exempted from accusation. Success was not in their hands alone. When opinion makers and even opponents approved and disseminated such claims, partisanship became patriotism. Conspiracy theory has also proven useful to Washington bureaucrats who stroke public insecurities as a means to building and maintaining a power base. When new realities led opinion makers to discard conspiracy thinking, grassroots activists wielded it to mobilize resources and expand the countersubversive core. Within this community, conspiracists revealed what had remained hidden, while shaping the conspiracy to fit recent events. Robert Welch and his John Birch Society were critical in this process. Their preaching merged with traditional fears of government domination and anti-elite populism, but confidence in authorities sealed their isolation. Still, they harbored the doctrine of global conspiracy and continued publicizing it, waiting for events and opinion makers to validate them. The behavior of their targets would bring fresh recruits and the cooperation of the influential would enhance credibility. New technologies raised their profile and facilitated commitment. In the 1990s the mainstream became tolerant and even accepting of reports of secret plans, cover-ups, and hidden agendas. Cynicism had replaced trust in the authorities. Mainstream Americans did not adopt the intense dedication of credentialed countersubversives or share their ability to recall the details of conspiracy. They had learned, however, to be vigilant at the very mention of the Council on Foreign Relations, the Trilateral Commission, the New World Order, and Insiders.

Robert Welch had fought a secular crusade against the globalists. Although he had made vague references to God and the Judeo-Christian ethic, Welch had not grounded his interpretation in Scripture or religious imagery. He had also repeatedly denounced religious chauvinism and sectarianism as Insider tactics to fragment the patriot movement. Recently, however, the John Birch Society has slightly shifted its line. Writing in the *New American* in 1999, Steve Bonta assailed the "New Age" religious roots of the New World Order. The conspirators, he argued, "have seen the need for providing a religious foundation for a global society under a global government." Tied to the worship of Gaia and a belief in voodoo, this "new paganism" promised to destroy souls and make women and men passive before the emerging dictators.[144] This gesture recognized a powerful religious current that was energizing American conspiracy thinking in the 1990s. Christians have long looked to events for signs of the rise of the Antichrist and the end of days. In recent America such apocalyptic thinking has merged with and heightened fears of the master conspiracy. The New World Order dictatorship is not the end of the world but a means to it. Only when this religious stream of countersubversion is joined to the secular is the fascination with the global conspiracy fully comprehensible.

CHAPTER 3

The Rise of the Antichrist

> The events of public policy are not the accidents or coincidences we are generally led to believe. They are planned. ... Impulses of that sort do not spring from the human heart, or for that matter from God's heart. They spring, instead, from the depth of something that is evil.
> —PAT ROBERTSON

> The unmistakable scent of what the Bible calls the antichrist spirit is in the air. It was present at the tower of Babel and at Sodom and Gomorrah. It was present in the French Revolution and in Nazi Germany. And it is present in Europe and the United States today.
> —PAT ROBERTSON

Christians in America have long sensed a special relationship with God. The nation was created to perform the Lord's will and surely was chosen as the site of the Second Coming and God's future kingdom. In preparation, Americans proclaimed their manifest destiny and built a transcontinental city upon the hill. When God delivered power into American hands, the mission grew to encompass the world. America was the Lord's redeeming sword in the war against the forces of darkness. The Bible, particularly the Book of Revelation, guided this vision and steeled men and women in their purpose. Each generation repeated the task of interpretation, juggling, juxtaposing, and merging biblical verses to expose coded messages and to fit preconceptions. The resulting interpretive template transformed current events into fulfillment of biblical prophecies. Events, in turn, completed the circle, becoming new evidence of the literal truth of Scriptures and the working of the divine plan. Not surprisingly, each generation found itself in the unique position of reaching the end of days and leaving history.

Postwar Americans also felt an urgency, as key events signaled that the end was near. Using diverse means, evangelists aggressively beseeched the unforgiven to repent before Judgment Day. Christian conspiracists set the pace and tone for this new great awakening. With televangelist Pat Robertson playing a critical role, they infused the call for personal salvation—and often overwhelmed it—with the cry of conspiracy. Borrowing from the dogma of secular counter-subversives, the Christian crusaders gave the plot a spiritual spin. America, awash in sin, had betrayed its calling and fallen away from the Lord. Its leaders had sacrificed national sovereignty to the Antichrist and sworn allegiance to Satan's New World Order. To mobilize the faithful they stroked the belief in exceptionalism, distrust of government, and a sense of national decline. The imminence of the millennium spurred them to greater spiritual and secular effort, and they succeeded in advancing their cause from the periphery to the center of American politics and society. Support came from an unexpected source. The entertainment industry, seemingly steeped in humanist heresy, mainstreamed the apocalyptic message and its conspiracy theme by instructing Americans in biblical prophecy and conjuring up their worst fears.

To track God's work through history and to divine the future, believers turned to his prophets in the Bible. Biblical prophecy was history before its time. Scriptural passages that foretold the end of days, though, were difficult to decipher. Prophets had repeatedly shared their visions, but they spoke allegorically. Their obscure images and admonitions were tied to people and places far removed from the present. This ambiguity demanded that believers sift the literal words imaginatively to make God's plan comprehensible. The New Testament's Book of Revelation was particularly rich in imagery and thus invited vigorous interpretation. Its importance was obvious to believers. As the Puritan minister Cotton Mather noted, "'Tis the last Advice that we have had from Heaven, for now sixteen Hundred years."[1]

Revelation gives readers the vision of John, who was exiled to the Greek island of Patmos in A.D. 95 for preaching Christianity to pagan Rome. John writes of an angel who beckoned him to the "door" of heaven to see "things which must be hereafter." Before him appears a succession of images of tribulations and calamities in sequences of seven. Earthquakes, storms, polluted rivers and seas, falling stars, locust, famine, and plague devastate the faithless but are only a prelude to the final battle. Satan confronts God and takes the shape of "a great red dragon having seven heads and ten horns, and seven crowns upon his heads." On a base of ten kingdoms, the dark lord elevates his heir, the "beast" or Antichrist: "And they worshiped the dragon which gave power unto the beast: and they worshiped the beast, saying Who is like unto the beast? Who is able to make war with him?" Joined by his coconspirator, the false prophet, the Antichrist creates an economic system that requires every person to "receive a mark in their right hand, or in their foreheads: And that no man might buy or sell, save he that had the mark, or the name of the beast, or the number of the beast . . . Six hundred threescore and six." God pours out his wrath on those who accept the mark, while the faithful suffer through forty-two months of persecution. The physical return of Jesus brings redemption, and he leads the heavenly host to victory over the beast and false prophet. The evil ones are cast into a lake of fire and their master Satan is captured and confined to a bottomless pit for one thousand years. Christ reigns with the true believers by his throne until Satan's return at the end of the millennium. His escape is brief and he is condemned to an eternal dousing in the lake of fire. God then passes final judgment on the human race and ushers the holy into paradise.[2]

Bible students were especially inspired when other verses seemed independently to confirm such prophecies or provide elaboration. Evidence accumulated rapidly, for the Scriptures offered more than 1,800 predictions about the Messiah, the Second Coming, and the end of days. The Old Testament prophet Daniel dreamed of a horned beast at war with God. The beast would spawn ten kings, and "another shall rise after them," who would "wear out the saints of the most High." Believers were not surprised that his prophecy of a reign of terror lasting forty-two months synchronized exactly with John's timetable. Ezekiel filled in the details of the battle of Armageddon, surveying the vast armies of Magog, Meshech, Gomer, and Tubal as they converged on Israel from the north and south. Others like Matthew corroborated signs of the end time: "Ye shall hear of wars and rumors of wars. . . . For nation shall rise against nation, and kingdom against kingdom: and there shall be famines, and pestilences, and earthquakes, in diverse places." He quoted Jesus: "Verily I say unto you, This generation shall not pass, till all these things be fulfilled." But Jesus also admonished believers: "Of that day and hour knoweth no man, no, not the angels of heaven, but my Father only."[3]

Christ's caution did nothing to temper speculation. Puritans settled New England in the seventeenth century convinced that they were the terminal generation. Fleeing the satanic papists and their Anglican allies, they commenced building the new Jerusalem prophesied in Revelation as the center of the coming millennial kingdom. Because they were God's faithful, the devil poured his wrath on their enterprise, and they suffered conspiracies of Indians, dissenters, and witches. All these tribulations confirmed their holy mission and the lateness of the hour. Sunday sermons offered earthquakes, comets, plagues, and reports that the Jews were returning to the Holy Land as additional evidence of God's intentions. Puritan minister Increase Mather rattled off other symptoms of the end time: "Men shall be covetous . . . unthankful . . . Truce-breakers . . . Traytors."[4] To many the Second Coming was palpable. The sense is conveyed in America's first best-seller, Michael Wigglesworth's 1662 poem *Day of Doom:*

> For at midnight breaks forth a light,
>   which turns the night to day,
> And speedily an hideous cry
>   doth all the World dismay.
>   . . . .
> They rush from beds with giddy heads,
>   And to their windows run,
> Viewing this light, which shines more bright
>   than doth the noon-day Sun.
> Straightway appears (they see't with tears)
>   the Son of God most dread
> Who with his Train comes on amain
>   to judge both Quick and Dead.[5]

In this context, minister Cotton Mather repeatedly set pulses racing with his predictions that the Kingdom of God was at hand in 1697, then 1716, and finally in 1736. As he wrote in his diary, *"They are coming! They are coming! They are coming! They will quickly be upon us; and the world shall be shaken wonderfully!"*[6] Beyond the Puritan settlements, other colonists were well aware of the cosmic struggle that framed their lives. As historian Perry Miller observed about the Virginia plantations, "adventurers and planters felt in every disaster the hoof of the devil."[7]

Congregationalist minister Jonathan Edwards pursued Cotton Mather's eschatological or end-time message. Like Mather, he heard the approaching hoofbeat and singled out New England for a pivotal role in apocalyptic events. Edwards, with other American Protestants, identified the Roman Catholic pope as the Antichrist and kept a suspicious eye on his base in French Canada. Worried about the decline of spirituality at so critical a time, he welcomed the revival meetings of the Great Awakening of the 1730s and 1740s as the means to replenish God's armies. The new enthusiasm was surely a divine sign that would not only signal but hasten the Second Coming. Although Mather predicted that the Antichrist and his coconspirators would not be subdued until 1866, the outbreak of the French and Indian War in 1754 was surely the beginning of the end.[8]

America's sense of exceptionalism merged in the 1760s with a developing tradition of distrust of central authority to fuel the Revolutionary impulse. Colonists now discovered Satan conspiring through an oppressive civil government to punish God's people; they linked English King George III with the pope as likely candidates for the Antichrist. Members of the Boston Sons of Liberty certainly knew the consequences of a speaker's warning given in the wake of the passage of the Stamp Act: "I beseech you then to beware as good Christians and lovers of your country lest by touching any paper with this impression, you receive the mark of the *beast,* and become infamous in your country and throughout all generations."[9] John Adams also turned to the Book of Revelation during the Stamp Act crisis and raised familiar images when he reminded colonists "that popular powers must be placed as a guard, a control, a balance, to the power of the monarch and the priest, in every government, or else it would soon become the man of sin, the whore of Babylon, the mystery of iniquity, a great and detestable system of fraud, violence, and usurpation."[10] In the holy crusade that was the American Revolution, victory was another step toward the millennial kingdom, with the United States ready to serve as Christ's earthly throne.[11]

Americans knew that Satan's retreat would be brief. In the 1790s, New England Federalists exposed the Illuminati, the devil's latest device to turn the nation from its mission. Timothy Dwight, president of Yale College, warned on July 4, 1798: "The sins of these enemies of Christ, and Christians, are of number and degrees which mock account and description. All that the malice and atheism of the Dragon, the cruelty and rapacity of the Beast, and the fraud and deceit of the false Prophet can generate or accomplish, swell the list."[12] Nativists revived the idea of a satanic conspiracy of kings and popes in the nineteenth century to enflame sentiment against waves of Catholic immigrants. Protestant ministers opened their Bibles to chapter 17 of the Book of Revelation and railed against the menace, portraying the Catholic Church as "MYSTERY, BABYLON THE GREAT, THE MOTHER OF HARLOTS AND ABOMINATIONS OF THE EARTH" who sits upon the seven mountains of Rome.[13]

Such combative millennialism remained significant, but in the decades before the Civil War many tempered the conspiratorial overtones of the rush to the end. The focus now was on rebirth as Americans prepared to create or await the heavenly kingdom. Millennialism spread rapidly, with the Second Great Awakening igniting mass repentance and a ferment of social reform promising to end sin and corruption. In 1823 Joseph Smith believed that he had encountered an angel in upstate New York who revealed that the Second Coming was at hand. It was his task to gather the Mormon saints and prepare for the last days. Baptist preacher William Miller studied the books of Daniel and Revelation, did the arithmetic, and announced the date of Christ's return. His followers, estimated to have numbered almost one million men and women, repeatedly sang the hymn "And Smile to See a Burning World" as the appointed hour and subsequent alternatives failed to bring deliverance. Other Bible students had also been too specific, setting the day and the hour in 1816, 1832, 1857, and 1861. In spite of these great disappointments, few doubted America's chosen role in the divine drama. The Civil War, and its four years of bloodletting, sobered expectations. Nevertheless, as Julia Ward Howe's "Battle Hymn of the Republic" reflects, Americans remained immersed in the apocalyptic images of their inheritance:

> Mine eyes have seen the glory of the coming of the Lord;
> He is trampling out the vintage where the grapes of wrath are stored;
> He hath loosed the fateful lightning of his terrible swift sword:
> His truth is marching on.
> . . . .
> He has sounded forth the trumpet that shall never call retreat;
> He is sifting out the hearts of men before His judgment seat;
> Oh, be swift, my soul, to answer him! Be jubilant, my feet!
> Our God is marching on.[14]

In the second half of the nineteenth century, Americans gradually lost faith in human agency as the means to the millennium and placed their redemption in divine hands. Clarifying their thinking was British minister John Nelson Darby's new interpretive design, which claimed to solve apocalyptic mysteries. Certain that prophecy was history to come, Darby meshed, mixed, and reordered diverse biblical passages to create a linear and logical sequence of events that culminated in a detailed end-time scenario. He began by crafting biblical milestones into a series of seven dispensations, periods of time of unequal length that began with Adam and proceeded to the millennium. The crucifixion of Jesus brought the fifth of these ages to completion. Time marched on, but the prophetic clock then stopped when Jews failed to accept Christ as the Messiah and delayed the coming of his kingdom. In the current age, the last before judgment, God beckoned the community of true believers to spread the gospel and secure souls. The cause was urgent, for the divine countdown to Armageddon would resume without warning with the Rapture of the church, when believers would enter heaven without dying, "meet[ing] the Lord in the air; and so we ever shall be with the Lord."[15] The tribulation scenario moved quickly after that and climaxed in seven years: the emergence of a ten-nation confederation, the rise of the Antichrist and his subsequent perfidy, the machinations of the false prophet, the conversion of the 144,000 Jews who would preach the gospel and die for their labors, an invasion of Israel, the assault of the armies of the East, the return of Jesus, and the defeat of Satan and his followers.[16]

Darby's understanding of the final reckoning was not only intellectually satisfying but spiritually comforting. Knowledge of God's plan armed believers against uncertainty, tightened identities, and steadied faith. The concept of the Rapture worked on several levels, putting the faithful on alert, extinguishing the fear of death, and offering painless deliverance. In this state of raised expectations, the daily newspaper heralded fresh evidence of God's plan. Darby's detailing of coming events also put the Antichrist and false prophet into sharper focus. In stressing their conspiracy, he moved it back to the center of the narrative. This added tension even as the Rapture escape had removed the heat of tribulation fires. Nor did his framework daunt American exceptionalists who still believed that God had chosen their nation for a special role. Darby's framework now required only finishing touches and updating and a legion of guides would rise to the task in each succeeding generation.[17]

As important as Darby's creation was its dissemination within and beyond the ranks of the faithful core. Cyrus Scofield accomplished the task with his *Reference Bible,* first printed in 1909 and selling more than two million copies in a 1967 edition. Scofield canonized Darby's decoding by printing it in the margins of the King James Version of the biblical text. The result was "a new system of connected topical references . . . to which are added helps at hard places."[18] Human agency had ensured the Bible's infallibility. The literal word had been interpreted, and the interpretation was now raised to the level of the literal word. Through Scofield's effort, Darby became the intellectual father to ministers and their congregations even unto the final generation of the twentieth century.[19]

The spread of the word made the end time even more visible in current events. As Cyrus Scofield reminded believers, prophecy "is history written beforehand."[20] World War I was an ominous portent. Kaiser Wilhelm fit the description of the Antichrist, and the Bolshevik Revolution in Russia set a key protagonist on stage for the final drama. The faithful also knew that Woodrow Wilson's League of Nations offered only a brief solution to global tensions. At the same time, they marveled at the fulfillment of prophecy in Great Britain's Balfour Declaration that recognized Palestine as a Jewish homeland. International crises in the 1930s profiled Adolf Hitler, Benito Mussolini, and Joseph Stalin as possible Antichrists. Alternatively, Baptist evangelist Gerald Winrod used the Bible to discern the Jewish-satanic influences on Roosevelt's New Deal. The Blue Eagle symbol of the National Industrial Recovery Act sprouted seven feathers on one wing and ten on the other, a reflection of the seven-headed and ten-horned beast of Revelation. The Antichrist, Winrod knew, was a Jew, and *The Protocols of the Elders of Zion* "a newly discovered Bible scroll" that revealed the scheme.[21] Eschatological thinkers were convinced that Bible verses foretold of World War II, and they found additional proof in its consequences. The godless communists now commanded an empire that threatened not only the Middle East but the world. The atomic bombing of Hiroshima in 1945 was literally fire from heaven.[22]

Even more significant were the activities of the Jews, God's "timepieces" in the end times.[23] In 1948 Jews proclaimed the birth of the state of Israel and ended their two thousand–year exile. For believers, this was prophecy come to pass, the long-foretold restoration of the Jews to their promised land. They knew to turn for insight to Matthew 24:32 and realized "that summer is nigh"; the generation that witnessed this event would surely live to see the Second Coming. In 1967 further confirmation of God's hand in history appeared when Israeli soldiers captured the Old City of Jerusalem and united the capital under Jewish rule. As written in Luke 21:24: "And Jerusalem shall be trodden down of the Gentiles, until the time of the Gentiles be fulfilled." This potentially extended the timetable by twenty years, depending upon one's calculation of a generation's length. Clearly, the millennium was at the door.[24]

Events in Israel were more than sufficient to alert the faithful to divine possibilities. Enhancing their power was a multiplicity of signs, growing in intensity, that convinced many Christians that Rapture was imminent. Perhaps the trumpets were so insistent because as Judgment Day approached God sought the salvation of even the most prodigal of his children. With all happening according to their interpretative plan, believers were awed but not surprised by the accuracy of prophecy. The threat of a nuclear exchange hung over the world, and wars raged in the Middle East, Africa, and Vietnam. Prosperity brought materialism, which extinguished spirituality and widened the gap between rich and poor. A wave of lawlessness had submerged authority, and an army of police battled rioters for control of city streets and college campuses. Television and motion pictures encouraged sexual promiscuity and drowned the nation in wickedness. The population "bomb" augured a future in which sheer numbers of men and women overwhelmed the world's resources. As the Bible predicted, communication systems had created a knowledge web and facilitated the instant relay of information. Nonbelievers had declared God dead, and the appeal of eastern religions brought the worship of "false Christs" and "false prophets" and threatened to "deceive the very elect."[25] Witches and astrologers practiced their black arts openly and without fear of righteous retribution. The devil was surely abroad, and his hand was visible in escalating divorce rates, drug use, feminism, and gay liberation. Meanwhile, the United Nations had cleared the path for global unification, and internationalists fashioned a growing worldwide network of economic, political, and religious organizations. God was pouring out his wrath: great earthquakes, damaging floods, and killing storms were merely redundant reminders of what was to come.[26]

In this storm, afflicted America had lost its bearings—and worse, God's grace. Evangelists echoed rightists who blamed national leaders for not only failing to stem the tide but increasing its strength. The Supreme Court ended prayer in school, protected criminals, defended pornographers, and ordered the killing of the unborn. Presidents pursued a foreign policy of failure, fostering détente with the atheistic Russian and Chinese Communists while squandering men and resources in a no-win war in Southeast Asia. Personal misbehavior exacerbated policy mistakes. Rather than acting as role models, they had stained the nation and torn the moral fiber. More disturbing, American leaders had betrayed God's favor by relinquishing national sovereignty in international efforts to build a world government that would exercise supreme economic and military power. Christians had become strangers in their own land. As it would come to pass according to Jeremiah 44:22: "Because of the evil of your doings, and because of the abominations which ye have committed; therefore is your land a desolation, and an astonishment, and a curse."[27]

Awakening to God's frown, Christians prepared to get right with the Lord. Evangelical churches, stressing a born-again experience, the inerrancy of the Bible, and a mission to spread the gospel, took advantage and grew as their liberal counterparts declined in membership. During the 1970s and early 1980s, the United Presbyterian Church lost 21 percent of its members, the Episcopal Church 15 percent, and the United Methodists 10 percent while the Southern Baptist Convention registered an increase of 15 percent, the Church of the Nazarene 22 percent, and the Assemblies of God 71 percent. If America had fallen into apostasy, the faithful could yet claim a place by Christ's throne. But faith alone would not secure that claim, and evangelicals moved with a new confidence and aggressiveness to confront the modern world. Pledged to spread the holy word, they poured money into missionary efforts at home and abroad to save souls and build up the church. Important work could also be done in the political arena. To buy time for proselytizing, delay the devil's forces, and advance God's will, believers organized to cure the moral plague afflicting America. An America returned to righteousness would shelter Christians against the closing dark times before the certain but unknown moment of Rapture. Envisioning themselves as the church in politics, organizations like Moral Majority, America for Jesus, the National Christian Action Coalition, and later the Christian Coalition mobilized the faithful core in support of Israel and against the Equal Rights Amendment, abortion, gay rights, and the Trilateral Commission. Working through the Republican Party, Christians were able not only to control local and state organizations but to shape national platforms. Such works, combined with faith, were the keys to the kingdom.[28]

With the righteous secured, evangelists reached into the mainstream and challenged secular perspectives. Several advantages energized their proselytizing. They stood on the authority of the Bible, which four in five Americans believed was the "literal" or "inspired" word of God. Eight Americans in ten held that God still worked miracles and that on Judgment Day he would call men and women "to answer for our sins."[29] The matter of the Apocalypse—four horsemen, Antichrist, mark of the beast, and Second Coming—was part of the religious inheritance of even the most complacent Christians. Few would dispute evangelists' claims, either because of indifference or because of a lack of acquaintance with scriptural criticism and even the Bible's contents. Frequent repetition of the message, carried by diverse voices, not only blurred the line between biblical authority and interpretation, but testified to its truth. This homogenized version of the end time, with the devil in the details, succeeded in quieting doubts and proved difficult to rebut. Ministerial credentials also privileged their message and allowed entry denied other countersubversives. Meanwhile, media savvy enabled evangelists to exploit a variety of technologies to influence a national audience. Nor did the conspiracy message embedded in end-time prophecy produce dissonance. In a national climate of conspiracy, satanic machinations proved Americans' exceptionalism and validated their traditional distrust of central authority. Anticipating cosmic implications as a new millennium approached, mainstream Christians accepted their word as both spiritually and politically empowering.[30]

This campaign for souls and soldiers raised a new generation of evangelists. They came from the grass roots, obtaining their ministerial credentials from small Bible colleges or, in the absence of formal training, realizing their callings after the intercession of the Holy Spirit. Elaboration and dissemination, not creation, were their primary tasks. As Darby's disciples, they cast dispensationalism to fit modern sensibilities. Repackaging involved not only an updating of evidence but a revision of the language to enhance accessibility. Again, current events were distilled of their nuances and shaped to confirm rather than to test interpretation. In preaching Darby, evangelists also intensified their stress on conspiracy, mirroring the rising influence of secular countersubversives. Their calls for repentance revealed the plot to manipulate American government and foreign policy as steps in the creation of the evil one's kingdom on earth. Balancing hope with fear, they counterposed the lure of Rapture against the dread of the beast. Contemporary Darbyism thus worked to clarify the stakes of confrontation and, in exposing the enemy, fostered the community of saints. In the end, their efforts bore fruit in a coalition that crossed denominations and armed for both secular and spiritual Armageddons.[31]

One of the most prolific and influential of the new breed of fishers of women and men is Hal Lindsey, a graduate of the Dallas Theological Seminary and former staff member with the Campus Crusade for Christ. His first book, *The Late Great Planet Earth*, was published in 1970 and caught the wave of growing evangelical fervor. Finding its way into supermarkets and shopping mall bookstores, *Late Great Planet* became an immediate best-seller and the most successful nonfiction book of the decade. By the early 1990s it had been translated into fifty-two languages and sold more than twenty-eight million copies. Those unwilling to read the short book could take advantage of a documentary film narrated by Orson Welles that appeared in 1978. Success and his sense of mission motivated Lindsey to recycle and elaborate the message in a continuing series of books, the most recent published at the end of the 1990s. While Lindsey's debt to Darby was readily apparent, so, too, was his contribution. Here was a short, breezy account that did not hesitate over difficult passages or suggest the controversy inherent in biblical interpretation. In fact, Lindsey maintained that the Bible revealed itself and he advised readers not to be "bothered by the figures of speech which are used[;] you will see that the Bible explains the meaning."[32] Without self-consciousness, Lindsey confidently transformed Magog into the Soviet Union, locusts into helicopters, and fire and brimstone into nuclear war. He just as easily found the current proof of scriptural prophecies, with Israel, the European Common Market, and Communist China testifying to biblical infallibility. His fit of prophecy to events not only awed the ignorant but disarmed the cynical and skeptical who had never realized that the Bible was actually a history textbook. As he explained in a sequel, John's Revelation "must have been an experience of *time travel* to the beginning of the 21st century."[33]

In *Late Great Planet*, Lindsey sets the stage according to convention with a discussion of the pre-Rapture "birth pangs," or signs of the end times, distilled from the books of Ezekiel, Daniel, and Revelation. His decoding reveals, in the foreground, the Jews in Israel with their capital united. In the shadows are the Soviet Union and its Islamic and black African allies, preparing to pounce on Israel. From the East comes news that a powerful Chinese Communist army is preparing to march. Separate, but paralleling these developments, is the emergence of a ten-nation European confederation under the stewardship of the Common Market. In the background can be heard the gathering storm of wars, earthquakes, and plagues that is increasing in magnitude as time draws to a close.[34]

The sudden but expected Rapture of the community of believers ratchets up crisis momentum. Without the church to stay the dark lord's hand, the Antichrist assumes power in Europe, pretending to be the deliverer of peace and prosperity. The seven years of Tribulation begin when the Antichrist forges an alliance with Israel that he has no intention of honoring. Jews, misjudging the intentions of the beast, begin rebuilding their temple in Jerusalem. Meanwhile, the Antichrist extends his dominion, incorporating the United States into his global kingdom. His accomplice is the false prophet, whom Lindsey identifies as a Jew, perhaps because of his skill in creating and managing the new cashless economic system. The two also organize a one-world church that feeds on worship of the occult. Reflecting old prejudices, Lindsey advises readers to maintain their focus on the Vatican, for the pope will "become even more involved in world politics." For forty-two months, peace reigns while men and women succumb to devil worship and accept the mark of the beast. Christians left behind after Rapture and now reborn reject the new order and are persecuted and murdered. Tensions mount when the Antichrist journeys to the Jerusalem temple and proclaims himself god. This repels Jews, who finally turn to Jesus as the Messiah. As the second half of Tribulation dawns, the Islamic coalition, angered by the construction of the Jewish temple on its holy ground, attacks Israel from the south while the Russians invade from the north. God protects his chosen people and slaughters the invaders, but a new danger threatens when two hundred million Chinese advance on Megiddo, the site of Armageddon. The Antichrist prepares a last stand, mobilizing American and European troops in the defense. On the brink of world destruction, Jesus returns and in a "thermonuclear blast" destroys "all ungodly kingdoms." Those who took the mark are then dispatched, making way for the believers and the new millennium.[35]

Conspiracy imaging is apparent but subtle in *Late Great Planet,* which ignores the specifics of subversion. In subsequent books, Lindsey drew inspiration from sources other than the Bible to flush out the conspiracy. As he continued the "countdown toward Armageddon," he deciphered the code to biblical prophecies that foresaw the Trilateral Commission as a foundation stone of the sinister world government and economy. He predicted: "What the trilateralists are trying to establish will soon be controlled by the coming world leader—the anti-Christ himself." Further study pressed him to condemn the United Nations' "grab of global sovereignty" and NAFTA and the European Union as "precursors of world government."[36]

With *Late Great Planet* as their model, other evangelists added to the outpouring of end-time information. Differences over the timing of Rapture, the sequence of Tribulation events, and the religious identities of the Antichrist and false prophet notwithstanding, a contemporary consensus emerged by the late 1970s that assured believers that the truth was at hand. The united front also stoked salience by bringing America into the action, regardless of its apparent absence in biblical verse. Conspiracy, too, was assigned a more prominent role. The Reverend Jerry Falwell, founder of the Moral Majority, offered his views in books, on tape, and before national television and radio audiences on his *Old-Time Gospel Hour* program. His account confirmed that God had sent the AIDS plague to punish the city of San Francisco for its wickedness and warned that abortion sins would bring down more of his wrath on the United States. He speculated that Secretary of State Henry Kissinger might be the Antichrist because of his peace efforts in the Middle East and a numerical code that totaled his name to 666. Falwell corroborated Lindsey's suspicions about the Trilateral Commission and condemned its plans to merge the economies of Japan, the United States, and Europe in preparation for world government. He had his eye, as well, on Pope John Paul II, whose global travel "serve[d] to demonstrate the future religious achievements of the one world church during the coming tribulation."[37] Satan's progress and arrogance stunned televangelist Jack Van Impe. He noted ominously in his book *11:59 . . . and Counting* that New York City, the site of the United Nations, computed mathematically to 666 "and is also a base for the international bankers." He insisted that employees of the Bureau of Alcohol, Tobacco, and Firearms already wore badges displaying the number 666 and that U.S. Selective Service cards bore the same numerical code. The "one-world government is almost upon us," declared Van Impe, who counted fifteen global organizations that dominated the planet.[38] His report on the religious front was equally distressing: "Beware! The present ecumenical effort, attempting to unite all religions under a so-called 'banner of brotherhood,' regardless of one's belief about Christ, is the forerunner of a monstrous fornicator who makes all nations drink of the wine of her wrath."[39] Salem Kirban's *Guide to Survival,* which sold more than one half-million copies through 1991, verified the beast's advance, finding that the Social Security number was now "universal" and might become the mark through "an invisible tattoo number system."[40]

Advancing technologies brought new evidence of the devilish menace. Mary Relfe, the secretary-treasurer of the Montgomery, Alabama, Airport Authority, detected a sinister purpose in the universal product code, which made machine-readable the prices of items for sale. She uncovered a "consortium" of international bankers that suspiciously affixed on all products a bar-code symbol with lines grouped in aggregates of six. Alarmed, she wrote "*Many people are already 'buying' and 'selling' using the Anti Christ's number '666.' His system is already here! His number is already in use!*" The world was but a short step from "an amplified system to IDENTIFY every person with similar technology."[41] After additional research, Relfe was convinced that this was but one of the beast's ploys to effect the cashless society. Credit and debit cards, hand-scanners, and electronic funds transfers testified to the literal fulfillment of passages from Revelation. Relfe went public with her concerns and found she was not alone; her self-published book *When Your Money Fails* sold three hundred thousand copies within three months of publication in 1981 and six hundred thousand in total. The market was so good that she published a sequel the next year. Other authors later discerned the Antichrist's mark on smart cards, ATMs, microchip implants, and fiber optics. Certainly consistent was the revelation that "computer" had a numerical value of 666 and that the beast had programed a supermachine in Brussels to monitor the earth's billions.[42]

With the conviction of the chosen and the end in sight, evangelists went in hot pursuit of the unforgiven. Armed with offerings from the faithful core, they carried their messages of redemption and conspiracy door to door and around the world. Christian bookstores mushroomed and supplemented book selections with such periodical offerings as *It's Happening Now, Rapture Alert Newsletter, Countdown, Bible in the News, Bible Prophecy News,* and *Endtime Messenger,* among others. The "electric church" of radio and television, long a vehicle of American preachers, complemented the power of the written word in summoning converts and resources.[43] Surveys found that one-third of American adults in 1983 and nearly half in 1987 had watched all or part of at least one religious program during the previous thirty days. Ten percent of these viewers had made donations to sponsor the host's work. More than three hundred television and radio stations broadcast Jerry Falwell's interpretation and pleas for repentance. Americans also tuned in Pat Robertson, Oral Roberts, Rex Humbard, Jack Van Impe, Jimmy Swaggart, and Tammy and Jim Bakker for instruction. Televangelism recovered quickly from scandals in the late 1980s and prospered in the 1990s, when as many as 221 television stations and three cable networks were dedicated to the Christian cause. Meanwhile, 1,370 radio stations carried Christian programing, with more than 300 featuring the message full-time. Locally, Sunday sermons echoed the call, with weekly reminders to repent and escape the fiery lake that would swallow the unregenerate. Even freeway drivers could not escape the barrage. Christians proclaimed their salvation with bumper stickers reading "The Rapture: What a Way to Go," "Ready or not, Jesus is Coming," and "Beam Me Up, Lord."[44] Merchandisers offered T-shirts, key chains, and wristwatches with similar sentiments.[45]

Facilitating their acceptance in the mainstream was the true believer in the White House. As early as 1971, Ronald Reagan realized that "everything is falling into place. It can't be too long now. Ezekiel says that fire and brimstone will be raining upon the enemies of God's people. That must mean they'll be destroyed by nuclear weapons. They exist now, and they never did in the past. Ezekiel tells us that Gog, the nation that will lead all of the other powers of darkness against Israel, will come out of the north. Biblical scholars have been saying for generations that Gog must be Russia. What other powerful nation is to the north of Israel? None."[46] In 1984 the *Los Angeles Times* quoted the president: "You know, I turn back to your ancient prophets in the Old Testament and the signs

To maintain their focus and celebrate identity with a touch of humor, born-again Christians scooped up key chains, bookmarks, T-shirts, bumper stickers, among assorted other items with the proper evangelical messages.

of foretelling Armageddon, and I find myself wondering if—if we're the generation that is going to see that come about. I don't know if you've noted any of these prophecies lately, but believe me, they certainly describe the times we're going through."[47] To be on the safe side, Reagan had city officials change the "666" street number of his house in California to a more mundane address.[48]

The evangelical offensive had its effect. Gallup pollsters reported in 1979 that one in three Christians bore testimony of a personal conversion experience. Forty percent had been born again by 1984, increasing the ranks of evangelicals to an estimated forty million to fifty million women and men. Ten years later, surveys found that 60 percent of Americans had concluded that biblical passages about Judgment Day should be taken "literally," while two-thirds of those polled believed in the Devil. Half were similarly convinced of the truth of prophecies concerning the Antichrist.[49]

The appeal of the evangelical message was obvious. It had brought comfort and inner peace, as millions of Americans reexamined their lives and were born again in a personal commitment to Christ. Fear was also vanquished as Rapture promised heaven without death. Simultaneously quickening the repentance of the faithful was their knowledge of the wages of sin. Tribulation acted to intensify greatly the power of Rapture; those left behind would find no shelter from the Antichrist and an angry God. Breathing life into the Tribulation conspiracy, evangelists had returned God to history and given the supernatural human shape and form. Satan, the Antichrist, and the false prophet were no longer figurative adversaries but real beings presently scheming in existing organizations and international ventures. Although evangelical Christianity was not synonymous with conspiracism, the overlap was apparent. Faithful and secular Christians were familiar with the countersubversive message of evangelicalism and accepted or at least tolerated its premises.

By making evangelical conspiracism even more explicit and persuasive, the Reverend Pat Robertson was instrumental in both hastening commitment to and fostering public indulgence of countersubversion. It was Robertson who grounded evangelical conspiracism firmly in secular countersubversion, pronouncing the New World Order satanic. His media power and political activism guaranteed a broad audience and bestowed legitimacy on his contribution. This work carried Robertson beyond Hal Lindsey and Jerry Falwell and made him the most influential of the conspiracist trinity.

Pat Robertson was born in Lexington, Virginia, in 1930, the son of a congressman and later three-term U.S. senator. His father and mother, who raised him as a Southern Baptist, parented at a distance, and he was sent to military school for much of his secondary education. In spite of enjoying fraternity life to the full, he graduated Phi Beta Kappa from Washington and Lee College, then entered the Marine Corps with a reserve officer commission during the Korean conflict. Although he described himself in his autobiography as a "combat officer," Robertson saw service only in rear-echelon division headquarters. After the war, he entered Yale Law School, where classes took lower priority than a packed social calendar. He married his pregnant fiancée in 1954 and graduated to a promising business career in New York. The Robertsons soon acquired the trappings of success, and his "swinger" lifestyle and "jet set tastes" included a Modigliani nude, contour chairs, and Courvoisier brandy. This, however, left Robertson "empty," and he contemplated suicide. Searching for direction, he chose to do God's work. The decision was so abrupt that his startled wife suggested: "I guess if you're going in the ministry, we ought to start going to church and find out what it's all about."[50] Church shopping offered no guidance, and he hesitated about the future. Turning to his mother for encouragement, he was stunned when she discounted his sincerity, saying that he was not "born again" and did not "know" Jesus.[51]

What was empty was soon filled when Robertson prayed and received Christ as his lord and savior. Awaiting God's "next move," he "walked by faith."[52] Robertson stopped swearing and drinking, disposed of many of his worldly possessions, and asked those he had wronged for forgiveness. With little formal religious education, he attended Bible camp and enrolled at the evangelical New York Theological Seminary, where he learned the intricacies of dispensationalism. Spare time was spent poring over Scripture and spreading God's word on New York City streets. On graduation from the seminary, Robertson fasted and prayed for seven days, "waiting on the Lord" to provide a divine sign to guide his life.[53] His calling came with news that an abandoned UHF television station was available for purchase in Portsmouth, Virginia. God spoke, he remembered: "Go and possess the station. It is yours." Contributions, flexible financing, and a divinely inspired negotiating position enabled Robertson to complete the deal. On January 11, 1960, he received a charter for his "end-time ministry," the Christian Broadcast Network (CBN). In October he was on the air.[54]

It was a humble beginning. The operation was hardscrabble: inadequate funding, a leaky roof, antiquated equipment, and untrained staff. In front of a single camera and makeshift sets, Robertson broadcast for three hours daily, offering sermons and Bible commentary, fielding call-in questions, and hosting local guests. The network was viable by 1963, and Robertson moved to professionalize the operation and expand his audience. He organized a telethon that gathered seven hundred "faith partners" willing to pledge ten dollars a month to support the television ministry. This financial transfusion enabled the station to double broadcast time and birth the *700 Club,* the flagship of its schedule. A ninety-minute daily Christian talk show formatted to resemble the popular *Today Show,* the *700 Club* featured Robertson as a minister of the Lord, affable host, and conservative news commentator. Bypassing the national and established networks, it offered an unmediated Christian perspective on current events. The program pioneered interactive television, as viewers called on-screen telephone operators with prayer requests that were then read on the air. Viewers at home joined Robertson in asking God to perform miracles of spiritual and physical healing. Often Robertson provided instant testimony, as God directly revealed to him the working of his will. By the end of the 1960s, CBN was broadcasting twenty-four hours a day over a five-station television and six-station radio network to a potential audience of ten million people.[55]

Pat Robertson's fortunes rose quickly. In the early 1970s CBN expanded its range by distributing four-hour packages of programs for rebroadcast by other Christian television stations, and viewers could now watch Robertson in Baltimore, Philadelphia, Chicago, Houston, and Los Angeles. The *700 Club* was seen on fifty stations in twenty-five of the thirty largest metropolitan television markets in 1976, and on 150 U.S. and thirty-five foreign stations two years later. By 1980 CBN was available on three thousand cable systems. Five years later CBN was the fifth-largest cable network, and two hundred television stations carried the *700 Club* to an estimated weekly viewing audience of twelve million. In 1990 it was the third-largest cable network, feeding 5,300 systems.[56]

By the early 1980s the *700 Club* was the only explicitly Christian program on CBN, as the network devoted the rest of its schedule to family entertainment. The show, still telecast live for ninety minutes but now rebroadcast twice at night, had evolved to fit changing viewer tastes. The talk show format gave way to a professional magazine-style presentation that featured international and domestic news, financial advice, and human interest stories, all with a conservative Christian slant. Pat Robertson had also evolved, making the transition from ardent televangelist to sage commentator. Following each of the news segments, he would tender seemingly off-the-cuff grandfatherly advice, insider details, and often a biblical perspective, while program anchors nodded in agreement. Miracle work remained a prominent feature of the show, as callers phoned in their ailments, and Robertson, eyes closed, breathless, and awed, proclaimed that healing had begun. The subsequent announcement of cures testified to Robertson's continuing influence with the Lord. In 1983 alone, the *700 Club* received three million calls from viewers, and between 1980 and 1986 it recorded six hundred thousand decisions for Christ. Surveys indicated that Robertson's audience was white, married, and churchgoing. Compared with other televangelists, he secured the highest percentage of viewers in the thirty-to-fifty age group and the lowest number with only a grade school education.[57]

Restrained on the air, Robertson gave full expression to biblical prophecy in the *700 Club* newsletter to members. In the February–March 1980 issue, for example, he sensed the immediacy of the end time and wrote: "Consider these events after 1967: A humiliating U.S. loss in Vietnam, the first military loss in our history; virulent worldwide inflation; the fall of the dollar; . . . the world oil crisis; Communist advances throughout Africa; upheaval in Iran; panic in world gold markets; . . . a plague of abortion, homosexuality, occultism, and pornography; a widespread family disintegration; genocide in Cambodia; Russian troops and planes in Cuba; the Afghan invasion; impending worldwide depression; potential Middle East War or even World War III." Meanwhile, Robertson spied the Antichrist lurking in the shadows: "there is a man alive today approximately 27 years old, who is now being groomed to be the Satanic messiah."[58] Occasionally, he felt the urgency to go public with the news, as on the *700 Club* program of June 9, 1982: "This whole thing [the battle of Armageddon] is now in place. It can happen any time [to] fulfill Ezekiel. . . . It is ready to happen. . . . The United States is in that Ezekiel passage, and . . . we are standing by."[59] In a 1984 book Robertson continued to track developments and enhanced his description of the Antichrist: "He will be like a combination of Adolf Hitler, Joseph Stalin, Genghis Khan, Mao Tse-Tung, and other dictators who have butchered millions." More ground had been lost: "The demons have what are called 'principalities and powers.' It is possible that a demon prince is in charge of New York City, Detroit, St. Louis."[60]

Media work had made Pat Robertson a national opinion maker and sparked his political activism. In 1987 he announced his candidacy for the Republican nomination for the presidency. God, he told supporters, had pressed him to run years before. He had heard "that still voice I had known so well: *You will not want to do it, but I want you to be President of the United States.*"[61] Robertson found a confirming sign in 1985 when God answered his prayers and spared Virginia from Hurricane Gloria. His platform was familiar to the faithful community. He attacked liberal academics, feminists, and government bureaucrats for promoting the doctrines of "militant humanism," which undermined America's Christian heritage and belief in God and biblical truth.[62] The assault was long-standing, and Robertson traced the decline from the creation of the Federal Reserve System in the early part of the twentieth century, through the "imperial presidency" of Franklin Roosevelt, to Vietnam and the Supreme Court's decision legalizing abortion. The Council on Foreign Relations and the Trilateral Commission were current threats, and he called on voters to elect candidates "who would stand up for America and stop trying to move us toward a one-world socialist government."[63]

To win, Robertson had to mobilize his evangelical constituency and then draw secular Republicans to the crusade. Pragmatically, he modified the contemporary end-time scenario by softening pessimism, postponing Rapture, and evoking a nineteenth-century optimism that bound Satan while the nation repented and reformed before the Second Coming. The election of "spirit-filled" candidates dedicated to ending abortion, restoring prayer to the schools, and resisting the New World Order would renew God's love for America. Robertson, grabbing the president's coattails, credited the outgoing Ronald Reagan as the spur to his new faith. Americans were "finding [their] way again" under Reagan's leadership and returning to their Christian and conservative roots.[64] The "shining city on a hill" was not behind but before America.[65]

Robertson went into the fray well financed and with strong grassroots support, particularly among white, married women who had been born again. Rallies were enthusiastic, with chants of "Go Pat Go" alternating with "Praise the Lord." In spite of his sense of divine election, Robertson did not win a single primary. Evangelical Christians would not unite behind him, and fundamentalists were wary of his charismatic belief in the gifts of the Holy Spirit, like miracle work, faith healing, and speaking in tongues. Fallout from the televangelist scandals involving Jim Bakker and Jimmy Swaggart and questions about Robertson's military service in Korea, his claim to have saved Virginia from hurricane, and his unfounded charges that Soviet missiles stood on Cuban launch pads also helped clinch his defeat. Robertson, however, did not retreat. He formed the Christian Crusade after the 1988 general election to contest control of the Republican Party and to maintain an organized Christian presence in national politics. It mobilized under the motto: "Think like Jesus, lead like Moses, fight like David, run like Lincoln." By the mid-1990s, the organization had established chapters in all fifty states and claimed almost two million members and sympathizers. It played a dominant role in eighteen state Republican organizations and exerted significant influence in thirteen more.[66]

The line between politics and religion remained faint as Robertson resumed the war against the enemies of Christianity on all fronts. Pleading for a "renaissance" of repentance, he turned his guns again on the dark forces. His 1990 publication *The New Millennium* railed at the "deliberate and methodical assault" by "humanists" determined to plunder Americans of their sovereignty and private property. The government, universities, public schools, media, and courts had fallen victim, "captured by the forces of anti-Christian rationalism." Equally sinister were humanists' plans to bring forth a "secular religion" with "New Age-type concepts." He discerned a "satanic root" in the human potential movement of EST, Silva Mind Control, and Dianetics. The "force" from the motion picture *Star Wars,* ESP, and astrology were also suspicious. Reviewing the Book of Revelation, Robertson wondered whether "these kinds of cults might not be the origin of the Anti-Christ? It certainly seems that way." The signs of God's anger were clear: the assassination of John Kennedy, Vietnam, Watergate, the Iran-Contra scandal, and the savings and loan debacle, among others, were "not coincidental." Robertson asked, has "a watchful God given us up?" News reports from abroad aroused concern as well. "Was the demise of the Soviet Union occurring as if on cue to coincide with the 1992 European Union? . . . Could the bright hope we share for the future of a United Europe be dashed in the new millennium by the appearance of a charismatic leader who, like Adolf Hitler, resembles the Anti-Christ of the Bible? Only time will tell." The clock was surely ticking. Calculating a generation from the Israeli takeover of Jerusalem in 1967, Robertson suggested that 2007, four hundred years after America's founding at Jamestown, might be the fateful year.[67]

The war in the Persian Gulf against the resurrected Babylon convinced Pat Robertson that prophetic time was accelerating. The conflict, he believed, was not merely a confrontation over Kuwaiti independence and oil but "a set up," with "hidden motives." Robertson realized its cosmic significance: "We are witnessing the unfolding of a historic age, 'a time of troubles,' if you will, of biblical proportions." With insights gathered from the Bible and countersubversive sources, he found the answer in a world conspiracy whose origins were satanic. For Robertson, "events of public policy are not the accidents or coincidences we are generally led to believe. They are planned. . . . Impulses of that sort do not spring from the human heart, or for that matter from God's heart. They spring, instead, from the depth of something that is evil, neither well intentioned nor benevolent." Like other countersubversives, Robertson had no patience for explanations that stressed the randomness of events, or accident, or institutional process. Motivation was always clear and loyalties never divided. Conspiracy was the dominant thread that ran through history, with its practitioners reaching for power single-mindedly and without restraint.[68]

In 1991 Robertson made a full presentation of his case in *The New World Order*, which stayed on the *New York Times* best-seller list for weeks and sold more than half a million copies. Like the John Birchers before him, Robertson tracked the beast to its Illuminati lair and again conjured up the Devil's minion Adam Weishaupt as the father of the plot. Weishaupt, Robertson discovered, had "polluted" the Rothschild family with Illuminated Freemasonry "occultism," thus forging the link between the secret society and the international bankers. The "Satanists" used Rothschild money to finance revolution in France and undermine Christianity and authority in Europe and the world. Karl Marx and his fellow communists were loyal servants, and Wall Street banker Jacob Schiff sponsored Lenin in his conquest of Russia. Deceptively, their goal was not to promote communism but to saddle Russia with an inefficient system that would eventually make it dependent on international financiers.[69]

In the United States, President Woodrow Wilson had been the first "front man" of the "tightly knit cabal" of international bankers and Wall Street lawyers. Under its direction, he schemed to deliver the United States into the League of Nations, the beginnings of "a new order for the human race under the domination of Lucifer and his followers." The Council on Foreign Relations carried forward the plot for world government, and with Ford and Rockefeller foundation money took control of the departments of State and Treasury and the Federal Reserve Board. From their posts in Washington, CFR members, and later, their Trilateralist cousins, worked to subvert the Constitution and American independence en route to the New World Order. Similarly, they promoted the Communist takeover of Eastern Europe and China in their phased construction of the global economy. The Vietnam war, in this scenario, was simply a ploy to weaken America spiritually and financially in order to facilitate the globalists' power grab. The Cold War was also a plot element designed to drain U.S. resources and make the nation ripe for submission. Presidents Carter and Bush continued the tradition of their predecessors, serving the conspiracy "without fully understanding what they were saying or doing." (Interestingly, Dwight Eisenhower escaped Robertson's censure.) Meanwhile, leading newspapers and the major universities, having fallen under the subversives' spell, extolled the virtues of world peace and cooperation. With military and financial operations speedily transferring to New World ownership, the plotters moved to the last item on their agenda. As the Bible prophesied, they raised New Age messiahs to undermine Judeo-Christian theism and cloak the world in Satan worship. Asked Robertson: "How does the word of the Bible relate to the events of today? It is clear that the counterfeit world order will be waiting for the satanic dictator." In spite of his forebodings, Robertson kept the faith with other countersubversives: "There is power in truth. ... If the full ramifications of what is being planned for every family in America comes out, their house of world order will splinter apart like so many match sticks."[70]

Following Pat Robertson's lead within a national context of growing secular countersubversion, evangelicals continued their probe into the global conspiracy. They validated each other by repetition, recapitulating the premises of the contemporary scenario, reviewing the same evidence, and coming to similar conclusions. Baptist minister Tim LaHaye argued that in spite of the collapse of the Soviet Union, Russia was still poised to attack Israel. Glasnost and perestroika were "hoaxes" meant to deceive the West into complacency and generosity, with international loans diverted to rebuilding military power.[71] Lay minister Dee Zahner added Aaron Burr to the ranks of the Illuminati and the Whiskey Rebellion to the litany of its mischief making. He also tied the federal siege at Waco into the plot as "a test run to see if Americans have been sufficiently conditioned to accept military attacks by the government upon religion."[72] Gordon Kah concluded that Burr's opponent Alexander Hamilton was a leading member of the Illuminati and that health food stores were "fronts" for New Age "pantheism." Like many others in the postwar years, he tried to link the deaths of leading politicians like Congressman and Bircher Larry McDonald and senators and CFR members John Tower and John Heinz to a secret scheme. "Could they have known too much?"[73] Donald McAlvany, formerly engaged in "undercover intelligence work" offered pre-Tribulation advice: find Jesus, get out of debt, store food, amass gold, and stockpile guns.[74] The list of Satan's coconspirators continued to grow, with computer hackers and advocates of hate-crime legislation joining Catholics, Mormons, the World Council of Churches, the Church of Scientology, the Unification Church, Hare Krishnas, Jehovah's Witnesses, and Christian Scientists. The roster of possible Antichrists grew as well, including King Juan Carlos of Spain, Great Britain's Prince Charles, President Bill Clinton, and Iraqi President Saddam Hussein. Not unexpectedly, Pat Robertson's media power and political ambitions made him similarly suspect.[75]

Particularly effective in spreading the word was the fictionalization of prophecy. Pat Robertson's novel *The End of the Age* (1995) opened with a giant meteor streaking through space toward the ocean off California, which was already baking in a heat wave and suffering water shortages and energy brownouts. The born-again Christian protagonist is keenly aware of the significance of the signs. She pleads with her less-observant husband: "Don't you see? It's not a made up story. Revelation was a prophecy about what would happen at the end of the age, and in one part it says that an angel is going to throw a burning mountain into the sea. . . . Don't you get it?" The husband does, especially after the meteor collides with the earth and triggers tidal waves, earthquakes, volcanic eruptions, forest fires, and core breaches in nuclear reactors. Tens of millions die as trumpets sound and vials pour. Robertson adds his own touches to the apocalyptic formula, making the Antichrist an American and having the faithful wait for Rapture in redoubts protected by angels and Poseidon missiles. Most original is his transformation of prophecy into sports metaphor: "It's played in four quarters with no break for half-time. During the first half, God controls the action. In the first quarter, the good guys run up a score that you can't believe. Then the second quarter gets very physical and a lot of players get hurt. In the third quarter, the opposing coach sends in a . . . crew of hairy-legged, muscle-bound gorillas who beat up the good guys and then scare the socks off every fan in the bleachers. In the fourth quarter, God sends in a fresh team of special good guys with wings and halos. They round up the gorillas and lock 'em up. Finally, God's team wins the trophy and gets to keep it for all time."[76]

Even more successful commercially was the *Left Behind* series, by Tim LaHaye and Jerry Jenkins. The novels follow airline pilot Ray-ford Steele and journalist Buck Williams, left behind in the post-Rapture world, as they find Jesus and learn to "only believe what the Bible says." They soon realize that intense study of biblical prophecy and Illuminati history are the keys to surviving the trials of Tribulation and effectively confronting Antichrist Nicolae Carpathia, a Romanian political leader who resembles "a young Robert Redford."[77] Taking power as secretary general of the United Nations and with the help of a David Rockefeller-like financier, Carpathia forges a false peace and crafts the New World Order. The times grow dark, but the Tribulation Force, with Steele and Williams in the lead, puts its faith in God and battles toward final redemption. The combination of fast-paced conspiracy intrigue, murder mystery, and love story helped the authors sell more than ten million copies by 1999. The series expanded to meet demand; two additional installments appeared in 1999 and one in 2000. Three more are promised by 2003. The novels are also published in abridged versions and on cassette tape. LaHaye and Jenkins also announced a *Left Behind* series for children and a movie based on the first volume. *People Get Ready,* a collection of music inspired by the series, was available on CD and tape.[78]

While most messengers reached into the mainstream, some turned inward and fortified strongholds against the Antichrist. Reiterating the claims of anti-Semites Gerald L. K. Smith and Wesley Swift, the Reverend Richard Butler preached to his Aryan Nations flock that the Anglo-Saxons, Celts, and Scandinavians were the "children of light," God's real chosen people. He traced their lineal descent to Adam through Abraham, Isaac, and Jacob and was convinced that they had migrated as the ten lost tribes of Israel to northern Europe. With fellow Christian Identity activists Louis Beam and Tom Metzger, Butler followed the trail of these Aryans to the United States, thus carrying the idea of American exceptionalism to its logical extreme. Where other evangelicals had given Jews a necessary but supporting role in the last-days drama, Christian Identity leaders positioned them at the heart of the Devil's conspiracy. Jews were mongrel usurpers, the literal spawns of Satan, who birthed them when he mated as a serpent with Eve in Eden.[79]

As the *Protocols of the Elders of Zion* had revealed, Jews schemed for world power, and to further their plot they had promoted the

Black Plague, the Roman Catholic Church, Illuminati, Masonic lodges, communism, the Federal Reserve System, Council on Foreign Relations, international banking, and such modern medical treatments as vaccination and chemotherapy. According to sympathizer Bo Gritz, the Star of David exposed the Jews' true loyalty: "The number of the Antichrist system is 666, a six within a six within a six. Six sides, six angles, six points."[80] Serving the Jewish-satanic masters were the subhuman mud people—Blacks, Hispanics, and Asians, God's failed experiments before perfecting the Aryan man and woman. Ruby Ridge and Waco alerted Aryan warriors to the accelerating Jewish advance, and they hastened their preparations. Rejecting the hope of Rapture, they stockpiled guns and ammunition and practiced sharpshooting, sabotage, and ambush in anticipation of the last battle. Leaders organized a Christian Identity coalition that joined Aryan Nations; the Church of Israel; White Aryan Resistance; the Covenant, the Sword, and the Arm of the Lord; skinhead groups; the Posse Comitatus; survivalists; Ku Klux Klan klaverns; and neo-Nazi units. Retreating to a redoubt in the northwest United States, believers would resist the satanic armies of ZOG, the Zionist Occupation Government in Washington, D.C., until Christ's return brought rescue and salvation.[81]

The bunker that the Reverend Texe Marrs's end-times ministry erected in preparation for the Tribulation siege was also noninclusive. An Illuminati "secret brotherhood" of ten men had formed a global corporate board whose chief executive officer was the Devil himself. Their impressive organizational chart included the Masonic Order, the Vatican, the Mafia, the CIA, the FBI, the Trilateral Commission, the Israeli Mossad, the United Nations, the International Monetary Fund, and Skull and Bones fraternity, among many others. With the help of Jerry Falwell and Pat Robertson, the masters would appoint a "religion czar" to organize a global faith based upon the occult. Programmed biological warfare in the form of the AIDS and ebola viruses would have the earth's billions soon suing for peace and world government. By December 31, 2000, Project L.U.C.I.D. (Lucifer's Universal Criminal Identification System) would be fully operational and every person on earth would be forced to carry a "universal biometrics I.D. card" and "worship the image of the Beast." The plot was well along in the United States, with presidents Ronald Reagan and George Bush having devotedly served the brotherhood. Under them, "a FEMA-managed regional Federal Prison Transfer Center" had been readied to hold religious dissidents.[82] President Bill Clinton, as well, had succumbed to the dark side. He was under the control of first lady Hillary Clinton, a Jewish coconspirator. The brotherhood had also played the "Esther Option," using Monica Lewinsky to blackmail the president into following orders or resigning in favor of the compliant Vice President Al Gore. Hedging their bets, a "cabal of Talmudic Jewish Rabbis" had placed a "curse" on Clinton that called for his destruction, with the Israeli secret police, the Shin Bet, assigned the contract on his life.[83]

If such anti-Jewish voices were extreme, their echoes could be heard within the evangelical establishment. The Reverend James Robison, who had given the opening prayer at the 1984 Republican Convention, observed that "an anti-Semite is someone who hates Jews more than he's suppose to." The Reverend Jerry Falwell, known for his efforts on behalf of the state of Israel, played on stereotypes and joked, "I know why you don't like the Jew. . . . He can make more money accidently [sic] than you can on purpose."[84] Critics of Pat Robertson's *New World Order* had chided him, as well, for his "anti-Semitic fellow traveling" in placing inordinate stress on the alleged Illuminati connections of Jewish bankers.[85] The messages, then, formed a continuum differing from one another in degree rather than in kind. Few listeners could escape the impression that Jews were, at worst, suspect and guilty of complicity and, at best, stiff-necked before the light and due for divine retribution.[86]

Taking advantage of the approach of the new millennium, their entrepreneurial skills, and a culture of conspiracism, evangelists had clearly made great strides. They had established a strong base on which to exert political power and had gathered significant support within the mainstream. Often they found that unlikely allies had already prepared the ground for the planting of their beliefs. Scientists, America's secular holy men, substantiated evangelists' claims of a future cataclysm with their own scenarios of global catastrophe. They ominously warned of the greenhouse effect, ozone depletion, overpopulation, the loss of the rain forests, asteroid hits, Y2K technological breakdown, and toxic waste and nuclear contamination. Every scientific report of a volcanic eruption or earthquake or hurricane offered new grist for the evangelical mill. So, too, did medical warnings of diseases now resistant to modern drugs and plagues that threatened millions and ravaged the social structures of nation-states. None of this surprised evangelists, who confidently noted that they had read it in the Bible. The long war with the scientists was over. They had made science their acolyte, vital to the reclaiming of lost souls.[87]

Popular recording artists also validated and spread the evangelical message with lyrics that pirated images from the Bible. Audiences that were seemingly beyond the reach of traditional preachers would absorb the word painlessly and without generational resistance. In 1969, Creedence Clearwater Revival released the Vietnam-era icon "Bad Moon Rising," which set the Book of Revelation to music:

> I hear hurricanes ablowing
> I know the end is coming soon
> I fear rivers overflowing
> I hear the voice of rage and ruin.
>
> Hope you got your things together
> Hope you are quite prepared to die
> Looks like we're in for nasty weather
> One eye is taken for an eye.[88]

The rock group Black Sabbath's version of the Apocalypse appeared the following year on its *Paranoid* album, which featured "War Pigs:"

> And as God has struck the hour
> Day of Judgement, God is calling.
> On their knees the war pigs crawling
> Begging mercy for their sins
> Satan, laughing, spreading his wings.[89]

Other artists in the seventies, like Jackson Browne, Genesis, and the Sex Pistols, would find such imagery similarly inspiring. In the 1980s the lyrics of heavy metal band Iron Maiden prompted Bible study of several cuts on *Number of the Beast* (1982), *Piece of Mind* (1983), and *Seventh Son of a Seventh Son* (1988). Judas Priest, Danzig, Manowar, and Blue Öyster Cult could carry the same tune. Meanwhile, Morbid Angel offered the devil's perspective:

> We spit on the Virgin lamb
> and mock the words he spoke
> his ways not worthy of me
> We chose to burn in the pits of hell.[90]

Marilyn Manson's theater of the demonic attracted 1990s audiences, and his *Antichrist Superstar* brought to millions news of the beast's birth and a world in adoration. The apocalyptic message of Revelation, with its theme of conspiracy, had adapted well to the popular music medium. From easy listening to heavy metal, it impinged subliminally on the American consciousness. Like rock and roll, it was here to stay.[91]

Television viewers who surfed through Christian programing could take lessons on Revelation from the Fox Network. Chris Carter's *X-Files* conjured up the Devil on more than one occasion and birthed his child in a 1999 program. The "Duane Barry" episode may have been inspired by warnings of the beast's plan to make everyone machine-readable. Viewers watched Agent Dana Scully place an implant with markings resembling the bar code under a supermarket scanner and, like her, were shaken when the cashier's register recorded streams of data. Of course, federal authorities were in the know. More deeply steeped in apocalyptic images was *Millennium,* another Chris Carter production. Filmed in the shadows, this series followed Frank Black as he fought a secret group with government ties that conspired to control the world during the millennial crisis. His computer logon was "the time is near" and the program offered confirmation with frequent references to Revelation's horsemen, famines, plagues, earthquakes, and demons. *Brimstone* made a brief appearance in the Fox Friday night lineup, scheduled as a lead-in to *Millennium.* The show featured police detective Ezekiel Stone, condemned to hell but given a second chance at life if he could track down 113 evildoers and return them to the nether regions. The Devil made frequent appearances in the flesh to explain the rules of the hunt, with appropriate biblical imagery giving the show color and context. Even the cartoon series *The Simpsons* broadcast endtime allusions. When a bulldozer rumbled near his home, a startled

Homer cried, "It's the Rapture." The four horsemen rode in another episode, and this time the Rapture came to pass, with Lisa and the Flanders family ascending to heaven.[92]

Hollywood has long made a killing at the box office with disaster and global catastrophe movies. *On the Beach, Dr. Strangelove,* the *Mad Max* series, the *Planet of the Apes* series, *Earthquake, Volcano, Waterworld, Outbreak, Deep Impact,* and *Armageddon* are among many films that focus on the global endgame. Though secular in their script lines, the movies effectively demonstrate and reify with state-of-the-art sound and special effects the evangelical doomsday scenario. The occult has also proved cinematically profitable since the late 1960s, with such films as *Rosemary's Baby,* the *Exorcist* series, *The Devil Within Her, The Amityville Horror* series, *The Unholy, Witchcraft* and its sequel, *The Prophecy,* and *The Ninth Gate* joining an ever-growing genre. While summoning the devil, these movies lack apocalyptic context and do little to merge the two themes. Lucifer usually appears in a cameo role, freelancing his mayhem without clear intent. He has become another monster-plot device, though far more formidable than the more common werewolves and vampires. Still, as evangelical proselytizing intensified, Hollywood worked in a supporting role, giving big-screen billing to Satan and keeping viewers apprised of his whereabouts.[93]

Some moviemakers did forge the link between the Devil and the end-of-the world genre. The script of *Holocaust 2000* (1978) is anchored in the Bible and follows the plot of the Antichrist to construct a nuclear power plant as a doomsday device to destroy the world. *Prince of Darkness* (1987) has Catholic priests interpreting the signs of Satan's growing power and standing against the growing menace. *The Seventh Sign* (1988) is a short course in the Book of Revelation. Seals are broken and lakes are polluted, snow falls in the Israeli desert, oceans die, water turns to blood, disease spreads, and earthquakes, hailstones, and violent winds wreak havoc. A Jewish child brings the audience up to speed on these "signs of the end" and asks the uninformed, "Didn't you at least go to Sunday school?" The plot thickens in *Devil's Daughter* (1991), *Warlock: The Armageddon* (1993), *The Devil's Advocate* (1997), and *End of Days* (1999), in which the Devil is repeatedly frustrated in his determination to mate and spawn the Antichrist. In *Servants of Twilight* (1991) religious zealots discover that the Antichrist is alive and has nine lives. They die violently as he remains healthy and ready for a sequel. *Rapture* (1991) offers believers convincing evidence that faith will see them through to their heavenly reward.

Especially critical in acquainting a generation of viewers with the details and sequence of the apocalyptic conspiracy is the popular *Omen* series. Frequently quoting from the Book of Revelation, *Omen* scriptwriters, like the evangelists, were not hesitant to take liberties with the literal word. The *Omen* (1976) begins the saga of Damien, the Antichrist, identifying his mother as a jackal and recording his birth in Rome on the sixth day of the sixth month at 6:00 A.M. Satan's servants position the child for success, engineering his adoption by the wealthy U.S. ambassador to Great Britain and his wife. Both father and mother are blind to the clues of their son's real identity: Damien is never ill, he has tantrums near churches, animals fear him, sinister henchmen and women protect him, and 666 is birthmarked on his head. Knowledge means death to his foster parents, and Damien is left unencumbered at movie's end to proceed on his career track. So that no one misses the movie's underlying message, a priest bluntly warns: "He who will not be saved by the lamb will be torn by the beast."[94] In the background, the Common Market is made operational as the Antichrist's lever for world power. *Damien: Omen II* premiered in 1978 and finds the Antichrist on the verge of adolescence and self-awareness. Reading the Book of Revelation for guidance, he leads the audience in study of the whore of Babylon and the horns of the beast. Bodies continue to fall in graphic display while Damien grows comfortable with his powers and purpose. Meanwhile, the script provides a new means to world domination. With a "future in famine," his multinational conglomerate buys agricultural land and makes plans to farm the ocean floor to corner global food supplies.[95] *Omen III: The Final Conflict* appeared three years later to fast-forward Damien's rise. He has added nuclear weapons production to his agribusiness interests and is currently serving as the U.S. ambassador to England. Following his biblical lines, he is busy cultivating a reputation as a peacemaker in an attempt to defuse a Middle Eastern crisis. The Antichrist's plot, however, unravels as predicted. Jesus returns to save the faithful, and Damien is unceremoniously assassinated. Yet another installment of the story was shown on cable television in 1991. Insipid and convoluted, its only contribution was a gender change for the Antichrist.[96]

The Apocalypse and its accompanying conspiracy proved so popular and profitable that the supermarket tabloid *Weekly World News* made them regular features. The *News* reported multiple signs that the Second Coming was imminent. Its correspondent in Israel observed that the sky over Jerusalem "is turning green. . . . [This] happens at random and lasts from less than a second to as long as five minutes."[97] A U.S. space probe photographed a moon becoming "blood red."[98] Angel sightings were increasing, with the heavenly figures frequently heard to utter: "He is coming."[99] Simultaneously, halos were appearing over the heads of young children, Virgin Mary statues were bleeding, and a deceased demon was discovered in Africa, complete with cloven hooves, horn, and tail. From confidential sources, the *News* learned that the U.S. government would begin implanting an identity chip in every man and woman by June 1999, that the first wave of believers had already been Raptured, and that Jesus has been back since 1967. Refusing to leave its readers in the lurch in perilous times, the tabloid advertised the "Last Days Handbook: Your Guide to the End Times," which answered such much-asked questions as "Who is the anti-Christ?" and "Is there going to be a one world government?"[100] It counseled men and women anxious about protocol on meeting Jesus: Christ eats only kosher food, can be touched, and enjoys humor, but not off-color jokes. Meanwhile, the *News* kept readers current on the hunt for the Antichrist. An Illinois professor was readying for mass production an "Antichrist detector" that looked like a television remote, operated on batteries, and had an effective range of up to five hundred yards. Until it was on the market, the paper suggested that anyone identifying the beast should call 911 and a minister or priest for rebaptism. Further anxiety was allayed by reports that U.S. intelligence agencies had narrowed the search to Saddam Hussein, Bill Gates, Sun Myung Moon, and Vladimir Zhironovsky and planned to "take the Anti-Christ into custody soon."[101] In an unprecedented scoop, the tabloid published the Antichrist's "first interview."[102]

Popular culture, in pursuit of art and profit, had sounded a strong drumbeat in support of the evangelical offensive. In music and film, entertainment experts packaged the Apocalypse and the biblical conspiracy with a style and verve that reinforced the beliefs of the faithful while conditioning the mainstream to the message. Repetition only enhanced salience and credibility. So, too, did the image makers. Tuned to current tastes, secular authorities could sway the young and uncommitted more easily than traditional mentors. For some, the craving for end-time news was so intense that even tabloid reporting became reliable.

Apocalyptic anticipation heightened as the 1990s became history, with no break in the search for signs. The assassination of Israeli Prime Minister Yitzhak Rabin, wrote the Reverend John Hagee, "launched Bible prophecy onto the fast track." Playing into the Antichrist's hands, Israel would now pursue peace "with a passion that throws caution to the wind."[103] Evangelicals marked as high priority reports that a Jewish group in Jerusalem was practicing temple ceremonies and organizing to rebuild on the Temple Mount. Jack Van Impe announced "closing time," noting that the European Union's supercomputer bore the name *Belgian Electronic Accounting Surveillance Terminal* and that the Euro meant continental currency union.[104] Pat Robertson perceived in the Y2K crisis the Antichrist's opportunity to grab world power. By solving the computer glitch, he would win the allegiance of billions. Robertson also worried about the cosmic impact of events at home, charging that the federal government had covered up the murder of White House aide Vince Foster, Ruby Ridge, the siege of the Branch Davidian compound at Waco, the Oklahoma City bombing, and the death of Secretary of Commerce Ron Brown. American immorality, he was certain, "will bring about terrorist bombs, it'll bring earthquakes, tornadoes, and possibly a meteor."[105] Sightings of UFOs and reports of alien abductions and cattle mutilations had believers studying Scripture for insight. Moody Bible Institute graduate Timothy Dailey uncovered the meaning of the extraterrestrial sign: "We are not dealing with another planet, but with demonic forces from a parallel dimension."[106] Correlating with such concerns, in 1999 the Vatican reaffirmed the reality of the Devil and revised its rite of exorcism in anticipation of demand. Most Americans needed little convincing. Opinion polls at the end of the century found that 56 percent believed in the Devil's existence, 19 percent that the Antichrist was currently plotting on Earth, and 40 percent that the world faces a final battle at Armageddon.[107]

The failure of the new millennium to end history did not break evangelical momentum. Eyes were now on 2007, forty years after the Israeli recapture of Jerusalem, and on 2033, the two thousandth anniversary of Christ's crucifixion and resurrection. Evangelists continued to sow seeds, opening more than two hundred millennial web pages and producing scores of new books and audio- and video-tapes. Television remained a powerful weapon in the Christian arsenal, and pleas for repentance and promises of salvation played daily on living-room screens. Meanwhile, the fifteen million members of the Southern Baptist Convention, the nation's largest Protestant denomination, committed themselves to accelerated efforts to convert Jews. The search for souls led Jack Van Impe to produce full-length motion pictures that dramatized the end-time scenario. His *Apocalypse* video series wears a professional sheen and features Hollywood stars Gary Busey and Margot Kidder. A similar production, *The Omega Code* (1999), with endorsements from Hal Lindsey and Pat Robertson, ran briefly in theaters and is available for rental at the neighborhood video store. For those seeking a tighter hold on current events, a 900-number Tribulation hotline with news flashes is available at $2 per minute. Responding to the call, the number of men and women waiting for Rapture and escape from the Antichrist conspiracy continues to build.[108]

Believers have long meditated on biblical passages to discern God's plan. Creative reading brought flexibility to the words, and their meanings were contoured to fit the age. Holding the Bible as a mirror, each generation could see itself chosen as the final one. Thus Christians in recent America have convinced themselves that the signs are now self-evident that the end is nearer than ever before. Particularly compelling is the specter of national and international conspiracy. Spiritual guides demonize enemies within the federal government as deeply enmeshed in the Antichrist's plot to mark and enslave the earth's billions. As Pat Robertson, Jerry Falwell, and Hal Lindsey maintain, the conspirators betray their Illuminati–New World Order agenda in a host of international organizations such as the Trilateral Commission, United Nations, the

European Union, and International Monetary Fund. Their preconceptions shape biblical prophecy and remove history from its context. As John Buchanan, the director of People for the American Way, observes, the religious Right has "baptize[d] the mentality of the John Birch Society."[109] Such tactics are critical to mobilization, for they put into bold relief the stakes of confrontation and strengthen the commitment of the saints. In the quest for souls, evangelists thus magnified the role of the Antichrist in the drama of salvation. Belief in conspiracy has become as essential to repentance as faith in Jesus. To be born again means both delivery from the beast and a place by God's throne. Even those who are vague on conspiracy's details and tightly focused on their personal salvation feel the tension and fear the plot that prods them into Rapture's escape hatch.

CHAPTER 4

The View from the Grassy Knoll

> That's the real question isn't it—Why?—the how is just sce-
> nery for the suckers. . . . Oswald, Ruby, Cuba, Mafia, it
> keeps people guessing like a parlor game, but it prevents
> them from asking the most important question—Why?
> *Why was Kennedy killed? Who benefited? Who has the power to*
> *cover it up?*
> —"X" IN *JFK*

> Keep in mind, through this series of vitally important
> questions, that we are piling circumstance upon circum-
> stance. It is the body of circumstantial evidence that
> proves the existence of conspiracy.
> —FLETCHER PROUTY

> My God! They are going to kill us all.
> —JOHN CONNALLY

On November 22, 1963, six seconds of history transfixed America
and forged a community of grief. At 12:30 P.M. Central Standard
Time, President John F. Kennedy's motorcade passed the Texas
School Book Depository in Dallas's Dealey Plaza. Witnesses heard
shots and saw the president clutch his throat while Texas Governor
John Connally withered in his limousine jump seat from a wound
to the back. Seconds later, a bullet fragmented in the president's
head, and a red halo misted the tragedy. Time became telescoped
in a rush of events seared into memory by the power of television.
Dallas police officer J. D. Tippit was shot to death, and shortly there-
after, Texas School Book Depository employee Lee Harvey Oswald
was taken into custody for the murder. Doubt that Oswald was the
president's assassin quickly surfaced, but trial and closure were
frustrated when local nightclub owner Jack Ruby killed him in the

basement of Dallas police headquarters before a national television audience. Mourning continued through the weekend as the three television networks suspended regular programming and the nation participated vicariously in the president's funeral. Americans clung to the images of that November, convinced that history had turned away from promise.

The Kennedy assassination may be the most intensively studied event in U.S. history. It is flush with detail and offers hundreds of eyewitnesses, extensive ballistics evidence and autopsy results, and even a film that frames action to the split second. In spite of the attempt of a presidential commission to close the case, Kennedy's death remains hotly contested ground. Nearly two hundred books and articles appeared within thirty-six months of the assassination. Almost forty years later, bibliographies count more than three thousand entries, including films, plays, scores of television programs, and a dozen newsletters. Particularly influential was Oliver Stone's powerful motion picture *JFK,* which acquainted a new generation with the intricacies of assassination studies. Conspiracy thinking permeates most of these efforts. Born of bereavement and drawing strength from the memory of a lost Camelot, conspiracy theories challenged the conclusions of the official account that indicted the lone gunman. Once conspiracists were convinced that they had exposed the cover-up, new theories and a counterhistory appeared. The assassination, they contend, was actually a coup d'état that had robbed the nation of its future.[1] A long struggle for authority ensued, with opinion shapers and average Americans accepting the countersubversive argument. Opinion surveys testify to their success; conspiracy thinking about the death of John Kennedy was never a fringe phenomenon. To the great majority of Americans, the idea of an assassination conspiracy, if not its consequences, was conventional wisdom. This questioning of authority, moreover, proved contagious and accelerated the loss of faith in core institutions.[2]

No one deliberately planted the idea of conspiracy in the death of the president. It emerged spontaneously from the chaos of Dallas. Some presidential aides suspected a right-wing plot, recalling a recent incident in the city during which U.S. ambassador to the

United Nations Adlai Stevenson was roughed up. Others focused on Cold War tensions and saw the hand of the Soviet Union, or China, or Cuba in the tragedy. A breakdown in telephone service in the Washington, D.C., area thirty minutes after the shooting seemed to justify fear of a wider conspiracy. Under-Secretary of State George Ball remembered, "We were just scared to death that this was something bigger than just the act of a madman."[3] Understandably, the new president, Lyndon Johnson, was conspiracy conscious: "What raced through my mind was that if they had shot our president, driving down there, who would they shoot next? And what was going on in Washington? And when would the missiles be coming? . . . I was fearful that the communists were trying to take over."[4] FBI Director J. Edgar Hoover agreed, believing that Oswald was a communist conspirator. Numb and grief-stricken, Jacqueline Kennedy sensed a conspiracy. Referring to her bloodstained dress, she brought John Connally's cry during the assassination to mind: "Let them see what they've done. I want them to see it."[5] Bobby Kennedy also thought that the enemies were within. Just hours after the assassination, he asked CIA Director John McCone, "Did you kill my brother?"[6] As a precaution against further consequences of conspiracy, the pilot of Air Force One followed instructions to fly back to the nation's capital at an unusually high altitude and on a zigzag course. U.S. Air Force fighter planes flew escort, providing added security against attack. The Department of Defense issued a flash alert to every American military base in the world and ordered additional strategic bombers into the air. Meanwhile, Secret Service and Federal Bureau of Investigation agents failed to secure the presidential limousine for evidence, and it was refurbished before undergoing thorough inspection. They similarly neglected to seize Governor Connally's bloody shirt, which his wife subsequently had laundered.[7]

Exacerbating the confusion was the grief and shock of members of the press corps. The impetus of deadlines and career considerations turned hearsay and rumor into news fit to air and print. Consider the press conference at Parkland Hospital, which Dr. Malcolm Perry described as "bedlam": "A question would be asked and you would incompletely answer it and another question would be asked and they had gotten what they wanted without really understanding, and they would go on and it would go out of context."[8] As a result, television and newspapers bombarded the public with conflicting and inadequate information not only about the nature of presidential wounds but about the number of shots and locations of the shooters. An hour after the shooting, the evening edition of the *Dallas Times Herald* was on the streets, reporting that a "volley" of shots had downed the president, Governor Connally, and six or seven bystanders.[9] The next day, the *New York Times* headlined the arrest of Oswald as the lone sniper, but other information suggested additional assassins. The paper's report summarized statements by Parkland Hospital's chief of neurosurgery, Dr. Kemp Clark, and attending surgeon Perry that President Kennedy's throat wound "had the appearance of a bullet's entry." A typographical error marred a subsequent statement that the president had suffered a "massive, gaping wound in the back and one the right side of the head" [sic]. Eyewitnesses told reporters that Kennedy had been shot in the forehead as well. Later, the *Times* observed that the assassination "involved excellent marksmanship" but noted that Oswald "for a Marine, was not a crack shot" and that the discovered weapon was a "poor choice for a sporting firearm."[10] The media raised the question of conspiracy. At a press conference with Dallas County District Attorney Henry Wade, a reporter asked about Oswald: "Do you know that he had been recognized as a patron of Ruby's nightclub?"[11]

Clearly, the rush of events and contradictions in news reporting invited conspiracy thinking. Jack Ruby's murder of Lee Oswald added layers of complexity. Social scientists also found that Americans accepted conspiracy as an explanation not to balance the proportionality of cause and effect but because they believe collusion integral to a successful assassination. Plot imaging was, similarly, a coping mechanism. Visions of conspiracy enabled men and women to understand the tragedy as more than a simple twist of fate. When these factors are combined, the results of opinion polls taken during the week following the assassination are not surprising. Fewer than a third of those surveyed believed that Oswald acted alone, while as many as 62 percent were convinced that others were involved in the president's death. Cubans, Russians, segregationists,

John Birchers, and African Americans were among the suspects identified. In light of the public disquiet, on November 29, 1963, President Lyndon Johnson appointed a commission headed by Supreme Court Chief Justice Earl Warren to investigate the assassination. He also named to the body Senators Richard Russell and John Sherman Cooper, Representatives Hale Boggs and Gerald Ford, former CIA Director Allen Dulles, and former president of the International Bank John McCloy.[12]

Even before the Warren Commission began its work, administration officials, the FBI, and mainline journalists pressed what scholar Bonnie Zelizer calls the "master narrative" of the lone gunman "to lend closure."[13] Key to this effort was a *Life* magazine article entitled "End to the Nagging Rumors," which appeared on December 6. *Life* was an authoritative source because it had purchased Abraham Zapruder's amateur film of the assassination, which it would release only to authorized personnel. Printing selected and disconnected frames, it made the case that "a trained sharpshooter" had sufficient time to shoot Kennedy in the throat and head and Governor Connally in the back. The magazine contorted the photographic evidence to explain Kennedy's throat wound: "His throat is exposed—toward the sniper's nest—just before he clutches it."[14] A five-volume FBI report also indicted Oswald but played a different three-bullet scenario: the first struck Kennedy "deep in the shoulder," approximately six inches below the collar, and did not exit; the second hit Connally; and the third caused Kennedy's head wound, with a fragment penetrating his throat.[15]

Some opinion makers did not follow the government's lead. *St. Louis Post-Dispatch* reporter Richard Dudman, who was on the press bus in Dealey Plaza, remained troubled by Kennedy's throat wound. Citing Parkland Hospital doctors who described it as a bullet entry, he asked, "How could the president have been shot in the front from the back?"[16] Jack Minnis and Staughton Lynd raised other questions in a piece in the *New Republic* on December 21, 1963. If only three shots were fired, how had investigators found four bullets? How did one of the bullets materialize on a Parkland Hospital stretcher? How could Oswald fire so fast and accurately at a moving target with a clumsy, bolt-action weapon? Liberal journals *Commentary* and *The*

Nation also went on record with their skepticism of the official line. Clouding issues further, Texas Attorney General Waggoner Carr forwarded a report that Oswald was a paid informant for the FBI.[17]

Early conspiracy theories came from both the left and right wings of the political spectrum. In 1964 German leftist Joachim Joesten published *Oswald: Assassin or Fall Guy?* which revealed a purported plot of the CIA, the FBI, and Texas oil millionaires to kill Kennedy. Oswald, who was both a CIA agent and "an FBI informant and *agent provocateur*," pulled the trigger to prevent Kennedy from repealing the oil depletion allowance, dismantling the CIA, and seeking reconciliation with Fidel Castro.[18] The John Birch Society's Revilo Oliver probed deeper and unearthed the more intricate work of the global conspirators who ordered the assassination "as part of a systematic preparation for a domestic take over." The conspirators had become impatient with Kennedy when his efforts to foment domestic chaos through the civil rights movement and "economic collapse" had fallen behind schedule. Blaming "right-wing extremists" for the assassination would eliminate opposition and accelerate their plans. The Warren Commission was merely an instrument of cover-up, blinding Americans to the real menace.[19]

On September 24, 1964, Chief Justice Warren presented his commission's report. The product was visually impressive and official, consisting of a summary of nearly 900 pages with more than 6,700 footnotes, backed by twenty-six volumes of hearing transcripts and exhibits, and emblazoned with the golden presidential seal. The authors testified to their thoroughness, displaying statistics that recorded approximately 26,500 FBI interviews and testimony from more than 550 witnesses. Findings of fact delivered in strong, declarative sentences elevated the document's authority still further. Oswald had purchased the rifle recovered in the Texas School Book Depository, had posed with it, had carried a suspicious-looking package into the building, and had left his palm print on the gun stock. Oswald had the skill to fire the weapon accurately and in sufficient time for what commission experts judged "an easy shot." Settling conflicts between their witnesses and extrapolating from the number of spent cartridge shells recovered, the commissioners resolved that Oswald, alone, fired three times from the sixth floor window of the depository. Coming from above and behind, a bullet hit John Kennedy in the back of the neck, exited his throat, and then struck John Connally, causing multiple wounds. This bullet (Commission Exhibit 399, dubbed the "magic bullet" by critics) was later found on a hospital stretcher, almost intact. Another shot blew apart the president's skull. One bullet missed. Fleeing the scene, Oswald later killed Dallas police officer J. D. Tippit. Although they had intensively reviewed Oswald's family history and constructed psychological and ideological profiles, the commissioners arrived at no "definitive determination" of the killer's motives. In a thirty-page appendix, the report addressed "speculations and rumors." Here it dismissed as hearsay, mistaken identification, and hoax any relationship between Oswald and Jack Ruby, sightings of a "second" Oswald, and Oswald's alleged FBI and CIA connections. There was, concluded the commission, no "credible evidence" of a conspiracy. Public interest was intense and the report was an immediate best-seller. It quickly ran through two printings that produced one million copies.[20]

The establishment press was lavish in its praise. The *New York Times* welcomed the report with front-page banner headlines and applauded the Warren Commission for its "comprehensive and convincing account. . . . The facts—exhaustively gathered, independently checked out and cogently set forth—destroy the basis of conspiracy theories that have grown weedlike in this country and abroad."[21] The *Times* went further and published the entire summary report as a forty-eight-page special supplement to its September 28 edition. It also collaborated with Bantam Books to print a paperback edition and then a companion book, *The Witnesses,* with selected highlights from the testimony. *Time* magazine similarly extolled the effort as "amazing in its detail, remarkable in its judicious caution and restraint, yet utterly convincing in its major conclusions."[22] *Life* magazine showed its support by choosing commission member Gerald Ford to appraise the report. CBS News concluded that "no investigation could have been more painstaking" and broadcast a two-hour special hosted by Walter Cronkite that uncritically reviewed the Warren Commission's findings.[23]

The united front of authorities and media briefly masked from public perception the human nature of the investigation. Seemingly autonomous in pursuit of the facts, the panel operated under restraints both self-imposed and beyond its control. From the first, the commissioners felt the pressure of immediate historical circumstances to close the nation's wound quickly. In the climate of the Cold War, and with the Bay of Pigs fiasco, erection of the Berlin Wall, and the Cuban missile crisis still recent history, they set an agenda to restore public confidence, dispel rumors of foreign intrigue, and protect the national interest. John McCloy spoke for the others in declaring a priority to "show the world that America is not a banana republic where a government can be changed by conspiracy." Such a plan set a hurried pace for a complex investigation of three murders. Scores of witnesses offered conflicting and incomplete testimony. Seeing was not believing, and photographs and film of the assassination were open to interpretation. Similarly, the FBI report on the president's wounds and their locations was at odds with the Bethesda Naval Hospital autopsy results, with little effort made to reconcile the two official documents. A loss of focus was apparent in other areas. The re-creation of the assassination featured stationary targets and did not accurately replicate distances. No army marksman could duplicate the speed and accuracy of the November shooting. Such inconsistencies caused only brief pause in the investigation.[24]

Meanwhile, disagreement, negotiation, and compromise necessitated several document redrafts by the already-harried staff. For example, a critical issue to the report's theory of the assassination, and especially troubling to some members of the commission, was the path of CE 399—the so-called magic bullet—which was conjectured to have struck both Kennedy and Connally. A single bullet was essential to the lone-gunman theory because Oswald's bolt-action rifle prevented him from having fired another round that could have hit Connally in the necessary time interval set by the Zapruder film. John Connally was adamant that he had been struck by a different bullet from the one that had exited from Kennedy's throat. Panel members Hale Boggs and John Sherman Cooper also had reservations, and John McCloy complained that evidence contradicting the single-bullet theory "is not fully stated" in the report.[25] The panel debated words like credible and compelling before settling on "very persuasive" to describe their scenario.[26] Commissioner Richard Russell, however, remained unconvinced and only reluctantly signed the document. He vented his frustrations to President Lyndon Johnson: "I'm just worn out, fighting over that damned report. Well, I don't believe it." Johnson responded, "I don't either."[27]

The commission's self-restraint short-circuited probes into sensitive areas deemed off-limits in the interests of national security. Similarly, the panel frustrated staff challenges to agencies reluctant to make full disclosure. The CIA was particularly resistant and determined to protect sources and disguise foreign intrigues. The CIA considered its Kennedy-era assassination attempts against Cuban leader Fidel Castro privileged and offered no information to staffers curious about possible connections. Bobby Kennedy and commission member Allen Dulles, who were privy to these secrets, also remained silent. The commission was dependent for fact finding on the FBI, which operated according to its own imperatives. J. Edgar Hoover was adamant about protecting his organization and deflecting any accusations of a security breakdown in the death of the president. To avoid embarrassment, Oswald had to be a "lone nut" without connection to any subversive group under the surveillance of the FBI. Concealing a previous investigation of Oswald, the Dallas FBI office began, in the words of one agent, "tidying up loose ends" and even destroyed evidence to cover up its negligence.[28] Hoover secretly censured seventeen agents for what he considered their dereliction of duty in failing to pursue Oswald more vigorously. FBI agents, in line with Hoover's agenda, ignored, discounted, and shaped witness testimony that contradicted the official version of events. For example, they rebutted presidential aide Kenneth O'Donnell, who told them that he heard two shots coming from the grassy knoll in front of the motorcade. He changed his story at their prompting, remembering that "the family, everybody wanted this thing behind them."[29] Other witnesses complained that their testimony had been altered without their knowledge. Secretly, panel member Gerald Ford kept Hoover apprised of the commission's deliberations.[30]

In its context of national mourning and high expectations, the Warren Commission report proved a failure. Heavy-handed, it bullied rather than persuaded and succumbed to the partisanship of a prosecutor's brief. Haste and contradictions left gaps in the evidence that could not be closed by dense prose or leaps in logic, some of which defied common sense. Most significant, the report left the case open and demanded re-creation by abdicating on the most important question, *why?* The report was, as novelist Norman Mailer suggested, "a species of Talmudic text begging for commentary and further elucidation."[31] In grief and searching for comfort, Americans could not simply dismiss the document as human and flawed. They would not resign themselves as Bobby Kennedy had to the commission's "poor job."[32] Rather, many prepared themselves to believe that the panel members were accessories to the crime after the fact. The commission had already aroused suspicion in the process of investigation when it closed hearings to the public. The writers of the report appeared deliberately to have concealed their work in not providing an index to the volumes that would have enabled readers to cross-reference testimony, exhibits, and conclusions. Storage of the evidence also raised concerns. Investigators sealed the material in the National Archives away from public scrutiny for seventy-five years. Security was tight for the top secret documents. According to the New York *Herald Tribune,* "the Kennedy assassination material will be stored in an inner vault equipped with highly sensitive electronic detection devices to guard against fire and theft. . . . The combination to the vault will be known by only two or three persons."[33] At the same time, *Life* magazine concealed the Zapruder film, while autopsy photographs and X rays remained in the custody of the Kennedy family. Neither hubris, incompetence, time pressure, propriety, nor bureaucratic imperative seemed sufficient to explain the mechanics of the investigation. Instead, limitations of the investigative process and instances of secrecy assumed the appearance of deception. They, in turn, became the matter of conspiracy.[34]

Critics had networked into a community long before the report's publication. As Kennedy admirers and liberals, they were distressed by the loss of the president. Almost as unsettling were the doubts that would not fade. The diverse group included lawyers Mark Lane and Vincent Salandria; retired U.S. Senate investigator and now Maryland farmer Harold Weisberg; graduate students Edward Epstein and David Lifton; government worker Sylvia Meagher; Oklahoma housewife Shirley Martin; bookkeeper Lillian Castellano;

and Penn Jones, Jr., a small-town newspaper editor. By letter, telephone, and in person they shared information, reviewed inconsistencies, read drafts of each other's work, and brainstormed possibilities. These researchers shared a mission to discover the truth and became enmeshed in the case. The sheer volume of materials, eventually reaching more than one million pages of documents, precluded access to all but the most committed. Painstakingly, they followed the trail of details, convinced that every piece of evidence betrayed a pattern and that every action shouted implications. Few could match their knowledge; many of the critics' claims became matters of faith for the less observant. Although each left fingerprints and suggested a unique scenario, the work reflected their collaboration and the various interpretations merged into a joint brief. Their case, judged against the report, proved easier to make. When the critics pounced, the American jury was already suspicious of the official account and receptive to a reasonable doubt. In the end, it was the lingering images of a "magic bullet" and a gunman on the grassy knoll that swayed the verdict.[35]

Critics drew blood as they picked at the specifics of the Warren Commission report. While disputing every link in the chain of evidence that connected Lee Oswald to the rifle, they focused on marksmanship and contended that the "easy shot" was beyond his ability. The weapon's sight was misaligned, and FBI claims that the error gave the shooter an advantage seemed hollow. Even after adjusting their aim, expert marksmen could not repeat the deed. Other links raising suspicion were photographs of Oswald holding the weapon. Conspiracy-minded critics dismissed them as obvious forgeries; shadows fall oddly, while Oswald's head appears out of proportion to his body and he stands in a contorted pose. Searching the volumes of testimony, the researchers discovered that the only person to identify Oswald as the shooter was one hundred feet away and admitted that his eyesight was "not good."[36] He claimed that Oswald had shot from a standing position, impossible from the sniper's nest in the depository. Wasn't there a photograph, the critics asked, taken just seconds before the shooting that showed Oswald on the steps of the book depository observing the motorcade? They found other Dealey Plaza witnesses who claimed that shots were fired from the grassy knoll and elsewhere. Didn't pictures of the assassination capture hidden gunmen aiming rifles? The Tippit murder similarly produced unreliable witnesses and contradictory testimony of one or more shooters. Was Oswald involved in this crime? Could he have covered the distance from his rooming house to the site of the shooting in the allotted time? Warren Commission opponents privileged accounts of an impersonator who posed obtrusively as Oswald at a gun shop, at a shooting range, at a car dealership, and with anti-Castro activists. If these accounts were true, the conspirators had for months craftily framed Oswald as a patsy who would take the rap. What of testimony that Oswald had been seen in the company of Jack Ruby? Why had the Warren Commission ignored Ruby's ties to organized crime? In the same vein, how could Ruby have so easily penetrated police security to position himself to kill Oswald?[37]

The Dallas Police Department faced other indictments as well. Police officers skewed witness identification of the suspect by placing a bruised and disheveled Oswald in lineups with well-dressed police employees. Oswald's repeated bickering with authorities in front of the witnesses took the guesswork out of corroboration. Curiously, the department had no tape recorder, and only written notes and memories documented Oswald's twelve hours of interrogation. In this context, critics could barely suppress their disbelief that a member of the department was able to lift Oswald's palm print from the gun only after the FBI lab had searched in vain and declared the weapon clean.[38]

The critics' most inviting and important target was Commission Exhibit 399, which they had derisively labeled the "magic bullet." If sustained in their argument, they had a prima facie case for conspiracy.[39] According to the Warren Report scenario, a bullet had hit John Kennedy in the back, exited from his neck, and then wounded John Connally. Staff members posited this path because the Zapruder film caused a "time squeeze" in the assassination sequence.[40] That is, the film clocked a maximum 1.8 seconds between the time the president clutched his throat and the time the governor slumped in his seat. Yet the sniper working his bolt-action weapon required a minimum of 2.3 seconds to fire twice. Only two explanations were possible. Either a single bullet had caused the wounds, or a second gunman had been firing simultaneously at the men.

Print, film, and television were the primary media for the telling of the Kennedy assassination story. More unusual was this postcard, produced in the immediate aftermath of the shooting, which presented the Warren Commission's theory of the murder.

Conspiracists scoffed at the official theory and mocked an imagined bullet trail: after leaving the president's neck, it "evidently stopped in midair, made a ninety-degree left-hand-turn, traveled on a few inches, stopped again, made a ninety-degree right-hand-turn, and then plunged into Governor Connally's body."[41] The bullet drove downward through Connally at a 25-degree angle, smashed his fifth rib, exited the chest below the right nipple, struck downward again shattering the radius bone in the wrist, and came to rest briefly in his thigh. Critics bolstered their claims with John Connally's assertion that he had been hit by a second bullet. They also cited Secret Service agent Roy Kellerman, who heard John Kennedy cry out, "My God, I am hit," impossible if he had been wounded in the windpipe.[42] Kellerman's memory was consistent with the FBI's initial contention that a subsequent bullet had caused Connally's wounds. Curiously, the recovered bullet had seemingly lost only three grains of weight, less than doctors had measured in the several fragments embedded in the governor's wounds. It appeared to critics, considering the injuries suffered, to be remarkably "pristine." The bullet's retrieval from a Parkland Hospital stretcher also heightened suspicion and convinced the conspiracy-minded that it had been planted.[43]

There was even stronger evidence to refute the bullet's purported course. According to the FBI's summary report, Secret Service and Bureau agents observing the Bethesda Naval Hospital autopsy placed the president's back wound in the soft part of his shoulder approximately six inches below the shirt collar. The physicians' autopsy diagram locating the wound confirmed their description. So, too, did the bullet holes left in Jack Kennedy's shirt and jacket. The agents also noted that the doctors probed the wound but could penetrate it less than a finger's length with no apparent exit track. Unknown to the agents, however, their observations ran counter to the subsequent autopsy report. Head physician Naval Commander James Humes changed his preliminary findings after consulting with Parkland Hospital doctors, who informed him that their emergency room tracheotomy hid the president's throat wound. Humes then conjectured that the bullet had actually exited through the front of the neck. He also repositioned the shoulder wound to the back of the neck, later declaring that the autopsy diagram marked the wounds' locations "in general. . . . They [sic] are never meant to be accurate or precisely to scale."[44] The location of the president's head wound was similarly misreported. Soon after the autopsy, Humes burned his notes, which had been stained by the president's blood, because "I did not want them to become a collector's item."[45] Failing to resolve the conflicts in autopsy observations, the Warren Commission gave more fuel to the critics, who discredited Humes's intentions and expertise, accepted the FBI's report, and rejected the official autopsy findings.[46]

More dramatic because of its visual power and emotional impact was the Zapruder film's apparent confirmation of a grassy-knoll gunman. Frames 314 and 315 of the film seem to show John Kennedy's head snapping first forward and then backward, apparently from shots fired almost simultaneously from different angles. Not only did critics believe their eyes, but a Warren Commission error further convinced them that they had uncovered critical evidence. The report printed the Zapruder frames in reverse sequence, giving the impression that the president's head had been thrown forward from a shot from behind. FBI Director Hoover had dismissed this as a "printing error," but conspiracists were convinced that a cover-up was in place and holding.[47]

From the details emerged implicitly and explicitly the circumstantial evidence of conspiracy. Harold Weisberg counted gunmen on the grassy knoll and in the book depository building but denied Jack Ruby a role in the plot. Sylvia Meagher believed that the conspirators, Ruby included, had framed Oswald, firing from behind and in front of the motorcade. Her prime suspects were anti-Castro Cubans. Early on, President Lyndon Johnson came under suspicion. Barbara Garson's satirical play *MacBird* was based on that premise:

> Earl of Warren: Small doubts still flit like fleas through the nation.
> MacBird: That's why I'd like a full investigation.
> Conducted by a man of such repute
> That we may put an end to all these doubts.
> That man is you.
> Earl of Warren: Oh cursed spite
> That ever I was born to set things right.
> MacBird: I don't believe you understand the job.
> I wouldn't say you're asked to set things right.
> I think you get the point.[48]

Mark Lane, who was hired by Oswald's mother to defend her son at trial, was the most specific. In his book *Rush to Judgment,* which went through seven printings in five months and sold more than one million copies, Lane featured a right-wing conspiracy, and included Ruby and police officer J. D. Tippit, that set up the innocent Oswald. Issuing orders and funds were Texas millionaires with support from the John Birch Society, the conservative Young Americans for Freedom, and the Dallas Police Department. The Warren Commission did its part, offering cover in an attempt to quiet the controversy. Also part of the plot were unnamed authorities, engaged in an "anonymous terror" campaign to intimidate witnesses.[49] Without establishing a tight chain of evidence, Lane claimed that a number of key witnesses had died mysteriously. In tolling the casualty count, neither Lane nor later conspiracy theorists saw any reason to factor in variables of age or cause of death. They also disregarded the increasing likelihood of death with each passing year. Lane's conspiracism may have intensified when he discovered that FBI agents had tapped his telephone and taken notes during his lectures. Opponents of the Warren Report drew the attention of the CIA as well. Agents were instructed to "employ propaganda assets to answer and refute the attacks of the critics. Book reviews and feature articles are particularly appropriate for this purpose."[50]

Opinion leaders attached their names to the critics' effort and gave it additional weight. British historian Hugh Trevor Roper wrote the introduction for *Rush to Judgment,* and Lane acknowledged Bertrand Russell and Arnold Toynbee for reading the manuscript in draft. Novelist Norman Mailer reviewed Lane's book and praised it for unearthing "staggering facts. If one-tenth of them should prove to be significant, then the work of the Warren Commission will be judged by history to be a scandal worse than the Teapot Dome."[51] Edward Epstein's *Inquest,* which joined *Rush to Judgment* on the *New York Times* best-seller list for six months, carried the endorsements of John Kennedy's assistant special counsel Richard Goodwin and Arkansas Senator J. William Fulbright, with the introduction written by veteran journalist Richard Rovere. In a somewhat lighter vein, comedian Woody Allen joked that these two books constituted the "nonfiction version of the Warren Report."[52] Mainstream opinion makers William F. Buckley, Jr., Richard Cardinal Cushing, Murray Kempton, Walter Lippmann, Arthur Schlesinger, Jr., and Tom Wicker also went public with their doubts.[53]

The Warren Report still troubled President Lyndon Johnson. When told of the Kennedy administration's assassination plots against Fidel Castro, he was convinced that the Cubans had drawn first blood. Only after leaving the presidency did Johnson make public his private disquiet. Bobby Kennedy remained circumspect to the end. He confided in friends his suspicion of conspiracy, naming Castro's Cubans and the Mafia as suspects. Meanwhile, the KGB, the Soviet secret police, fingered Johnson as a coconspirator.[54]

The critics made believers of former supporters of the Warren Report. On the third anniversary of the assassination, the *New York Times* distanced itself from the official version. The newspaper's editor noted that "there are enough solid doubts of thoughtful citizens . . . to require answers."[55] He called on the Warren Commission to end its policy of "further dignified silence, or merely more denials." *Life* magazine asked on its November 25, 1966, cover, "Did Oswald Act Alone?" and answered, "A Matter of Reasonable Doubt." The *Saturday Evening Post* also urged a reopening of the investigation. The magazine's editor wondered: "Is the question really too ugly to be raised or are we just too childish to face reality?"[56] In December 1967 the *Post* published excerpts from philosophy professor Josiah Thompson's book *Six Seconds in Dallas,* which insisted that John Kennedy was gunned down in a triangle of fire with assassins on the grassy knoll and in the book depository and federal records building.[57]

Other authorities held onto the official line. Attorney General Ramsey Clark convened panels of pathologists in 1966 and 1968 to review the autopsy findings. Although the doctors relocated the bullet's entry wound four inches higher in the president's head, they upheld the Warren Commission conclusion about the direction of the shots. The investigations, however, aroused new suspicions, revealing that Kennedy's brain was inexplicably missing, as were tissue slides taken from his wounds. In 1967 CBS News broadcast a four-part documentary that reviewed the Warren Report's findings and conducted new ballistics and firing tests. Oswald was again pronounced guilty and the account of the lone gunman confirmed.

These attempts and a few book-length defenses failed to sway public opinion. Polls indicated that the Warren Report remained unconvincing and that the grip of conspiracy thinking had not relaxed. The Harris and Gallup organizations found that nearly two-thirds of Americans believed that a conspiracy had brought down the president. But demonstrating an unwillingness to confront the consequences, only one-third of those polled favored reopening the investigation.[58]

The attack clearly had effect. Basing their case on the Warren Report itself, critics exposed an investigation that did not match expectations or public relations efforts. Opponents pressed on all fronts, cross-examining hostile medical findings, ballistics evidence, and witness testimony. Nothing was as it seemed; photographs had been doctored, physicians intimidated, and firing tests manipulated. The conspiracists' case displayed a mathematical exactness, with precise equations offered and trajectories carefully plotted to illustrate the points of contention. Such details filled the foreground and gave legitimacy to the theories of conspiracy that underwrote the brief. The conspirators' execution had been flawless. Not only had they framed an innocent man and escaped unseen, they had intimidated federal investigators to cover up their crime. The critics' offensive was so vast and multipronged that authorities were thrown on the defensive and overwhelmed. Mainstream opinion makers moved to retract their support of the Warren Report, and Americans were convinced that their fears were real. In the end, not only was the report tarnished, but trust in the authorities eroded.[59]

The critics built a foundation of doubt, but had they approached closer to justice or truth? Like the commission staff, the researchers were selective in marshaling evidence for their case. They scorned the investigative ability of the FBI, yet had absolute faith in its summary report that disputed the official autopsy findings. While cross-examining witnesses supportive of the lone-gunman account, they took testimony to the contrary at face value. This meant rejecting the statements of 88 percent of the witnesses who heard three shots and instead championing those who remembered more. They repeated claims that a flash of light and puff of smoke were observed on the grassy knoll, even though modern weapons discharge without such signs. Nor did they grow suspicious when new witnesses surfaced or seasoned ones embellished and changed stories over time. As Oswald's coworker Danny Arce suggested, the assassination's collective memory made this a risky strategy: "I have read so many things, it mixes together. You don't know if it's your own memory or it's somebody else's. We all read a lot of things, and sometimes inadvertently adopt things we hear from others. It's hard to separate the two and can get real confusing."[60]

In pursuit of the facts, the conspiracy-minded had lost perspective. They ignored the confusion that was Dallas and set an agenda that made no allowance for incompetence or sins of omission. Thus critics suspected sinister motive when the FBI failed to close gaps in the chain of evidence. They expected a flawless autopsy even though the pathologists felt the enormity of their task and were aware that the president's widow was impatiently waiting in the outer hallway to retrieve her husband's body. The frantic escape from Dallas, failures in evidence gathering, and hurried nature of the official investigation had to be plot elements and not the signs of men and women in crisis. Conspiracy thinking crafted assumptions. Would the bullet remain magical if the positions of Kennedy and Connally were shifted to accommodate other possible alignments? The fatal head shot was not easy, but could it have been lucky? In searching for the clues of conspiracy, they yielded to the lures of circumstance, hearsay, and uncertain identification. Asking questions had exposed the weaknesses in their adversary's position, but critics had not offered a more convincing explanation or proven their case.[61]

Frustrated in their efforts to reopen the investigation, conspiracists in 1967 seized the opportunity when New Orleans District Attorney Jim Garrison announced that he had solved the case with the arrest of prominent local businessman Clay Shaw. Mark Lane, Edward Epstein, and Harold Weisberg, among others, enlisted as advisers and offered their detailed knowledge of the assassination to the cause. They were soon disappointed, for Garrison followed his own agenda and accepted little counsel. The district attorney focused on Lee Oswald's activities in his city and conjured up a network that linked the accused assassin to Shaw; former FBI official and archconservative Guy Bannister; and David Ferrie, an eccentric pilot who had trained Cuban exiles for the CIA-organized Bay of Pigs invasion. In Garrison's scenario, Oswald was an expendable CIA asset, then an agent provocateur for the FBI, and became the patsy for "an organized clandestine force" of the "military-intelligence complex." Diverse groups participated in the plot. Rogue elements of the CIA, anti-Castro Cubans, and White Russians prepared the ambush, with the assistance of members of the Secret Service, the FBI, the U.S. military, and the Dallas Police Homicide Unit. At the district attorney's count, a sixteen-member death squad had taken up positions in Dealey Plaza. The fatal head shot, he was convinced, was delivered at point-blank range, fired upward from the sewer on Elm Street. Jack Ruby, meanwhile, worked as the liaison and utility man, planting evidence, driving gunmen to the grassy knoll, and snuffing out the life of the scapegoat. For Garrison, the Warren Commission investigation "was nothing less than a continuation of pre-assassination planning"; a perversion that screened the conspiracy from exposure.[62] It was quite a tangled web, Garrison acknowledged: "The key to the whole case is through the looking glass. Black is white; white is black. I don't want to be cryptic, but that's the way it is."[63] More obvious was the reason for Kennedy's murder. Garrison believed that the president's plan to end the Cold War "threatened the survival of the war machinery." The Nuclear Test-Ban Treaty of 1963, a thaw in relations with Cuba, planned withdrawal from Vietnam, defense spending cuts, and the dismantling of the CIA created a community of interests and opponents. Killing Kennedy would protect those who really ruled America.[64]

The jury could not follow Garrison through his looking glass. The district attorney's speculations were all-encompassing and grounded more in faith than evidence. His claim of conspiracy appeared fanciful, its intensity dulled by being spread among so many perpetrators. He relied heavily on allegation, insinuation, and innuendo to weave a conspiracy narrative. Proximity in time, location, or interest became determinative of collusion and guilt. Every telephone call, trip, and meeting took meaning from their conjectured relation to following events in Dallas. Overruling issues of credibility and corroboration, Garrison accepted the dubious testimony of a heroin addict, an alcoholic, and a Ku Klux Klansman to detail the conspiracy. Countercharges of witness tampering, planting evidence, and bribery further contaminated his case. So, too, did Garrison's apparent protection of Carlos Marcello, the reputed family head of the New Orleans Mafia. Marcello hated the Kennedy brothers and certainly had means and motive to make the plotters' list. Garrison deflected criticism by accusing the power elite of conspiracy to silence his effort to expose the truth. Staff dissension, he maintained, was CIA-driven. In the end, the jury acquitted Clay Shaw after less than an hour of deliberation. This was not simply a defeat for Garrison. Spotlighted before the nation, his public posturing, questionable tactics, and unmitigated failure to convict had compromised the standing of all critics and broken their momentum. Tarnished by their embrace of Garrison, they now rejected him as "a populist demagogue," a "megalomaniac" who had perpetrated "a monstrous, grotesque hoax, a charade."[65]

Yet Garrison's impact on assassination studies was significant. He added a New Orleans segment to the Oswald story, a subplot with its own cast of characters. By finding associates for Oswald, naming names, locating addresses of secret rendezvous, and logging dates and times of purported plot events, he gave new impetus to conspiracy thinking. Most important, he shifted attention from the mechanics of the shooting to the questions, why and who benefited? This began the transformation of conspiracy thinking about the assassination into a counterhistory of recent America. As all countersubversives knew, John Kennedy's death was not simply the act of a lone madman, devoid of broader implications. The nation lost both its president and its way at Dallas. Conspirators had stopped Kennedy from making peace with America's adversaries and withdrawing from Vietnam. The young president, moreover, wanted to dismantle the military-industrial complex and the surveillance state and return the nation to its democratic virtues. A Kennedy dynasty, with brothers Bobby and Teddy following the path to the White House, would have secured the legacy. Instead, the enemies of the people had not only escaped justice but captured the seat of national power. Their lust for profits ensured the agony of Vietnam and maintained world tension and the resulting arms race. Here was a vision of Camelot, prompted by the promise of change. If touched by romanticism, conspiracy thinking as counterhistory was a contest for authority with those who offered America less noble direction. This yearning for an imagined present and future grew more intense with escalation in Vietnam, the Watergate scandal, and the conservative revolution of the 1980s. As counterhistorian, Garrison was reclaimed and elevated by a new generation of critics as the founding father.[66]

Feeling marginalized, yet fearing the loss of salience as time passed, members of the conspiracist core persisted in their efforts to gain vindication and avenge the president. Often frustrated and made suspicious by delays and official resistance, they used the recently passed Freedom of Information Act to petition for the release of government files. In 1968 they organized the Committee to Investigate Assassinations to coordinate efforts and serve as a clearinghouse for information. At the same time, the critics took solace from opinion polls that confirmed public commitment to the idiom of conspiracy, if not its implications.[67]

Hollywood also provided sustenance. In 1973 it offered *Executive Action,* which was based on a novel by Mark Lane and credited Warren Report critics David Lifton and Penn Jones for their research efforts. With stars Burt Lancaster and Robert Ryan cast as the conspirators, the film worked through the intricacies of the plot on Kennedy's life. The president had to die because he supported cuts in the oil-depletion allowance, antitrust action against business mergers, military base closures, withdrawal from Vietnam, and the civil rights movement. The conspirators were well placed, pulling levers that fixed the motorcade route, silenced the Washington, D.C., telephone system, and allowed Ruby to slip through police security. Oswald was a mere puppet who had been chosen by computer to play the patsy. Not only did the real assassins escape, but the film suggested that the conspiracy continued. At the end of the movie, pictures of deceased witnesses filled the screen, with a voice-over giving the astronomical odds of one hundred quadrillion-to-one that their deaths could have occurred naturally. The more disturbing *Parallax View* (1974) also forced viewers to reconsider the Kennedy assassination. The film opens with the murder of a Kennedy-like politician and a subsequent Warren-like commission that blames a lone gunman. Tension builds as the protagonist stumbles upon a deep-cover corporation that trains misfits as assassins.

The end does not bring relief, and the audience leaves the theater unsettled in the knowledge that the corporation has not only implicated the hero in an assassination and killed him, but escaped punishment to continue its work.[68]

Fresh commitment from media opinion makers enabled conspiracy theorists to resume the offensive. In March 1975 Geraldo Rivera's *Goodnight America* show on the ABC television network premiered the Zapruder film for a national audience and repeated the telecast several weeks later. In slow motion, enhanced, and with commentary from Warren Report critic Robert Groden, the images suggested murder by conspiratorial crossfire. A flurry of news documentaries and a made-for-television movie followed and teased interest. Articles validating the conspiracists and petitioning for review of the Warren Report also appeared in *Rolling Stone, New Times, Saturday Evening Post, Playboy,* and *Penthouse.* The public was receptive. In the context of Watergate disclosures, suspicion of government cover-up was a mainstream phenomenon. So, too, was a sense of history as conspiracy. A CBS News poll found that almost one-half of Americans believed that the shootings of John and Robert Kennedy, Martin Luther King, Jr., and George Wallace were connected.[69]

Also priming interest, Bantam Books published an updated study of the assassination that framed the issues and brought the curious up to speed. Veteran journalist Robert Anson, verifying the Warren Report critics' factual foundation and building on the counterhistory, put Cuba at the center of the plot. He argued that a "tripartite pact" of "overlapping interests" united Cuban exiles, the CIA, and organized crime against President Kennedy's apparent policy of detente with Castro. "Each group helped the other," wrote Anson. "In their free-floating association, members drifted out of one group and into another and then back again." Sealing their agreement was additional pressure from the Kennedy administration. The mob worried about a crackdown on its gambling base in Nevada and a withdrawal from Vietnam that threatened the "heroin connection." The CIA feared a shake-up in the wake of its intelligence failures. If Oswald could be framed as a Castro agent, the putative plan went, Americans would demand war on Cuba to avenge their martyred president. Invasion delivered the prize, with the exiles returning home, organized crime reopening its casinos, and the CIA reclaiming lost prestige. Meanwhile, time was running out on uncovering the truth; "witnesses were dying like flies," with the death toll at more than fifty.[70]

Entwined with these developments were official probes in Washington, D.C., that exposed the dark side of America's intelligence community. First the Rockefeller Commission investigation of the CIA and then the Senate Select Committee on Intelligence hearings on the CIA and FBI revealed covert domestic and foreign operations that violated American principle and law. These included illegal wiretap and bugging actions, the disruption of dissenting groups, and mail opening and cable interception programs. The CIA had also scripted an "executive action" option that plotted the assassination of foreign leaders.[71] Of special significance were repeated attempts on the life of Fidel Castro, some of which involved CIA recruitment of Mafia hit men. This was an important finding, and the investigators condemned the FBI and CIA for withholding pertinent information from the Warren Commission. Yet the probes offered researchers little else. Confirming the Warren Report's main points and discovering no official complicity in the assassination, the investigators dismissed the relevance of the new evidence.[72]

Critics took heart when the House of Representatives, outraged by the revelation of intelligence abuses, immediately ordered an investigation of the murders of John Kennedy and Martin Luther King, Jr. Completed in January 1979, the final report of the House Select Committee on Assassinations brought no closure. Investigators resolved that the Warren Report was inadequate, yet confirmed that Lee Harvey Oswald had, indeed, fired at the president three times from the book depository, with the fatal head shot coming from above and behind. Judging the autopsy diagram of the back wound inaccurate, they placed the bullet's entry closer to his neck. With their bodies aligned properly, the president and the governor could have been struck by the same bullet. Committee investigators also decided that the head snap visible on the Zapruder film was a neuromuscular reaction and not the result of a double impact. Yet newly discovered evidence forced the committee to deny the lone gunman theory and conclude that the president "was probably assassinated as a result of a conspiracy." The radio of a Dallas motorcycle police officer had jammed in the "on" position, and a dictabelt tape recording was available of the open channel. Reviewing the material, acoustical experts detected sound patterns suggesting four shots and giving "a high probability that two gunmen fired at President John F. Kennedy." Investigators were unable to identify the second shooter or the masterminds of the plot. They uncovered no proof of CIA, FBI, or Secret Service involvement and found that evidence linking Cuban exile organizations or the mob to the crime was insufficient.[73]

In spite of years of labor, the House committee had failed to restore confidence in the authority of the official investigative process. Its mixed message, of course, was unsatisfying to the conspiracy-minded. Gaeton Fonzi, an assassination researcher and former member of the House committee staff, criticized the investigation as "simply not broad enough, deep enough, ambitious enough, nor honest enough."[74] Michael Kurtz dismissed it as "limited and faulty as that of the Warren Commission."[75] More than unmet expectations discouraged them. The conspiracists sensed that a cover-up was still in place, for the committee sealed its investigative materials for fifty years, and its chief counsel allegedly muzzled his staff with mandatory secrecy oaths. Even worse, a government-sponsored panel of scientists subsequently reviewed the acoustical evidence and concluded that the tape recording did not demonstrate a shot from the grassy knoll. More likely, the tape had picked up sound patterns made after the assassination and at a considerable distance from Dealey Plaza. If disappointing, the committee's findings were remarkably politic in mirroring the popular consensus. Pollsters noted that more than 80 percent of Americans, regardless of gender or socioeconomic differences, believed in an assassination conspiracy. The Gallup organization concluded, "The belief that Lee Harvey Oswald acted alone . . . is now almost totally without adherents."[76] Still, few outside the conspiracist core could positively identify Oswald's accomplices or relate the specifics of the plot.[77]

A new stream of Kennedy assassination books appeared even before the release of the House committee's report and continued to flow through the 1980s. Each repeated the critics' mantra of the grassy-knoll gunman, the magic bullet, the head snap. Some fleshed out more details of Oswald's life, attempting to cement the intelligence community connection. The role of organized crime similarly received additional attention. Others attached scenarios to the counterhistory of what might have been. A shift was also apparent in the thrust of the new work. The countersubversives no longer railed against the authorities for misrepresentation or misunderstanding the evidence. Malevolence had replaced incompetence in the explanations; the focus now was on how perpetrators of the official cover-up had fabricated or planted the materials to advance the conspiracy. Autopsy reports, ballistics evidence, and the photographic record confirming a lone gunman became, in themselves, further proof of subversion. In part, this came from the conspiracists' quest for truth that demanded intense scrutiny of every facet of the case. They had to probe deeper, for what was revealed might disguise evidence still concealed. Longtime frustration also nourished an awe of the enemy. Justice denied pressed them to summon up visions of a federal army of disciplined conspirators lock-stepped in their mission, sealed in silence, and prepared for every contingency. In spite of the enormity of the task, countersubversives never yielded their certainty that exposure would rout the foe from the machinery of the state. Entrepreneurial considerations were involved as well. Competition demanded more sensational revelations in search of a lucrative market share. In the main, the conspiracists' voices went unchallenged. Few defenders of the Warren Report were invested in carrying on the debate. For the curious, one read usually sufficed, and initiation into the mysteries of the conspiracy was hard to resist.

Political scientist Edward Epstein, an early critic of the Warren Commission, returned to the assassination research field in 1978. Like *Inquest*, his new book, *Legend: The Secret World of Lee Harvey Oswald*, was measured in its claims and eschewed the hyperbole usually found in the genre. Epstein's focus was the relationship between Oswald and the KGB and the role of the Soviet Union in the Kennedy assassination. A committed Marxist, Oswald as a young U.S. Marine defected to the Soviet Union and may have compromised military communication secrets to demonstrate his good faith. Could this breach, asked Epstein, have given the Russians the necessary data to shoot down the U-2 spy plane in 1960? Oswald's abrupt departure from the USSR was also suggestive. Did the KGB recruit him as an agent to go deep cover in the United States until positioned for an intelligence mission? Did this plan go awry when marital difficulties and a thwarted defection to Cuba pushed Oswald beyond his handlers' control and into murder? For Epstein, the defection of a senior Soviet official in the wake of the Kennedy assassination was hardly coincidental. Could his mission have been anything but a clumsy attempt at disinformation to obscure Oswald's allegiance and deceive the Warren Commission? Circumstance was determinative in rendering judgment, for Epstein's proof rested only on plausibility and a narrow base of evidence.[78]

David Lifton, also among the first Warren Report critics, broached a more provocative theory. Lifton's puzzle was to square the different pieces of evidence that pointed to a grassy-knoll shooter with the final autopsy report that had bullets striking John Kennedy from behind. To unlock the mystery, he returned to the president's body—the "Rosetta Stone to Dealey Plaza." Deciphering it, he uncovered a conspiracy that was unprecedented in its omniscience, power, arrogance, and apparent invisibility. Lifton is convinced that just before Air Force One departed from Dallas, the conspirators sealed off a section of the aircraft, opened the casket, transferred the president into a body bag, and stowed it until landing in Washington, D.C. As the world watched the casket being lowered from the left side of the plane, conspirators removed John Kennedy's body from the right and hustled it to a waiting helicopter for transport to Walter Reed Army Medical Hospital. Within ninety minutes of landing, the surgical wing of the conspiracy modified the head wounds to appear that the president was shot from behind. The body was then delivered to the official autopsy, with the Bethesda Naval doctors frightened into silence. Of course, all X rays and photographs were subsequently altered and the president's brain stolen to secure the "medical forgery." The cast of characters had expanded geometrically, with doctors, pilots, drivers, intelligence agents, and forgers, among others, added to the plot. These findings stunned even Lifton: "The scene conjured up was unbelievable—the lid of a coffin raised at some secret location, unknown hands on the body, tools brought to bear cutting into the corpse of John F. Kennedy." He was amazed, as well, by the genius of the perpetrators, who even cut a shoulder wound to match the bullet recovered on the Parkland Hospital stretcher: "I was startled at the level of detail at which the plotters could fabricate evidence, the verisimilitude such a scheme could afford." Nor was he dismayed when interview subjects dismissed his assertions as "ridiculous" and "fantastic" and members of the president's entourage insisted that they had never left the body unattended. Truth had become stranger than fiction: "It doesn't matter whether the hypothesis was logical," wrote Lifton. "The barrier was psychological. Conspiracy was a ladder that had to be climbed step by step." Readers eagerly took Lifton's hand and made the climb. *Best Evidence* was a Book-of-the-Month Club selection, sold one hundred thousand copies in hardcover, and made the *New York Times* best-seller list for three months. It was also available in a "collector's set" edition, complete with video and autographed copy.[79]

Listening to the "whispers of faint clues," writer Henry Hurt dove into the "murk" of the Kennedy assassination in 1985. His book *Reasonable Doubt* insisted, in contradiction to Edward Epstein, that Lee Oswald was an American intelligence–community asset ordered to the Soviet Union as part of a false-defector program. Oswald's later pro-Castro activities were part of his cover. Hurt speculated that Oswald may have been involved in CIA-sponsored LSD experiments and that he could have obtained his rifle while serving as an investigator for a congressional committee looking into mailorder gun purchases. He was also convinced that Oswald was involved in the Kennedy assassination, but was uncertain of his handlers' identities. Accepting CIA and FBI denials, Hurt hypothesized a "branch of U.S. intelligence that to this day remains hidden from the public." Hurt's main contribution, however, was an interview with one of Oswald's accomplices. Schizophrenic and a self-confessed multiple murderer, the assassin unfortunately offered little evidence that Hurt could verify "in traditional fashion."[80]

Jim Garrison updated his take in 1988. In *On the Trail of the Assassins* the former New Orleans district attorney portrayed Oswald as an FBI informant who penetrated a right-wing, anti-Castro plot to kill Kennedy. When the FBI proved unresponsive to his urgent pleas for intervention, he may have "telegraphed some kind of warning to the secretary of the Navy." This sealed his fate: "He had clearly acquired more information than the assassination engineers could tolerate. That is why he had to die so suddenly in Dallas." Revision had come full circle. Through Garrison's looking glass, the patsy was transformed into a patriot, with the truth still obscured by order of the conspirators.[81]

Conspiracism went to a higher level in Don DeLillo's novel *Libra*. DeLillo's richly textured plot involved former CIA operatives bent upon revenge for their defeat at the Bay of Pigs. They could reverse the tide with an attempted assassination of the president, "a spectacular miss," that would rouse the public to war with Cuba. Their expendable asset Lee Oswald was critical to the scheme, for he tightened the link to the Cubans. "His role was to provide artifacts of historical interest, a traceable weapon, all the cutting and hoardings of his Cuban career." At the critical time, Oswald performs as expected, but a second shooter on the grassy knoll is too accurate. In the end, the plotters are left with neither victory nor honor.[82]

David Scheim's *Contract on America* fixed the spotlight on organized crime. The mob put out a contract because of a Kennedy brothers' double cross. Mafia leaders believed that they had delivered on their promises of victory in the 1960 election and procurement of women to satisfy the new president's lust. In return, Kennedy would invade Cuba and allow the rebuilding of the mob's gambling empire on the island. Kennedy reneged, however, when he backed away from the Bay of Pigs invasion and then sought rapprochement with Castro. Justice Department investigations targeting Mafia kingpins Carlos Marcello and Santo Trafficante and Teamsters boss Jimmy Hoffa pressed them to arrange a hit on Kennedy. Once the president was removed, Attorney General Robert Kennedy would cease to be a threat. Jack Ruby, "a buddy of mafioso," was their man on the scene. Scheim reviewed Ruby's travel schedule and found suspicious his trips to New Orleans, New York, Chicago, and Miami, "four key Mafia bases." Scheim also looked at Ruby's telephone records and detected a high volume of calls to men with underworld ties. Particularly telling, these activities increased in frequency with the approach of Kennedy's trip to Dallas in November 1963. The circumstances were so compelling that Scheim could brook no other explanation than conspiracy. Thus he readily discounted as "a collusively fabricated alibi" Ruby's repeated statements that he was calling in favors to solve his financial and union troubles. Scheim found more proof in subsequent Justice Department behavior. By 1967, in contrast to the Kennedy years, the organized crime section of the department had reduced its field time by 48 percent, time before grand juries by 72 percent, and district court briefs by 83 percent. But in almost one hundred pages of footnotes Scheim could cite no authoritative sources to substantiate the Kennedy-Mafia deal or the conspiratorial substance of Ruby's telephone conversations.[83]

Robert Groden and Harrison Livingstone offered "new" evidence of the conspiracy and promised the definitive word in their book *High Treason* (1989). They could do this because the insiders—"various former ranking (and dissident) intelligence officials, military officers, political figures, and other powerful persons in a position to know the facts"—had finally revealed all. Rejecting David Lifton's claim that John Kennedy's wounds could be altered, Groden and Livingstone nevertheless faced the same quandary, how to account for autopsy findings that excluded shots from the front of the motorcade? The answer was plain to anyone who would see the conspirators' "greasy thumbprint." The autopsy photographs of Kennedy's wounds had been doctored. After thorough study, Groden and Livingstone detected a telltale matte line that exposed the composite image transforming the exit to an entrance wound in the back of the president's head. This was confirmed by "the one deliberate or unintentional mistake the conspirators made. The x-rays are totally incompatible with the photographs and a key to the case." The naval physicians were aware of the ruse, but the threat of court martial silenced them. Meanwhile, the "Ultra Cold Warrior Sect" rewarded the compliant; Warren Commission staffer Arlen Specter was elected to the U.S. Senate, Gerald Ford rose to the presidency, and Marina Oswald "suddenly" became wealthy. Equally amazing were other disclosures delivered in the authors' breathless pace by staccato sentences in short paragraphs. As many as ten shots were fired at the president by several sniper teams, a fact deduced from the number of times a startled Zapruder reflexively jerked his camera in response. Watergate burglars Howard Hunt and Frank Sturgis were involved in the plot, as was Richard Nixon, a member of the shadow government that secretly ruled America. The eighteen-minute gap in a Nixon tape may have covered up assassination chatter. Groden and Livingstone could not even dismiss the suggestion that the Secret Service agent riding in the front seat of the limousine shot the president. "Although this seems to be a fantastic idea, it is not beyond the realm of possibility. They are certainly covering up a lot of things."[84]

Jim Marrs's book *Crossfire* ended the 1980s barrage with few new insights but heightened sensationalism. Some of the questions he pondered suggest the tone of his work. Was Oswald replaced by a double on leaving the Soviet Union? Was Oswald a subject in a CIA mind-control program? Did doctors inject Jack Ruby with cancer cells to cause his "sudden and convenient death?" Did Lyndon Johnson and J. Edgar Hoover contract with the mob to remove Kennedy? The last question, Marrs noted, was at the heart of the matter, for this scenario "goes farther in tying together the disparate bits of assassination evidence than any other theory offered to date and cannot be easily dismissed." Marrs had his finger securely on the nation's pulse. *Crossfire* later joined Garrison's *On the Trail of the Assassins* and Groden and Livingstone's *High Treason* on the *New York Times* best-seller list.[85]

Sales were good for the countersubversives, who continued to bask in opinion polls that reflected the popularity of conspiracy thinking. Still, closure eluded them. Although their merging scenarios found a wide audience, an aroused constituency failed to materialize. They felt hamstrung by official resistance to the Freedom of Information Act; small victories were rendered pyrrhic by long delays, high copying costs, blacked-out sections on released documents, and continued restrictions on classified materials. Such standard bureaucratic procedures so frustrated the researchers that they incorporated them into their conspiracy scenarios. More disheartening, the Justice Department in 1988 ruled that there was "no persuasive evidence" to justify reopening the Kennedy investigation.[86]

A breakthrough, however, was imminent. Filmmaker Oliver Stone welcomed the opportunity not only to confront the authorities but to rescript the history of recent America. Coming to terms with the Kennedy assassination would be his quest; the personal became political. Stone was so skilled in his work that those born since the assassination felt like eyewitnesses to events. His film images reignited the debate on the assassination story and helped power the wave of conspiracism that enveloped the 1990s.

Oliver Stone was born in New York City in 1946 to a former World War II army officer and his French bride. Although an only child raised in upper-middle-class surroundings, Stone felt "born into conflict."[87] His parents were self-absorbed, his father emotionally distant, and his mother physically absent. At age thirteen Oliver was sent away to boarding school. Shy and insecure, he felt like "an outsider," unable to establish close relationships. Two years later, his parents' divorce (which was revealed to him by the school's headmaster) caught him unawares and devastated him. His mother left the country without seeing him, and his father moved into a hotel. "The family was over"; his moorings were gone.[88] Attempting to cope with the loss, he retreated emotionally: "Everything was metallic. All the adults were dangerous, not to be trusted. I reassessed everything. I had a sense that everything was stripped away. That there was a mask on everything and underneath there was a harder truth, a deeper more negative truth." John Kennedy's assassination two years later became part of his personal script. His response paralleled the impact of his parents' divorce: "It left me with the feeling that there was a mask on everything, a hidden negative truth. . . . I'm still groping my way, trying to figure it out."[89] In retreat from these emotional upheavals, Stone lost himself in a flurry of activities. Dropping out of Yale University after only a year, he taught English in Vietnam, joined the Merchant Marine, and attempted a novel. In April 1967 he enlisted in the U.S. Army and was sent to Vietnam, a member of the 2d platoon of Bravo Company, 25th Infantry Division. Stone saw combat and was wounded twice, receiving the Purple Heart and the Bronze Star for bravery. Vietnam had a profound influence, "the major shaping event of my life."[90] He remembered: "I walked away from that war, 21 and benumbed and something of an anarchist. It took me several years to recover some form of social identification."[91]

Stone found his bearings in film school under the tutelage of director Martin Scorsese. He wrote eleven screenplays in six years, but none attracted financial backers. His piece "The Coverup," which exposed a government conspiracy to discredit and disrupt radical groups, suggested his frame of mind as well as the times. Fame came in 1978 with an Academy Award for his screenplay for *Midnight Express*. In quick succession he made *Salvador* (1985), the autobiographical *Platoon* (1986), *Wall Street* (1987), *Talk Radio* (1988), and *Born on the Fourth of July* (1989). All exposed a dark and gritty side of recent history. Honor and faith had lost their power and the tight focus was on decline and loss.[92]

Feeling the weight of his past, Oliver Stone turned to the Kennedy assassination and bought the film rights to Garrison's *On the Trail of the Assassins* and Marrs's *Crossfire*. Jim Garrison, Stone recalled, "opened my eyes" to what he had long suspected.[93] Even more important, Garrison introduced him to Fletcher Prouty, who elaborated the conspiratorial context of the assassination. Prouty's credentials impressed Stone. As chief of special operations (1955–64), first for the air force and later for the joint chiefs of staff, he had outfitted CIA operatives with military support for covert activity. In linking Kennedy's death to Vietnam, memories heavily freighted with emotion for Stone, Prouty made a convert. He told the filmmaker that John Kennedy had renounced the Vietnam war in October 1963 and authorized the withdrawal of all U.S. forces by the end of 1965. This raised a direct challenge to the "power elite," which since World War II had orchestrated events to create "a new world power center of transnational corporations." Seeking to maximize profits, these "master manipulators" prompted their "puppets" on the "Roosevelt-Churchill-Stalin level" to initiate the Cold War and fight on brushfire battlegrounds like Vietnam. Removing the threat to their coffers proved a simple affair. They set in motion their CIA operatives to kill Kennedy and then ordered the more tractable Lyndon Johnson to reverse the U.S. withdrawal. The official record was then modified to cover up Kennedy's plans and tar him with the war. The conspirators chose the assassination option again, and attempts on the lives of Presidents Gerald Ford and Ronald Reagan taught them "how the game is played." Since Kennedy's death, Prouty insisted, the conspirators had accelerated their drive to replace nation states with the New World Order.[94] He saw their hand clearly in the energy crisis, drug traffic, downing of Korean Airlines flight 007, air strikes against Libya, aid to the Contra rebels in Nicaragua, and Operation Desert Storm. With the assassination, Vietnam, and the counterhistory now plot devices, Stone was ready to make his movie: "For us, it starts with the Kennedy stuff, that's where the betrayal began. Our lifetime is about betrayal as Americans."[95] He named Prouty his technical adviser for the film and wrote him into the script.[96]

As a believer, Stone had to look past important contradictions. The John Birch Society had already proposed this conspiracy theory, with gaps in evidence and lapses in logic still unattended. Prouty was associated with the Liberty Lobby, a far-right organization that critics had censured for racism and for accusations that American Jews were guilty of divided loyalties. When probing the reasons for the assassination, Stone also had to ignore information deleted from Prouty's counterhistory. In the speech that John Kennedy had planned to deliver at the Dallas Trade Mart, he cloaked himself in the mantle of a Cold Warrior. Kennedy took pride in the accomplishments of the military-industrial complex and boasted of having increased the number of Polaris submarines by 50 percent, strategic bombers on fifteen-minute alert status by 50 percent, and nuclear weapons in the American stockpile by 100 percent. Nor did he publicly espouse withdrawal from Vietnam or any ally threatened by communist aggression: "Our assistance to these nations can be painful, risky and costly—as is true in Southeast Asia today. But we dare not weary of the task."[97] Well schooled in the ideology of containment and a firm believer in the domino theory, Kennedy was convinced of the importance of Vietnam to U.S. interests. His talk of withdrawal, according to the historical consensus, was a ploy to pressure the unpopular government of Premier Ngo Dinh Diem into making reforms. Diem's failure did not hasten withdrawal, but instead brought about his American-sanctioned assassination just weeks before Kennedy's death. Similarly, the Kennedy administration did not tire of plots to remove Fidel Castro.[98]

Stone's film *JFK* (1991) offered no new evidence to crack the Kennedy case. Members of the countersubversive core and those familiar with the details easily recognized events and characters. As he acknowledged, "the film brings together several layers of research from the '60s, '70s, and '80s, we hope in a seamless jigsaw puzzle that will allow the audience, for the first time, to understand what happened and why."[99] This entailed merging the four levels of the assassination story—Oswald's history, Kennedy's death in Dealey Plaza, the Jim Garrision investigation, and the conspiracist counterhistory. In pursuit, the three-hour film moves quickly "in the *Rashomon* style," a juxtaposition of various perspectives of the same incidents.[100] Stone implicates the traditional suspects, including but not limited to mobsters, Texas oil millionaires, Cuban exiles, Dallas police officers, Pentagon officials, and intelligence operatives. The magic bullet and head snap receive standard if exaggerated play. Nor is Stone's sketch of assassination mechanics original. Three teams of snipers triangulate their fire on Kennedy, hitting him from the front and rear. More innovative is his Fletcher Prouty character, who speaks with authority and conjures up the "Deep Throat" informant of Watergate fame. An insider operating among the Washington power brokers, "X" outlines "black operations," which range from the overthrow of foreign governments to the rigging of elections to assassination. He plays a vital role in the film, steering not only Jim Garrison but the less perceptive through the complex plot.

Stone's brilliance was in the presentation, and his work confirmed that the twentieth century's most influential historians are filmmakers. While the opening credits are still rolling, he dispatches rapid-fire "splinters to the brain," with vintage newsreel footage that frames the issues.[101] Outgoing president Dwight Eisenhower begins the tale, warning the nation of the overweening influence of the "military-industrial complex." Seemingly heeding the words of the old warrior, new president John Kennedy commits himself not only to end the Cold War but to bridle the power of the militarists and their comrades in the intelligence community. The anti-Kennedy coalition rises in response and carries out his "public execution" in Dealey Plaza. The cover-up is now in place, the conspirators in control, and the nation numb in disbelief. Stone scripted the previously disgraced New Orleans District Attorney Jim Garrison as the martyred president's avenger and America's savior. This would be convincing only if he cast well. Recalling the Frank Capra film *Mr. Smith Goes to Washington,* he looked for an actor whom audiences trusted without hesitation and who exuded the integrity necessary for a quest against the hidden conspirators. Kevin Costner, still basking in the success of *Dances with Wolves,* accepted

Stone's offer. "Kevin was the perfect choice for Jim Garrison," Stone believed, "because he reminds me of those Gary Cooper, Jimmy Stewart qualities—moral simplicity and a quiet understatement. . . . Through Kevin playing Jim you get on the fifty-yard line for the Kennedy assassination."[102] Jim Garrison was Stone's irony-laden choice to play Earl Warren.[103]

With Costner in the foreground and suspicion written into every scene in the script, Stone worked his skills as a filmmaker. He blurred the line between life and art, costuming extras in clothing similar to that worn by Dealey Plaza witnesses, filming from the sniper's nest in the Texas School Book Depository, and reenacting Oswald's murder in the basement of the Dallas Police Department headquarters. Mixing film stock, moving from color to black and white, merging archival and simulated grainy footage, and using quick cuts and slow motion, Stone created a document that breathed life into the conspiracy and covered it with a veneer of historical authenticity. So convincing were the images that Stone's conjectures became a new reality for many viewers. "Isn't history," asked Stone, "a distorted hall of mirrors that depends on the kind of surface that reflects its essence and its events?"[104] Pounding his point home, the movie concluded with the conspiracists' motto of choice: "Eternal vigilance is the price of liberty." Stone revisited the assassination in a later film, *Nixon* (1995). In a scene set in Texas in November 1963, Richard Nixon receives pledges of support for a run against Kennedy in the coming election. Nixon demurs: "Nobody's gonna beat Kennedy in '64 with all the money in the world." Knowing glances are exchanged, and one of the conspirators asks, "Suppose Kennedy don't run in '64? . . . These are dangerous times, Mr. Nixon. Anything can happen." Later in the film, Nixon awakens to the hidden reality: "It's taken me twenty-five fucking years in politics to understand. The CIA, the Mafia, the Wall Street bastards. . . . The Beast."

JFK is complex, thick with place details, character flashes, and assassination information. Several times Stone has to pause the plot to allow Garrison or "X" to clarify and dissect the conspiracy. Even then, the perpetrators remain mysterious and their scheme lacking in specifics and tight connections. Schooling Americans in the intricacies of the plot, however, was not Stone's primary goal. Rather, his achievement is to make history present and personal. He forces viewers to own the past, to invest themselves emotionally in the outcome of national events. Already cynical and streetwise, audiences were receptive to a counterhistory pitted with deceits, betrayals, and lost opportunities. With America's sense of its past so weak and affording little protection, history was reborn as conspiracy.

Warner Brothers strongly backed *JFK* and launched a fifteen million–dollar publicity campaign. Spots appeared in the fifty major television markets, two-page advertisements ran in the *Los Angeles Times* and *New York Times*, and posters decorated buses and subway stations. Opening in December 1991, *JFK* grossed more than fifty million dollars by the first week in January 1992 and eventually took in two hundred million dollars. Along the way it gathered eight Academy Award nominations, including best director and best picture. Warner Brothers also sent boxes of the companion "*JFK* Classroom Study Guide" to thirteen thousand school districts to facilitate student discussion. Stone supplemented this with a nearly six hundred–page book that included the annotated screenplay, research notes, and commentaries on his film.[105]

Established opinion makers would not yield authority to Stone and the conspiracy theorists without a fight. Clearly, the stakes were high and involved the allegiance of a new generation coming of age. Critics broke their silence even before the film was released and accused Stone of concocting evidence, fabricating characters and events, and deceiving viewers with trick photography. Denying Stone both license as an artist and his voice in the debate, they privileged themselves as the defenders of historical truth. Nor would they refrain from personal attack. *Newsweek* magazine's Kenneth Achincloss condemned the "work of propaganda" for "distorting history." It was better, he argued, to rely on the "imperfect but painstaking government investigation."[106] Columnist George Will, writing in the *Washington Post*, dismissed *JFK* as "cartoon history" and its maker as "an intellectual sociopath indifferent to the truth."[107] Charles Krauthammer, Will's colleague at the *Post*, concurred: the film was "paranoid fantasy."[108] Taking the offensive, CBS News broadcast a *48 Hours* segment on the assassination, with Dan Rather again confirming the official version. Later it offered "Who Killed Kennedy," showcasing Gerald Posner, the most persuasive advocate of the Warren Commission Report. The *New York Times* joined the chorus of denunciation, printing nearly thirty articles, columns, editorials, and op-ed pieces about the motion picture. The *Times*, however, did concede Stone's points that government secrecy fanned conspiracy thinking and that still-restricted documents should be released.[109]

Stone responded in a host of public forums, including television appearances on *Larry King Live, Nightline,* and *C-Span.* He defended his right to interpret the past against the "priesthood. . . . They bludgeon newcomers, wielding heavy clubs like 'objectivity' and charging high crimes like 'rewriting history.'"[110] Others came to his support. The intensity of the media assault disturbed film critic Roger Ebert: "Saddam Hussein did not receive half the vituperation the op-ed crowd has aimed at *JFK* and nothing Oliver North did was remotely as shocking to them."[111] Shortly after the release of the motion picture, the *American Historical Review* published a symposium on *JFK* in which a commentator declared that the film was "surprisingly accurate" and "holds its own against the Warren Commission."[112] In seeming validation, the Democratic Party invited Oliver Stone to address its 1992 convention, where he called for the elimination of government corruption, the dismantling of the CIA, and the opening of federal assassination files. Stone declared victory when an aroused Congress created a board to review all assassination-related, federal documents in preparation for their release. By September 1992 the National Archives had unsealed eight hundred thousand of an estimated four million pages of material. Conspiracists, of course, remained skeptical. Said Fletcher Prouty, "This was well intentioned; but in reality it is a sham. The answers to the source of the decision to murder John F. Kennedy are not in government files."[113]

The counterattack changed few minds. Opinion polls continued to register strong belief in an assassination conspiracy, with one-half of those questioned denouncing the CIA for its involvement. Although it is hard to gauge the impact of *JFK* on movie audiences, some evidence is suggestive. Political psychologists interviewed a small sample of *JFK* viewers and surveyed attitudes before and after seeing the film. They found that the motion picture aroused anger and made men and women more receptive to conspiracy thinking specific to the assassination. The data also revealed "a general help-lessness effect," characterized by a significant decrease in viewers' intention to vote, volunteer, or make political contributions. Surprisingly, two-thirds of the respondents reported a history of conspiracies in their own lives, especially in the workplace. More generally, the popular film certainly contributed to the 1990s milieu of suspicion and distrust of government.[114]

JFK and the thirtieth anniversary of the assassination in 1993 spurred fresh enthusiasm and energy in the countersubversive core. Ten new studies of the assassination appeared, and publishers reprinted Lane's *Rush to Judgment* and Lifton's *Best Evidence*. In *Crime of the Century,* historian Michael Kurtz concluded that Castro had ordered Kennedy's execution in retaliation for plots on his life. Kurtz suspected that the hit men were Mafioso, but admitted, "the evidence is certainly incomplete."[115] The subsequent FBI and Secret Service cover-up, Kurtz wrote, had come at the behest of Lyndon Johnson. Confrontation with Cuba, Johnson had feared, might escalate into world war. More sensational were Harrison Livingstone's *High Treason* and later *Killing Kennedy,* which called into question all previous investigations. Livingstone insisted that the Zapruder movie was "the biggest hoax of the twentieth century" and that the real film was still under FBI seal. The Oswald pictures, CE 399, the autopsy X rays and photographs, and the recovered rifle were also "red herrings" set to deceive. The scale of the conspiracy caused Livingstone to look beyond the FBI and CIA to perpetrators "higher" than the federal government. Moreover, the assassination was just a single step in their plan. "Even now, the pot is being stirred in our country, with drugs and sports and rock and roll the deadly mix. It's all deliberately set loose, like the dogs of war." Fellow researchers did not escape his censure: "I believe that some of the leading critics . . . are wittingly or unwittingly part of the cover-up." This included Oliver Stone, whom Livingstone sternly rebuked for making "a circus of the case" and perhaps scheming with Jim Garrison in a "second level of cover-up."[116] The research had now come full circle, devouring not only the authorities but the rebels as well.[117]

Popular-culture media returned to the assassination several more times during the 1990s and kept the conspiracy in the public eye. Hollywood producer Steve Golin's *Ruby* (1992), as can be inferred from the title, positions Jack Ruby in the middle of the web with connections to the CIA, FBI, and organized crime. According to the film, Ruby was not only involved in attempts on Castro's life but romantically linked to the woman who served as Jack Kennedy's intermediary with the mob. *In the Line of Fire* (1993) features Clint Eastwood as an aging Secret Service agent who is haunted by his failure to react quickly enough to save John Kennedy's life. Hidden microfilm in *The Rock* (1996) reveals who killed Kennedy and government secrets about UFO landings. *The Omega Code* (1999) deciphers the date of John Kennedy's assassination from biblical verse. Banking on the audience's familiarity with the plot, television moved the assassination into prime time. *Quantum Leap* had time traveler Sam Beckett materialize in the body of Lee Harvey Oswald. Reviewing and rejecting the conspiracy theories, the show fixed the blame on the lone gunman. Beckett fails to prevent the president's assassination but still changes history. He saves Jackie Kennedy, who had died with her husband the first time around. A *Seinfeld* episode satirized Oliver Stone's film and featured a spitting incident replete with a "magic loogie." With a Zapruder-like video photographer and a mysterious "umbrella man" in place, the event is reenacted repeatedly and in slow motion, with Seinfeld concluding, "There had to have been a second spitter."[118] *The X-Files* made John Kennedy the first victim of its villainous cigarette-smoking man. Recruited by hidden conspirators to avenge Kennedy's betrayal at the Bay of Pigs, he crouches in the storm drain in Dealey Plaza, waiting for the limousine to come into range. The "umbrella man" on the grassy knoll signals, and the gunman delivers the fatal head shot from the front. In another episode, FBI agent Fox Mulder listens to a telephone message about a digitized version of the Zapruder film. Says the caller: "You'll never believe where the third shot came from. Erase this once you hear it." Meanwhile, savvy viewers know that appearances of the conspiracy-minded Lone Gunmen, Mulder's unofficial deputies, are repeated slaps at the Warren Commission's theory of the assassination. Sensing the possibilities for an *X-Files* spin-off, Fox Network officials offered the Lone Gunmen their own series in 2001.[119]

The death of John Kennedy breathed new life into other conspiracy theories. Countersubversive Milton William Cooper believed that the Secret Service agent driving the presidential limousine turned and shot Kennedy point-blank on orders from Majesty Twelve (MJ-12), the shadow government of the United States. Kennedy had drawn fire because he threatened to reveal secret dealings with extraterrestrials. The hidden group also saw to the cover-up, murdering all witnesses able to identify the real assassin. Meanwhile, members of the Council on Foreign Relations formed the majority of the Warren Commission and diverted the investigation from the master perpetrators. MJ-12 later forced Richard Nixon to resign the presidency, fearing that an impeachment trial would expose secret extraterrestrial files. NBC's short-running *Dark Skies* floated the plot in the mainstream in 1996. According to the script, Kennedy planned to reveal MJ-12-alien negotiations in his 1964 state of the union address. Jack Ruby killed Oswald after an alien infected his body and took control of his mind. Assassination researcher Jim Marrs, appearing on the Art Bell radio program in 1999, gave credence to such allegations. He discovered that in November 1963 Kennedy asked the CIA to provide the White House with its UFO files in preparation for a planned joint space exploration program with the Soviet Union. Marrs concluded that this effort to ease international tensions "may have been, indeed, yet another straw that broke the camel's back." As if the Kennedy enemies list was not long enough, Marrs noted the president's difficulties with "international bankers." Alien abduction expert Whitley Strieber, guest-hosting that night for Bell, found it suspicious that while Kennedy's Texas itinerary had scheduled a feast at the LBJ ranch the evening of the assassination, no preparations had been initiated. "That is," observed Strieber, "a glimpse of something."[120] *Weekly World News* reporter Mike Foster uncovered even more startling news. Kennedy had planned a public address on November 23, 1963, to reveal the alien presence on Earth. He carried the speech, printed on note cards, to Dallas and entrusted the text to Governor John Connally. Following the assassination, the governor's aide hid the blood-stained notes in a safety deposit box, finally breaking cover in 2000. Kennedy's purported speech was to have revealed that in 1947 the military had recovered an alien spacecraft in New Mexico. Contact had subsequently been made, and Kennedy would have reassured his listeners, "We have determined that they are not foes, but friends. Together with them we can create a better world."[121]

The Kennedy assassination merged into various global conspiracies. Ralph Epperson's video "The Driver Shot President Kennedy!" put the Mafia, the CIA, and the FBI in the service of the Illuminati. The military-industrial complex was merely a ruse, exaggerated by the suspect Dwight Eisenhower to distract patriots. Holocaust denier Michael Piper exposed a Jewish plot. John Kennedy had angered Prime Minister David Ben-Gurion by refusing to support Israel's nuclear weapons program and by endorsing Palestinian rights. In operation HAMAN, the Israeli Mossad used Meyer Lansky's criminal connections to arrange the hit. Steven Frogue offered a similar scenario, adding that Lee Harvey Oswald worked for the Anti-Defamation League. Christian evangelist Texe Marrs created fusion by laying responsibility on "Jewish-born Illuminati characters." Specifically, he condemned "Jewish-born" Warren Commission investigator Arlen Specter for deviously creating the magic bullet "snow job."[122] Such disparate elements made the different conspiracy theories more tightly coherent and mutually reinforcing. By nurturing distrust and suspicion, conspiracists wrought a collective effect, and the whole proved greater than the sum of its parts.[123]

In the background, the congressionally mandated Assassination Records Review Board went about its task. In the six years of its existence, the panel declassified sixty thousand documents accumulating to more than four million pages from the files of the Warren Commission, the CIA, the FBI, the House Select Committee on Assassinations, the Senate Select Committee on Intelligence, and the Rockefeller Commission. It also added to the record, deposing the Parkland and Bethesda physicians, sponsoring new ballistics tests, obtaining Jim Garrison's records, and authenticating and making available the Zapruder film. Although more than three decades had passed since the assassination, public and opinion makers' fascination was such that revelations in the released documents secured broad coverage. The media reported on the diverse CIA-prompted assassination attempts on Castro's life. Bobby Kennedy's zealous attempt to shield his brother's reputation by covering up these plots was made clear. Similarly exposed was the then–attorney general's intent to protect the family's privacy with tight restrictions on the autopsy. The president's supposedly missing brain had never been lost, but was given to his brother Bobby and placed in the casket.

Records also documented the imprecision of the autopsy and the lost photographs, but explanation diminished the substance of conspiracy. In its final report issued in 1998, the board confirmed the finding of a lone gunman. It nevertheless censured the government's "penchant for secrecy," which had sapped confidence in authority and bred conspiracy thinking. The Freedom of Information Act, the board concluded, offered little relief; designed to encourage openness, it often created the opposite impression. Officials "heavily redacted" FOIA requests, exempted CIA operational files, and stubbornly protected FBI records. To change this culture of secrecy, the panel recommended a new openness, with restrictions on the number of officials charged with classifying secrets and a time limit on the sealing of records.[124]

The assassination's hold was so great, however, that the case did not close. The review board had worked diligently, but James Lesur of the Assassination Archives and Research Center noted pessimistically, "For those who hoped that the release would quell the controversy, I don't think that will happen. We have an unsolved assassination of a president of the United States that is not being investigated. This will never be over unless someone comes up with a believable solution."[125] Insulated and resonating to their own rhythms, the conspiracists continue to search for Kennedy's killer. In addition to the Research Center, the Coalition on Political Assassinations and the Association of Assassination Researchers provide structure for the countersubversive community. Newsletters *Deep Politics Quarterly, Fair Play,* and *Fourth Decade* persist in combing assassination materials for clues. Chain bookstores still offered half a dozen assassination titles, with the conspiracist interpretation receiving the most shelf space. On the web, the "Kennedy Assassination Home Page" furnishes links to more than one hundred sites and news groups. The site "The Kennedy Assassination for the Novice," which was no longer active at the end of 2000, received almost thirty-five thousand hits in the twelve months beginning May 1999. Internet surfers can also log on to www.jfk.org, which offers a live "earthcam" scanning Dealey Plaza from the sniper's nest.[126]

Outside the conspiracist core interest remains high and skepticism strong. CNN News concluded a report on the Assassination Records Review Board by editorializing, "History continues to attach question marks to events in Dallas."[127] In August 1999 and March 2000 the History Channel rebroadcast the six-part 1980s British documentary *Men Who Killed Kennedy*. Fox network's *Mad TV* offered a skit in which comedians quizzed children on the letter *C*, which stood for "conspiracy, cover-up, and Cuban connection." Teaching that the "real" shot was fired from the grassy knoll, they cautioned students to "read between the lines" and not be "sellout pig[s]."[128] The April 4, 2000, edition of *Weekly World News* found Lee Harvey Oswald alive and well in Russia and willing to tell all in exchange for "total immunity." Characterizing him as a CIA mole, the reporter testified to Oswald's patriotism and credited him with doing "more than any other American agent to ensure the collapse of the Soviet empire."[129] In homage, six million pilgrims visit the site of the assassination each year. Thousands stay to tour the Dallas Museum of Conspiracies, which opened in 1995 just three blocks from Dealey Plaza. It offers exhibits on the Kennedy assassination, the death of Mary Jo Kopechne at Chappaquiddick in 1968, and the downing of Korean Airlines flight 007. At the dawn of the new millennium, opinion polls indicate little change in public sentiment and an audience receptive to conspiracy claims. Seventy-five percent of Americans still reject the Warren Commission's lone-gunman theory. The results betray no significant gender or socioeconomic differences. Nor do political leanings markedly affect the percentages. Thus in conservative Utah, where the counterhistory finds few proponents, 78 percent accept a conspiracy explanation.[130]

The assassination of President John Kennedy was prime for conspiracy thinking. The past verified the reality of successful assassination plots in America and elsewhere, and belief required neither leaps of faith nor logic. Emotional rupture and the sense of a historical turning point nourished significance and suspicion. With so many eyewitnesses and ballistics, forensics, and autopsy details, the solution appeared within reach. That opportunity was quickly lost. The tragedy bred confusion and mistakes in judgment, while individuals and agencies covered themselves to protect reputation. A hurried report, exposed in its inconsistencies, offered no closure and eroded confidence in the authorities. Public uneasiness sustained the conspiracy community from the beginning, with momentum added when opinion makers broke ranks and validated critics' claims. In command of growing resources, the conspiracists waged a decades-long war of attrition against only intermittent resistance. Government secrecy and later revelations of official misdeeds sanctioned conspiracy theories and made believers even more tenacious in their suspicions. This bid for authority proved successful, and Americans folded their memories into a collective wisdom of conspiracy. A younger generation, following the script in book and film, was similarly enticed. Nevertheless, there was a passivity to popular conspiracism. Belief outside the countersubversive core did not compel action but gave evidence of resignation with the passage of time and to the power of the enemy. In raising a reasonable doubt, conspiracists would have to be content with fostering a pervasive alienation and heightening public sensitivity to other potential sources of subversion.

Yet conspiracy thinking was more than a means to emotional closure and crime solution. Inherent in the work of the critics is an alternative history of recent America. As Oliver Stone observed, if the Warren Commission Report is "a great myth," then "in order to fight a myth, maybe you have to create another one, a counter myth."[131] With the unraveling of liberalism in the 1960s, progressives mourned what was and what might have been. They said that Kennedy's death had robbed Americans of a commitment beyond the self, a desire to sacrifice for the greater good. Conspiracy had left Camelot in ruins. If Kennedy had lived, the nation would have been spared the agony of Vietnam and racial divide. Conspiracists were convinced that Kennedy had been poised as the people's champion to challenge the military-industrial-intelligence complex. The Watergate crisis, the AIDS plague, the crack epidemic, and the Iran-Contra scandal would never have occurred. The New Frontier had been betrayed and its promise killed at birth. So steep a fall from grace could not be a matter of circumstance, but could only be the work of the self-interested and malevolent. In contesting the present and future, conspiracy theorists offered a vision of the good society. That made countersubversion a mighty weapon in the struggle for authority and power.

Jewish Devils and the War on Black America

> The Jewish lobby has a stranglehold on the government.
> . . . Whatever they want they get it because the president
> himself is actively punking out . . . selling America right
> on down the tube.
> —LOUIS FARRAKHAN

> The Uzis, the AK-47s, your enemy is feeding you auto-
> matic weapons now. You don't make any weapons,
> Brother. Where did you get the weapons? . . . This is
> all calculated. This is all part of the conspiracy.
> —LOUIS FARRAKHAN

Opinion polls give evidence of the conspiracist zeal that flares in modern America. They also mark the demographic communities that glow most intensely with countersubversive fire. Collective experiences may entice groups to conspiracy thinking, with those who feel their place in American society most precarious primed to be the most suspicious. Disproportionately among the vigilant are African Americans. Opinion surveys in the 1990s found that more than 60 percent of African Americans believed that the CIA had flooded their neighborhoods with drugs and one-third were convinced that government scientists had created the AIDS virus to ensure black genocide. On the streets, word passes that the Ku Klux Klan or the government has placed chemicals in food and drink to render black men sterile. Such beliefs are not confined to the poor or ignorant. In the black community, rumors of white plots are essential matter of the folk discourse. Collaterally, opinion polls since the 1960s have consistently shown that African Americans are twice as likely as whites to harbor strong biases against Jews. For outsiders, conspiracism not only offers self-protection and empowerment but reiterates shared values and asserts a collective defense.[1]

Conspiracism is also a weapon in the struggle for power within the black community. Most striking, it has been instrumental in the quest for authority of the Nation of Islam and particularly its minister Louis Farrakhan. Dismissing the Nation's leaders as paranoid extremists and Jew baiters ignores their agility in using countersubversion as a lever to leadership and a means of social movement mobilization. Their claims of conspiracy draw energy from the African-American past and present and loudly resonate with community experiences and perceptions. Louis Farrakhan's combat rhetoric combined with a message of self help, moreover, clearly delineates the Nation of Islam's agenda, attracts opinion shapers, and firms members' loyalties. Farrakhan's attack and the habitual white counterattack only enhance his and the Nation's reputation as defenders of the race. Essentially risk-free, this racially divisive conspiracy thinking embraces previous generations of black leaders while distancing proponents from a discredited integrationist ideology. Farrakhan and the Nation, uncompromising before white power and its alleged black lackeys, appear the community's most defiant and effective advocates, making them immune to challenges from within.

Follow the theme of conspiracism in the ideology and appeal of the Nation of Islam. The first members of the Nation, more popularly known as Black Muslims, were born again in Allah, who appeared to them in the person of Wallace D. Fard during the Great Depression. A man of mystery, claiming birth in Mecca, Fard peddled household goods door-to-door in the Detroit ghetto, but he found more customers for his ideas. He taught followers that God was black and had created man and woman in his image. Under the guidance of twenty-three god-scientists, the chosen people, led by the tribe of Shabazz, raised great empires in Africa and the Middle East. These were, said Fard, the foundation stones of modern civilization. A threat, however, arose to the peace and prosperity of the black world. "Mr. Yacub," an evil god-scientist, devised genetic experiments to create a devilish white race. The conspiracy was exposed and Yacub and his disciples were exiled to the island of Patmos. This did not deter Yacub, who after six hundred years succeeded in creating a wicked white people by successively killing the darkest born and breeding the color and humanity out of generations of subjects. Fierce and brutal, the blue-eyed devils were driven away and confined to ice caves in Europe, where they walked like animals and ate raw meat. Allah took pity and sent his prophets Moses and Jesus to civilize the savages. While tempering their feral behavior, God's messengers could not change their hateful nature. Over time, whites multiplied in number and grew powerful, while blacks became sinful and corrupt. In anger, God turned away and allowed the white savages to humble and enslave his people. Blacks were stripped of their culture and lost sight of their history. White masters bent them to the "dirty religion" of Christianity while tampering with the Bible to disguise all traces of the truly chosen. So total was the white victory that blacks even adopted the names of their owners.[2]

Fard offered hope, revealing that God had not forgotten his people. Allah had decreed white domination to last six thousand years and end in 1914. A brief period of grace had begun for the once lost, now found tribe of Shabazz to reclaim its birthright. This meant a return to the worship of Allah and the rejection of the slave masters' "spook" god of Christianity. To be worthy also meant coming to a new knowledge of self by rejecting sin, building financial resources, strengthening family life, resisting unclean foods, and discarding slave names. Attentive to the Christian apocalyptic beliefs of his followers, Fard warned that the time was at hand and that only 144,000 black men and women would escape the final conflict between God and the white devils. On the day of reckoning, Allah would send a giant spaceship to lift the chosen to safety and destroy the cursed. As he told his disciple Elijah Poole (renamed Muhammad), the god-scientists had created the "mother plane," which now hovered in position: "He pointed out a destructive, dreadful-looking plane that is made like a wheel in the sky today. It is a half-mile by a half-mile square; it is a humanly-built planet. It is up there and can be seen twice a week; it is no secret." On God's command, the mother plane would launch 1,500 smaller craft that would firebomb the earth and destroy all life. The chosen would wait in the mother plane for one thousand years and then return to inherit paradise. Elijah Muhammad had no reason to doubt, for Fard had convinced him that "My name is Mahdi; I am God."[3]

Although Wallace Fard's following remained small, the Detroit police would not long tolerate his "cult."[4] Officials arrested Fard three times and then summarily banished him from the city. His departure caused no leadership vacuum, for he had chosen the loyal Elijah Muhammad as his "messenger" to carry on the work. Muhammad deified his mentor and mixed Fardism with Christianity and the black nationalism of Marcus Garvey. He reached to the "so-called Negro" using familiar images: "The human beast—the serpent, the dragon, the devil, and Satan—all mean one and the same; the people or race known as the white or Caucasian."[5] In line with Protestant tradition, the pope was the Antichrist of the Book of Revelation and the mastermind of the white conspiracy. The new Social Security numbers were marks of the beast, and Muhammad called on blacks to resist their temptation. He chided those who questioned the existence of the mother plane and reminded them of the wheel of Ezekiel, quoting the relevant biblical passages to validate his claims. Waiting for Armageddon and offering salvation, Muhammad preached self-help, thrift, personal dignity, black economic independence, and racial purity. He pooled resources to open a mosque, educational institutions, and black-owned and -operated apartment houses, grocery stores, and restaurants. Contesting for authority, he attacked established black leaders for plotting with whites to keep the ghetto submerged in alcohol and drugs. Clergymen, however, were the most dangerous of the white man's puppets, for they blinded blacks to the true god. Defiant and relentless, Elijah Muhammad offered not only a message of pride and dignity but a challenge to the racial status quo. As the Reverend Jesse Jackson later praised him: "During our Colored and Negro days, he was black."[6]

The authorities' response to the movement heightened Elijah Muhammad's sense of siege and provided additional proof of the white conspiracy. During World War II, the Nation of Islam came under FBI surveillance for its refusal to defend America against foreign attack. Muhammad and dozens of Black Muslims resisted the draft and were jailed for the duration. In the 1950s the FBI petitioned the attorney general to add the Nation to the Justice Department's list of subversive organizations but was denied on failing to establish the group's subversive credentials. Agents did wiretap the messenger's telephone and recruit informants to expose Nation secrets. They also attempted to devastate the movement by channeling to a reliable reporter information that exposed Wallace Fard as both white and a petty criminal. When national magazines went on the offensive in 1959, Black Muslims were not surprised. Said Jabril Muhammad, "They conspired to deceive the public. . . . Members of a large orchestra do not accidently [sic] play the same tune." Meanwhile, federal files on Elijah Muhammad accumulated, documenting his extravagant lifestyle and sexual promiscuity. These would be the grist for the disruptive FBI Counter Intelligence Program against the Nation of Islam during the 1960s.[7]

With eyes turned toward the South in the 1950s and the black community overwhelmingly supporting the integration campaign, the Nation's message lacked salience to all but a few. Commitment demanded too great a leap of faith. Regimentation and restrictions on personal habits deterred many others. After twenty years of organizing, Elijah Muhammad could count fewer than a thousand followers. Fortunes changed dramatically with the emergence of Malcolm X. Born Malcolm Little, he brought to the movement a new intensity and authenticity. His power was in his suffering, which probed the wounds of collective black victimization. He told of the night that the Ku Klux Klan rode and terrorized his family. His father, an organizer for Marcus Garvey's Universal Negro Improvement Association, had made white enemies and died under mysterious circumstances. White authorities confined his mentally ill mother to a state institution and left the family broken. Failed by a school system that offered no hope to black children, Malcolm Little turned to crime. He pimped, dealt drugs, ran numbers, and eventually robbed his way into prison. There he found Allah and was reborn a faithful servant of the messenger. Charismatic and passionate, Malcolm X took to the streets to raise up a Muslim following. He preached the Nation's agenda, echoing Elijah Muhammad's calls for self-improvement and black power and against race mixing. He modeled the influence that the messenger exerted on the repentant. His success was easy to gauge. By the early 1960s the

Nation boasted one hundred thousand members and sixty-nine temples in twenty-seven states.[8]

Both in vision and in image, Elijah Muhammad and Malcolm X posed a challenge to civil rights leaders. They preached that integration was a false path and trumpeted black purity and superiority. Self-defense, they argued, roused an adversary's respect, while nonviolence only curried contempt. Showing no deference, the Nation's leaders confronted whites while defending blacks without hesitation or qualification. Their loyalties were certain; they felt no pressure to cultivate the white media or the power brokers. As defenders of the race they were unassailable. And they made the white man flinch. With this authority, they attacked civil rights activists as Uncle Toms who did their master's bidding. Malcolm X dismissed the 1963 March on Washington as a "farce" and "circus" contrived by the black bourgeoisie in league with white financiers. "Hoaxed again by the white man," the integration scam went about "weakening, lulling, and deluding" black men and women about the real enemy.[9] Elijah Muhammad denounced the sit-in campaign as groveling before the white devils. The Reverend Martin Luther King, Jr., was a "fool" who, acting like a dog, "just waddles all around the door" to gain the master's approval. Muhammad did not desist even after King's death. He was convinced that Allah had condemned the civil rights leader to hell for "trying to satisfy his white enemies." The black establishment struck back hard. Thurgood Marshall of the National Association for the Advancement of Colored People condemned the Nation of Islam's leadership as "a bunch of thugs organized from prison and jails, and financed I am sure, by . . . some Arab groups." King cautioned African Americans about "hate groups arising in our midst which preach a doctrine of black supremacy" and pleaded with them not to "stoop to the low and primitive methods of some of our opponents."[10]

In their attempt to undermine the integrationist leadership, Nation of Islam separatists pursued a strategy that resonated with traditional black attitudes and community experiences. The Civil Rights Movement, they were convinced, was a fraud perpetrated by Jews, the longtime exploiters of ghetto America. Malcolm X made the connection: the Jews "know how to rob you, they know how to be your landlord, they know how to be your grocer . . . they know how to join the NAACP and become the president. . . . They know how to control everything you've got."[11] Pulling the strings, Jews supported the freedom campaign because "all of the bigotry and hatred focused upon the black man keeps off the Jew a lot of heat that would be on him otherwise."[12] At the same time, the Jewish integration plot would keep African Americans impotent by subverting black nationalism and weakening the race through assimilation. Jewish means and ends, as usual, were economic: "With money donations, the Jew gains control, then he sends the black man doing all this wading-in, boring-in, even burying-in—everything but buying-in. Never advises him how to set up factories and hotels. Never advises him to own what he wants. No, where there's something worth owning, the Jew's got it."[13] Jeremiah X, minister of the Atlanta temple, concurred: "The Jews are the Negro's worst enemies. . . . Unlike other whites, Jews make it a practice to study Negroes, they are able to get next to him better than other whites . . . thereby being in a position to stab him with a knife."[14] Black leaders were merely puppets in the scheme, guilty by association, who betrayed their own people for personal gain. The black-Jewish coalition—fragile, intermittent, and often expedient—assumed in Black Muslim rhetoric a sinister design. In stoking anti-Jewish feelings, the Nation had both fused the black establishment with a familiar antagonist and positioned itself to profit. Had not Wallace Fard first condemned the chosen pretenders? Was not the tribe of Shabazz united with its Arab comrades in the war against Zionist aggression? The Jewish counterattack played shrilly in the ghetto and acted to validate the Nation's accusations of overweening influence in the news media. At the same time, it bolstered the Muslims' claim to a vanguard position in defense of the black community.

These seeds fell on fertile ground, for throughout the twentieth century relations between blacks and Jews had often been contentious. On the surface, the two minorities appeared to have similar interests; they shared the status of outsiders and suffered common enemies. Jewish and black elites had built alliances rooted both in idealism and self-interest, and Jewish philanthropists proved generous in their support of black educational and welfare institutions. At the grass roots, activists created interracial organizations to advance a progressive agenda. Yet the two groups approached the future at a different pace. America was a land of slavery for blacks and a promised land for Jews. A white skin gave Jews the advantage, the token of opportunity and acceptance that would distance them from the oppressed. Ghetto life put the unequal relationship into bold relief and fostered in the vulnerable not only bitterness but a sense of secret power and control. Cries of anti-Semitism and conspiracy were thus raised in unison, with each confirming and reinforcing the other. Coalitions persisted throughout the century, but disparities in resources between the two peoples made not comrades but unequal partners—or more typically, antagonists.[15]

Every day, Jews and blacks met on uneven ground in the northern cities. Jews had built a financial base on rental property and small retail establishments serving poor blacks newly arrived from the South. Both groups interpreted natural and personal conflicts of interest in collective terms, and stereotypes quickly established the lines of engagement. With major white corporate interests invisible in the ghetto, the Jew was for blacks the symbol of oppression and the master of their subordination. The black newspaper *The New York Age* declared as early as 1913: "It is a peculiar race . . . parasitical and predatory . . . preying upon and devouring the substance of others rather than creating and devouring the substance of itself. This is essentially the race characteristic of all parasites, all race fungi."[16] Blacks accused Jewish landlords of exacting exorbitant rents for overcrowded apartment space and padding profits by neglecting repairs. "Antagonism toward the 'Jewish landlord,'" psychologist Kenneth Clark observed, "is so common as to have become almost an integral aspect of the folk culture of the northern urban Negro. To him, almost all landlords are automatically Jewish."[17] Blacks registered similar complaints against Jewish shopkeepers who disproportionately served the ghetto. Overcharging, short-weighting, high interest rates, and shoddy goods were among their litany of accusations. Wrote James Baldwin: "The grocer was a Jew, and being in debt to him was very much like being in debt to the company store. The butcher was a Jew and, yes, we certainly paid more for bad cuts of meat than other New York citizens. . . . We bought our clothes from a Jew and, sometimes, our secondhand shoes, and the pawnbroker was a Jew—perhaps we hated him most of all. . . . All of them were exploiting us, and that was why we hated them."[18] Observe how Malcolm X personified the situation: "Goldberg always catches ya'. If Goldberg can't catch ya', Goldstein'll catch ya'. And if Goldstein don't catch ya', Greenberg will."[19] From such daily interactions came the perception of Jewish control, a reflection of the vulnerability of economic and political outsiders who were disproportionately ill-housed, ill-fed, and ill-clothed. None of this should have surprised Jews, who also participated, sometimes subconsciously, in stereotyping. Essayist Ben Halpern thus remarked: "The age-old Shylock image becomes in Negro city folklore, Goldberg, the slumlord, the extortionist storekeeper, and his wife who hires the *shvartze* cleaning woman off the street or at the employment exchange."[20]

Religious antagonism exacerbated economic conflict. Novelist Richard Wright, growing up in Chicago, recalled that "we had been taught at home and Sunday school that Jews were 'Christ killers.' With the Jews thus singled out for us, we made them fair game for ridicule."[21] In this vein, black children played games to rhymes like:

> Virgin Mary had one son
> The cruel Jews had him hung
> Bloody Christ killer
> Never trust a Jew
> Bloody Christ killer
> What won't a Jew do?[22]

Wright concluded, the distrust of the Jews "was bred in us from childhood; it was not merely racial prejudice, it was a part of our cultural heritage."[23]

In the 1920s Marcus Garvey's Universal Negro Improvement Association pressed for black-owned and -operated businesses and challenged Jewish merchants with a "Buy from a Negro" campaign. When this effort failed and his "Back to Africa" movement suffered setbacks, Garvey detected a Jewish plot. He was sure that his conviction for mail fraud and subsequent deportation were arranged by Jews. During the Great Depression, Harlem's Businessmen's Club and Housewives League helped organize community boycotts in "Don't Buy Where You Can't Work" demonstrations that targeted Jewish stores for their failure to employ African Americans. Black merchants in Chicago complained of unfair Jewish competition and were convinced that they were "victims of a Jewish conspiracy."[24] Nor did the work of Jewish leftists in black causes mitigate the anger. In fact African-American Communists denounced their Jewish comrades as arrogant, paternalistic, and willing to sacrifice black interests for the good of the party. Tension gave way to violence in race riots during the 1930s and 1940s, with Jewish property singled out for economic revenge.[25]

Jewish resistance to black residential inroads and subsequent exodus also fueled antagonism. Meanwhile, Jewish mobility created new levels of unequal interaction. Civil rights activist Bayard Rustin remarked, "If you happen to be an uneducated, poorly-trained Negro living in the ghetto you see only four kinds of white people— the policeman, the businessman, the teacher, and the welfare worker. In many cities, three of these four are Jewish."[26] The Reverend Adam Clayton Powell, Jr., blamed Jews for the troubles: "Everybody knows that the Jew on the way up, when he has to scuffle and scramble for pennies, . . . can say he is the friend of the Negro. However, once he is free of the shackles of poverty, the Jew turns white. Negro anti-Semitism was regrettable but the Jew himself is the author."[27] Blacks entertained Jewish stereotypes across class and educational lines. In a 1941 poll African-American college students most frequently listed "progressive, shrewd, ambitious, and grasping" as distinctively Jewish traits.[28] These results mirrored a similar survey taken among men at Princeton University. Without amelioration, bitterness flared in new generations. Growing up in the Cleveland ghetto in the 1950s, author Barbara Smith confessed, "I am an anti-Semite. . . . I have swallowed anti-Semitism simply by living here, whether I wanted to or not."[29]

Black-Jewish cooperation during the civil rights movement of the 1960s was not sufficient to ease distrust or change perceptions. Viewed in the shadow of African-American history, Jewish liberalism was inadequate compensation and remained shrouded in self-interest and paternalism. For their part, Jews continued to pride themselves on contributions to the struggle, making heavy financial donations to black organizations and putting their bodies on the line in the freedom rides and during Freedom Summer in 1964. Civil rights leaders were appreciative; a poll found that 71 percent considered Jews "helpful" to the cause. Even in 1963, during the movement's seemingly harmonious period, however, such sentiments were not shared in the wider black community. Only 42 percent of African Americans agreed with their leadership on the Jewish role; 9 percent believed Jews "harmful," with the remainder unsure or reserving judgment. Just 29 percent of blacks deemed Jews as "favorable" to integration, with 15 percent regarding them as opposed. Interestingly, 42 percent of African Americans rated Catholics as supportive of their goals.[30] Many could agree with a Harlem black man who mused, "You know all those Jews in the civil rights marches and going down South—you know why they do it? They did it to take the heat off themselves. They've got a bad conscience because they live on black dollars. We had the riots because of the Jews."[31] Martin Luther King, Jr., denounced anti-Semitism: "It is used to divide Negro and Jew who have effectively collaborated in the struggle for justice. . . . The individual Jew or gentile who may be an exploiter acts out of his greed as an individual, not his religious perception."[32] More politic was Roy Innis of the Congress of Racial Equality, who later noted, "A black leader would be crazy to publicly repudiate anti-Semitism."[33]

These tensions played into the hands of the leaders of the Nation of Islam, who were practiced in exploiting anti-Jewish feelings for leverage. They escalated their attacks on King and the NAACP's Roy Wilkins as the "phony leadership" of the civil rights movement, fronting for the Jews, who manipulated events.[34] Looking beyond the black community for allies, Malcolm X and Jeremiah X reached out improbably to the Ku Klux Klan for support against the Jewish menace. In a meeting with Klan leaders, the two Muslim ministers expressed their opposition to integration and dismissed the movement as a Jewish plot. Elijah Muhammad also invited George Lincoln Rockwell to the Nation's Saviour's Day Convention (Fard's birthday), where the American Nazi leader spoke and donated money to their common cause. The Black Muslims, meanwhile, set the Jewish problem in a wider context. Their newspaper *Muhammad Speaks* condemned the "international economic conspiracy" plotted by the Rothschilds, the Sulzbergers, the Guggenheims, and other Jewish bankers.[35] Israel was their tool in the Middle East, eager to seize the oil resources of its Arab neighbors. In a more theological vein, Malcolm X reminded listeners that Abraham was not Jewish, nor were Jews the biblical slaves of Egypt. The Bible is written "in such a tricky way," he cautioned, that the true Israelites have been erased from its pages.[36] Vying for authority in victimization, he mourned slavery's one hundred million black deaths but was contemptuous of the six million Jews lost during World War II: "Now everybody's wet-eyed over a handful of Jews who brought it on themselves."[37] These comments seared Jews, but many African Americans were too absorbed with their own pain or too proud of their defender to empathize. In light of past antagonism and growing conflict, the Jew became a convenient and effective fulcrum on which to raise the Nation of Islam to influence.[38]

The Black Muslims, meanwhile, combated enemies closer at hand than Jewish conspirators. FBI wiretaps and informants, some within Elijah Muhammad's inner circle, revealed that the messenger had had extramarital affairs with six women and had fathered thirteen children. To discredit Muhammad and neutralize the Nation, agents sent anonymous letters to his wife and spread the news among Black Muslims, including Malcolm X. Muhammad's hypocrisy stunned Malcolm, and the true believer lost faith in his teacher. At the same time, agents provocateurs convinced Muhammad that his chief minister was plotting to take over the movement. The FBI also fomented dissension by planting doubts about the worthiness of other Muslim ministers and leaking information about the Nation's troubles to the *Chicago Tribune*. The Internal Revenue Service and the Central Intelligence Agency augmented these efforts with probes of their own. In a climate of induced and endemic paranoia, Malcolm X was assassinated by conspiracy, with or without FBI complicity. The murder did nothing to deter federal agents, whose counterintelligence program continued. Authorities even targeted the rank and file and in one instance attempted to close down a Muslim grade school for zoning and health reasons while compiling dossiers on the students' parents. The federal attack was effective, and the movement sustained heavy losses. Repression scarred survivors, who became even more vigilant and guarded. Not only had their fears of secret plots been confirmed, but the enemy had breached the walls of the Nation and had recruited within.[39]

Besieged, the Nation took solace in the confirmation of other

FBI targets, the more militant organizations of the civil rights movement. As the struggle shifted its base of operations to the North after 1965, groups like the Student Nonviolent Coordinating Committee (SNCC) and the Black Panther Party embraced the Black Muslim stand against integration and pursued a separatist path. In the process, anti-Semitism figured more prominently as a mobilization tactic and in activists' efforts to confront and distance themselves from establishment leaders. Paralleling the Nation of Islam's strategy, SNCC and the Panthers reached for legitimacy not only by denouncing Jewish "slumlords" and store owners, but by joining the war against Israel's "Zionist Terror Gangs."[40] In fellowship with the colonized peoples of the world, they called on African Americans to repel Jewish imperialists at home and abroad. A SNCC broadside declared "that the famous European Jews, the Rothschilds, who have long controlled the wealth of many European nations, were involved in the original conspiracy with the British to create the 'State of Israel' and are still among Israel's chief supporters. . . . The Rothschilds Also Control Much of Africa's Mineral Wealth."[41] In reaction, Jewish donors closed their coffers to SNCC, while purges removed Jews from the membership list, hastening the general Jewish retreat from the civil rights movement.[42]

With the Black Muslims continuing to sound the alarm against the Jewish menace, rancor built over issues of community control and even museum exhibits. Urban rioters in dozens of northern cities repeatedly vented black anger, with Jewish stores taking the brunt of vandalism and looting. Opinion polls marked the clear divide between African Americans and Jews. Almost one-half of blacks, compared with one-third of whites, ranked among the most intensely anti-Semitic. By the end of the 1960s, the brittle interracial coalition was broken, communication severed. Now in defensive crouch, blacks and Jews turned inward and moved along different trajectories.[43]

The 1970s brought new tensions that increased the friction between Jews and blacks. As the American mainstream shifted to the right politically, issues critical to the black community were dropped from the national agenda. Jews secured ranking positions in government, the university, business, and the media, their mobility making them effectively "white" in the eyes of the Christian majority. As African Americans moved assertively in support of group interests, they protested that Jewish gains came at their expense. Thus blacks and Jews found themselves adversaries in the affirmative-action debate, with Jewish organizations playing prominent roles in opposing quotas in hiring and school admission. Although Jewish memory may have demanded such a position, such behavior exasperated blacks, who focused on the sharp economic disparity between the two communities. Poll results reflected their anger: more than 80 percent of black leaders believed that Jews "chose money over people."[44] The conflict began, the Reverend Jesse Jackson concluded, "when we started our quest for power. Jews were willing to share decency, but not power."[45]

Middle Eastern politics widened the breach. Jewish leaders had access to American decision makers, and their clout brought dramatically increasing aid to Israel during the 1970s. Adding insult to injury, Israel normalized relations with South Africa and became a major trading partner and arms supplier to the apartheid nation. Israeli policies in the occupied territories also drew black criticism. The matter came to a head in 1979, when Andrew Young, U.S. ambassador to the United Nations and the ranking African American in government, violated a Carter administration pledge by opening private talks with representatives of the Palestine Liberation Organization and was asked to resign his position. Black leaders met soon after in a national summit to support Young and issue what Kenneth B. Clark called a "declaration of independence" from American Jewry.[46] Thelma Thomas Daley, the national president of Delta Sigma Theta, a predominately black college sorority, emphatically echoed Young's stand: "We have been patient and forbearing in [Jews'] masquerading as friends under the pretense of working for the common purpose of civil rights. . . . Their loyalties are not compatible with the struggle of black Americans for equal opportunities under the law. Indeed, we question whether their loyalties are first to the State of Israel or to the United States."[47] The Reverend Jesse Jackson, labeling Young's resignation a "capitulation to the Jews," concluded that "the real resistance to black progress has not been coming from the Ku Klux Klan but from our former allies in the American Jewish community."[48]

Blacks offered still more proof of Jewish leverage. Congress made trade relations with the Soviet Union conditional on that nation's treatment of its Jewish citizens. At the prompting of the American Jewish community, the U.S. government followed up with a guarantee of private loans to Soviet immigrants resettling in Israel. America's black ghettos and Africa, in contrast, were given low priority and appeared the victims of a zero-sum budget game that seemed to favor Jewish causes. Once again, African-American leaders had been exposed as weak, unable to protect their vulnerable constituents. These instances gave new life to accusations of secret influence and strengthened traditional stereotypes. Polls repeatedly confirmed that blacks were more willing than whites to believe that Jews exercised too much power and were guilty of divided loyalties. A significant shift was also apparent. African-American opinion makers recorded levels of anti-Semitic belief nearly twice as high as the black rank and file.[49]

The Nation of Islam had long staked a claim to these issues, but to little effect. Though recovered from federal attack and estimated to have reclaimed its membership of one hundred thousand, the organization had entered a period of drift and transition. Movement energy ebbed with the advancing age of Elijah Muhammad, who held tightly to the reins of power. Disquieting to true believers, Muhammad appointed his son Wallace as successor, in spite of frequent clashes and doubts about his commitment to the faith. These doubts gained substance upon Elijah Muhammad's death in 1975. Immediately, Wallace Muhammad radically recast the movement, cutting the Christian roots of ritual and belief and replacing them with Islamic grafts. The war with the white devils was over, as was the Nation's focus on self-help and racial pride. In line with the new direction, the younger Muhammad deemphasized Fardism, invited whites to enter the Nation as equals, relaxed the dress code and restrictions on smoking and dancing, disbanded the paramilitary Fruit of Islam, and ordained women as ministers. By 1977 the Nation of Islam was no more, reborn as the World Community of al-Islam in the West.[50]

Such drastic change in so short a time caused heavy fallout. The messenger's forty years of rule had made him a divine presence to his followers. Their relationship with him was intimate, and his beliefs had shaped their daily lives and nurtured their dreams.

Beyond the personal, Elijah Muhammad had fashioned a tightly bound community of believers who refused to surrender to white devils or infidels. Naturally, there were rumors of conspiracy in the messenger's death: had Wallace Muhammad plotted with the U.S. government to kill his father and destroy the Nation from within? Many despaired, but a familiar figure in the Black Muslim community emerged to offer hope of restoration and salvation. Louis Abdul Farrakhan, the messenger's national spokesman and convinced that he was the true heir, soon broke with Wallace Muhammad, and Muslims rallied to his cause. As it was at the birth of the Nation, Farrakhan worked the mortar of black pride, self-help, and conspiracism to rebuild the community. In confronting traditional enemies, he would win support beyond the Muslim world and successfully claim the mantle of leadership.[51]

Farrakhan was born Louis Eugene Walcott in New York City in 1933, the second son of Mae Clark, a domestic servant and recent immigrant from Barbados. Convinced that her children's future depended on secure moorings, Clark moved the family to the Roxbury ghetto near Boston and settled into the West Indian community. She demanded much of Gene. He began studying the violin when he was five years old and even appeared on the *Ted Mack Original Amateur Hour,* where he won the competition for his age group. His intelligence brought admission to prestigious schools, and his grades in Latin, English, calculus, and history consistently placed him on the academic honor roll. He made friends easily, and among his circle were several Jews. Remarked a Jewish schoolmate, "I wish I could say otherwise, but Gene was a *mensch.*"[52] An early encounter with Malcolm X made little impression. A track scholarship took Gene Walcott to all-black Winston-Salem Teachers' College in North Carolina. Though acclimated to northern de facto segregation, he was not prepared for the color line that still sharply divided southern society in the early 1950s. Signs segregating blacks from whites and confinement to the "nigger heaven" balcony in movie theaters were his most profound college memories. He repressed these ordeals as he had his northern encounters with racism, but he could not deny their impact for long. Walcott may have been relieved when his seventeen-year-old fiancée became pregnant, and he left North Carolina to marry her without finishing his studies. The calypso craze of the 1950s brought new opportunities. He joined a band and performed under the stage name Calypso Gene, known also as the Charmer for his extroverted personality and flair for entertaining.[53]

While he was on tour in Chicago in 1955, his life changed. Meeting an old friend who had joined the Nation of Islam, he accepted his invitation to hear Elijah Muhammad speak. Curious and probably amused, Walcott later remembered hiding a marijuana cigarette in his hatband in deference to the Nation's prohibitions. He was initially unimpressed with Muhammad, put off by his dry style and poor syntax. Then the messenger, who had been alerted to the presence of a college man in the audience, looked toward him and said: "Brother, don't pay attention to how I speak. Pay attention to what I'm saying. I didn't get the chance to go to the white man's fine schools, because when I tried to go, the doors were closed. But if you take what I say and place it into the beautiful way of speaking you know, you can help me save our people." Walcott was awed, and he and his wife converted immediately. A few months later, he dismissed second thoughts about leaving a successful calypso career after hearing an impassioned Malcolm X outline the cause and his new mission—race pride, self-help, and separatism.[54]

An ambitious man with even a modicum of college education could go fast and far in the Nation. Walcott, now known as Louis X, fell under the tutelage of Malcolm, serving as his assistant in the Harlem mosque. He said of Malcolm X, "He was my mentor, he was a man that I deeply loved and deeply admired, and I really adored him as my father in the movement."[55] Soon he was assigned to the pulpit of Mosque #11 in Boston as minister to a congregation of approximately one hundred worshipers. Within five years, he had almost tripled the mosque's membership and caught the attention of Elijah Muhammad. In addition to regular ministerial functions, Louis X found an outlet for his musical talents; he put the Nation's creed to song in "A White Man's Heaven Is a Black Man's Hell," which sold more than ten thousand copies by 1960. He also wrote and directed two stage productions. *Orgena* ("a Negro" spelled backward), performed in Carnegie Hall in New York City in 1961 with Louis X in the starring role, tells the story of black slavery and the transformation of the tribe of Shabazz into the degraded Negro. *The*

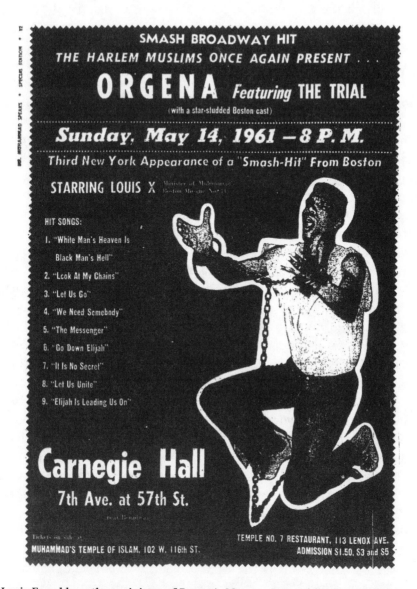

SMASH BROADWAY HIT

THE HARLEM MUSLIMS ONCE AGAIN PRESENT . . .

ORGENA *Featuring* THE TRIAL

(with a star-studded Boston cast)

Sunday, May 14, 1961 — 8 P. M.

Third New York Appearance of a "Smash-Hit" From Boston

STARRING LOUIS X Minister of Muhammad Boston Mosque No. 11

HIT SONGS:

1. "White Man's Heaven Is
   Black Man's Hell"
2. "Look At My Chains"
3. "Let Us Go"
4. "We Need Somebody"
5. "The Messenger"
6. "Go Down Elijah"
7. "It Is No Secret"
8. "Let Us Unite"
9. "Elijah Is Leading Us On"

Carnegie Hall
7th Ave. at 57th St.

Tickets on sale at
MUHAMMAD'S TEMPLE OF ISLAM, 102 W. 116th ST.

TEMPLE NO. 7 RESTAURANT, 113 LENOX AVE.
ADMISSION $1.50, $3 and $5

Louis Farrakhan, then minister of Boston's Mosque #11 and known as Louis X, played the lead in *Orgena* ("a Negro" spelled backward) in 1961 in New York City, The play re-creates the history of black slavery and the debasement of the tribe of Shabazz. He also wrote *The Trial*, performed at Carnegie Hall in conjunction with *Orgena*.

From the author's collection

Trial brings the white man to justice for his sins against the black race. The jury's verdict is anticlimactic and the sentence of death well deserved.

Already on the rise, his fortunes within the Nation improved dramatically with the fall of his mentor. Malcolm X had confided to his "little brother" the truth of Elijah Muhammad's infidelities. Louis X, however, would not join him in revolt and reported Malcolm's words to the messenger. Not only did Louis pledge allegiance to his leader, he pitched the death of the "hypocrite." Just a few months before Malcolm's assassination, Louis wrote in the Nation's newspaper *Muhammad Speaks:* "Only those who wish to be led to hell, or to their doom, will follow Malcolm. The die is set, and Malcolm shall not escape, especially after such evil, foolish talk about his benefactor. . . . Such a man as Malcolm is worthy of death."[56] He discounted his responsibility later: "We were all pawns. . . . Our own sincerity and ignorance was used by a wicked government, who wanted Malcolm dead, but wanted the blame on Elijah Muhammad, so they could kill two birds with one stone."[57] The messenger rewarded his loyalty, appointing him Malcolm's replacement as minister of Harlem's Mosque #7 and national representative. Muhammad also honored him with the name Farrakhan.[58]

Louis Farrakhan served the messenger faithfully. He crisscrossed the Black Muslim world to steel the faithful and rebuild congregations, reiterating the history of the original man, the diabolical Mr. Yacub, and the tribe of Shabazz. To potential recruits he held out salvation through the Nation's program of separatism, equal justice, community control, and economic self-determination. While taking blacks to task for their problems, Farrakhan placed ultimate responsibility on the devil race: "Just remember what white America is doing when she floods the Black community with dope. She knows this is the time of your rise, but you can't rise nodding, brother." He sparred, as well, with familiar enemies. Jews, he insisted, had in 1959 taken "control of every major Black organization: the NAACP; the Urban League; and Martin Luther King's SCLC."[59] Civil rights leaders who denounced Elijah Muhammad were just following orders. Black Muslims could discount information gleaned from television, radio, and newspapers for Jewish ownership made them unreliable sources. Looking to the future, in 1975 two of Louis Farrakhan's daughters married grandsons of the messenger.[60]

The death of Elijah Muhammad reversed the fortunes of the man many considered the heir apparent. Securing his position, Wallace Muhammad removed Louis Farrakhan from his bases of support on the East Coast and put him under close watch in Chicago. Confined to his "dirty little place on the west side," Farrakhan was frustrated as he became a stranger in the Nation: "Every day, I'm slipping further, trying to preach what Wallace preached. . . . I'm trying to reason this out. . . . Mean to tell me for twenty years I've been preaching lies?"[61] After two years, he left the organization, refusing to be "a prostitute for anybody, any more."[62] He beckoned Muslims to follow and return to the true path, assuring them that the messenger had confided in him: "The Nation is going to take a dive for the second time. . . . But, don't worry Brother. It will be rebuilt and will never fall again. . . . Go exactly as you see me go and do exactly as you see me do."[63] To those who hesitated, Farrakhan revealed the hidden plotters: it was the FBI, then the Jews who "planned that . . . a fight would break out over who would be the real heir. . . . They felt that this would tear the Nation up."[64]

To rally the faithful, Farrakhan reclaimed the discarded teachings of Wallace Fard and Elijah Muhammad. He preached self-reliance, self-control, and race pride in the old style. While chiding blacks on their fall from grace, he reserved blame for whites and predicted the imminent return of the mother plane and Allah's final judgment. Even the name of his movement's newspaper, The Final Call, suggested the lateness of the hour. Farrakhan promoted solidarity through conspiracism and joined the Nation of Islam and himself to the history of black resistance. The authorities, he claimed, had brought down Marcus Garvey, spied on Martin Luther King, condemned Malcolm X, and attempted to ruin the reputation of Elijah Muhammad. In defending his teacher, Farrakhan reminded his followers that their enemies still lurked in the shadows: "You sought to destroy his work. You paid informers among us to try and destabilize our work. You . . . feed stories into the news and television media to make us look like convicts and thugs and criminals."[65] By 1981 Farrakhan had made important strides, and six thousand believers attended the reborn Nation of Islam's first

Saviour's Day convention. A few years later, the membership had climbed to an estimated ten thousand men and women. In 1983 African-American leaders acknowledged Farrakhan's growing influence and invited him to speak at ceremonies marking the twentieth anniversary of the civil rights movement's March on Washington. Picking up speed on the path to legitimacy, Farrakhan bought Elijah Muhammad's homes in Phoenix and Chicago and the Nation's original mosque and school. He also invited the messenger's six mistresses and their children to join the once lost, now found movement and take their proper places as leaders.[66]

The Nation was the means, not the end of Louis Farrakhan's quest for authority. In 1984 he broke from his sectarian world and reached for influence through Jesse Jackson's campaign for the Democratic Party's presidential nomination. Charismatic and articulate, Jackson was an attractive candidate. His civil rights movement credentials appealed to white moderates and liberals, while his advocacy on behalf of the African-American community fired black enthusiasm. Farrakhan, sensing the symbolic meaning and practical possibilities of Jackson's candidacy, reversed Elijah Muhammad's injunction forbidding members from voting and participating in politics. He vigorously endorsed Jackson: "If you listen to Jesse talk, he sounds like the Christ. If you listen to him talk, he sounds like the Mahdi."[67] He also gave speeches on Jackson's behalf and offered precinct organizers and a security detail to the campaign.[68]

In mobilizing his black constituency and meeting its needs, Jackson clashed with American Jews, key members of the Democratic Party coalition. Jews had long distrusted Jackson. He had first startled them in the early 1970s, singling out four of President Richard Nixon's closest advisers as Jewish and his chief aides John Erlichman and H. R Haldeman as "German Jews."[69] In 1979 he embraced Palestine Liberation Organization leader Yassir Arafat and called for a civil-disobedience campaign against Israeli authority in the occupied territories. After visiting the Holocaust memorial of *Yad Vashem* near Jerusalem, he had rubbed sensitivities raw with a remark about the Jewish "persecution complex."[70] Widely reported in the Jewish community was an alleged Jackson comment that he was "sick and tired of hearing constantly about the Holocaust."[71] More immediate was a story that broke during the campaign. On a trip to New York City,

Jackson in an unguarded moment used a derogatory term for Jews and complained, "All hymie wants to talk about is Israel; every time you go to hymietown, that's all they want to talk about."[72] His apology carried no weight with Jews, who felt vindicated in their outrage. Threats were made on his life. In a context of seething black anger, Jackson had only spoken truth to the powerful.[73]

Louis Farrakhan rushed to Jackson's defense. He pronounced judgment on the black reporter who made Jackson's remarks public: "At this point, no physical harm. . . . In sufficient time we will come to power, execute the law of God on all of you who fall under our jurisdiction. We're going to keep on going until we make it so that he cannot enter in among any black people." When his comments were aired, he denounced the "wicked machinations of the media . . . who have twisted my words out of context."[74] Then Farrakhan confronted American Jews—"They intend to kill our brother"— and declared their collective guilt in making the climate ripe for violence. He set the stakes: "Its not just Jews against Jesse. Its Jews against millions of black people who are lining up with Reverend Jackson. We are tired of feeding our leaders like raw meat to the open mouths of sharks."[75] He threatened: "If you harm this brother, I warn you in the name of Allah, this will be the last one you harm."[76] Nor did he forget Jewish economic sins, condemning "the tyranny of Jewish shopkeepers and landlords who swarmed the ghetto communities to prey upon our people in their wretched condition of helplessness like vultures."[77] Few voices in the black community challenged Farrakhan, and his prestige grew. In the midst of the controversy, he addressed the National Conference of Black Mayors and received a standing ovation. A survey of African-American delegates to the 1984 Democratic National Convention recorded that 47 percent approved of the Black Muslim minister. An aide to New York Congressman Charles Rangel read the community: "Now he's a bigger draw than Jackson. . . . If whites are that upset, it must be good for black people."[78]

Louis Farrakhan was the clear winner in this skirmish. In escalating the clash of interests, symbolic and real, he vented black anger and defied the community's traditional antagonist. "It was war," he later noted. "I was vicious in those days."[79] These tactics brought him escape from the fringe and ended his isolation as the leader of an eccentric Muslim faction hustling for members and influence. Farrakhan was now on the rise, a proven champion of the race whose words commanded respect. Even to close observers, the speed of his ascent was startling and gave evidence of an African-American hunger for vindication after years of apparent retreat. The attack of Jewish defense organizations merely corroborated black judgment and confirmed his position. The white majority took notice. National magazines did profiles, polls surveyed opinion about him, and he appeared on *Nightline* and before the National Press Club.[80]

He made no retreat. In 1985 Farrakhan ratcheted up the rhetoric in a fourteen-city speaking tour that attracted audiences of nineteen thousand in Atlanta, fifteen thousand in Chicago, and seventeen thousand in Los Angeles. The high point was his speech to twenty-five thousand men and women at New York City's Madison Square Garden. "The germ of murder," he declared, "is already sown in the hearts of Jews across the nation and across this world. . . . It is not I who have said it, the Scriptures has said, it is the time of war." Now, Farrakhan demanded, African Americans must force the "bloodsuckers" to remove their "stranglehold" on the U.S. government and "rid themselves of black leaders, these silly toms [who] run out to do their master's bidding." Farrakhan cautioned Jews: "I am your last chance. . . . The Scriptures charge your people with killing the prophets of God. . . . I come in the footsteps of those worthies and if you rise up to try and kill me, . . . all of you will be killed outright." The time of redemption was at hand and he called blacks to action: "Jewish control of black organizations has to be busted up and broken. The old Jewish relationship with black people has to be changed. We don't want to relate to Jews on a master-slave relationship [be]cause our time to be free black men and women has come."[81] Among the honored guests who attended stops on the tour were Thomas Metzger, a former Ku Klux Klansman and founder of the White Aryan Resistance, and Arthur Butz, who had achieved fame as a Holocaust revisionist.[82]

Having struck a chord, Farrakhan continued to exploit the Jewish conspiracy. For him, Jewish influence meant control, common interest proved collusion. He accepted the premises of the *Protocols of the Elders of Zion* and postulated that a small group of Jews meeting in New York City and Hollywood already dominated the world: "I would respectfully submit that in my judgment 85 percent . . . of the people of earth are victimized by a small clique who use their power and knowledge to manipulate the masses against the best interests of the people."[83] More specifically, weak sales of the Nation of Islam's cosmetic and toiletries product lines were proof of the plot to frustrate black enterprise and strengthen the Jewish grip on his community's purchasing power. Where once Jews controlled the ghetto, now "you are our managers, you are our agents. You run the institutions quietly behind the scenes. You pull the strings where education is concerned. You're the scriptwriters. You're the Hollywood promoters that promoted us as Little Black Sambo with the bug-eyes and Stepin' Fetchit. . . . But I ask you, who taught us to hate ourselves?"[84] He repeated allegations that Jewish doctors had infected African-American children with diseases and had conducted AIDS experiments on black subjects. When asked whether he understood why Jews were offended by his remarks, Farrakhan responded, "because the truth hurts."[85] Bible truth that closely paralleled the ideology of the Christian Identity movement would similarly set his people free: "This Caucasian who claims to be the Jew, Israel, had been masquerading as the chosen of God. He has been scattered all over the world, that is true, but he's not the real Israel. . . . The real Israel, according to the Bible, that has been scattered to the ends of the Earth is the black man and woman of America and the world."[86]

Farrakhan also touted the Nation of Islam's *The Secret Relationship Between Blacks and Jews,* a heavily footnoted three hundred–page study that exposed Jews as the masterminds of black slavery. According to the book, Jewish rabbis committed the original sin, having fabricated the "Hamitic myth," which identified blacks as the descendants of Ham cursed forever to be servants of the white devils. This biblical imperative gave Jews free rein, and in their hunger for gold they became the "key operatives" and earned "monumental culpability" for the black holocaust. In fact, Jewish crimes stained the pages not only of black but of American history. Among other crimes, the authors charge that Jews had raped and exploited black women "with abandon," furnished smallpox-infested blankets to Native Americans, "openly defied" the American Revolution, helped put down Nat Turner's revolt, dominated the "white slave trade," and sabotaged the family farm.[87] Black Muslims further alleged that Jewish influence kept the book off the shelves of mainstream bookstores and out of high school and university classrooms. Readers could still obtain copies from Nation of Islam outlets, which peddled *The Protocols* as well.[88]

If Jews were the prime movers, they were not alone in engineering the conspiracy. Looking to the past, Farrakhan found abundant evidence that federal officials had plotted genocide. There was, he insisted, a concerted and carefully planned campaign to eliminate resistance by preventing the rise of a "Black Messiah." Among its victims had been Denmark Vesey, Marcus Garvey, Paul Robeson, Malcolm X, Adam Clayton Powell, Jr., Martin Luther King, Jr., Huey Newton, and Angela Davis. African-American leaders who had not been executed, imprisoned, or discredited had been co-opted into betraying their race. Farrakhan was convinced that he was the next target and that federal agents had already set "the stage for my incarceration or assassination."[89] With white America entering its last days and soon to face divine retribution, the federal government was moving toward a final solution of the black problem. "So I am saying," insisted Farrakhan, "we are dying. Blacks are dying in America at an inordinate rate. Is there a plan? We believe there is."[90] The plot was devious and merciless. Birth control, abortion, sterilization, and a high black infant mortality rate would carry out the "death plan at birth."[91] Those who survived faced planted traps. Pornography, liquor, and drugs were calculated to lower black defenses. "If you watch the crack epidemic, it did not start till after Louis Farrakhan became the voice of the poor."[92] "They're using chemical warfare," he warned, "biological warfare, germ warfare already on black people. AIDS is not an accident any more than smallpox was an accident with the Indians. Sending them blankets and killing them with disease. . . . You need to wake up and see that your life is threatened."[93] He also detected a secret hand behind ghetto violence: "The Uzis, the AK-47s, your enemy is feeding you automatic weapons now. You don't make any weapons, Brother. Where did you get the weapons? . . . This is all calculated. This is all part of the conspiracy."[94] Media silence about the "death march" was similarly planned by those who ran America.[95] "Nobody talks about black suffering. We don't own CNN, ABC, NBC, CBS, Fox Broad-casting."[96]

How does Farrakhan use the past to lend credence to the war against black America? Repeatedly, he cuts historical moorings and conjures up slavery, lynchings, and Jim Crow laws as proof of the machinations of a secret cabal. Conspiracy gives purpose to gener-ations of persecution and exploitation, a plausible explanation to those far from the practice of power. Farrakhan also summons more recent and convincing evidence of federal intrigue to expose the hidden pattern. Between 1932 and 1972 the U.S. Public Health Ser-vice conducted a study in Tuskegee, Alabama, in which black men were told they had "bad blood" and were used as guinea pigs in syphilis research. The test subjects received hot meals, free medical care, and burial stipends but were denied the benefits of advances in treatment. Invoking the Tuskegee experiment, Farrakhan then makes history repeat, accusing federal authorities of continuing to exploit the black population for medical research. Thus he alleged that polio inoculation programs for black children in the 1960s were covers for spreading cancer. A "polio contaminant . . . gave those little babies cancer. Now twenty-five years later cancer is run-ning throughout the black community. You see the experiments that have been done on our people with syphilis and all other kind of diseases and drugs. . . . Your holocaust is going on hourly, daily, nightly."[97] Continually placing news items in a Tuskegee context, *The Final Call* has featured articles about medical experiments on black prison inmates and editorials demanding to know whether the U.S. Army "massacred" black soldiers during World War II.[98] A columnist warned that although the federal birth control program "is not as well known as the Tuskegee Experiment, it involves the same kind of falsehoods and manipulations." Obviously, recent vac-cination programs against childhood disease aroused suspicion. Na-tion of Islam minister Abdul Alim Muhammad, M.D., cautioned in his *Final Call* medical advice column that African Americans have for a long time been "victims, in many ways, of deceitful and wicked plots. . . . How can any rational person conclude that we are acting irrationally when such historical evidence can be cited?"[99]

Farrakhan offers the FBI's Counter Intelligence Program (COINTEL-PRO) of the 1960s as more proof of the conspiracy. As we have seen, the covert operation targeted black activists and groups, using wire-taps, agents provocateurs, and disinformation in an attempt to discredit, disrupt, and neutralize protest. Elijah Muhammad and Malcolm X were under surveillance, as were Martin Luther King, Jr., Fannie Lou Hammer, and Stokely Carmichael, among many others. In 1968 the FBI counted more than thirty-two hundred paid informants in black communities across the United States. Local authorities supplemented that secret army with legions of their own spies. Close encounters with these hidden operatives and the more visible police forces fostered the suspicion and sense of siege that were conducive to conspiracy thinking. Like Tuskegee, COINTELPRO is a historical marker for African Americans, heavily laden with cultural and emotional significance. Neither is perceived as an aberration or a mistake; they take meaning as flash symbols of black America's chronic pain. When moored to such powerful markers, Louis Farrakhan's conspiracy message develops credibility and legitimacy. Speaking in the third person, he has observed, "What Farrakhan is doing, is touching where it hurts."[100]

Louis Farrakhan's style enhances the intensity of his conspiracy thinking. He conveys an image of fearlessness, a man willing to tell the truth and close with the enemy regardless of the consequences. He knows his audience well and declares in the third person: "Now you see Farrakhan, you say, boy he got courage. Look at him. . . . He don't back down from what he says. He stands."[101] His delivery is passionate, urgent, and sincere, gripping his audience for speeches that may last for two hours and more. Beginning with a religious text, whether the Bible or the Qur'an, he works the message to fit the daily lives of black Americans. Alternately comforting and accusatory, his soft-spoken delivery becomes the charged discourse of the jeremiad, with its catechism of sins and demands for repentance. In his rebuke of black men and women, however, the focus quickly shifts to the hidden corrupters. Farrakhan's conspiracism is never the core of his discourse, and he presents it in brief paragraphs or even a few sentences. His case lacks details, development, and careful sequencing. Careless with nouns and pronouns, he is often unclear about who the actual culprits are and what crimes were committed. Once Farrakhan has sketched the plotters and their plans, he hurries to other topics, only to return again and again and in a similarly abbreviated manner to those who operate in the dark. Astutely, he realizes that little more is necessary. The power is in the word, not the explanation. Once voiced, the charge fixes attention, releases rage, and anchors support. Knowledge empowers the victims, their eyes now open and hearts pure before the devious foe. Attacked, Farrakhan never gives ground. He probes, instead, for new weaknesses, stinging his antagonists with verbal taunts sure to provoke another cycle of recrimination. Cleverly, he denies prejudice and turns the energy and accusations of critics to his defense. "We're not the racists," declares Farrakhan. "We come to end racism once and for all. . . . So, why put it on me?"[102] Countersubversion in Farrakhan's hands is thus a renewed commitment to self and community through a leadership that is racially authentic and difficult to outflank by competitors.[103]

The Nation of Islam's message of self-improvement and community affirmation built tolerance for conspiracism and furthered Farrakhan's quest for leadership. Counting twenty thousand members and several hundred thousand supporters in the early 1990s, the Nation won praise for its program of self-determination, black pride, and bootstrap capitalism. Muslims put words into action, operating a soap and cosmetic distribution company, a chain of retail establishments, and a federally funded security company that patrolled housing projects in low-income areas against drug dealing and violence. Farrakhan also organized a national antidrug campaign and a "Stop the Killing" speaking tour, which enhanced his and the Nation's reputation. The city councils of the District of Columbia and Philadelphia passed resolutions acclaiming his work, and he received keys to the city from the mayors of Tacoma, Washington; Compton, California; Prairie View, Texas; and Tuskegee, Alabama. Farrakhan critic Benjamin Hooks of the NAACP conceded his capture of the issues: "When Farrakhan talks about black solidarity and economic independence, you can't dispute that. I would look like a fool."[104] Also bringing legitimacy was a meeting with Nelson Mandela and trips to Ghana, Libya, and China, where Farrakhan met with heads of state. An opinion survey of African Americans in 1994 found that 62 percent considered him "good for the black community," 63 percent believed that "he speaks the truth," and 67 percent that he made "an effective leader."[105]

After years of distance and caution, the black establishment acknowledged Farrakhan's influence and accepted his leadership credentials. The Reverend Cecil Murray of the First African Methodist Episcopal Church and Baptist Minister Hycel Taylor spoke at Black Muslim gatherings, as did Reverend Benjamin Chavis, executive director of the NAACP. Educators Derrick Bell, C. Eric Lincoln, and Cornell West wrote endorsements for Farrakhan's book *A Torchlight for America*. Farrakhan received invitations to address the Blacks in Government convention and the African-American Leadership Summit meeting. In 1993 the Congressional Black Caucus established a "sacred covenant" with the Nation of Islam "to work for real and meaningful change," though the alliance was soon terminated when new charges of anti-Semitism surfaced.[106] White America also recognized Farrakhan and gave him numerous platforms in the print and television media. He appeared on *Meet the Press, Donahue, Larry King Live, ABC Prime Time, CBS This Morning, 20/20*, and *C-SPAN*. *Time, Newsweek*, the *Los Angeles Times*, the *Washington Post*, and the *Washington Times* interviewed and featured him. In 1994 more than 40 percent of all major network news stories about African-American leaders and organizations profiled Farrakhan. The mainstream media remained focused on the sensational. Research engines combing newspapers still found that more than one-half of the stories concerning Farrakhan reiterated his charges of a Jewish conspiracy against black America.[107]

Farrakhan reached higher. In 1995 he issued a national call for a Million Man March on Washington, D.C. Black men, he declared, had to take control of their lives to save not only themselves but their communities. With homicide the leading cause of death for black males between fifteen and thirty-four years of age, with one in three of these men in prison or on parole, and with nearly one-half of black teenagers functionally illiterate, Farrakhan spoke to real concerns. His authority proven, few questioned his prerogative. Civil rights activist Rosa Parks, the Reverend Jesse Jackson, and the Reverend Joseph Lowery of the Southern Christian Leadership Conference, among many others, joined him and endorsed the event. Catching the imagination, the movement became a crusade, and hundreds of thousands of African Americans—more than a million, according to the organizers' estimates—responded and participated in a day of atonement, reconciliation, and responsibility. Eyes were on not only the past but the future, and the men collectively pledged to lead moral lives, respect their families, end the violence, and support black businesses. The march secured Louis Farrakhan's leadership rank and firmly anchored him in the mainstream. Only Jesse Jackson commanded more support. Just months after the march, Farrakhan continued his image building, leaving on a twenty-three nation "World Friendship Tour."[108]

Meanwhile, Farrakhan drew inspiration from white countersubversives. He read and recommended to members of the Nation of Islam the John Birch Society standard *None Dare Call It Conspiracy* by Gary Allen. Not surprisingly, he singled out the Rothschilds and other Jewish members of the New World Order conspiracy for special emphasis: "They worked and maneuvered until they gained control of the central banks of England, France, Austria, Italy and Germany. . . . They would loan money to both sides in the conflict cause they really didn't care who won or lost." American banks came under Rothschild control in 1913, when at the family's prompting Congress passed the Federal Reserve Act. Looking closely, Farrakhan grew more suspicious, for the Internal Revenue Service, the Federal Bureau of Investigation, and the Anti-Defamation League of B'nai B'rith (ADL) were also established that year. He asked, "Is that a coincidence? Or is there a tie in?" He followed the countersubversive script from there, noting that "the same group of people" developed capitalism and communism, and that Marx, Lenin, and Trotsky were "financed by wicked bankers, many of whom were Jews."[109] He even implicated Jews in the rise of Adolf Hitler and the final solution: "Poor Jews died while big Jews were at the root of what they call the holocaust. . . . Little Jews being turned into soap while big Jews washed themselves with it."[110] In follow-up, readers of *The Final Call* could order *The Ugly Truth About the ADL* and learn that B'nai B'rith was "a pivotal player" in the assassination of Abraham Lincoln and that the ADL was involved in the spread of "secular humanism" and "New Age religion" and shared office space with the Trilateral Commission.[111] Available as well were such countersubversive offerings as *Behold a Pale Horse, The Unseen Hand, The New World Order,* and Texe Marrs's *Circle of Intrigue.*[112]

Farrakhan's comments about the Jewish Holocaust helped reignite the controversy between blacks and Jews. Adding fuel were new signs of Jewish influence in the federal government. The Justice Department established an office to hunt down and expel Nazi war criminals who had entered the United States illegally. Later Congress mandated the building on federal land of the Holocaust Museum in Washington, D.C. A memorial to European Jews in the most African-American city in the United States aroused Farrakhan supporters, who diminished Jewish pain and demanded official recognition of black suffering. Confrontation became acrimonious and quickly degenerated into Holocaust denial. Farrakhan surrogate Khalid Abdul Muhammad went on the offensive in a 1993 address at Kean College: "Everybody always talks about Hitler exterminating six million Jews. But don't nobody ever ask, what did they do to them folks? They went in there, in Germany, the way they do everywhere they go, and they supplanted, they usurped. . . . They had undermined the fabric of society."[113] At Howard University the following year, Khalid Muhammad again expressed black rage: "You talk about the death marches. What about the death marches in Africa? . . . You say you lost six million. We question that. But for the sake of argument, we'll give you that. We lost 600 million. . . . Not one dollar has been put aside for our holocaust, which is still taking place."[114] Maintaining the pressure, Khalid Muhammad's aide Eric Muhammad publishes *The Holocaust Journal,* which offers readings from the anti-Semitic tract *The Turner Diaries* and commentary from Holocaust denier Arthur Butz, author of *The Hoax of the Twentieth Century.* Internet users can access the Nation of Islam's "Blacks and Jews News" website and follow a link to Butz's revisionist Institute of Historical Review. In natural progression, the Nation of Islam wrought the conversion of Jews from victims to predators. Khalid Muhammad discovered that "Jew doctors" ran the Tuskegee experiment.[115] *Final Call* columnist Ali Baghdadi reported that Israel was engaged in that now seemingly routine Jewish practice of germ warfare: "The Israelis are using the AIDS virus [against Palestinians]. The method of delivery is not through sex, which is currently being used to spread the disease amongst the Egyptians by the Mossad, Israeli intelligence, disguised as tourists. The Israelis are using the needle. . . . The slow and painful murder of Palestinian kids is being carried out in Israeli hospitals."[116]

The coming end of the millennium also captured Louis Farrakhan's attention and put him in an apocalyptic mood. Time was running out on the white devils, and the "divine destruction of America" would soon begin. Referring to the Book of Revelation, Farrakhan prophesied judgments of rain, hail, snow, and earthquake, with America the object of God's wrath: "No city or people answer the description of a mystery Babylon better than the cities and people of America."[117] As America's close encounter with the mother plane approached, members of the Nation of Islam gave credence to those who watched the skies for UFOs. After one such report, *The Final Call* interpreted: "The size and shape of the crafts ... leave no doubt that the so-called UFOs ... sighted were the Mother Plane and two of the 'baby planes' which the Honorable Elijah Muhammad taught about."[118] Black Muslims needed little convincing, and Louis Farrakhan himself could bear witness to an encounter. In 1985, he said, he had been beamed aboard the mother plane and had conversed with Elijah Muhammad, who authorized him to lead the people into the latter days. For more information, Muslim leaders recommended Timothy Good's book, *Above Top Secret: The World-Wide U.F.O. Cover-Up,* and the motion picture *Independence Day. Final Call* film critic James Muhammad observed that the movie's spacecraft "resembled" the mother plane and its attack ships. Hollywood produced the film, he conjectured, as a public service "to make us so familiar with them that we won't get hysterical when we see them."[119]

Rather than weaken his influence, such claims enhanced it. In fact, Louis Farrakhan's conspiracism helped put him in the mainstream of a community rife with suspicion. Centuries of white domination and oppression had scarred blacks with the reality of their powerlessness. First as slaves and then as citizens, they had been convinced by encounters with often malevolent authorities that economic and political rights, and even their lives, were beyond their control. Decisions came from above, made by groups unseen for reasons arbitrary, devious, or unexplained. From the pulpit, on the radio, in the newspaper, or on the street, rumors of danger circulated that demanded solidarity and raised a collective defense. Twentieth-century changes in the racial status quo were too recent and fragmentary for African Americans to abandon their survival skills. Farrakhan was hardly a solitary voice, but instead joined a chorus of black countersubversives.

Blacks united against a host of conspirators. Looking back to the 1960s and before, African Americans believed that the federal government had systematically persecuted their leaders. Conspiracy, insisted almost 70 percent of blacks, had killed Martin Luther King, Jr. His widow, Coretta King, and Ambassador Andrew Young accepted that verdict and were certain that the alleged assassin was a patsy covering up for official perpetrators. Malcolm X was another FBI target, and many outside Nation of Islam circles demanded a probe of COINTELPRO to ascertain official complicity in his assassination. The editor of the *Chicago Defender* supported such an investigation, "especially in light of recent suspicion of FBI impropriety at Waco."[120] California Congressman Mervyn Dymally said, "The fact that we are paranoid about the FBI doesn't make us wrong."[121] Was the federal government still targeting black leaders? Did investigators single out Washington, D.C., Mayor Marion Barry and Secretary of Agriculture Mike Espy because they were black? Was Secretary of Commerce Ron Brown murdered? Even the establishment NAACP and the Congressional Black Caucus raised concerns about the official explanation of Brown's death, and Jesse Jackson called for an inquiry "to quiet people's doubts."[122] Sensing the pattern, the attorney defending Jamil Abdullah Al-Amin (formerly H. Rap Brown) declared, "He will not be the first or the last black man framed by the system."[123] O. J. Simpson concurred, laying his victimization to a Jewish plot: "I've heard 'em on those talk shows actually say it— 'A Jewish life has to be avenged.' "[124]

Accompanying the offensive against black leaders was a ruthless campaign of mass extermination. Newspaper reports that the CIA had conspired to flood the ghetto with crack cocaine, though later retracted, raised a firestorm of black protest. When a CIA report denied charges of drug trafficking, U.S. Representative Maxine Waters of California rejected it as "lack[ing] credibility" and said that "its conclusions should be dismissed."[125] Jesse Jackson found the accusations of CIA wrongdoing "painful but believable."[126] The rank and file backed up these claims. More than 60 percent of African Americans saw the government's hand in the drug epidemic as part of a conspiracy to kill or make blacks docile. AIDS was another means of execution. Film producer and director Spike Lee declared, "All of a sudden a disease appears out of nowhere that nobody has a cure for and it's specifically targeted at gays and minorities. The mystery disease, yeah, about as mysterious as genocide. I'm convinced AIDS is a government-engineered disease."[127] New York City physician Barbara Justice echoed Lee: "All of a sudden here comes this raging virus that seems to have a propensity for Black people. If you stand back and look at it and you also look at the history of this country, at the very least you have to be suspicious."[128] These beliefs were widely shared; nearly one in three African Americans told pollsters that AIDS "was deliberately created in a laboratory in order to infect black people."[129] Filmmaker John Singleton addressed other community concerns and infused them with new energy. Action in his *Boyz N' the Hood* takes place in the South Central Los Angeles ghetto, where numerous liquor stores and gun shops betray the system's plot—"They want us to kill ourselves." The Reverend Cecil Williams of San Francisco's Glide United Methodist Church surveyed the coordinated assault and decried the AIDS epidemic, crack cocaine, and easy access to weapons as "genocide, 1990s style. We can't put our finger on any one person or group, but many of us are convinced that . . . there is a conspiracy to anesthetize and ultimately do away with as many blacks in American society as possible."[130] In line with the conventional wisdom, Barbara Bell, the founder of Massachusetts Blacks for Life, made Jews the agents and abortion the means of genocide: "It is the Jewish doctors that are the ones trying to wipe out black society."[131] Such accusations had impact, for anti-Semitic feelings were running high—37 percent of blacks in 1992 scored among the most prejudiced, with young and educated African Americans ranking highest.[132]

Shared conspiracism boosted Louis Farrakhan and muted his opponents. In similar fashion, Spike Lee shaped the screen images of Farrakhan and the Nation and facilitated their acceptance by both black and white audiences. In his film *Mo' Better Blues* (1990), Lee casts actor Denzel Washington as a talented but struggling jazz musician at the mercy of fast-talking Moe and Josh Flatbush, Jewish club owners with no interest in anything but the bottom line. Ratifying Farrakhan's charge of Jewish exploitation of black artists, the Jews grow rich on the jazz man's talent but won't yield to his reasonable requests for a pay raise or profit sharing. The threat of legal action holds the musician in their service, and his black manager, portrayed by the director, is ineffectual on his behalf. Perhaps, the two Jews suggest, a Jewish manager could help? The next year Lee made *Malcolm X*. Closely following Malcolm X's *Autobiography,* he created a sympathetic portrait with Denzel Washington in the title role. The film praises the Nation of Islam's program of racial solidarity and self-determination, and the logic of conversion is quite obvious: Muslims offer solutions to drug and alcohol addiction, crime, and prostitution. At the same time, the doctrine of Mr. Yacub's work in genetic engineering is well sanitized, and the audience is given little reason to squirm. As Malcolm, Denzel Washington calls black men and women to self-knowledge: "You have been duped," he contends, and he exposes the Jewish exploiters and the white plot "to pacify us." The conspiracy takes shape in the hands of federal agents, who bug his room and foment trouble in the Nation. As the time of his assassination approaches and Muslim turns against Muslim, Malcolm is certain that "they are not working alone" but are pawns of white intrigue. Louis Farrakhan is noticeable by his absence from the picture.

Nor does Farrakhan make an appearance in Lee's *Get on the Bus* (1996), yet he is the driving force of the film. In response to Farrakhan's call for the Million Man March, a group of California black men boards a bus "bound for glory" and the nation's capital. As the credits roll, Michael Jackson performs the song "Put Your Hurt on the Line" to images of black men in slavery's chains and police handcuffs. The men who choose to "ride into history" reflect the age, class, religious, color, and sexual heterogeneity of black America. With a Black Muslim among them bearing witness, the men find their common humanity and forge a new sense of solidarity that suggests the promise of change. Only a self-hating black Republican who "disses" black colleges, affirmative action, Jesse Jackson, and Louis Farrakhan is denied brotherhood. Repeatedly, Lee editorializes about the relationship between blacks and Jews, with his characters ritualistically rehashing the debate over victimization. The denouement comes when the Jewish bus driver departs, his lack of understanding and racial bigotry exposed. In comparison, rednecks are open to the travelers and relieved when told that Farrakhan does not condemn whites as devils but is simply "pro black." Spike Lee judges Farrakhan in absentia and bluntly delivers the verdict to viewers: "He was the only black leader who had the balls to call for this march. . . . Louis Farrakhan is the only free black man in America. And you know why? Because his only allegiance is to his God Allah and his people."

Hip-hop and rap music artists relayed the word to younger generations. Working with Prince Akeem, his national minister to youth, Louis Farrakhan developed a rapport with musicians Sister Souljah, K-Solo, Defiant Giants, Brand Nubians, KAM, Ice-T, and Chuck D. Mach-10, Snoop Doggy Dogg, and WC have appeared at Nation rallies. In the liner notes to *It Takes a Nation of Millions to Hold Us Back* (1988), Public Enemy acknowledged Louis Farrakhan and Khalid Muhammad for their inspiration. Poor Righteous Teachers, in the cut "I'm Comin' Again" on their *Pure Poverty* album, (1991), gave voice to Black Muslim theology:

> These devils lying to blacks
> so through the teachers' truth will come
> The black man's God, what's grafted is devil
> And Jesus not Christian
> . . . .
> You lack you lose you lose you lost the knowledge of yourself
> And if you don't know who you are, you won't know no-one else
> I'm comin' again, Wise G's comin'—again-again-and-again[133]

The liner notes to Ice Cube's *Death Certificate* (1991) decried the "LIMITED KNOWLEDGE OF SELF" that created "A NIGGA MENTALITY. THE BEST PLACE FOR A YOUNG BLACK MALE OR FEMALE IS THE NATION OF ISLAM. SOON AS WE USE OUR KNOWLEDGE OF SELF TO ADVANTAGE WE WILL THEN BE ABLE TO BECOME AND BE CALLED BLACKS." More lyrical was "When I Get to Heaven" on the *Lethal Injection* album (1993):

> Cuz God is comin' on day number seven
> N' they won't call me a nigga when I get to heaven
> . . . .
> But Elijah's got a plan
> Got the white man screamin': "Damn that Farrakhan!"
> Cuz one day these babies are uprise

Much worse than bowties n' bean pies
Kickin' knowledge at the 7-11
N' they won't call me a nigga when I get to Heaven.[134]

With his influence at high tide, Farrakhan pressed for greater advantage. He appeared on *Meet the Press* in 1997 and adamantly refused to apologize for offending Jews: "If I can defend every word that I speak, and every word that I speak is truth, then I have nothing to apologize for." He then went on the offensive, claiming that Jews have controlled every president since Franklin Roosevelt and that the NAACP and the Urban League were in the Jews' grip. He returned to *Meet the Press* the following year and discerned a suspicious pattern in current events: "I look at Lucianne Goldberg, Linda Tripp, and Monica Lewinsky, and I ask myself, 'Why was this introduced at this time when [Israeli Prime Minister Benjamin] Netanyahu was being pressured by the president to give up more land on the West Bank?' . . . I think we need to look deeper into this than just what appears on the surface." Distance from the more traditional activists of the civil rights movement was still useful. When Julian Bond of the NAACP accused him of anti-Semitism, Farrakhan was contemptuous: "That's a slave talking. Who was he talking to? He was talking to his masters."[135]

Farrakhan's notoriety helped the Nation of Islam thrive. Observers estimated membership at between fifty thousand and one hundred thousand in the late 1990s. Among the recent converts was Benjamin Muhammad, formerly the NAACP leader Benjamin Chavis, who blamed Jews for his ouster as the organization's director. *The Final Call* continued the countdown for the mother plane, still beckoning members of the tribe of Shabazz to self-knowledge before judgment day. Meanwhile, the publication alerted blacks to the continuing plot. Reporter Johnnie 5X warned of the drug depo-provera, "the latest medical weapon in a population control campaign targeted for Black women." Zionists, *The Final Call* was convinced, had staged a coup d'état and seized control of U.S. foreign policy: "Mr. Clinton is being held hostage by people who have no loyalty to America. Israeli agents who occupy the White House are in the driver's seat." The Jews, meanwhile, were developing an "ethnobomb" that specifically targeted the DNA of Arabs and Muslims.[136] Interested readers could find *The Final Call* on sale at Borders Books in thirty-one cities across the United States. Supplementing the published word, websites and links kept users current on news in the Nation and on Jewish schemes.[137]

In 1999 Louis Farrakhan was rushed to the hospital after suffering complications from a radioactive seed implant prescribed to combat his prostate cancer. Surgery removed him from harm's way and occasioned an outpouring of interfaith support. One hundred African-American ministers in Chicago organized a nondenominational prayer service in his honor. Christian clergy in seven other cities followed suit. Explained the Associated Press, "The Muslim minister is beloved by many in the black community as an uncompromising voice in the fight for black empowerment."[138] Nation leaders proclaimed his recovery a miracle but denounced the "wicked plan" to stir discontent among Black Muslims during the crisis. Tynnetta Muhammad continued: "The Hatred of some of the Jews and their Sponsors from within the United States Government and elsewhere in High Places is revealing their own sinister plot to kill the Beloved Messenger and Servant of Allah."[139]

While recuperating, Louis Farrakhan moved to secure his position in the black community. He reconciled with Elijah Muhammad's son Imam W. Deen Mohammed and the two hundred thousand members of the recently renamed Muslim American Society. He acknowledged to Malcolm X's daughter Attallah Shabazz: "I may have been complicit in words that I spoke . . . and regret that any word that I have said caused the loss of life of a human being."[140] A year after his surgery, the sixty-five-year-old Muslim leader was back in the vanguard. He proclaimed before eighteen thousand followers at Saviour's Day 2000 a plan to re-create the triumph of the Million Man March with a Million Family March in October for "atonement, reconciliation, responsibility, freedom and equality." In a bold stroke, he also announced a far-reaching National Agenda 2000–2008, which championed political empowerment; equal health, economic, and educational opportunities; welfare reform; an end to violence and the drug traffic; investment in developing Africa and Latin America; and the protection of human rights around the world. Farrakhan and the Nation had completed their climb. Once outsiders, they were now shaping the future of black America. Conspiracism had been essential to the ascent.[141]

At the end of the twentieth century, an internet rumor spread among African Americans that they would lose the vote when the Civil Rights Act expired in 2006. Chat rooms buzzed and talk radio hosts were deluged with calls from anxious listeners. Concern was such that members of the Congressional Black Caucus held a news conference to denounce the rumor and defuse baseless fears. In the wake of the incident, House member James Clyburn of South Carolina sadly observed, "I think this tells us how precarious African-Americans feel in their status in this society."[142] A history of racial oppression shadows America, and centuries of public and private incidents of humiliation still cause pain. Change in contemporary America's racial dynamic may be tangible, but it is also halting and uneven. In a recent piece entitled "The Good News About Black America," a *Newsweek* reporter concluded with a sobering insight: "We look with equanimity, even pride, upon a statistical profile of black Americans that, were it of whites, would be a source of horror and consternation."[143] Conspiracism thrives when power is exercised at a distance by seemingly selfish groups zealous in their authority. When the present continues to reveal the past, all are susceptible to the prompting of conspiracy thinking, with class and gender lines offering no barriers.

Louis Farrakhan's authority emerges from this context. His conspiracy theories cannot be dismissed simply as examples of the paranoid style, symbols of pathology that have no basis in reality. Farrakhan's rhetoric of countersubversion is a call to battle that identifies friends and targets foes while marking off the distance from rival leaders and groups. Conspiracism demands confrontation and breeds activism and social-movement mobilization. Essential to its reception is a grounding in past markers and the ability to represent current experiences and voice collective fears. When Louis Farrakhan becomes a lightning rod for countercharges by traditional antagonists, he builds a reputation and assumes the role of defender of the race. Few rivals can challenge his earnestness or passion. Good works, in turn, enhance this aura and facilitate the acceptance of his conspiracy ideas. Power flows to such an individual and cements his hold on leadership.

CHAPTER 6

The Roswell Incident

> I saw a lot of wreckage but no complete machine. . . .
> The wreckage was scattered over an area of about three-
> quarters of a mile long and several hundred feet wide.
> —MAJ. JESSE MARCEL

> No rational person can claim there is no government
> cover-up. . . . Yes, Virginia, there is a Cosmic Watergate.
> —STANTON FRIEDMAN

In July 1997, tens of thousands of Americans made pilgrimage into the New Mexican outback to Roswell, the most sacred shrine of the UFO phenomenon. There they commemorated the incident of fifty years before, when, they believed, an alien craft had crash-landed and confirmed the existence of extraterrestrial life. In spite of one hundred–degree–plus temperatures, the pilgrims were in a festive mood, and Roswell entrepreneurs served up a cornucopia of treats. An "Aliens Welcome" sign decorated the Arby's fast-food restaurant, while Bud's Bar described itself as the "Unofficial UFO crash recovery site" and Church's Fried Chicken promised "Best Alien Chicken in Town." Owners of the crash site offered fifteen-dollar guided tours, and dirt bags from the debris field could be purchased for an additional $3.95. A stroll through town brought close encounters with vendors of assorted extraterrestrial knickknacks and shirts, one of which read, "I crashed on Earth and all I got was this crappy T-shirt." More serious believers viewed crash dioramas at the International U.F.O. Museum and Research Center and its rival the UFO Enigma Museum. Meshing naturally and adding to the ambience were the pleas of street-corner evangelists who insisted that the aliens were "demonic beings" and UFO sightings fresh evidence of the approach of Judgment Day. An air of defiance was also palpable. On the eve of the celebration, the U.S. Air Force had launched a preemptive public relations strike to debunk the incident and deflate ballooning interest. This only heightened suspicion of government intentions and made believers more adamant in defense of their scenarios. At center stage of the Roswell encounter was a press conference scheduled for Independence Day, attended by reporters from twelve countries representing 220 news organizations and videotaped by crews from the ABC, CBS, CNN, NBC, and FOX networks. On screen was a slide of a metal chip that purportedly came from the spaceship. After careful analysis, Dr. Vernon Clark had concluded that the fragment was "both manufactured and extraterrestrial in origin."[1] Filmmaker Paul Davids, Clark's colleague, said, "This is as rare as the shroud of Turin." Although no chain of evidence linked the metal to the crashed saucer, Davids declared the Roswell "case closed" and the mystery solved. The men left the conference hall soon after, refusing to take questions from the press.[2]

The commercialism and hype of the encounter masked Roswell's significance. For believers the Roswell incident is the holy grail, and many have joined the search, making it the most studied event in UFO history. The mystery begs solution, and a quest for truth and fame compels researchers, who have flushed out hundreds of witnesses testifying to things extraterrestrial. Enhancing the drama of this interpretation is the theme of conspiracy. As a researcher noted, Roswell has produced "a virtual mini-industry . . . paralleling in almost every respect that spawned by the Kennedy assassination."[3] Believers contend that a secret group within the federal government is engaged in plot weaving, covering up the evidence of extraterrestrial contact, and conspiring to discredit them and deceive the public. Roswell was, moreover, only the first instance of deception, setting the pattern for official denials about UFO sightings, abductions, cattle mutilations, crop circles, and even hidden alien bases. No famous men or women drive this challenge to government authority. It comes, instead, from the grass roots, raised by individuals with few resources and little reputation outside the UFO community. In mainstreaming their belief in a Roswell cover-up, the conspiracy-minded welcomed the embrace of the me-

In a weeklong series of strips, cartoonist Garry Trudeau offered his view of the 1997 celebration of the Roswell incident. Believers were mixed in their response, amused by Trudeau's deft sarcasm yet suspicious that he was part of the cover-up.

dia. They relied heavily, as well, on the behavior of the authorities to prove their case.

The modern UFO phenomenon began in 1947, when Americans from nearly every state reported sightings of what pilot Kenneth Arnold had described as "saucer-like" flying objects. Visual encounters peaked over the July 4 holiday, with thousands of women and men, many characterized as "reliable" witnesses, notifying authorities of a wave of more than 850 sightings. Newspapers were impressed with the similarities in observations; the objects were round or oval shaped, reflected light brilliantly, and traveled at high speeds. Skepticism and derision greeted these accounts but were quickly muted on July 8, when the intelligence office of the 509th Bombardment group stationed at Roswell Army Air Field announced that the unit had "come into possession of a flying saucer." According to news accounts, rancher Mac Brazel had found saucer debris on his land, and intelligence officer Maj. Jesse Marcel was dispatched to retrieve the wreckage. The "disk" had then been flown immediately to "higher headquarters" for analysis. The Roswell Daily Record offered collateral evidence, reporting that local resident Dan Wilmot had seen "a large glowing object" moving in a northwesterly direction "at a high rate of speed." Wilmot described it as soundless and oval in shape, "like two inverted saucers faced mouth to mouth. . . . The entire body glowed as though light were showing through from inside." The newspaper vouched for Wilmot's credibility: he was "one of the most respected and reliable citizens in town." Such news traveled fast, and telephone calls from around the world flooded Roswell switchboards demanding saucer information.[4]

The story died the next day. Air Force Gen. Roger Ramey announced that the flying saucer wreckage had been misidentified and was merely a "harmless, high-altitude weather balloon." As Ramey spoke, Marcel silently testified to the official account by posing with the debris for photographers. Perhaps embarrassed for him, none of the reporters followed up with the major about his apparent failure to distinguish between an ordinary weather balloon and something more exotic. Roswell reporters did interview Mac Brazel, who told them that he had initially discovered the debris on June 14 but found little unusual. The wreckage, spread over an area two hundred yards wide, consisted of strips of synthetic rubber, tinfoil, cellophane tape, paper, and sticks, measuring together "about as large as a table top" and collectively weighing approximately five pounds. When a neighbor suggested that the material might fetch a reward if it were flying saucer–related, Brazel had gathered pieces for a trip to Roswell on July 6. Curiously, reporters did not question the rancher about a statement he had made in the wake of the commotion. Having recovered air force balloons on his land before, he remarked: "I am sure what I found was not a weather observation balloon." The Roswell newspaper accounts are the only shards of physical evidence that exist to document these happenings.[5]

The Roswell incident was dead and almost forgotten, with only a handful of brief references to these events appearing in the thirty years after 1947. Harold Wilkins's *Flying Saucers on the Attack* (1954) made only brief mention of Roswell and was cited in Frank Edwards's book *Flying Saucers, Serious Business* (1966). Edwards ignored the air force explanation and elaborated on the extraterrestrial theme. He has Brazel telephoning Chaves County Sheriff George Wilcox to inform him that "a blazing disc-shaped object had passed over this house at low altitude and had crashed and burned on a hillside within view of the house." In *Identified Flying Saucers* (1968), Robert Loftin similarly maintains that a flying saucer "crashed and burned" near Roswell and derisively asks, "*Was a flying saucer crash in the United States explained away as the crash of a burning box kite with a non-inflammable pie pan tied to its tail?*"[6] Frank Scully's *Behind the Flying Saucers* (1950) took no notice of Roswell but did find that the "silencers" had covered up reports of a crashed spacecraft at Aztec, New Mexico, that left sixteen extraterrestrials dead in 1949.[7]

The manner of Roswell's rediscovery ensured its importance and credibility. In 1978, during a national lecture tour, nuclear physicist–turned–professional ufologist Stanton Friedman was given several leads that triangulated Roswell as an important site for investigation. In California he interviewed Lydia Sleppy, who worked as a teletype operator for KOAT radio in Albuquerque in the post–World War II years. Sleppy informed Friedman that in July 1947 she had received a call from Roswell reporter Johnny McBoyle about a flying saucer story to be sent nationally by teletype. She remembered McBoyle telling her, "I've been there and seen it." As he dictated and she typed his story on to the wire, the warning bell on her machine rang and a command preempted her: "DO NOT TRANSMIT THIS MESSAGE. STOP COMMUNICATING IMMEDIATELY." Vern and Jean Maltais disclosed to Friedman that civil engineer Barney Barnett, since deceased, had spoken of finding a crashed saucer on the Plains of San Agustin in New Mexico, about two hundred miles northwest of Roswell. Friedman's third contact was even more important. In Louisiana he found retired Air Force Col. Jesse Marcel, the Roswell Army Air Field intelligence officer who had played a prominent role in the 1947 incident. Marcel, after years of silence, was eager to talk. He recalled that the wreckage on Brazel's ranch was scattered over an area "three-quarters of a mile long and several hundred feet wide." The debris offered up no spaceship but did yield a collection of materials resembling "metal like tinfoil" and "balsa wood," and "parchment." Scanning the pieces, he noticed symbols "that we had to call hieroglyphics because I could not understand them." Efforts to cut, burn, dent, or tear the metal were fruitless. Declared Marcel: "I was pretty well acquainted with most everything that was in the air at that time, both ours and foreign. I was also acquainted with virtually every type of weather-observation or radar tracking device being used by either the civilians or the military. It was definitely not a weather or tracking device nor was it any sort of plane or missile. What it was, we didn't know." Ordered to remain silent, Marcel had stood by as General Ramey floated the cover story for the press. The news reporters "saw very little of the material—none of the important things that had hieroglyphics, or markings, on them. They didn't see that because it wasn't there."[8]

Stanton Friedman, long involved in UFO matters, was not easily impressed. Born in Elizabeth, New Jersey, in 1934, Friedman had taken an early interest in science. On graduating from high school, he pursued a physics major first at Rutgers University and then at the University of Chicago, from which he received his bachelor of science degree in 1955 and his master's the following year. His expertise made him quite marketable; General Electric, Westinghouse, and McDonnell Douglas, in turn, assigned him to work on nuclear and space system development programs. Flying saucers caught Friedman's attention in 1958, and he became an avid reader of books and reports about the phenomenon. He was soon convinced of its authenticity and after ten years of study began lecturing on the subject. In 1970, when funding ended for a project on which he was working, Friedman saw his opportunity and went on the lecture circuit full-time. Entering a field notorious for hoaxes and frauds, he proclaimed, "My goal is truth," and promised to apply the scientific method rigorously to his subject. He was well aware of the pitfalls and kept his eyes wide open: "In the UFO world, you can't take anything at face value."[9] In the matter of Roswell, however, his skepticism quickly faded. Its eyewitness accounts and corroborative testimony seemed convincing proof of extraterrestrial contact. Friedman had no doubt that he had uncovered one of the "biggest stories of the Millennium."[10]

Without publishing connections and research funds, Friedman was uncertain how to proceed. He found direction after a lecture in Minneapolis and a chance encounter with an old friend named William Moore. The son of a steelworker, Moore was born in 1943 and like many children of his generation developed an interest in space and even resolved to become an astronaut. He refined his focus as a teenager, reading books and attending lectures about flying saucers. Later he joined the National Investigations Committee on Aerial Phenomena (NICAP) and did on-site research of UFO sightings. Moore graduated from Pennsylvania's Thiel College in 1965 and took a job teaching English and French to high school students in upstate New York. Restless and unfulfilled, he moved his growing family first to Minnesota and then to Arizona. UFOs continued to be a priority in his life, and in Arizona he became a MUFON (Mutual UFO Network) state section director. In 1979 he left teaching to become a freelance writer and published the successful *Philadelphia Experiment: Project Invisibility* with Charles Berlitz, the author of *The Bermuda Triangle: An Incredible Saga of Unexplained Disappearances* (1974). *Philadelphia Experiment* recounts the military's alleged effort in 1943 to cloak the USS *Eldridge* from enemy radar by manipulating magnetic fields. The project went terribly awry and had to be covered up when the ship was transported in time and space, with some sailors rematerializing inside bulkheads.[11] Bill Moore represented an opportunity that Stan Friedman could hardly resist. With Moore's entrepreneurial talent and proven record of publishing success, Friedman could claim the fame and fortune for which he worked so hard.[12]

As the two men chewed on pizza, Friedman revealed the Roswell findings to his friend. Moore was impressed and fashioned a deal. He would take charge of the Roswell inquiry, joining Friedman in the research, financing the investigation, and securing a publishing contract. Naming Charles Berlitz as his coauthor and chief writer, he pitched the idea to representatives from G. P. Putnam's Sons, who offered a contract. No hard sell was necessary; all parties were aware of the tale's appeal. Moore was blasé and recalled, "The press bought the story, having no reason not to."[13]

The Roswell Incident appeared in 1980, supported by interviews with almost one hundred individuals, one-third of whom claimed firsthand knowledge of the crash. Piecing together the various accounts, the authors contended that on July 2, 1947, a lightning strike had shattered a UFO, leaving a debris field seventy-five miles northwest of Roswell. The spacecraft had managed to stay aloft, but crashed 125 miles farther west on the Plains of San Agustin. Ten witnesses testified that they had seen the UFO, and five remembered handling pieces of the wreckage. Barney Barnett, according to his friends, had come upon the crash site and seen aliens with large, round heads and small, oddly spaced eyes. An archaeological team from the University of Pennsylvania was also rumored to have been nearby. Appeals to patriotism and threats had secured their silence. Mac Brazel's son William claimed to have handled the unusual wreckage: "The odd thing about this foil was that you could wrinkle it and lay it back down and it immediately resumed its original shape." He kept some of the foil as a souvenir, but military authorities quickly confiscated it. William Brazel was certain that the military detained his father and "swore him to secrecy," and that he "took the most part of what he knew to the grave." The debris made a lasting impression on the young son of Jesse Marcel, who recalled the "foil-like stuff" and the "hieroglyphic-type characters." Other witnesses offered tantalizing clues. The wife of base commander Col. William Blanchard maintained that her husband "knew it was nothing made by us." Lt. Louis Bohanon insisted that no photographic record remained documenting the incident. Robert Porter had seen the armed-guard escort that accompanied the debris on its flight to "higher headquarters." Col. Thomas DuBose, General Ramey's aide, revealed that the weather balloon story was concocted to "put out the fire" and get the press "off [the general's] back in a hurry." Authors Moore and Berlitz anticipated skeptics who might wonder why remote Roswell was the site of a UFO encounter. "Inside sources" revealed to them that the ship was a "space probe" targeted on New Mexico's array of atomic research and defense installations. As the base of the only combat-trained atomic bomb group in the world, Roswell was a prime attraction. The television pseudodocumentary *In Search Of . . .* followed-up the best-seller, broadcasting the Roswell message in an episode on government cover-ups of UFO contact.[14]

This scenario held sway until the end of the 1980s, when others joined the research rush for gold in Roswell. The team of Don Schmitt and Kevin Randle posed the most serious challenge. Schmitt was the director of Special Investigations for the Center for UFO Studies and well connected in the community. Remembering the assassination of John Kennedy as a formative event in his life, Schmitt linked allegations of a Warren Report cover-up to official denials of extraterrestrial contact. Mockingly, he asked, "Can you trust the government?" Kevin Randle had graduated from the University of Iowa and served as a U.S. Air Force intelligence officer. Earning his living as a science fiction and adventure writer, he had published scores of books and articles with a focus on UFOs, alien abductions, and cattle mutilations. In 1988 the two men traveled to Roswell to "look into it first hand" and determine whether the story warranted another take.[15] The opportunity proved too great to pass up.[16]

In 1991 Randle and Schmitt published *UFO Crash at Roswell*. Though clearly indebted to their predecessors, they found an additional one hundred witnesses and offered another scenario of the incident. Quickening the pace of their narrative and enhancing its appeal was a more sinister twist to events. In context with their time, the authors detected the secret hands of federal authorities in orchestrating the recovery of the spacecraft and the subsequent cover-up. Randle and Schmitt emphasized accounts of military authorities browbeating witnesses, practicing disinformation, and destroying official records. How frightening was the government's campaign of intimidation? "Those threats have silenced people for more than forty years." Coercion in tandem with official denial, the authors were convinced, blanketed the incident in spite of its significance and the large number of men and women involved. Nor was the Roswell case unusual. Hadn't the Manhattan Project's work on the atomic bomb, the code-breaking efforts of Project Ultra, and recent stealth technology remained hidden until officially revealed? They asked pointedly and circularly: "If nothing extraordinary happened at Roswell, why the extraordinary efforts to keep it secret?"[17]

In their book, Randle and Schmitt held to the accepted timeline and downed the alien spaceship on July 2, 1947. According to their scenario, the cause of the mishap was mechanical failure and not a lightning strike. The damaged ship attempted to lift off but fell again, leaving a gouge five hundred feet long by ten feet wide through the assorted space junk. Eventually becoming airborne, the UFO remained in flight only briefly and crash-landed two and one-half miles away. The gouge was a new detail attributed to Maj. Jesse Marcel but actually added by Mac Brazel's son. Seeking consistency, the authors repositioned civil engineer Barney Barnett and the Pennsylvania archaeologists from the Plains of San Agustin to the new site. The authors persuaded more of the rancher's neighbors to break cover, and the witnesses offered signed affidavits attesting to having seen or touched space debris. There was also telling information about Mac Brazel's activities. The military was said to have kept him in isolation for eight days while officers coached his account and made him take an oath of secrecy. When a radio reporter questioned Brazel about inconsistencies in his stories, the rancher supposedly deflected him, pleading "It'll go hard on me." Off the record, however, Brazel revealed cryptically, "You know how they talk of little green men? . . . They weren't green." Suspiciously, Brazel was subsequently seen driving around Roswell in a new truck. Roswell mortician Glenn Dennis added a startling tale. He remembered an unusual series of telephone calls from the airfield asking about preservation techniques and small, hermetically sealed caskets. Hoping to be of help, he went to the base hospital only to be forcibly removed and followed back into town by military police. An air force nurse he was dating later revealed that the victims were not human but aliens, with large heads, concave noses and ears, and no visible sex organs.[18]

Military police, meanwhile, were alleged to have turned away deputy sheriffs from the cordoned-off debris field and crash site while lines of soldiers swept for alien items on their hands and knees. Airplane crew member Robert Smith told Randle and Schmitt that "security was extremely tight" when sealed boxes were loaded on as many as eight flights out of Roswell. Still, some witnesses claimed to have peeked into the containers and under tarpaulin and reported seeing dead aliens with large heads and hands with only four fingers. Changing the script, Schmitt and Randle demoted General Ramey from his commanding role in the affair and gave hands-on control to his superiors in Washington. In all, *UFO Crash at Roswell* sold 160,000 copies.[19]

Stanton Friedman, now in partnership with Don Berliner, an author of aviation and space books, rejoined the debate in 1992 with *Crash at Corona*. Friedman, too, had new witnesses, and they did more than confirm the strange properties of alien tinfoil, the whereabouts of Barney Barnett, and tales of government intrigue. Based on his witnesses' testimony, Friedman insisted that two flying saucers had crashed in the New Mexican desert. He revealed that military personnel recovered an alien spacecraft a few miles from the Brazel ranch debris field, four escape pods near the downed UFO, and another saucer down on the Plains of San Agustin. The crash toll was high, with six aliens dead and two more injured and taken into federal custody. Like his fellow researchers, Friedman condemned the powerful who controlled events. In operation, then and now, was a "brilliant covering-up by the entire American government, quite possibly with the cooperation of other governments, including the disgracefully clever trick of creating an atmosphere in which anyone showing more than a casual interest in UFOs was made to look like a fool."[20]

His was not the final word. Kevin Randle and Don Schmitt responded with their 1994 sequel *The Truth about the UFO Crash at Roswell*. To accommodate fresh testimony, the authors were forced to revise their original scenario. The alien craft now had fallen from the sky on July 4, not July 2. The debris field remained stationary, but the crash site moved to within thirty-five miles of Roswell. The archaeological team was still on site but hailed from Texas Tech, not the University of Pennsylvania. Regardless of their affiliation, military authorities intimidated the students into silence by threatening to cut off their funding from the G.I. Bill of Rights program.

Barney Barnett had vanished in the revision, his story no longer viable and dismissed as a hoax. Glenn Dennis added more details, but the authors could not locate his nurse friend, who had suspiciously "disappeared from the face of the earth." Although one eyewitness recalled seeing only a balloon, the authors confidently explained that this was part of the cover-up: "It would mean that the army had to bring one in. In other words, they were salting the area. . . . It would mean that the army had something to hide." Other sources updated flight information, noting that a C-54 cargo plane had taken alien bodies to Andrews Field outside Washington, D.C., to satisfy Gen. Dwight Eisenhower's curiosity. Apparently, President Harry Truman was busy or uninterested or did not have sufficient security clearance to peek. In spite of the fresh evidence, the authors were becoming increasingly frustrated with the federal government's cunningly foresighted and thorough cover-up: "Files were altered. So were personnel records, along with assignments and various codings and code words. Changing serial numbers ensured that those searching later would not be able to locate those who were involved in the recovery. The trail was being carefully altered." Randle and Schmitt clung more tightly than ever to an extraterrestrial explanation of the Roswell incident. Mundane answers featuring atomic bomb accidents, experimental aircraft, captured V-2 rockets, or weather balloons were unconvincing in light of missing official records and the accumulating testimony of hundreds of eyewitnesses.[21]

This, with several variations, is the case of the Roswell researchers. Clearly, something happened in the desert outside Roswell, New Mexico, in July 1947. The question is, what? Seeking the answer, competing research teams combed town and country for eye- and hearsay witnesses to the alleged crash and government recovery efforts. They met with much success. Investigators located more than a dozen men and women who claimed to have handled unusual crash debris. Another ten informants said that they had examined the crashed saucer. Six professed to have seen alien bodies. In all, more than three hundred people detailed their pieces of the puzzle—a flash in the sky, the debris field, military roadblocks, the shattered craft, duty at the debris field retrieving fragments of the saucer, the recovery of alien bodies and their examination at the hospital, ground transport of sealed crates and their temporary storage under armed guard in an empty airplane hanger, and flights of B-25s, B-29s, and C-54s with bodies and saucer parts to Fort Worth, Wright Air Field, Los Alamos, and Andrews Field. Military officers were said to have invoked national security to silence some witnesses. Others remembered death threats, which frightened them into silence or the surrender of extraterrestrial souvenirs. For those studying Roswell, such intimidation and the labor-intensive retrieval discounted all but the most extraordinary of explanations for the incident. In sum, researchers are convinced that an alien spacecraft crashed, extraterrestrial biological entities were retrieved, and the incident covered up by federal authorities. If correct, they have uncovered the story of the millennium.[22]

The Roswell tale stood apart from nearly all other accounts of extraterrestrial encounters. The incident does not rely on accounts of anonymous "friends" or leaks from mysterious second- and thirdhand "highly placed sources." Its believability springs from the number of ordinary, respectable men and women, with little to gain but ridicule, who have come forward to bear witness. The investigators' tight packaging of the testimony brought coherence and maximized corroboration and credibility. Amplifying the power of these recollections was the number of books and articles generated about Roswell, the very volume of which hinted at the significance of the event. Continually changing scenarios, meanwhile, suggested a fast-breaking story, with each revision a new episode in an unfolding saga of discovery. The Roswell researchers, while not trained as scholars, appeared earnest and legitimate. This was a reflection of their extensive fieldwork, their reputable occupational and educational backgrounds, and their affiliations with UFO think tanks. While still without a single fragment of alien metal foil, they made their treasure troves of witness recollections into convincing evidence of first contact. Nor has the failure to resolve disputes and create a common scenario detracted from their influence. Don Schmitt dismissed this problem by drawing a parallel: "We know Jesus Christ was crucified, we just don't know where."[23] Following that logic, few outside the UFO community were interested in tracking the discrepancies within and between narratives. With differences compressed and inconsistencies unexplored, Roswell events spun easily into a single, seamless web.[24]

A tale well told may disguise its weaknesses. Researchers have integrated themselves into the story, removing any barrier between participant and observer. In premising their work on the reality of alien visitation, they have persuaded witnesses to reject more plausible alternatives. If an alien encounter was a vulnerable premise, so too, was their conviction that the federal officials could keep a secret and silence thousands of people for more than fifty years. Forced to rely on elderly men and women to recall events decades in the past, researchers prompted subjects with leading questions and drew questionable conclusions from cryptic and paradoxical responses. They eagerly embraced sensational accounts on their face, with skepticism fading in the race to sell books. In pursuit of their agendas, researchers also disregarded the memory contagion that comes with repetition and pollutes the recall of new witnesses. Radio reporter Frank Joyce remarked in frustration: "I was there when it happened and I've read so much about it, but darned if I know what's true anymore."[25] Inconsistencies were similarly abided, as were witnesses who embellished testimony over many tellings, especially if new details scooped competitors. The truth for Don Schmitt was, in fact, wrapped in contradiction, for consistency was a sure "sign of a hoax."[26] At the same time, investigators failed to probe sensational findings with more mundane recollections, instead manipulating them in support of a conspiratorial explanation. Nor have the researchers recognized the power of publicity and celebrity status to cure reticence and elicit exaggeration.

Rules of evidence were disregarded or broken as well. Does it matter that Barney Barnett's diary makes no mention of the Plains of San Agustin or alien life forms? Is it important that the person whom mortician Glenn Dennis named as his nurse friend never served at Roswell Air Field? The papers of the identified Texas Tech archaeologist offered no corroboration of his assumed saucer-related activities, yet Kevin Randle still reached for confirmation: "By the same token, there was nothing in the records to refute the idea."[27] Circular reasoning infected the research process; absence of evidence was neither proof of its existence nor of conspiracy. Fast-paced writing suitable to the adventure genre leaped logic to disguise gaps in evidence. False leads brought charges of cover-up. Kevin Randle had a telling insight: "Until we begin to apply the strict standards of science, until we begin to review the evidence objectively, and until we allow our conclusions to be drawn solely from the evidence, we are not going to gain ground. Our findings are rejected, and rightly so."[28] Most readers of the Roswell story, however, did not hold the researchers to such exacting criteria and were quite willing to believe.[29]

No other Roswell investigator could hope to match the effort of these research teams. Still, truth and opportunity beckoned those who could reconcile inconsistencies and offer a solution. Karl Pflock reviewed the evidence and merged the stories, concluding that Mac Brazel had found both a government balloon *and* space debris. Perhaps the flying saucer collided with the balloon or lost control and crashed trying to evade it? Writer John Keel believed that the cause of the commotion was terrestrial, a Japanese fugo balloon launched during World War II to set American forests aflame. This satisfied few, for it did not explain sightings of bodies or spacecraft or, with the war over, the need for a weather balloon cover story. Was it the classified "Silver Bug" project, a saucer-shaped, vertical-lift vehicle that flew 2,300 miles per hour at an altitude of eighty thousand feet? In the same vein, Jacques Vallee wondered whether Roswell had resulted from a government attempt to protect a security-sensitive top secret program: "It would not have been difficult to plant an egg-shaped device in the desert to divert attention from the real debris, and even to scatter a few diminutive bodies to represent dead aliens."[30] There was more information on the craft's origin. A surviving alien pilot revealed to an anonymous source that the disc was a "probe ship" launched from a "lander ship" stationed at the "dimensional gateway to the Terran solar system, thirty-two light years away."[31] Courtney Brown recommended "remote viewing," an extrasensory perception technique that allowed access to areas distant in time and space. From this "psychic information gathering," Brown perceived that the Roswell aliens' mission was "to crash and thus force humans to investigate ET questions."[32] The aliens then returned to the scene of the crash and secretly retrieved the evidence. More conventional were the methods of the Allen Hynek Center for UFO Studies. Its researchers did three days of field work, sinking approximately two hundred test holes in the debris field. Nothing extraterrestrial was found. Whitley Strieber, the best-selling author of stories of alien abduction, turned to Roswell in his novel *Majestic*. The crash, he maintained, was no accident but the beginning of alien manipulation of humans. "It was bait. . . . And now they were going to reel us in."[33] The crash also operationalized government procedures to discredit and remove those who revealed the threat: "You will use flat, blanket denials as your primary means of covering the truth, and orchestrate a program of ridicule against any individual who makes public statements. You are officially authorized to use all necessary means to insure absolute and continuing silence from witnesses. The use of extreme or final means must be approved by this office."[34]

With Roswell harvested, investigators moved to the next task, unraveling the conspiracy that has hidden the incident for fifty years. They had already found numerous clues. Extensive testimony exposed the military presence at the debris field and the sealing off of the crash sites. Interviews repeatedly documented government attempts to silence and intimidate witnesses. Several officials refused to talk with the researchers, insisting that they were still bound by oaths of silence. From the very beginning of his investigation, Stanton Friedman was sensitive to intrigue and cover-up. Recalling the interruption of Lydia Sleppy's teletype machine when she had attempted to spread the Roswell story, Friedman insisted that an "extensive" monitoring and surveillance system "must have already been in place in Washington which reached out to all parts of the United States." It was, he believed, created after "an earlier crash" and designed to buy time while officials allayed public concern and grappled with a response. National security, moreover, demanded that the federal bureaucracy "compartmentalize" intelligence, with only a few privy to the most sensitive secrets. Continued Friedman: "The news that a system existed for detecting alien crashes and then controlling all information about them would, of necessity, have to be kept secret from almost everyone in the government as well as outside it." The Roswell military commanders, then, were clearly out of the "intelligence loop" and revealed their capture of the flying disk without consulting higher authority.[35] General Ramey had to move quickly to close the breach, and

he smothered public and press excitement with the weather balloon story. Ramey, however, was just following orders. The cover-
up of Roswell and the UFO phenomenon was plotted at the highest
levels of the federal government.[36]

Mysteriously, confirmation of the conspiracy arrived in the mail.
On December 11, 1984, Jaime Shandera, a research associate of Stan
Friedman's and Bill Moore's, received an envelope with no return
address containing a roll of exposed but unprocessed black-and-
white 35mm film. When developed, the film revealed eight pages,
the most important of which were portions of an alleged briefing
paper dated November 18, 1952, and prepared for newly elected
President Dwight Eisenhower. The briefing detailed the Roswell incident and the retrieval of four alien bodies as well as a second crash
of a spacecraft in 1950. It further reported that in Roswell's wake, on
September 24, 1947, President Harry Truman authorized Operation
Majestic Twelve (MJ-12). Under the direction of an oversight committee composed of representatives of the military, scientific, and intelligence communities, this program was tasked with the analysis of
crashed saucer data and the conduct of future alien relations. The
document prompted those in on the secret to maintain the "strict-
est" security to avoid public panic and to ensure America's lead in
the exploitation of alien technology.[37]

The news stunned Moore, Friedman, and Shandera, who feared
that they were being used to spread disinformation and discredit
UFO research. "Was it meant," asked Friedman, "to occupy the time
and energy of the best people in the UFO community and thus draw
their attention away from some other government UFO event or
non-UFO project that was considered more sensitive?" Intensive
study, however, convinced Friedman that the material was genuine,
leaked by a rogue group determined to reveal the truth to the American people. Proactively and circularly, he contended that even if
it were a hoax, "there must be something very similar in existence.
. . . Why fake a document when a real one with substantially similar content may be in the next filing cabinet?" In follow-up, the
researchers received postcards with riddles whose solutions revealed the location of documents in the National Archives obviously
planted to bolster the legitimacy of the briefing papers. Bill Moore,

in secret communication with men claiming to be members of the U.S. intelligence community, was shown additional materials that testified to the papers' authenticity.[38]

Also validating the find was a previous encounter that documentary filmmaker Linda Howe had with Moore's secret contact, Sgt. Richard Doty, who claimed affiliation with the Air Force Office of Special Investigation. In a meeting at Kirtland Air Force Base in Albuquerque, Howe remembered, Doty confirmed the existence of MJ-12 and explained that his superiors wanted to awaken the public to the extraterrestrial reality. His was only a small part of the operation, and government "programming" was occurring through a variety of mass media sources. Doty showed Howe an undated document titled "Briefing Paper for the President of the United States," which summarized the details of a series of UFO crashes. Although forbidden to take notes, Howe recalled that the report described the alien pilots as gray-colored, approximately four feet in height, with no noses or ears. Doty had even more tantalizing information to share. For broadcast on an HBO television special, he pledged to release several thousand feet of classified film showing crashed saucers and an interview with a surviving extraterrestrial who hailed from the Zeta Reticuli star system. The promise was never fulfilled, and Sergeant Doty and the air force denied all of Howe's claims.[39]

These revelations fractured the UFO community. Critics pounced on Moore and Friedman, accusing them of perpetrating a fraud. Worse, they were denounced as willing dupes in a government disinformation operation to undermine and neutralize the UFO cause. Unable to determine authenticity through ink-and-paper tests, skeptics focused on inconsistencies and errors of style and spelling within the briefing papers. Evidence of malfeasance was plentiful. Critics noted that the date format did not conform to governmental style, the papers carried no top secret registration number, military titles were improperly noted, and signatures appeared to be grafted onto the document. Anachronistic usages like *media* and *impacted* further betrayed the find. Such obvious errors convinced Jacques Vallee that "*The MJ-12 source operates as the manipulator of a contrived disinformation leak* rather than as a real whistleblower with something at stake, or as the deeply concerned person who has decided to expose a genuine scandal once and for all."[40] Mark Rodeghier concurred: "I suggest the intent was to confuse the UFO community, make us look gullible . . . and, most important, destroy the credibility of the Roswell event."[41] Competitor Kevin Randle was especially irate: "The MJ-12 documents, all of them are fakes. There is not a shred of evidence to support any other conclusion. . . . And if the documents weren't created by those inside the UFO community to promote themselves . . . it is possible they were invented by others to divert attention from Roswell."[42] In spite of his objections, Randle echoed his antagonists, suspecting the existence of just such a secret operation: "There clearly was a directed program from inside the government whose job it was to obscure the truth. The room is littered with smoking guns."[43] Supporters of Moore and Friedman, in turn, demonized their detractors. "It would now seem essential," declared Whitley Strieber, "for them to prove that they are not working in furtherance of a conspiracy of silence before they can be trusted further."[44] In the end, consensus eluded the community. Yet the bloodletting concentrated attention on the common enemy. Alleged government intrigue implied that the truth was out there and that researchers were closer than ever before. While continuing to watch the skies, they suspiciously eyed the government in anticipation of new machinations.[45]

Conspiracism is a strong current within the UFO mainstream. Nevertheless, the community distances itself from the most passionate countersubversives. New World Order foe William Cooper condemned Bill Moore and Stan Friedman as CIA operatives and their MJ-12 briefing paper as a fraud. Yet his book *Behold a Pale Horse* reveals "Majesty Twelve," a shadow government that is the driving force for Illuminati world rule. As a naval intelligence officer in the 1970s, Cooper claimed to have read reports listing twenty-six flying saucer crashes between 1947 and 1953, with an alien death toll of ninety-one. A sole surviving "insect-like being" with a "tendency to lie" was plucked from the Roswell wreckage. Cooper added chilling details to the story, describing "a large number of human body parts stored within" the craft. He also noticed an alien emblem known as the "Trilateral insignia" displayed on the ship and space traveler's uniform. To deal with the situation, President Dwight Eisenhower approached Nelson Rockefeller to create Majesty Twelve, a secret agency for "alien-task supervision." Rockefeller saw his opportunity and staffed it with members of the Council on Foreign Relations. The top secret agency then brokered a treaty with the aliens that bartered extraterrestrial technology for the right to build secret, underground bases where biological experiments on abducted humans could be conducted. World dictatorship is the eventual goal, and Majesty-12 is coordinating with the Bilderberg group to facilitate the creation of similar alien-Illuminati partnerships in other nations.[46]

Even more ominous were the warnings of "Commander X." "High-level contacts" revealed that the alien "puppetmasters" had captured control of the government from gullible federal officials, guilty of "cosmic treason" for betraying American freedom. With impunity, aliens ignored treaty obligations limiting their access to cattle and humans and engaged in a wholesale harvest of body parts and secretions. They precipitated President Eisenhower's heart attack when he balked at their demands. They put a contract out on President John Kennedy because he threatened to reveal "secret government/Grey alien collaboration." Patiently, they prepared for conquest, stocking their bases under the Navajo Indian Reservation and Area 51 in Nevada with disorientation lasers, mind control devices, and electromagnetic zap guns. Now in league with the Illuminati and Masons, they face little opposition to their "world conspiracy" and their plan to establish a new order. Although other researchers are less imaginative and concentrate more specifically on "men in black" and "black helicopters," Roswell and the federal betrayal are required story lines.[47]

Just beneath the surface of sensationalism, the controversy over UFOs is a battle for authority between believers and federal officials. Roswell is only the latest incident to pit the seekers against the keepers of the truth. Similarities with the concurrent controversy over the assassination of President John Kennedy are obvious. Like critics of the Warren Commission Report, UFO researchers presented witnesses to the facts and efficiently unraveled official explanation to plant a reasonable doubt. Washington has attempted to frustrate the challenge with secrecy restrictions, bureaucratic maneuvers, silence, ridicule, and counterattack. An arrogance of federal power has fueled a sense of injustice, igniting the conspiracist fire while eroding public trust. With suspicions escalating, even acts of official incompetence were interpreted as clever signs of intrigue. No wonder that by the end of the twentieth century a majority of Americans embraced Stanton Friedman's charge of a "cosmic Watergate," the alleged cover-up of not only Roswell but all extraterrestrial contact.

The air force command, along with average Americans, took an active interest in the 1947 wave of flying saucer sightings. In response, it authorized Project Sign and then Project Grudge to collect and evaluate information and determine whether the phenomenon posed a threat to national security. Official investigators open to an extraterrestrial explanation were in the minority, and Project Grudge formally concluded in 1949 that the solution was mundane. The sightings represented a "mild form of mass hysteria and war nerves," which caused misidentification of conventional objects. Often the incidents were "hoaxes" perpetrated by psychopathic personalities.[48] The report found nothing to suggest that the objects were extraterrestrial craft or compromised American defenses. Still, in spite of an effort to explain all of the cases investigated, Grudge left almost one in four unidentified. This provoked critics to dismiss the investigation as incomplete and to grow suspicious when secrecy regulations blanketed the report. Subsequent official silence only aggravated public concerns and encouraged those who believed that the government was hiding secrets. Belying its official stance that flying saucers were not serious business, the air force continued quietly to collect and study UFO information.[49]

A wave of more than fifteen hundred sightings created a public uproar that forced the air force into the open and to renew investigation with Project Blue Book in 1952. The Central Intelligence Agency also responded by forming the Robertson Panel the following year. This group of scientists and intelligence analysts reviewed sighting data for twelve hours and readily confirmed Project Grudge's conclusion that UFOs were neither extraterrestrial nor a security risk. A danger existed, however, because the flood of sighting reports threatened to clog military communication channels. In the midst of the Cold War, military authorities feared that the Russians might exploit the UFO hysteria to launch a surprise attack on the United States. Measures must be pursued, the panelists agreed, to strip "the aura of mystery" from the sightings and thus reduce the interference with American defenses.[50] Officials censored the Robertson Panel report, which remained classified until 1975, when it was pried from government files by UFO researchers. The Federal Bureau of Investigation, the National Security Agency, and assorted military organizations were also curious about UFOs and similarly kept their documents under wraps.[51]

In line with the Robertson Panel's recommendations, Project Blue Book dropped its investigative mission and initiated a public relations offensive against UFO believers. Air force officers were determined to reduce the number of unknowns to a minimum by quickly resolving all sightings and debunking witnesses. New air force guidelines that prohibited the release of any information about a sighting, unless positively resolved, kept up appearances. So, too, did dubious bookkeeping practices. While keeping their files classified, project officers put the best face on their work by recategorizing possible and probable explanations as "definitely established." This led the air force to boast that more than 80 percent of the sightings were "solved." When the statistics were refigured, however, unsolved sightings ballooned to 60 percent of the thirteen thousand cases reported. Its public relations mission, underfunding, a small staff, and leadership by junior officers meant that Project Blue Book lacked power and priority and never became the investigative tool that Americans were led to believe was in place. Superficial and inept explanations invoking temperature inversion or swamp gas showcased these shortcomings. Nevertheless, U.S. Air Force Chief of Staff Gen. Thomas White declared, "Under this program all unidentified flying objects are investigated in meticulous detail by Air Force personnel and qualified scientific consultants."[52] Secretary of the Air Force Harold Brown concurred in a report to Congress in 1966: "Let me assure you that the Air Force is both objective and thorough in its treatment of all reports of unusual aerial objects over the United States."[53] Project commander Maj. Hector Quintanilla was closer to reality, conceding, "We don't investigate much.... We collect data. It's a misnomer to think we investigate."[54]

Such bureaucratic faults and command expectations, of course, played little role in cover-up scenarios. Thus UFO researcher Maj. Donald Keyhoe decried in the 1950s the "top-level blackout" by the "silence group."[55] Kevin Randle was also wise to military ways and gave events a suitable spin: "The best cover for them was to look as if they didn't know what they were doing, all the while gathering their data. Incompetence is the project name for the conspiracy."[56] Questions flowed logically from this: if Project Blue Book was "nothing more than a public relations outfit," what government agency was tasked with extraterrestrial matters?[57] Where were the documents that proved contact?[58]

In search of the elusive documents, researchers attempted in the 1970s to open government files with the Freedom of Information Act (FOIA), which Congress had passed to facilitate access to federal records. The ordeal, in what Don Schmitt called "the black hole," would only deepen the conviction of conspiracy.[59] In the face of repeated denials of involvement or even interest by the FBI, CIA, and National Security Agency, among other government organizations, the act brought the grudging release of more than three thousand pages of previously classified materials. Of no surprise to believers, the cache proved of little value, as it was composed mainly of sighting reports clipped from newspapers, letters seeking information about UFOs, and duplicated materials. Still, researchers had caught the authorities in an obvious lie. Thousands of pages of documents and the number of agencies involved left the impression that federal officials had been deeply concerned about UFOs for decades.[60]

Continuing to probe for other materials withheld on security grounds, researchers encountered stiff bureaucratic resistance. Typical in its expense of time and money, was Stanton Friedman's tangle with the CIA. He requested twenty-three documents but received only nine after a delay of thirty-five months. An appeal brought the release of fragments of three additional documents two years later, their censored pages so blacked out that they were undecipherable. Friedman could only surmise from his encounter that the cover-up was still in place and that only the "barest tip of the iceberg" had been revealed.[61] In 1980 researchers brought suit in federal court to compel the National Security Agency to declassify its files. District Court Judge Gerhard Gesell denied them access, however, ruling that release "could seriously jeopardize the work of the agency and the security of the United States."[62] The plaintiffs found some solace in the decision. A threat to American security surely implied an extraterrestrial reality, and researchers readily rejected the less sensational interpretation that exposure might compromise intelligence sources and data-gathering techniques. Perhaps even more illuminating, the paper chase had found no evidence about Roswell: "No letters, no notes, no investigative forms, no official weather balloon explanation, nothing but [a] lone [press] clipping."[63] Clearly, the shadow government was above the law and made quite a formidable foe.[64]

On occasion, FOIA revealed hidden snares that entangled UFO researchers. On September 23, 1947, just months after the alleged crash at Roswell, Lt. Gen. Nathan Twining of the Air Force Air Material Command responded to a letter from Assistant Chief of Staff for Air Intelligence Brig. Gen. George Schulgen. Schulgen was seeking information about UFO sightings, and Twining had much to report. The objects, he wrote, were "something real and not visionary or fictitious." Circular or elliptical in shape, they had been seen flying in formation, capable of "extreme" rates of climb, and traveling at high speed. Twining offered the possibility that the craft was a top secret project of either the United States or a foreign government. Although there was no crash debris available for analysis, he proposed that air force intelligence undertake "a detailed study" of the phenomenon.[65] If Roswell was a reality, Twining's letter was curious. Alien bodies or ship debris would surely have been sent to his laboratories at Wright-Patterson Field for examination. Officers assigned to Projects Sign and Grudge and members of the Robertson Panel certainly would have been informed of the incident. This was an absence of evidence in reverse, and it demanded the utmost in mental agility from UFO investigators. Bill Moore had no doubt that Roswell was the context of Twining's letter. A study was necessary because a disk had been recovered. Twining was attempting to conceal this from Air Force intelligence and detour its energies into a more general investigation of UFOs. Kevin Randle and Don Schmitt pointed to the letter's low "secret" classification and suggested that Twining would be especially discreet in a communication accessible to many readers. Nor did it surprise them that high-ranking officers like Schulgen or those in Projects Sign and Grudge would not have a "need to know" about Roswell. Similarly, the air force was protective of its domain and later wanted to keep the CIA in the dark. Like Moore, they believed that Twining was "shutting off one area of investigation" so that the Roswell analysis could proceed unhindered. Such reasoning, they were convinced, offered "room for Roswell to slip through the cracks. Or to be pushed through them."[66]

In spite of appearances, so important in shaping perceptions, researchers' experiences with the Freedom of Information Act may reflect nothing more sinister than bureaucracy in action or the contested terrain of national security. Yet believers tell other tales that go beyond denial to suggest government malevolence. In the 1970s filmmakers Robert Emenegger and Allan Sandler recalled an invitation to visit Norton Air Force Base in California from members of the Office of Special Investigation and an offer of film documenting an alien encounter. No footage materialized. Well known in the UFO community was the alleged "bait and switch trick" that Sgt. Richard Doty had played on Linda Howe during the 1980s.[67]

More disturbing were the experiences of Bill Moore. After publication of *The Roswell Incident*, men claiming to be air force intelligence officers approached him with a proposal. Soviet operatives had infiltrated the aerospace industry and threatened to steal defense secrets. His country needed Moore to help ferret out these spies and protect national security. Patriotism alone may have enticed Moore's cooperation, but the men offered more. Noting that his book was "on the right track" and identifying themselves as members of a group who wanted the secret out, they promised him information about crashed saucers and alien retrievals.[68] Moore hesitated: "The thing I had on my mind the whole time was this smells like a con game." Yet the lure was irresistible. "If I don't play the game, I learn nothing. If I do play the game, and play by their rules, I stand to learn more and continue to play." He took the bait and was recruited as an "asset," with Sergeant Doty as his liaison. To fulfill his part of the pact, Moore was told "to watch carefully" and "gather information" among UFO researchers.[69]

Moore's tasks soon evolved. His contact required him to report on the effectiveness of a government campaign to discredit a UFO investigator fed with stories of secret alien bases, extraterrestrial implants, and treaties with abduction clauses. Nor was he above informing on fellow researchers, planting false leads, and attempting to destabilize UFO organizations. Moore never was let in on the secret and became trapped in his own game. In 1988 his handlers appeared on a television program titled *UFO Cover-UP? Live!* With faces shadowed and voices distorted, they revealed solemnly that three alien space travelers were guests of the federal government and that they enjoyed Tibetan music and strawberry ice cream. Moore's public confession soon after caused an uproar in the UFO community, with many members charting the progress of deceit back through the Eisenhower briefing papers and the MJ-12 revelations. Others rose to defend the documents, arguing that the essence of disinformation was the masking of truth with lies. Such happenings only convinced researchers of the importance of their work. If the investigation was of no consequence, why would government agents operating independently or under orders go to such lengths to discredit their efforts?[70]

Those focused specifically on Roswell also found grist for their conspiracy theories. Having failed in their efforts through the Freedom of Information Act to obtain official communication traffic records concerning Roswell Air Field, researchers in 1994 approached New Mexico Congressman Steven Schiff, who promised to intervene. The air force, however, stonewalled his efforts, ignoring requests for briefings and referring him to the National Archives for information. Schiff then requested that the General Accounting Office (GAO) investigate. The GAO discovered that all administrative records and "outgoing messages from Roswell were destroyed without proper authority."[71] Was this another bureaucratic foul-up? Had a standard procedure record-clearing operation gone too far? Perhaps, but the conspiracy-minded knew better. Researchers found it curious that the GAO search uncovered no Roswell materials in the papers of the White House, the National Security Council, or the Central Intelligence Agency. MJ-12 documents were also missing. This necessitated a more vigorous search, and Stanton Friedman called for a congressional investigation "to really dig into the subject."[72]

To close the case before the GAO went public, the air force produced a thousand-page report in 1994. It acknowledged for the first time that General Ramey's weather balloon story was false. What Mac Brazel found was probably test flight balloon #4 from the top secret Mogul Project that was designed to develop a long-range system to detect Soviet atomic detonations and ballistic missile launches. The intelligence sensitivity of the device had to do with its secret mission and not its construction material, which consisted of nonclassified balsa wood sticks held together with Elmer's glue, cellophane tape with decorative symbols, and shiny, aluminum radar reflectors attached to a six hundred–foot braided master line. UFO investigators raked the report, decrying the air force's failure to interview their hundreds of witnesses. Would Maj. Jesse Marcel, they asked, have mistaken a balloon for a UFO? How could a balloon leave a debris field or explain the "overreaction" of military authorities? Like Warren Report critics, UFO investigators also found suspicious the decision not to index the lengthy report. To the *New York Times* reporter covering the event, the air force statement was definitive and "to all appearances deflate[d] the conspiracy once and for all."[73] UFO investigators had a different take, insisting that the original sin of Roswell had been revealed and that their charges of cover-up now had more substance than ever.[74]

Government action, then, facilitated the building of conspiracy theories about Roswell in particular and UFOs in general. Sins of omission and commission tainted the federal record and enflamed suspicions that disregarded the workings of human nature or bureaucratic process in the historical account. While in close combat, authorities and believers never lost sight of those who interpreted the action for an audience invested in the outcome. The briefing was neither disinterested nor dispassionate. With an eye to market shares and box office receipts, media executives filtered and packaged information to privilege the more sensational stories of the countersubversives. The UFO phenomenon and Roswell became mainstream, not only icons of conspiracism but staples of American popular culture. In satisfying this craving for news of alien invaders and their human coconspirators, authorities were again casualties, bled of their credibility. Stanton Friedman acknowledged the UFO community's debt: "What's changed drastically is *Independence Day, X-Files,* all of these television shows—that makes it respectable."[75] The result is apparent not only at the bottom line but in opinion polls that testify to America's commitment to the conspiracists' tale.

Establishment print journalists, from the beginning, were the federal government's strongest supporters. Though not shy about revealing conspiracy in other contexts, newspapers repeatedly validated the air force version of events and pronounced official investigations thorough and worthy of public confidence. Project Blue Book thus escaped muckraking, and investigative journalists never exposed its public-relations cover. Only when official explanations blatantly defied logic and evidence did reporters break ranks. Meanwhile, witnesses who testified to alien encounters faced skepticism and ridicule, with the 10 percent of Americans who swore to similar episodes feeling the pain vicariously. Newspaper best-seller lists alone gave UFO investigators equal coverage.[76]

The tabloids have been less deferential than the establishment press, readily highlighting extraterrestrial events. They have continually updated readers about Mars bases, implants, abductions, crashed saucers, and other trends in UFO research. "Help Me Find My Spaceman Lover!" headlined a *Weekly World News* piece that described the search of a Cedar Rapids, Iowa, woman for Inor, a four-foot tall, rust-colored alien who had courted her for six years and then mysteriously vanished. Another article described the telltale signs of alien rape and offered women advice on avoiding abduction. The *News* also solved the Roswell mystery. The downed craft was not extraterrestrial but a time machine from Earth's future. As proof, it quoted the inscription on the wrecked fuselage: "Made in Greater America, 2458 A.D."[77]

More influential were the messages beamed from Hollywood. The science fiction film has had a long run with American audiences and conspiracy is a common theme. In the late 1930s Saturday matinees featured Flash Gordon confronting Emperor Ming the Merciless of Mongo, who plotted to enslave Earth. Captain Video and his rangers had their hands full, facing down Vazarium, Mook the Moon Man, and Kul of Eos. During the 1950s Hollywood launched repeated extraterrestrial invasions, with a peak between 1956 and 1958, when more than ninety movies were released. Though sometimes peaceful, movie aliens were more often engaged in evil conspiracies in which mind control was the means and world domination the end. The usual script had a foundation of realism but included alien encounters in its vision of reality. *The Blob* (1958) was typical. Teenagers get the brush-off from adults, who find their reports of a pulsating, human-eating goo from space as irritating as drag racing, rock and roll, and slang. Tension builds as the blob devours people while stubborn officials waste precious time searching for a logical, terrestrial explanation. Only close contact with the marauding gel changes perceptions, and the authorities, finally convinced, come to the rescue. After the alien attack on Santa Mira, California, in *Invasion of the Body Snatchers* (1956), once-complacent viewers were surely persuaded to watch friends and relatives closely and trust no one.[78]

Box office success has ensured the future of science fiction films in the decades since the 1950s, though in smaller numbers. Over the years aliens have accepted roles as parasites, predators, and playmates, according to audience tastes. The latest surge occurred between 1996 and 1998, when more than a dozen films appeared. By the end of the twentieth century, Hollywood had succeeded in making space a familiar setting. Movies showed viewers that intelligent life existed beyond Earth and made space travel a reality. The promise of space was apparent, but so were the dangers that lurked at its outer reaches. Moviegoers repeatedly confronted extraterrestrial travelers and became well acquainted with their chameleon-like nature. They also witnessed the aliens' powers of infiltration and subversion. Impatient with the teachings of orthodox science, Americans would find the claims of the UFO researchers more consistent with the lessons they had learned in the theaters. At the same time, the flood of recent films made some conspiracists uneasy. Was there a message in the repetition? Was Hollywood following Washington's lead and preparing Earthlings for momentous news?[79]

A break from the science fiction tradition of the 1950s has been apparent in more recent films. Traditional treatments preached public faith in police, military, and scientific authorities. Now, as conspiracists had surmised and Hollywood confirmed, outer space was no longer the sole source of conspiracy. Federal authorities have broken trust and are in on the secret, covering up alien activities. As Jack Nicholson's character in *Easy Rider* (1969) observed, aliens "have been livin' and workin' among us in vast quantities. . . . The government knows all about 'em." *Close Encounters of the Third Kind*

(1977) has the federal government engaged in an elaborate disinformation effort to cover up first contact. *Capricorn One* (1978) fakes a mission to Mars, with astronauts romping in red dust in a terrestrial warehouse. *Hangar 18* (1980) reveals the hiding place of a captured UFO. The women and men of the *Alien* film series (1979, 1986, 1992, 1997) confront not only extraterrestrial life forms but the more dangerous military-industrial complex, which is willing to sacrifice them for the sake of its bio-weapons division. A 1988 remake of *The Blob* reflected changing times. Teenagers save the town, while authorities are recast as corrupt and power-hungry officials interested only in their germ-warfare program.[80] In *The Rock* (1996) concealed microfilm reveals the truth about "the alien landing at Roswell" and the official cover-up. The blockbuster hit *Independence Day* appeared the same year and linked Roswell to ultrasecret Area 51, the newest site of researcher interest. According to the script, alien bodies and a ship were recovered at Roswell and sent to Area 51 laboratories for analysis. The president had not been told, so that he might have "plausible deniability." It is left to the character played by Judd Hirsch to bring every member of the audience up to speed on the 1947 incident: "Don't give me 'unprepared.' . . . You had that spaceship. That thing that you found in New Mexico . . . Roswell, New Mexico. You had the spaceship and you had the bodies."

As *The Faculty* (1998) suggests, movie viewing is a cumulative experience and has produced a composite picture. The audience is expected to know its film history to keep up with the script. Teenagers fighting the alien takeover of their high school mount a defense by referencing visual aids like *Invasion of the Body Snatchers, Independence Day,* and *The X-Files*. In the best conspiracist tradition, they second-guess their sources and raise the possibility of a plot within a plot: "How do you know there's not a conspiracy? Maybe the X-Files is right. Where do all of these movies come from anyway? How do we know Spielberg, Lucas, Sonnenfeld, Emerich haven't been visited by aliens? Maybe they're aliens themselves. Maybe they're preparing us for what is to come? . . . If you were going to take over the world, would you blow up the White House *Independence Day* style or sneak in through the back door?"

Television has supplemented film coverage, especially in its focus on the Roswell incident. Fighting for ratings and attuned to the draw of a mystery that features aliens, *Hard Copy, 48 Hours, Larry King Live, Good Morning America, CBS This Morning, Entertainment Tonight, Leeza,* and *Sally Jessy Raphael* have invited Roswell researchers and witnesses as guests. For entertainment's sake, the stress is on the secret, with critics' airtime carefully managed to avoid dampening the drama. Sometimes, a host provides the necessary balance. In other instances, they feed suspicion, as Larry King did when he compared Vietnam and Watergate to the UFO cover-up. At the end of a telecast, he asked, "Crashed saucers? Who knows? But clearly, the government is withholding something."[81] For nonreaders, Showtime broadcast *Roswell: The U.F.O. Cover-up* (1994), based on the research of Kevin Randle and Don Schmitt. The made-for-television movie follows the authors' crash scenario closely but adds, for dramatic effect, insider Martin Sheen, who lays bare the government cover-up for an aging Jesse Marcel. As an aside, Sheen reveals that the film *Close Encounters of the Third Kind* was a government plant, a Hollywood reenactment of the first formal contact between the United States and the aliens. *Roswell* also features a telepathic extraterrestrial survivor who imprints on U.S. Secretary of Defense James Forrestal the necessity of going public with the news of the crash. Forrestal is later found dead under mysterious circumstances, and his diaries have disappeared.

Equally important in shaping opinion are the recurring pseudo-documentaries about Roswell. The alien autopsy film, purportedly of a Roswell crash victim, was telecast on the Fox network in 1995 to an audience of ten million viewers. High ratings inspired an expanded version and reruns. More realistic were the Roswell features on *Ancient Mysteries, The Unexplained, Unsolved Mysteries,* and *Sightings* and specials on the Discovery Channel and A&E. The format of these programs was similar and framed with variations of the question asked during the alien autopsy telecast: "What does the government know and what aren't they telling us?" In the typical televised account, actors reenact the alleged events of Roswell, with witnesses reinterviewed and experts found to support or deny the reality of the incident. The tenor is objective and reasoned, and the story is seemingly played according to the scientific method, or at least in the best tradition of the police drama. Although the program presents the viewer with alternatives, the alien explanation remains viable at the conclusion of the broadcast, a product of the preponderance of eyewitness testimony and its dramatic presentation. If the audience still needs nudging, the voice-over offers an equivocal closer: "The question persists," or "Other information remains classified and unexplained," or "Is the government covering up something more secret?" or "Does Roswell prove we have been visited?" Rebroadcast and competing versions only validate the main story line and testify to a visual reality.[82]

Roswell has made appearances beyond the documentary and talk show circuits. An episode of the comedy show *Ellen* mentioned a side trip to Roswell to visit the site of the crash. *Star Trek, Deep Space 9* laid the 1947 incident to space-traveling Ferengi. As to the official weather balloon story, a character apologizes, "We had to come up with something quick."[83] The NBC series *Dark Skies* (1996) prepared viewers with an advertising campaign that announced: "Imagine everything you know about history is a lie. Tonight, you will stop imagining. And start believing."[84] According to the script, aliens had landed in Roswell and demanded the unconditional surrender of the United States. President Harry Truman responded by ordering the air force to blow them out of the sky. Now the aliens are back, and they are mad. Quietly infiltrating the federal government, they seize control of key agencies and reach for world domination. As President John Kennedy discovers, the aliens are ruthless and will brook no challenge to their plans. Some local newscasts could not resist the Roswell temptation. San Francisco station KTVU offered a series of segments in 1996 on Maj. Jesse Marcel's military record. KTVX in Salt Lake City discovered that a Roswell researcher had bought a ranch in Utah with a history of UFO sightings and cattle mutilations. A reporter speculated that the purchase was "maybe a cover for government activity."[85] In fall 2000 the Cartoon Network prepared the next generation, offering a trip for two to Roswell as the grand prize in a special promotion.[86]

In terms of market share, the most important carrier of the Roswell story is *The X-Files*. The government cover-up of the extraterrestrial presence has been a central theme of the show since its inception. As a familiar mystery and convenient historical marker, Roswell works well in a supporting role, and program writers have readily incorporated it as a touchstone to validate their conspiracy theories. The plot begins just after the crash in 1947, when insiders agree to collaborate with aliens in project "purity control." Using Americans as test subjects, extraterrestrials and program scientists clone human and alien biomatter to perfect a slave race in anticipation of colonization from outer space. As they gradually expose the conspiracy, FBI agents Dana Scully and Fox Mulder use Roswell as shorthand to help viewers fix their bearings and integrate new information in familiar ways. Thus in the "Fallen Angel" episode, a government retrieval team is dispatched to "sanitize" a site officially dismissed as a meteor landing. Like the agents, viewers are not fooled and realize that the scheme is "like the Roswell cover-up." An alien ship collides with a military plane in "Requiem," and the verdict is clear: "It's Roswell and Corona all over again years later." UFO researchers cheered when Mulder's source Deep Throat reveals: "Roswell was just a smoke screen." Says cigarette-smoking man, "We had a perfect conspiracy with an alien race. . . . They were good plans. Right plans. Kept secret for over fifty years ever since the crash at Roswell." The *X-Files* also showcased the Roswell Grays, a hometown baseball team of African Americans whose star player is a shape-changing extraterrestrial.[87]

Roswell offers the context in a pivotal trilogy of episodes ending the show's second season and beginning its third. In "Anazasi" a computer hacker penetrates secret Department of Defense files and downloads documents that expose the "global conspiracy of silence" about "Roswell, MJ-12, and beyond." Just before his death at the hands of government agents, the hacker gives the information to Fox Mulder, who immediately becomes the target of a federal "full alert." Meanwhile, an earthquake centered between Roswell and Corona reveals a hidden railroad boxcar filled with nonhuman corpses. The "Consortium" responds to the breach quickly, ordering cigarette-smoking man to plug the leak, get Mulder, and burn the evidence. "Blessing Way" develops the cover-up, with the conspirators "pulling the strings" of the military, FBI, and media. As one of the secret elite boasts: "We predict the future. The best way to predict the future is to invent it." "Paper Clip" ends the trilogy, offering solution but little closure. Mulder and Scully discover that in the wake of the Roswell crash, bioengineering experiments began under alien supervision. The insiders enlisted Nazi scientists for the work, permitting them to trade their expertise for asylum and immunity from prosecution for war crimes. Identifying human subjects was not difficult, for the government was gathering genetic data on millions of women and men under the cover of federal smallpox vaccination programs. Stored in a vast warehouse and at the disposal of the extraterrestrial invaders, the medical files were clear evidence of "an elaborate conspiracy against the American people." Viewers knew that the plot would survive the episode and welcomed the return of the government files in exchange for the lives of Mulder and Scully. Still, they could only agree with Agent Scully: "I've heard the truth, now what I want are the answers."[88]

Those wedded to computer rather than movie or television screens would not want for Roswell news. In the 1990s believers developed more than fifty websites dedicated to the Roswell conspiracy. In a thickly growing matrix, these linked to other sites specializing in UFO sightings, Area 51, alien abductions, and crop circles. Usernet groups and e-mail added intimacy and created community. Self-referential and mutually confirming, messages grew credible in isolation and through repetition. In spite of the appearance of openness and freedom, this was a sealed, self-policing world. Dissidents were not welcome; challenges to the basic paradigm were ignored. In a fight for truth against a powerful foe, such single-mindedness was a virtue and tolerance a heresy.[89]

Muting the dark tones, merchandisers completed the mainstreaming of Roswell and the aliens. U-Haul International unveiled a graphic on its New Mexico fleet of trucks depicting a green alien with a crashed saucer in the background. The caption reads, "What happened in Roswell?" More information was made available on the U-Haul website, which was formatted to look like an FBI file. Included in the dossier were eyewitness accounts, with sensitive information blacked out, and official explanations of the incident. Nevada U-Haul trucks, meanwhile, sported an Area 51 logo. Volkswagen, with commercial breaks during The X-Files, showed its automobiles spinning to the ground designed through "Reverse Engineering from UFOs." Pullman Bank in Chicago offered a VISA card embossed with alien figures. AT&T, Kodak, Polaroid, Arctic Circle, amazon.com, Absolut Vodka, AirTouch cellular calling cards, Hallmark's Shoebox greeting cards, Coca-Cola, U.S. West, Maytag, Chili's restaurants, and others also worked to domesticate aliens for consumers. Observed a *New York Times* reporter, "All in all, the marketing mania for everything intergalactic makes it seem as if Madison Avenue runs through Roswell, New Mexico."[90]

Children were even more comfortable in the company of extraterrestrials. In the Area 51 video game, youngsters join STAAR, the Special Tactical Advanced Alien Response team, to counter aliens and their "alien-infected" zombies. Their mission is to wade into the extraterrestrial horde and recapture control of a secret base. The Testor hobby company created "Grey: The Extraterrestrial Life Form," a nine-piece plastic model kit for assembly by those eight years and older. Hostess Ding Dongs and Quisp, Rice Krispies, and Captain Crunch breakfast cereals enticed consumers with alien imagery, while Butterfinger played on the Roswell cover-up to sell its candy bars. Three different kinds of Roswell alien action figures were available for purchase. One offered the history-minded a brief account of the incident: "By executive order, a special team of scientists and military personnel were sent to examine the wreckage. This top secret mission was classified Majestic-12. . . . The government created a cover up story. They claimed a weather balloon crashed in the desert. The location of the Extra-Terrestrial beings and the craft wreckage remain [sic] unknown." Toy soldiers from the "Tub of Generals" could be used for battle or "the suppression of important evidence concerning cow mutilations near Roswell." At Hansen Planetarium in Salt Lake City, patrons could buy the "Glow in the Dark Amazing Growing Alien." The Roswell story is outlined on the back of the package with the disclaimer, "There is no proof of this." The planetarium did not stock the related "Glow-in-the-Dark Alien Autopsy" figure or "Alien Babies," which were available, while supplies lasted, at the local mall. Alien candy pops, air fresheners, candy dispensers, refrigerator magnets, contact lenses, Hacky Sacks, washable tattoos, stuffed animals, hats, shirts, and key chains sold in wholesale lots and could barely keep up with demand. The alien visage was everywhere and truly became the smiley face of the 1990s. Only the human imagination limited the extraterrestrial presence.[91]

In the competition with government authorities for credibility,

U-Haul International, known for its imaginative rental-truck logos advertising moving destinations, did its part to publicize the Roswell incident. It featured Roswell with a dazed alien from a downed spacecraft and prodded passing motorists: "Evaluate for Yourself . . . The Air Force originally stated a flying saucer was found. They later claimed it was just a weather balloon."

Courtesy of U-Haul International

conspiracists and their media allies had made an impressive show-ing. As early as the 1960s, Gallup polls found that almost one-half of Americans discounted air force explanations and thought UFOs were real. Five percent of Americans even claimed to have experi-enced an encounter. By the 1970s believers had climbed to 56 per-cent of Americans and eyewitnesses had doubled to 11 percent. These numbers held through the 1990s, with no significant gender differences and with middle-class and college-educated respondents more likely than others to accept alien possibilities. A belief in con-spiracy was an obvious corollary. Seventy-one percent of Americans surveyed in 1996 responded in the affirmative to the question "Does the U.S. government know more about UFOs than it is telling us?" As to the Roswell incident, one in three Americans accepted the scenario of a crashed flying saucer, and nearly another 20 percent were uncertain. Americans rejected air force explanations of Ros-well by a margin of 64 to 25 percent. President Bill Clinton acknowl-edged the continuing public fascination with the incident during a state visit to Ireland: "No, as far as I know, an alien spacecraft did not crash in Roswell, New Mexico, in 1947. . . . If the United States did recover alien bodies, they didn't tell me about it either, and I want to know."[92] Conspiracists would find plenty to dissect in the president's statement. In fact, a reporter for the *Weekly World News* later discovered that President Clinton did know the truth about the Roswell incident. Just after taking the oath of office in 1993, according to the *News* story, Clinton had traveled to Area 51 in Ne-vada, where he was shown the remains of the four aliens killed in the crash. The military also briefed him on the invasion from outer space under way since 1947.[93]

The fiftieth anniversary of the incident in 1997 was an opportu-nity none of the players in the Roswell story could resist. Civic and business boosters in Roswell welcomed the world to their encoun-ter, predicting a crowd of more than one hundred thousand. In com-memoration, Testors Corporation debuted its new plastic model kit "The Roswell UFO," complete with four alien pilots. Doing its part to publicize the happening, Delta Airlines *Sky Magazine* informed passengers that "something weird went on that summer night, July 4, 1947, on the plains near Roswell, though nobody really knows— or is saying—what."[94] *Time* magazine cashed in on the excitement and put Roswell on its cover. Even *Popular Mechanics* gave space to the mystery. Meanwhile, A&E set the context, offering television viewers *UFOs vs. the Government* and *UFOs: The First Encounters.* The Discovery Channel rose to the challenge with *Are We Alone?* The Fox network's fall lineup included *The Visitor,* the story of a pilot, abducted by aliens over the Bermuda triangle in 1947, now returned, with aliens and federal agents in hot pursuit. Hollywood was also prepared. *Contact* picked up signals in prime number variations from deep space. Authorities hide a trip through the worm hole to the Vega System in "confidential findings" and mollify the space traveler with a "healthy grant." The *Men in Black* belong to a secret government agency that monitors alien residents in the United States. To ensure the cover-up, the agents are armed with a device that erases the memories of eyewitnesses. In *Waiting for Guffman,* Blaine, Missouri, takes civic pride in being the site of a pre-Roswell alien landing.[95]

Researchers also proved that all the gold had not been mined out of Roswell. Philip Corso's *The Day After Roswell* produced the most startling revelations, even upstaging the appearance of the metal chip purported to come from the downed spacecraft. Corso's credentials were impressive. A career soldier, he had served as an intelligence officer during World War II, on Gen. Douglas MacArthur's staff in Korea, and in the National Security Council under President Dwight Eisenhower. Rising to the rank of lieutenant colonel, Corso became chief of the army's foreign technology division. In this billet, he took command of a four-drawer file cabinet that contained "the cache of debris and information an army retrieval team . . . pulled out of the wreckage of a flying disk." Corso claims to have seeded these parts to defense contractors for back engineering, their origin later hidden under new patents. The results were revolutionary. Manufacturers deconstructed and rebuilt lasers, integrated circuit chips, fiber optics, Kevlar fabric, and night-vision goggles. Technology for the stealth bomber program and Strategic Defense Initiative was Roswell-based, as well. Other investigators added Velcro to Corso's list. If this was not sensational enough, Corso also insisted that he had seen alien bodies and autopsy results and been privy to MJ-12 matters. The news drew little attention from the establishment press but did get a four-page spread in the *Weekly World News.*[96]

Many in the UFO community embraced Corso's claims. Here was the long-awaited smoking gun, delivered by the hand of an insider. A reviewer declared, "To say this is a significant book, if not the most significant book to appear on a UFO subject in decades, can hardly be considered an exaggeration. If even a portion of Corso's extraordinary claims are true, the implications are staggering."[97] Official silence in the book's wake was interpreted as proof of Corso's veracity. According to William Birnes, the publisher of *UFO Magazine,* "No one in the government has decided, as of yet, to step forward to dispute anything the Colonel has said. . . . So the government is standing behind him without specifically saying that there are UFOs, a crash at Roswell, or a government program to exploit ET technology."[98] Others were not so easily persuaded. Corso could produce no paper trail to document any of his remarkable activities. Didn't Corso maintain that aliens had established bases on the moon, mutilated cattle, and buzzed American spacecraft? Was the Cold War, as the colonel wrote, merely a cover to develop a space defense system against hostile extraterrestrials? Nor did critics overlook his assertion that the Soviet KGB had infiltrated the federal government at the highest levels and his two-Oswalds theory of the Kennedy assassination. To William Moore, the book was a "work of fiction."[99] Don Schmitt was more suspicious: "Was Corso part of the disinformation? Was he used?"[100] Nevertheless, the book ran through an eighty thousand–copy first edition and within the year was in its sixth printing. Such success was inspirational, and nine more books appeared on the Roswell incident in 1997.[101]

Curiously, the air force could not let the occasion pass without comment. In a follow-up to the 1994 admission that the weather balloon story was a cover for the secret Mogul Project, the air force now proposed "to find all the facts and bring them to light." Roswell residents were confused, argued the air force investigators, and had morphed and conflated "many unrelated events" spanning more than a decade into a single incident. Rather than extraterrestrials, they had seen injured test pilots, casualties from an airplane accident, and crash-test dummies. A manned balloon mishap had caused a pilot's head to swell to alien proportions. Witnesses could easily have mistaken the dummies for aliens because their skin was a bluish latex and they had no ears, hair, or eyebrows. Pronouncing its lengthy report the last word, the air force again ruled the Roswell case closed. Americans, however, did not need the demurrals of countersubversives to realize that the investigation had been ill-advised on several counts. The release of the findings just a week before the Roswell encounter made the report appear self-serving. Its reasoning stretched belief, opening it to challenge and quick dismissal. Prosecutorial in tone, the report also dripped of self-righteousness and arrogance. The authors concluded, "It is the right—and indeed the duty—of the Air Force to challenge those who attempt to exploit these human tragedies." To do less would perpetuate "an affront to the truth" and tarnish "the proud history of the finest air force in the world." Said Stanton Friedman, "I couldn't believe the air force was so stupid."[102]

The Central Intelligence Agency had the last word that summer of 1997. The agency admitted that it and Air Force Project Blue Book had made "misleading and deceptive statements" about UFO sightings in the 1950s and 1960s to cover the activities of America's growing fleet of spy planes. Their false stories had disarmed more than one-half of the UFO reports, whose witnesses had really seen manned reconnaissance flights. To the dismay of federal officials, such admissions did not restore credibility but only deepened cynicism. Reporting the news in Salt Lake City, the Fox network anchor ended the segment asking, "Are they telling the truth now?"[103] Wrote David Wise in the New York Times: "You don't have to believe in little green men to see the admitted deception as yet another example of official lying that has eroded public trust in government."[104] Assuming their right to lie while holding fast to the privilege of secrecy, authorities had become accomplices to the plot weaving that they decried.[105]

The glow was off the Roswell incident after the golden anniversary, but entertainment executives still fan its celebrity in search of market shares. In 1998 Roswell: The Aliens Attack went quickly from theater screens to video. The movie has an attractive male and female alien couple crash near Roswell in 1947, brought down when an experimental rocket hits their spaceship. Quickly the audience realizes these extraterrestrials are up to no good. Dismissing humans as "just another colony of half-breed interplanetary trash," they activate the "Roswell Project" to reconfigure atomic bomb yields for a massive explosion that will clear Earth for colonization. When a human gets wise to the male alien's identity, the female comes clean: "He's not from around here, sweetie. And you're nothing more than a stopover in a galaxy that's worth more without your species than with them." As expected, the plot is thwarted, and the authorities cover up with new and revised explanations: "Just a weather balloon and a couple of crash dummies." The WB television network gave Roswell a high profile. Premiering in 1999, *Roswell* follows beautiful teenage aliens coming to awareness of their extraterrestrial origins while coping with growing pains and authorities determined to hunt them down. The clear message of the series is that teenage angst is a cosmic dilemma. For younger viewers, there is *Roswell Conspiracies,* a Sunday morning cartoon series. Each week it repeats the traditional scenario in a montage of scenes: a flying saucer, lightning strike, alien bodies, and official cover-up. Only recently have skeptics received equal time. After repeatedly showcasing the alien autopsy footage, the Fox network has now had it both ways, broadcasting *World's Greatest Hoaxes,* which debunked the film as a fraud. The History Channel produced "Roswell: Secrets Unveiled," dramatizing the air force version of the incident and giving short play to the "urban legend" of "diehard believers."[106]

Paralleling the Roswell story, the media focus on the UFO phenomenon has also continued, although with less intensity. In 1998 *The X-Files* went to the movies in *Fight the Future,* which updated the saga of the alien-insider conspiracy and gave the Federal Emergency Management Agency (FEMA) a more pivotal role in extraterrestrial relations. Mulder and Scully also continued their weekly encounters with the bizarre, slowly closing on the conspirators. Breaking the monopoly of the cable television networks, NBC broadcast the two-hour special *Confirmation: The Hard Evidence of Aliens Among Us?* in 1999. Viewers were well acquainted with the show's method and evidence. With alien abduction expert Whitley Strieber serving as executive producer, the program documented the removal of an alleged alien implant, claims of hidden government MJ-12 papers, and film of UFO sightings. Dramatic reenactment of the high points of UFO history and disproportionate airtime given to believers enabled the special to preach faith rather than skepticism. Meanwhile, A&E, the Discovery Channel, and even the Travel Channel kept current with UFO researchers' interests, deemphasizing Roswell for new features on crop circles, mysterious sightings, alien abductions, and Area 51.[107]

The Roswell researchers were also pulling up stakes, for the evidence was well-worn and growing cold. There were few witnesses left to interview, although "deathbed confessions" still offered hope. So, too, did an end to the official cover-up. Stanton Friedman complained: "They're playing hardball about Roswell. . . . If they weren't why would[n't] the secretary of the Air Force give a blanket amnesty to anybody who wants to talk?"[108] Meanwhile, Roswell researchers had learned from experience to be more wary of their evidence. Clearly questionable were new finds of MJ-12 documents, as many as two thousand pages produced by "anonymous sources."[109] Short on reliable material, several investigators turned to new technologies to reveal secrets. Using high-resolution digital imaging and photo enlargement, they attempted to decipher the telegram Gen. Roger Ramey was holding as he posed in the famous photographs with the weather balloon debris. The fuzzy results uncovered no smoking gun and proved ambiguous. Researchers believed they saw such words as "MJ" and "disk," and the phrases, "victims of the wreck" and "Emergency powers are needed." Others decoded "TURN OUT TO BE WEATHER BALLOONS" or were frustrated and could read nothing in "the darn things."[110] With energy draining from the Roswell search, Don Schmitt's promise of a new crash scenario aroused neither enthusiasm nor interest. In fact, Roswell revisionists gained momentum, dismissing the incident as "a red herring, diverting time and resources from research into the real UFO phenomenon" of sightings, abductions, and secret government bases.[111]

At the turn of the millennium, some in the UFO community saw their opportunity and pressed the shift from Roswell to their own agendas. The aliens were Satan's "high tech terrorists" and the rising tide of sightings proof of "burgeoning demonic activity."[112] The end time was surely at hand. More mundane, the aliens and the collaborating Illuminati were simply the latest marauders bent upon world conquest. Regardless of the scenario, the aliens proved flexible in meeting human needs.[113]

In 1999 Roswell's International U.F.O. Museum and Research Center welcomed its five hundred thousandth visitor and announced plans for a $7.5 million expansion to create a state of the art operation. Museum organizers had made great strides since 1992, when they served fewer than fifteen hundred visitors. Meanwhile, civic leaders had made the incident's anniversary an annual affair and were busy on Roswell Encounter 2000, with its theme, "On to the Millennium." Clearly, boosters were banking on Roswell's still-powerful grip on the popular imagination. Like Billy the Kid, the patron saint of nearby Lincoln, ET gave Roswell mythic meaning. Entering American folklore as the "mother of all UFO crashes," here was tangible, if elusive, proof that they were here. The strain of conspiracism only embedded Roswell more deeply in the national consciousness.[114]

The making of such an icon is a collective effort. With their eyes fixed on the heavens and fired by missionary zeal and economic necessity, grassroots men and women sifted for clues of the extraordinary kind. Their investigations uncovered hundreds of witnesses whose testimony of an alien encounter and government cover-up appeared authentic and uncontaminated. Making sense of the information and ensuring its marketability required some literary license. Selective quotation, circular reasoning, leaps of faith, exaggeration, and even fabrication marred the work but drew the attention of book publishers, documentary makers, and film producers. In the offices of the media players, the Roswell story was mainstreamed and repeatedly spun into gold. As aliens were processed into children's toys, plot weaving became a mind game offering entertainment for older generations. Authorities did their part. Contemptuous of challengers, wedded to the rituals of secrecy, and occasionally incompetent or malevolent, federal officials encouraged the conspiracy thinking of their adversaries. Robbed of historical and bureaucratic context, official actions became evidence of both the existence of a shadow government and the truth of the Roswell incident. In the end, Americans would look for Roswell only on a map captioned with a conspiratorial legend.

Mainstreaming Conspiracism

The Kennedy assassination, MIAS, radiation experiments
on terminal patients, Watergate, Iran-Contra, Roswell, the
Tuskegee experiments, where will it all end?
—Fox Mulder to "Deep Throat"

During the second half of the twentieth century, the alarm of American countersubversion grew louder and more insistent. It reached a crescendo in the 1990s, when a chorus of messengers gave warning, their pleas for defense merging, resonating, and reinforcing. Their construction of conspiracy, only loosely tethered to the legal definition, was broad and multifaceted. Diverse enemies, the conspiracy-minded claimed, had entered the gates and now bent history to their will. If some conspiracists could be dismissed as eccentrics, large numbers of women and men had awakened to the threat, convinced that secret groups plotted the assassination of a president, sought the suicide of the black community, or planned world domination in league with Satan. These fears crossed gender, racial, and socioeconomic lines to mass a broad constituency responsive to challengers and hostile to official explanations. The public ownership of such beliefs refutes an explanation that roots countersubversion in private paranoia. By the end of the century, conspiracism had become the watchword for a new nationalism, consistent with American traditions, that made belief the criterion of community.

Although conspiracy theorists hold center stage, their influence comes in relation to the drama's supporting cast. Long ago, media actors discovered the appeal of conspiracy and made it an audience favorite. Film and television confirmed and spread tales and even departed from the script to improvise imaginative and convincing scenarios. Frequent viewing prepared men and women to accept conspiracy possibilities while validating those who dreamed subversive nightmares. With Americans well steeped in the imagery, conspiracists were assured that their bid for authority would be neither brief nor tedious. Countersubversives, meanwhile, were in tight embrace with their targets, each maneuvering zealously to defend group interests while pressing for new leverage. Reaching for weapons, the conspiracy-minded discounted historical, bureaucratic, and idiosyncratic circumstances to construct a past record of deliberate abuse, with the present offering fresh hints of betrayal. Seemingly in confirmation, the powerful raised the cry of conspiracy to brand their adversaries as enemies of the people and rob their claims of legitimacy. Power, similarly, may breed contempt. Authorities comfortable in its use grew jealous of their prerogatives, deceptive, distant, and scornful not only of challengers but of citizens. Such arrogance made them tempting targets.

Conspiracy, wrote Oliver Stone, "is a bit like the bugs chomping in the grass in our backyards—it's everywhere, a natural outgrowth of human behavior, wherever or whenever people congregate to form societies."[1] Many Americans, like Stone, feared the blight that threatened their lives and country. The republic was under siege by the advocates of the New World Order, Satan, Jews, extraterrestrial invaders, or the insiders of the shadow government. Determined and ruthless, the plotters readily offered up American lives and sovereignty in sacrifice for power and gold. Control of the federal government only made them more menacing.

The risk, however, was not restricted to these encompassing plots. Taking an expansive view of the danger, Americans found conspiracy ubiquitous, and little was thought to escape the reach of hidden hands. Thus extraterrestrials were not the only group believed to be stealing children. Americans discovered a satanic underground that conspired to abduct young girls and abuse them in demonic rituals. Proctor and Gamble changed its corporate logo after charges that it displayed devilish symbols. Did Neil Armstrong walk on the moon, or was the world "Apolloscammed" by a terrestrial stroll through a movie soundstage? Allegations of economic conspiracies, frequent throughout American history, have punctuated recent decades. Spurred by the fear of modern plagues, pharmaceutical companies were accused of concealing breakthroughs and inflating prices on lifesaving drugs. The oil companies, conspiracists claimed, surely plotted to fix prices and keep them at inflated levels. Oil companies also were in collusion with rubber manufacturers and automobile makers to cripple mass transit systems. The conspiracy-minded found the death of nuclear plant worker Karen Silkwood suspicious and demanded an investigation of the industry to uncover responsibility and negligence.

Such accusations took on new life when juries found that the tobacco companies had conspired to hide the addictiveness and health hazards of cigarettes. Similarly, customer complaints that music recording and distribution companies were engaged in a price-fixing conspiracy were validated when federal investigators filed suit. Weren't the bombings at the World Trade Center in 1993 and the federal building in Oklahoma City in 1995 officially exposed as conspiracies? As *Newsweek* columnist Jonathan Alter cautioned, "Where it gets tricky is that even paranoids have real enemies, and even conspiracy theories can occasionally turn out to be true."[2]

Tragedy focused conspiracists, and Americans rarely closed their eyes when celebrities were involved. Initially, few questioned the coroner's finding that Marilyn Monroe had committed suicide. John Kennedy's assassination, however, suddenly gave greater meaning to the passing of the Hollywood actress. In the late 1960s, pop music fans fretted over the disappearance of Beatle Paul McCartney, searching for clues that he had died and his death had been covered up. Others are convinced that they have seen Elvis and that his death was elaborately faked to secure his seclusion. Within hours of Princess Diana's death, internet sites appeared offering conspiracy theories to explain the tragedy. Americans participated in the worldwide hunt for the plotters, narrowing the search by asking, Was it a royal intrigue? Did the merchants of death silence her to stop the anti–land mine campaign? Was her death faked so that, like Elvis, she could finally escape the paparazzi? If less grand than the major theories and often the substance of parlor games, such thinking did reveal the high comfort level Americans have with conspiracism.[3]

Political and government leaders, of course, figured prominently in conspiracy thinking. Did a brainwashed Sirhan Sirhan have an accomplice when he killed Bobby Kennedy? Did all the bullets fired that night come from Sirhan's gun? Who was the woman in the polka-dot dress? The family of Martin Luther King, Jr., is convinced that confessed assassin James Earl Ray was an innocent patsy, fronting for the same groups that had ordered John Kennedy's execution. Validation came thirty years after the civil rights leader's death, when a Tennessee jury returned a conspiracy verdict in a civil suit. The attempt on the life of presidential hopeful George Wallace in 1972 raised the question, Who benefited? In the context of the Watergate scandals, the conspiracy-minded tailed the plotters to the Nixon White House. For some, Watergate had the markings of a coup d'état. The search for culprits narrowed to the Rockefeller family, fresh from their manipulation of oil prices. Who other than brothers David and Nelson Rockefeller had both opportunity and motive to seize power? Ronald Reagan's 1980 victory over President Jimmy Carter raised suspicion. Did Reagan envoys strike a secret deal with the Iranian militants to hold American hostages until after the November election in exchange for future deliveries of military hardware and the release of frozen assets? Long after peace, the Vietnam war continued to haunt Americans. In the rush to retreat, were American soldiers left behind? Alleged sightings in the 1970s and 1980s suggested conspiracy and moral culpability. Vietnam veterans also charged government authorities with covering up the health hazards of Agent Orange, a defoliant used to clear jungle during the war. Ailing Persian Gulf war veterans would make similar accusations, certain that the U.S. military dodged liability by masking the combatants' exposure to toxic chemicals and nerve gas. When the Pentagon reported the disappearance of its chemical warfare logs detailing incidents during the war in 1991, the conspiracy-minded were not surprised.[4]

Conspiracy accusations poured down on President Bill Clinton. Tracking back to his college days, investigators found Clinton in the company of members of the CIA, the Council on Foreign Relations, and the Trilateral Commission. As governor of Arkansas, he had claimed a share of the take from money-laundering, gun-running, and drug-trafficking operations. The trail often went cold, perhaps because of the "statistically improbable" number of deaths of his associates. Clinton's record of misdeeds followed him to

Washington. Did White House aide Vincent Foster, the keeper of the Whitewater portfolio, commit suicide, or was he murdered to cover up Clinton crimes? A *Time/CNN* poll found two-thirds of Americans wary of the official ruling. Secretary of Commerce Ron Brown was another casualty. "Like Vincent Foster," concluded countersubversive Nicholas Guarino, "he knew too much . . . where all the money went for the pay-offs, bribes, scams, money laundering, cover ups, and side deals."[5] When charges of sexual misconduct were added to the barrage, Hillary Clinton rose to her husband's defense and reacted in kind. She explained before a national audience on NBC's *Today* show: "Look at the very people who are involved in this. They have popped up in other settings. The great story here . . . is this vast right-wing conspiracy that has been conspiring against my husband since the day he announced for president."[6] As proof, Hillary Clinton had material researched by the Democratic National Committee and issued from the White House counsel's office. The official release traced a "communication stream of conspiracy commerce" that showed how conservative think tanks had "bounced" fringe stories into mainstream publications for national distribution.[7]

Counterattack slowed the momentum of government critics only briefly. Speculation continued about the 1996 crash of TWA flight 800 that killed 223 people just after takeoff from Kennedy International Airport. Most prominent among the several conspiracy theories was a government cover-up of a missile test that had gone tragically awry. Government technicians certainly should have corrected the Y2K computer problem before it reached crisis stage. Who or what kept them from performing their duties promptly? In the twilight of the Clinton presidency, new conspiracy theories were spawned in Miami, Florida. The American relatives of six-year-old Elián González cried conspiracy, distraught after federal agents seized the Cuban boy from their home. Comparing photographs taken before and after the raid, his cousin was convinced that it was "not Elián. Look how short the hair looks when he was taken and look how long the hair is in the picture that they show today." U.S. Congressman Lincoln Díaz-Balart, who represents the Miami area, was convinced the photographs revealed the telltale signs of "brainwashing. . . . I think the drugging has already begun."[8]

The Clinton saga raised the heat in a decade already pulsing with conspiracism. Sophisticated, interwoven, increasing in frequency, and mutually reinforcing, conspiracy theories formed a tight interpretive web that frustrated contradiction. The enemy appeared everywhere and was advancing. Filmmaker Oliver Stone set the mood in 1991 with *JFK,* and the decadelong news flash of released information by the Assassination Records Review Board fixed American attention without closing the case. The confrontations at Ruby Ridge and Waco roused fears of federal terrorism and daily life in the New World Order. Lawsuits followed in the wake of both incidents and made headlines for years. Even after a jury exonerated federal agents of misconduct at Waco, Branch Davidian Clive Doyle was convinced suspicion would not recede: "It's kind of like the Kennedy assassination. You have the official version and you have what everybody else believes."[9] Nation of Islam minister Louis Farrakhan occupied the national stage in the 1990s, commanding the spotlight during the Million Man March on Washington, D.C., and again at the end of the decade. Feeding on Jewish and black anger, he repeatedly refused to back down from his charges of conspiracy. Excitement built for years in anticipation of the fiftieth anniversary of the Roswell crash, even when reports of alien abductions and crop circles competed for airtime. Overshadowing the decade, as it had the entire postwar period, was the quickening countdown to Armageddon. Rapture was always just an instant away, with the Antichrist impatiently biding his time in the shadows. Mainly, conspiracy allegations came from the grass roots, for the enemies were now within, having captured core institutions. If no longer in the forefront, the powerful still could be heard tolling the bell of countersubversion when it served their purposes.

The internet was critical to the rising intensity. With computer and modem, tens of millions of women and men daily accessed the World Wide Web, and its thousands of conspiracy sites became popular draws. Conspiracy megasites saved browsing time, allowing users at the click of the mouse to link to their plot of choice, whether Roswell, Waco, Area 51, Armageddon, New World Order, or Kennedy assassination, among others. Such web architecture suggested the interrelation of intrigue and perhaps even the perception of master manipulators. For students of the internet, evolutionary biologist Richard Dawkins's concept of the meme offered insight. Reproducing briskly and disseminating broadly, conspiracy theories mirrored epidemics that spread indiscriminately and evolve in unpredictable ways. As Richard Thieme observed, the meme of "Roswell," circulating and seeding progeny, thus became another of the many "contagious ideas that replicate like viruses from mind to mind. The internet is like a Petri dish in which memes multiply rapidly."[10] Proprietorship of memes defined communities governed by the principles of cyberdemocracy. Onscreen, everyone interfaced anonymously, and no privilege was accorded class, race, or gender. Still, there were limits, and dissenters were noticeably absent from the chat rooms. These trends concerned opinion shapers, who issued repeated warnings in the 1990s about the rapid breeding and mainstreaming of the messages. The mushrooming of suspicion also distressed John Birchers, sure that the static would distract patriots from the real enemy. In fact, they were convinced that the multiplication of theories "may itself be considered *prima facie* evidence of a larger conspiracy."[11]

Suggesting the future of conspiracism, 150 demonstrators gathered near Area 51 in Nevada on the sixth day of the sixth month of 1998 to protest the "evil oligarchy" in Washington. Commencing at 6 A.M. to complete the symbolic code, organizer Norio Hayakawa informed his audience, "This is not about UFOS. It's about something more serious. It's about the abuses of civil rights by the government. It's about unnecessary secrecy . . . and its about the New World Order." Follow-up speaker Anthony Hilder closed the circle. Federal agents had masterminded the Oklahoma City bombing to complete the trilogy of terrorism that included Ruby Ridge and Waco. Accused bomber Timothy McVeigh was as innocent as Lee Harvey Oswald.[12]

In spite of the widespread tolerance and even acceptance of conspiracy thinking, Americans remain dubious about the messengers. Extremists in the conspiracy community may leave a strong, negative impression that invalidates their cause. Also, authorities have often nullified countersubversive challenges with dismissive strategies. The recent film *Conspiracy Theory* (1997) mirrored popular attitudes. Actor Mel Gibson portrays the theorist in stereotype—marginal, friendless, and clearly suffering mental disorder. Obsessively, he rapid-fires mind games of intrigue and collusion about black helicopters, infiltrating U.N. troops, and government-implanted tracking devices. But the audience has seen this script before and knows, with star Gibson in the lead, to hold skepticism in check. Eventually Gibson routs the conspirators and traces his paranoia to mind-control experiments performed by a secret agency of the U.S. government. The truth had set him free and again stopped the plotters in their tracks. It also tempered viewers' ambivalence; perhaps in the rambling of the paranoid can be discerned the reality that lies hidden beneath.

Conspiracy thinking does not thrive in isolation. It takes power in the resonance of community. At the core are those who make countersubversion their occupation. They discover the plots, trace the intrigue, and sound the alarm in book, film, website, and video. Absorbed full-time with the details, their conspiracism is a habit of belief both involuntary and addictive. Commitment to nation or race or truth drives them, but financial need presses them equally hard. In a highly competitive market, a flair for packaging confers advantage. The mix of dedication, ambition, and entrepreneurship ensures intensity and a continuous stream of product, sequel, and rerun. The heart of the community is a male preserve inhabited by intelligent and creative individuals like Robert Welch, Pat Robertson, Oliver Stone, Louis Farrakhan, Bill Moore, and Stanton Friedman. Well educated and immersed in the organizational subculture, they are nevertheless disparate in background and political, social, and religious orientation. Their personal histories reveal fixation with a cause, but not mental disorder or marginality. Nor is the pursuit of conspiracism an end. In their hands, countersubversion is the weapon of choice in single-minded bids to save the world. The degree rather than the kind of their suspicion sets them apart from decision makers and other activists. Integrity, skills, and charismatic talents only enhance the appeal. Women at the center of the grassroots network play supporting roles. Reflecting the American social context, Phyllis Schlafly, Mary Relfe, Sylvia Meagher, and Linda Howe gained recognition but found their climb both steeper and slower. Women achieve equality as countersubversives not in leadership circles but only in the ranks of believers.

Moving away from the core, the focus on conspiracy blurs. Suspicion gradually becomes less intense and familiarity with plot details increasingly uncertain. Active believers digest anticonspiracy materials, discuss them, and put their own twists on plots. The more distracted rely on experts to interpret and synthesize information, with video or print sources a matter of taste and involvement. With further distance, perceptions of betrayal become more important to commitment than knowledge of its specifics. Theories bounce from the conspiracy-minded subculture when the national media homogenize them for the curious. On the banks of the mainstream, the message may overflow barriers of class, race, and gender and envelop the majority. Shared fears and common belief systems concerning the Antichrist, the assassination of John Kennedy, and the plot against black America have found such majorities and clearly built a consensus.

Conspiracy theories offer much to believers. If slippery in their logic and often careless of facts and assumptions, they order the random and make consistent the paradoxical. Theories find purpose in tragedy and clarity in ambiguity. Strength builds with repetition, and conditioning makes these tools hard to relinquish. Belief also enfranchises. Those distant from power may sense a loss of control, stripped of authority over the basic decisions that shape their lives. Feeling unable to effect change, they withdraw. Dramatic declines in political participation and membership in voluntary organizations suggest this broad retreat and the widespread apathy that has plagued millennial America. For many, conspiracy thinking proves an antidote to powerlessness. It lifts the despair of vulnerability and arms believers with the knowledge to understand and defeat the enemy. Whether men and women act on the information is less important than their sense of revitalization in discovering the truth.

Nor does ownership entail great risk, for conspiracism is a national tradition. For centuries, Americans have eagerly conjured up enemies to their experiment. Saints working in the vineyard of the Lord naturally assumed devils bent upon thwarting their holy labors. Ethnic and religious diversity fueled suspicion of enemies within, still loyal to king and pope. Whites maintained the racial order with conspiracy thinking while blacks used it for self-defense. Democratic chants condemned elites for plotting secret machinations to silence the people's voice. Jealous of their liberty, Americans have long been suspicious of federal intrigue. In support, they quoted Henry David Thoreau's *Civil Disobedience* (1849): "How does it become a man to behave toward this American government today? I answer that he cannot without disgrace be associated with it."[13] Americans also heeded warnings from the other side of the political spectrum. Arizona Senator Barry Goldwater declared in the 1960s, "Government represents power in the hands of some men to control and regulate the lives of other men. And power, as Lord Acton said, *corrupts* men. 'Absolute power,' he added, 'corrupts absolutely.'"[14] President Ronald Reagan echoed Goldwater in his 1989 farewell address: "As government expands, liberty contracts."[15] In personalizing the danger, countersubversion insulated the revered institutions of national life. Consistent with American experience, the solution lay not in revolution but in reform that chased the outlaws from the temple. Optimism fueled this effort, with conspiracists certain that the tide would eventually turn in their favor. As John Bircher Robert Lee wrote: "A point to keep in mind regarding the 'conspiracy theory' is that it offers far more hope for the future than does the 'accident' alternative. After all, if our major problems have reached their present crisis due to mere chance and/or well-intentioned mistakes in judgement by honorable men, the outlook for the future is indeed bleak, for we have little or no control over the situation. On the other hand, if these problems are . . . the result of . . . the willful actions of a relatively small clique of conspirators, there is hope that sufficient exposure can eventually rout the troublemakers and neutralize their influence."[16]

In the struggle for power, conspiracism proved an effective and flexible tactic. Robert Welch, a latter-day Paul Revere, used it to awaken Americans to alleged treason. His conspiracy thinking demanded a rededication to patriotic ideals and a new determination to ensure domestic tranquility and secure the blessings of liberty. Pat Robertson drew inspiration from the Bible to facilitate conversion by raising the demon of conspiracy. The end time was near, and evil not only darkened America but threatened the world. Rescue meant that the born-again had to accept both the divinity of Christ and the profanity of the Antichrist. Oliver Stone fought for authority with conspiracy as counterhistory. The assassination in

Dallas snuffed out the promise of a new beginning. It ended the Kennedy reign, and America's Camelot was betrayed from within. If only the president had lived, the nation would have been spared foreign tragedy and domestic anguish. Louis Farrakhan, like Robert Welch, made conspiracy thinking a means to social-movement mobilization and community power. His passionate style drew taut the battle lines, clarifying the identities of followers while targeting opponents. Meanwhile, Farrakhan's uncompromising stand and fearlessness in provoking the enemy proved effective in deflecting challenges to his authority. Stanton Friedman, Bill Moore, and the other Roswell researchers made conspiracy essential to their search for evidence of extraterrestrial contact. The shadow government was capable of all things, but the people of Earth demanded that the investigators succeed. Those who suggest that such examples are proof of personality disorder or status grievance provide little insight. Conspiracy thinking is grounded in real issues of power and authority and equips groups with the will and means to contest them.

What makes the conspiracist's claims believable? Why are some theories more credible than others? Experience conditions acceptance. The past reveals many examples of conspiracy, and new allegations that mirror such happenings fuel suspicion. Accusations gain even greater credence when anchored in personal and group histories. Countersubversives realize that details make their case. Eyewitnesses or those assumed to have firsthand knowledge, exact measurements of time and place, and the intricate interweaving of people and events are the meat of their theories. By fine tuning this matter of the ordinary, conspiracists are able to create a seamless web that defies obvious contradiction. Emotional involvement enhances the salience of conspiracy as well. The death of a young president and the sight of his grieving widow and children cry out for meaning. A choice between eternal life and damnation is also heavily freighted and heightens susceptibility. The messengers themselves have an impact on the credibility of conspiracy. Americans trust ministers of God, especially when they can bolster their assertions with sources as authoritative as the Bible or the Qur'an. Mixing messages of self-help, family solidarity, and group pride with conspiracy thinking similarly cements commitment. Filmmakers may create images so powerful that rules of logic and evidence are lost in the rush to believe. In the absence of equally provocative presentation of the official version, these pictures become the new reality. Countersubversives, meanwhile, realize that the public gives them broad latitude in making their case. Standing as the people's champions against shadow government or selfish interests, they come to contention with hearts pure and hands clean.

These men and women are necessary but not sufficient to explain the power of conspiracy thinking. A culture of conspiracy exists because their charges resonate with the words and deeds of those who shape opinion in modern America. The national media confirm their pleas and make conspiracism essential to an understanding of history and society. The federal government, at the same time, conditions the conspiracy response. Official behavior substantiates charges of intrigue. In legitimizing fears, authorities spent the public's faith and bankrupted trust. Subject to their collective influence, conspiracism poses a determined threat to the future of the American experiment.

Conspiracy stories choked the twentieth-century information stream. Supplementing nonfiction works about real conspiracies is a rich collection of novels. Authors Thomas Pynchon, William Burroughs, Don DeLillo, Joseph Heller, Joan Didion, John Grisham, Robert Ludlum, Kurt Vonnegut, Norman Mailer, Ken Kesey, and Margaret Atwood, among others, relied on conspiracy to snare readers. Conspiracy specialists Jonathan Vankin and John Whalen found the market so profitable that they enjoyed repeated printings of books revealing the fifty, then the sixty, then the seventy "greatest conspiracies of all time." Imitators flocked to get a piece of the action. Supermarkets made tabloids readily available for those who demanded weekly updates on the changing landscape of intrigue. Each night, fifteen million listeners tuned to *Coast to Coast AM with Art Bell* for the latest conspiracy alerts. Scores of other talk radio hosts found niches during workday commutes and weekends.[17]

Television's lineup of spy, crime, and space dramas added the spice of conspiracy to bring variety to the weekly fare. Conspiracism was central to *The X-Files,* which helped feed the intensity of the 1990s. The insiders of the shadow government surely had their hands full with cover-ups of extraterrestrial contact and plots to assassinate national leaders. Yet each episode found agents Scully and Mulder peeling away new layers of intrigue. Senator Joseph McCarthy's anticommunist crusade during the Red Scare of the 1950s was nothing but a ruse, a cover for the alien-cloning project. The puppet masters programed zombielike "Manchurian candidates," who killed on command. To create the perfect soldier, the insiders' surgeons operated on unknowing subjects, eradicating permanently the need for sleep. Iraqi dictator Saddam Hussein was a "government plant" who "rattles his saber when we need a distraction."[18] Meanwhile, the insiders still had time to manage the Rodney King trial, hand-pick Oscar Award winners, fix sporting events, and assign Monica Lewinsky to the White House. Adding more complexity, the show raised doubt about the core conspiracy stories it had been telling for years. In "Patient X," Mulder attains a higher consciousness: "The conspiracy is not to hide the existence of extraterrestrials. It is to make people believe in it so completely that they question nothing."[19] This insight is developed in "All Lies Lead to the Truth," when Mulder realizes, "For four years, we've been nothing more than pawns in a game; that it was a lie from the beginning." Following the "lie to find the truth, to find . . . the enemies within," he uncovers the military-industrial complex at the root. The cigarette-smoking man explains: "The U.S. military saw a good thing in '47 when the Roswell story broke. The more we deny it the more people believed it was true. Aliens had landed, a made-to-order cover story for generals looking to develop the national war chest."[20] Yet this epiphany brought no relief to viewers who still looked for a riddle within the riddle and a plot within the plot. At the beginning of the new century and new season, they were convinced that the truth was still out there. Less confusing were offerings on the cable television networks, which ran and reran countersubversion to high market shares. With conspiracy still profitable, executives were always looking for fall season prospects.[21]

Hollywood's influence, spanning the century, was even greater. Filmmakers used conspiracy as a plot line from the beginning and did much to condition Americans to suspect hidden groups behind events. Conspiracy attended *The Birth of a Nation* (1915), the film industry's first blockbuster. Breaking from the world of nickelodeons, D. W. Griffith presented the Reconstruction era according to a

Pat Bagley caught the public mood in a *Salt Lake Tribune* cartoon published in 1999. In cases such as the Oklahoma City bombing, the suspicious gave more credence to Fox Mulder of *The X-Files* than U.S. Attorney General Janet Reno.

Courtesy of Pat Bagley

southern conspiracist interpretation. Plotting against President Abraham Lincoln's policy of mercy, Radical Republican Austin Stoneman and his "mulatto" allies scheme to "Africanize" the South under black and carpetbagger rule. In counterconspiracy ride the hooded knights of the Ku Klux Klan, who not only rescue the South and the union but ensure the purity of the white race. Conspiracy survived the death of the silent movies and played well in the 1930s. Director Frank Capra's civic lessons *Mr. Smith Goes to Washington* (1939) and *Meet John Doe* (1941) outlined American ideals in opposition to the sinister forces of conspiracy. In the former, Jimmy Stewart plays Jefferson Smith, an innocent abroad in Washington, D.C., cynically named to fill a vacated U.S. Senate seat. His plan to create a national boys' camp collides with a conspiracy to profit fraudulently at the public's expense. Refusing to "play ball," Smith is implicated and nearly flattened by the "steamroller stuff" of the state political bosses, who manipulate public opinion and even the Senate. Truth wins out, however, when a key conspirator exposes the plot. In *Meet John Doe*, a newspaper gimmick to raise circulation becomes a plot to dupe the American people into electing an unscrupulous tycoon to the White House. Again, there are casualties, but the hidden hands "pulling the strings" are exposed, the plot thwarted, and the republic saved. Capra's message was clear. Freedom was fragile and the price of protecting it high. Americans had learned their lessons, and with the coming of World War II rarely doubted why they fought.

Conspiracy played well in all film genres. It was standard in science fiction films, with space invaders occasionally finding human allies eager to join their conspiracy and betray Earth. Satan and his minions were naturals for conspiracy roles in horror movies. Plot weaving was also an obvious device in crime films. As the term suggests, gangsters ran in groups and conspired to break the law, whether local or national. *Kansas City Confidential* (1952), *Las Vegas Story* (1952), *New York Confidential* (1955), and *Chicago Syndicate* (1955) spoke to audience interests, with viewers surely noting the resemblance between the denizens of the crime and Communist underworlds. In addition to common criminals, Hollywood showcased a diverse collection of murderers, thieves, and corrupt authorities. In *Bad Day at Black Rock* (1954), a suspicious stranger visits Adobe Flat and exposes the town's secret—the cover-up of the murder of a Japanese American supposedly evacuated to a relocation camp during the war. Cover-ups by crooked police officials were typical fare. *The Big Heat* (1953), *Serpico* (1973), *Witness* (1985), and *The Untouchables* (1987) tell the stories of honest cops bent upon justice regardless of the consequences. In *Blow Up* (1966), *The Conversation* (1974), *Chinatown* (1974), and *Night Moves* (1975) the task falls to men outside of civil service ranks.

Movies of international intrigue attracted large audiences. The classic *Manchurian Candidate* (1962) unravels an elaborate Communist plot to capture the United States from within. During the Korean War, Communists trap an American patrol and subject the captured soldiers to Soviet and Chinese brainwashing. Their purpose is to condition one soldier to murder on command. His prime target is a candidate for the presidency whose elimination will enable a man more amenable to the Communists' will to assume the top spot on the ticket. The conspiracy goes not only to the highest levels of the political system but to the heart of the American family: the assassin's secret handler is his mother. Through a series of motion pictures, British spy James Bond thwarted the drive of S.P.E.C.T.R.E.—Special Executive for Counterintelligence, Terrorism, Revenge, and Extortion—for world power. In *Missing* (1981) Jack Lemmon plays a distraught father attempting to find his son, who disappeared in the wake of a South American coup d'état. U.S. embassy officials are sympathetic but are clearly covering up their involvement in the overthrow of the government. *The Package* (1989) makes Gene Hackman a pawn in a joint Russian-American intelligence scheme to assassinate the Soviet secretary general. The Soviet official survives, as does the multinational conspiracy community, which continues the search for new assassination projects.

In Westerns, conspirators not only rode in outlaw gangs but played a variety of roles. In *They Died With Their Boots On* (1941), Errol Flynn portrays Gen. George Custer, enraged by a business plot to open the Sioux Indians' sacred Black Hills to white settlement. "It's a conspiracy," he cries, "to break the peace treaty." Ensuring that his death at the Little Big Horn will not be in vain, he writes on the eve of the battle "a dying declaration" to his wife, revealing the intrigue and expressing the wish that the Indians have the "right to existence." The dead don't rest when the guilty remain unpunished in *High Plains Drifter* (1972). Clint Eastwood's ghost chastises the citizens of Lago who murdered their sheriff for threatening to reveal that the mine that secured community prosperity was illegally dug on government property. *Silverado* (1985) transforms the familiar land war between cattle barons and homesteaders into a conspiracy when settlers are murdered and the claims office burned.

Plot making provides an occasional backdrop for the death and dying of war movies. *Attack* (1956) finds the battle-weary infantrymen of Fragile Fox Company at the mercy of "gutless" Captain Cooney. Friendly fire eliminates the danger, but the battalion commander attempts to cover his negligence with promises of a promotion and "phoney medals." Truth wins out when division headquarters is made privy to his scheme. The *Rambo* (1982, 1985, 1988) and *Missing in Action* (1984, 1985) series were premised on betrayal in Vietnam and suggest that victory eluded American troops because Washington bureaucrats stabbed them in the back. Conspiracy also appeared in fatigues during peacetime. Demi Moore is *G.I. Jane* (1997), accused of lesbianism by the secretary of the navy and a U.S. senator bent upon preventing the closing of military bases. *The General's Daughter* (1998) invokes article 32 of the Code of Military Justice, which makes it a conspiracy to conceal criminal activity. The general under indictment has concealed the rape of his soldier-daughter for the good of the army and West Point and to promote his career.

A new film genre focusing on government conspiracies emerged in the second half of the twentieth century. In *Seven Days in May* (1964), Burt Lancaster plays a disgruntled general angry with the president for signing a nuclear test ban treaty that leaves the United States vulnerable to Soviet attack. National security presses him to a military solution, but his bid to oust the president is defeated. Lancaster also appeared in *Twilight's Last Gleaming* (1977), this time as a military officer who threatens to launch a missile strike unless the president makes full disclosure of a secret document that explains the real reason America intervened in Vietnam. The United States, he knows, pursued the war only to maintain its credibility, "to prove we were capable of inhuman acts" and in spite of intelligence that the war was unwinnable. The president and Lancaster are expendable at the conclusion, and authorities keep the document under wraps. The CIA is the subject of *Three Days of the Condor* (1975). Robert Redford is an agency analyst who inadvertently discovers "another CIA inside the CIA." The rogue group is planning Middle East oil intrigues and attempts to plug information leaks by murdering everyone in Redford's research unit. As a last resort, Redford approaches the *New York Times* with the story, but he has no answer when asked, "How do you know they'll print it?" On a related mission, a renegade CIA cell in *Chain Reaction* (1996) blows up a university lab to secure a chemical formula that would end the nation's dependence on foreign oil. As *Eraser* (1996) demonstrates, even the witness protection program offers no safe haven from a government conspiracy that encompasses the Defense Department, the FBI, and assorted corporate accomplices. Still, these adversaries prove no match for Arnold Schwarzenegger, who protects his charge and delivers her in time for an appearance before congressional investigators. The secretary of defense must die in Brian De Palma's *Snake Eyes* (1998) because he opposes contractors and military officers who want a missile system approved and funded. Nicolas Cage discovers the plot and confirms the charge with the audience: "Five people are a conspiracy, right?"

Often, the White House was at the center of the action. *The Pelican Brief* (1993), based on the John Grisham thriller, identifies the president as a coconspirator in an oilman's plot to assassinate uncooperative Supreme Court justices too willing to rule in favor of environmental interests. With the offending judges out of the way and the FBI covering his tracks, the chief executive plans appointments more amenable to the needs of his biggest campaign contributor. When sex turns violent, the president in *Absolute Power* (1996) depends on Secret Service agents to dispose of the body and other incriminating evidence. The presidential murderer assures the agents that their actions "show that you love your country." For the same reason, the Secret Service covers the killing of the chief executive under a finding of suicide. "Everyone's lying around here," declares Wesley Snipes, the detective called to the White House to investigate *Murder at 1600* (1997). This time, insiders use the scandal to force the president to resign, elevating a vice president who will redeem national honor by ordering a raid on North Korea to free American hostages. The Secret Service proves more fickle in *Air Force One* (1997) when an agent conspires with Russian nationalists to hijack the president's plane. *Shadow Conspiracy* (1996) seemed to have developed its story line from the screenplays of *The Manchurian Candidate, Seven Days in May,* and *JFK.* A controversial plan to slash the defense budget puts the president in harm's way, and everyone from his chief of staff to the speaker of the House of Representatives is in on the assassination plot. In *Wag the Dog* (1997), presidential aides fabricate a foreign crisis to distract the public from a White House sex scandal. Knowing that "war is show business," the spin doctors naturally turn to Hollywood to stage-manage the crisis. *Dave* (1993) scripts the Secret Service to recruit a lookalike to stand in for the incapacitated president for "security purposes." As the plot evolves, the mentally deranged vice president is bypassed, a capable aide is appointed to the office, and Dave is ruled medically unable to govern, thus putting the country back on course. In a cameo appearance, Oliver Stone plays to character, noting inconsistencies in presidential demeanor and telling Larry King, "Yes, I think it is a conspiracy."

Few topics escaped a conspiracy spin. In *Jaws* (1975) Amity town boosters press the police chief to conceal a shark attack on an unfortunate tourist. "We need summer dollars," they cry, and insist that the incident was probably a boating accident. When a shark is caught, the mayor has it disposed of before an autopsy can be performed to determine whether it is the killer. The tourists go back into the water, and a second attack prompts an angry mother to expose the cover-up: "You knew there was a shark out there. You knew it was dangerous. But you let people go swimming anyway." Feminism proved too much for the husbands of *The Stepford Wives* (1975). They conspire to bring back the good old days by transforming their wives into docile automatons. *Who Framed Roger Rabbit* (1988) explains the birth of the Los Angeles freeway system as part of a plot to destroy Toontown. Roger Rabbit defeats the evil Judge Doom, but apparently fails to forestall urban sprawl. *The China Syndrome* (1979) and *Silkwood* (1983) convinced viewers that nuclear plants were dangerous to their health, with operators concealing safety hazards to pad profits. Other films profiled corporate conspiracies in broadcast news (*Network,* 1976), the tobacco industry (*The Insider,* 1999), and chemical production (*Erin Brockovich,* 2000). *Extreme Measures* (1996) indicted doctors in a scheme to abduct the homeless for medical experimentation. Sandra Bullock gets caught in *The Net* (1995) when conspirators erase her true identity and tag her with a criminal record. A secret society that is easier to join than leave attracts upwardly mobile college students in *The Skulls* (1999). Viewers shake their heads knowingly when a pledge disregards his friend's advice, "If it's secret and elite, it can't be good." From the American heartland come the right-wing conspirators of *Betrayed* (1988). Tom Berenger is the point man for an assassination plot to overthrow ZOG, only to be gunned down by the FBI agent he loves. *Arlington Road* (1999) pursues the same theme. The antigovernment conspirators have moved to the suburbs and live across the street. During the suspicious nineties, even *Sleepy Hollow* (1999) became a tale of conspiracy.

Packagers of popular culture had certainly drunk deeply at the conspiracist well. Novelists, tabloid journalists, and television writers turned repeatedly to countersubversives for inspiration and material and disseminated their ideas widely. Filmmakers proved especially adept and flexible in raising the public's consciousness of conspiracy. Media members, however, did not simply deliver the news. Leaving their mark on the message, they joined the debate with powerful word and picture images that energized belief and set the mood of suspicion. Yet an atmosphere alive with conspiracism required one other element. Feeding apprehension were federal actions that legitimized conspiracy cries, eroded accountability, and tarnished those who claimed authority.

While media actors and countersubversives harmonized, federal officials elicited a fear response from the American people. To wage Cold War, authorities mobilized the home front with the rhetoric of conspiracy. Politicians cried conspiracy for partisan advantage, and bureaucrats used it to leverage power. Conspiracy also proved, Supreme Court Justice Learned Hand observed, to be "the darling of the modern prosecutor's nursery."[22] The crime was in the agreement, vague or specific, not the performance of an unlawful act. Thus the government had only to prove intent to secure a con-

Readers have relied on the supermarket tabloid *Weekly World News* to serve up generous portions of conspiracy information. Editions repeatedly warn of government cover-ups regarding contact with alien visitors, the New World Order, and the rise of the Antichrist. The *News* also creatively merges conspiracy scenarios, here showing a "professor" who claimed that a secret group within the federal government plotted the assassination of President John F. Kennedy to prevent disclosure of the extraterrestrial presence on Earth.

viction. In conspiracy cases, courts gave wide latitude to prosecutors in introducing evidence, making exceptions to the hearsay rule, and choosing jurisdiction. Joint trials, moreover, enhanced the probability of guilt by association, for each of the accused was liable for the statements and deeds of the other defendants.[23]

A succession of widely publicized trials validated public suspicion and contributed to the atmosphere of conspiracism. On the docket in the 1940s and 1950s were conspiracy charges against members of the American Communist Party and atomic spies Julius and Ethel Rosenberg. Officials accused the Chicago Seven of conspiring to cross state lines to incite riots at the 1968 Democratic Convention. The Nixon administration alleged that the Harrisburg Seven had participated in an antidraft conspiracy, while Ku Klux Klansmen, neo-Nazis, and members of Aryan Nations went to trial for conspiring to overthrow the United States government in the 1980s. Recently, conspiracy indictments have been returned against militia group members. In addition to radicals, federal prosecutors have used the conspiracy charge repeatedly and successfully against men and women accused of racketeering, murder, robbery, and drug trafficking, among many other crimes. The message is clear from the official record. Conspirators never rest; their plots to betray the nation or prey upon the innocent are a constant reminder of the fragile nature of the American mission.[24]

For many Americans, the sixties prompted a crisis of faith. The death of John Kennedy and the subsequent Warren Commission Report shook confidence and raised concerns about the integrity of national leaders and institutions. The Vietnam war not only drained America of blood and resources but deepened cynicism and eroded trust. In pursuing the enemy at home and abroad, President Lyndon Johnson lost his bearings. His end justified the means, and persuasion blurred into deception. Mistrust crept into the debate at the very beginning, with many convinced that the president had duped the nation into war. Were American warships in the Tonkin Gulf on routine patrol in international waters as they claimed? Was the North Vietnamese attack unprovoked? Did an attack even occur? Three years after the 1964 incident, Secretary of Defense Robert McNamara appeared before the U.S. Senate Foreign Relations Committee and felt compelled to defend the administration: "I find it inconceivable that anyone . . . could suspect the existence of a conspiracy which would include almost, if not all, the entire chain of command in the Pacific, the Chairman of the Joint Chiefs of Staff, the Joint Chiefs, the Secretary of Defense . . . the Secretary of State, and the President of the United States."[25] The credibility gap was such, however, that thinking the unthinkable became almost instinctive. Questionable body counts, secret bombings, and short-sighted, official reminders that the light was visible at the end of the tunnel only reinforced skepticism. The release of the Pentagon Papers and government attempts to suppress their publication hinted further at a history of deceit and subterfuge. Nor was conspiracy thinking confined to the challengers. President Johnson sensed a Kennedy plot behind the unrest of the decade. He confided to a close adviser: "Bobby saw his chance. He saw I was in trouble so he put King on the Kennedy payroll to roil up the Negroes. That's why we had the riots."[26]

Candor did not return to the White House during Richard Nixon's tenure. Under the guise of national security, Nixon authorized so-called plumbers' units to plug leaks with illegal wiretaps, mail covers, bugs, burglaries, and break-ins. Explained Nixon: "We're up against an enemy, a conspiracy. They're using any means. We are going to use any means. Is that clear?"[27] Public support and faith ebbed with disclosure. An early casualty of the truth was the vice president, who resigned rather than face trial on corruption charges. By June 1974 the Watergate scandal had claimed seventeen members of the administration who had confessed or been found guilty; another ten still awaited trial. A few months later, Richard Nixon resigned when a tape recording revealed that he had conspired to obstruct justice by using the CIA to deflect an FBI investigation. For some, President Gerald Ford's pardon of Nixon was the final act of the cover-up. Chris Carter, the creator of The X-Files, suggests how formative an experience the scandal was: "My paranoia and mistrust of authority came of age during Watergate. . . . It helps when you pick up the paper every day and see how the government has lied to us."[28]

Watergate prompted calls for atonement, but revelations brought no closure. Instead, they intensified the cynicism of the deceived and confirmed conspiracy theories of a shadow government manipulating events. The Central Intelligence Agency was a primary target, and congressional investigation exposed repeated betrayals of trust. Cloaked in national security and insulated from accountability, the CIA had rigged elections, staged strikes, and planned assassinations to undermine governments in Guatemala, Iran, Ecuador, Cuba, Nicaragua, Vietnam, the Congo, the Dominican Republic, and Chile. At home, the agency had violated its charter by spying on American citizens, compiling thousands of files and operating a computer bank holding 1.5 million names. Its MK-ULTRA program of the 1950s involved the testing of cocaine, heroin, and psychotropic drugs like LSD on unsuspecting Americans to improve interrogation results. This sounded like a cover story to the more suspicious, who surmised that the CIA was grooming a "Manchurian candidate." Disclosure did not restore public confidence but only raised the question: was the CIA out of control or merely following presidential orders?[29]

Congressional probes also exposed the FBI's domestic counterintelligence program (COINTELPRO). Following practices developed in the 1930s, agents targeted the Communist Party, the New Left, the antiwar movement, the John Birch Society, the Nation of Islam, civil rights groups, and right-wing organizations for infiltration, disruption, and neutralization. They wiretapped the Reverend Martin Luther King, Jr., and attempted to use the information to blackmail him into silence. Mainstream leaders like Bobby Kennedy, Barry Goldwater, Eleanor Roosevelt, J. William Fulbright, and Edmund Muskie were also under surveillance. Resignations, indictments, and convictions of top FBI officials did not ease disillusionment. For a public long nurtured on the carefully cultivated television and film images of FBI integrity, the evidence of malfeasance deepened the wound. When embarrassing details of Director J. Edgar Hoover's private life became public, the FBI's reputation was thoroughly stained.[30]

The decade of the 1970s was a season of disclosures. The U.S. Public Health Service revealed that black men diagnosed with syphilis had remained untreated for forty years in the Tuskegee experiment. Critics persisted in battering the Warren Commission Report, drawing new supporters by making public previously sealed assassination materials. Camelot, meanwhile, lost its glow, tainted with exposés of the president's sexual misconduct. Inconsistencies in Air Force Project Blue Book bred new skepticism and continuing experiences of extraterrestrial contact persuaded growing numbers of a cosmic cover-up.

Polls recorded a renewal of public trust in federal authorities with the election of Ronald Reagan to the White House. The gain, however, was soon squandered in government scandal. In violation of congressional mandate, the Reagan administration creatively financed the Contra war against the government of Nicaragua by raising funds from arm sales to nemesis Iran. "Contragate" recalled Watergate, and America returned to the congressional hearing room to witness high-ranking government officials caught in lies and rogue operations. The spiral of mistrust accelerated in the 1990s. The Clinton presidency suffered, in now familiar nomenclature, "Whitewatergate," allegations that Bill and Hillary Clinton profited illegally from an Arkansas land deal. Was the White House covering up that scandal? Were there other episodes of financial chicanery they were desperately trying to conceal? Sexual improprieties tore further at Clinton credibility and draped the oval office in duplicity. Meanwhile, incidents at Ruby Ridge and Waco evolved into new conspiracy scenarios that further besmirched the reputations of government officials.

These historical flares illuminate the darker context that nourishes conspiracy thinking. For a half-century or more, a cult of secrecy has dominated the bureaucracy in Washington and distanced federal authorities from those beyond the beltway. Bred in World War II and nurtured in the Cold War, the secrecy state was driven by national security fears and a determination to preserve the American way of life. Institutional imperatives joined with outside pressure to firm the authority of secrecy. Making secrets conferred status and secured control. The decision to classify was also risk free and protected career goals. The results were predictable. By 1995 three million men and women were tasked with classifying as many as ten thousand documents per day. The secrets piled up, and by the end of the century an estimated ten billion pages had secrecy rankings, with 1.5 billion of them at least twenty-five years old. As nuclear physicist Robert Oppenheimer observed, "Secrecy once accepted becomes an addiction."[31] In the process, secret keeping gradually slipped the traces of necessity and ripened into reflex and, on occasion, abuse of power. Concealed information denied accountability and enabled the arrogant both to ignore public opinion and to manipulate it. Behind this veil, laws were broken and democratic values subverted. Even without the taint of malevolence, suppression of information aroused concern. Essayist Susan Griffin was insightful: "Wherever there is a secret there is a rumor."[32] Drawing sustenance from America's resilient fear of centralized authority, perceptions of sinister design became truth. As outsiders, the conspiracy-minded only intensified their gaze and watched for confirmation of their worst suspicions. How far the nation had fallen since its last crusade. During World War II, everyone was in on the secret, cautioned not to aid the enemy with loose lips. Now Americans sensed that they had lost the confidence of their own government.[33]

Aware of the relation between secrecy and conspiracy thinking, some decision makers sought institutional reform. President Bill Clinton issued an executive order in 1995 releasing all secrets at least twenty-five years in the keeping by the year 2000. The Assassination Records Review Board complied and opened millions of pages of documents to public view. Yet reports that authorities continued their rituals of secrecy fixed the attention of countersubversives. In 1997 historian George Herring, recruited by the CIA to serve on a panel declassifying agency files, resigned in disgust after six years of frustration. The CIA's promise to release information, declared Herring, was "a brilliant public relations snow job" and "a carefully nurtured myth. . . . I was being used to cover the agency's ass while having no influence."[34] More in line with its traditional practices, the CIA announced soon after that documents concerning its involvement in the 1953 Iranian coup had been destroyed or lost. In 1999 the Treasury Department broke a three-month silence and confessed to having shredded 162 boxes of potential evidence in a multibillion dollar lawsuit over Indian trust funds. Nor did conspiracists ever tire of stories detailing how the Freedom of Information Act opened government files but effectively denied access to researchers.[35]

Conspiracist claims, media images, and federal behavior had a cumulative impact. Public faith in government was shaken, and

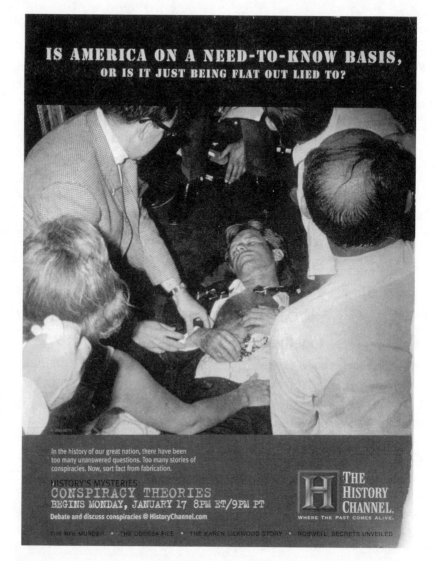

The History Channel, "where the past comes alive," responded to and fed the public hunger for conspiracy theories with a week of episodes in January 2000. Viewers had a variety of choices, ranging from the assassination of Bobby Kennedy to the death of Karen Silkwood to the Roswell incident.

Courtesy of THE HISTORY CHANNEL

opinion polls carefully surveyed the damage. In 1964 pollsters found that 75 percent of the American people trusted the federal government "to do what is right always or most of the time." Vietnam and then Watergate drained faith, and by 1976 only one in three Americans expressed similar thoughts. Women and men greeted the Reagan administration with new enthusiasm in the early 1980s, but confidence levels resumed their decline in the latter part of the decade. In 1995 public trust hit an all-time low. In mirror image of the 1964 findings, 75 percent of Americans expressed no faith in the government's ability to do what is right. Alternative phrasings did not alter the findings. The percentage of Americans who believe that the "government is pretty much run by a few big interests" more than doubled between 1964 and 1996, from 29 percent to 76 percent. Another 1996 survey found that 63 percent have little or no faith that government officials tell the truth. In just thirty years, a consensus of trust had become a minority position, with such sentiments registered across class, racial, educational, gender, religious, and age lines. Many, at the same time, were willing to believe the worst. One in four was convinced that the "government elite" was "involved in a conspiracy."[36]

Cynicism about government was only part of the broad-based pessimism that blanketed the nation at the end of the twentieth century. Americans had also lost faith in their corporate and labor leaders, university officials, military officers, physicians, and ministers. Mainstream journalists and reporters found that their voices commanded less respect. Newspapers and national magazines thus reported that readership was down and the news monopoly of the three major television networks had long been broken by CNN, the Discovery and History channels, talk radio, and the internet. Probes of local police forces uncovered flagrant evidence of bribery, racketeering, and unjustified beatings. DNA testing brought the release of dozens of prison inmates and raised doubt about the administration of justice by the American court system. If dismayed by the state of the nation and its leadership, Americans still clung tightly to their creed and mission. Almost nine in ten men and women were certain that America "had a special place in God's plan for history." Countersubversives, always optimistic that opinion would turn, filled the vacuum produced by this collapse of confidence and distrust of authority. In concert with the popular mood, they preached salvation once the enemies within had been routed.[37]

Rather than the sum of its paranoid parts, conspiracism is greater and more complex. It is part of the national birthright and offers community to believers. Conspiracy thinking gives hope, unity, and purpose in a world that often seems beyond the reach of the powerless. It factors into the deep discontent men and women feel about their leaders and the direction they have set for the Republic. This uprising against authority has touched all areas of national life, and conspiracy thinking has fed from the impulse and, in turn, stimulated new assaults. Yet those who preach countersubversion are not sufficient to explain its draw. Media merchandisers legitimize conspiracy thinking and give it broad appeal. Their images remain in the public mind, forever shaping new experiences into consistent patterns. Government authorities also support the conspiracist case by echoing the fear of subversion or offering proof of collusion by abusing power or betraying the people's trust. In essence, conspiracism is an American tradition. Yet there is danger in the observance. Conspiracism demonizes opponents and makes struggle internecine. Victories in such conflicts can only be pyrrhic. Conspiracy thinking has moved Americans beyond a healthy skepticism of authority. Lacking public confidence, core institutions become unstable and lose their ability to govern. The cancer of conspiracism has begun to metastasize. Without a new awareness of its character and quick intervention, countersubversion may overcome the body politic.

Notes

Preface

1. Alter, "Age," 47.
2. Kelly, "Road," 60–64, 66–70, 72–75; Safire, "Conspiracy," 24; Wills, "New Revolutionaries," 50–55.
3. Kelly, "Road," 63, 65; Eringer, *Conspiracy Peddlers*, 2; Johnson, "What?" 24; Goertzel, "Belief," 734.
4. La Fave and Scott, *Criminal Law*, 525.
5. Hofstadter, *Paranoid Style*, 3, 6.
6. For a valuable critique of Hofstadter, see Fenster, *Conspiracy Theories*.
7. Pipes, *Conspiracy*, 24, 49.
8. Robins and Post, *Political Paranoia*, 57, 95.

Chapter 1. An American Tradition

1. Cherry, *God's New Israel*, 58, 294.
2. John Winthrop, *Model of Christian Charity*, in Goldberg, Hinderaker, and May, *American Views*, 38.
3. Berkhofer, *White Man's Indian*, 81–85; Lepore, *Name of War*, passim.
4. Mather, *Wonders*, 16, 19, 58, 70, 80–81.
5. Demos, *Entertaining Satan*, 11, 310–11.
6. Boyer and Nissenbaum, *Salem Possessed*, 175.
7. Demos, *Entertaining Satan*, 93–94; Rosenthal, *Salem Story*, 81; Mather, *Wonders*, 140.
8. Hoffer, *Salem Witchcraft Trials*, 57, 80, 89; Demos, *Entertaining Satan*, 11; Karlsen, *Devil in the Shape of a Woman*, 44, 76, 116; Boyer and Nissenbaum, *Salem Possessed*, 15–16, 29, 69, 93, 100, 109, 177–78; Miller, *Crucible*, 26.
9. Robert Hunter to the Lords of Trade, June 23, 1712, in Hofstadter and Wallace, *American Violence*, 188–89.

10. Hofstadter and Wallace, *American Violence*, 188; Rosenthal, *Salem Story*, 211.

11. Bailyn, *Ideological Origins*, 11, 39, 43, 54, 56, 59, 119–20 (quotation), 144–59; Wood, "Conspiracy and the Paranoid Style," 410; Wood, *Creation of the American Republic*, 39–42; Breen, *Tobacco Culture*, 10–11.

12. Mayhew, *Snare Broken*, 9, 34.

13. Bailyn, *Pamphlets*, 86.

14. John Dickinson, *Letters of a Farmer in Pennsylvania*, 1768, in Ford, *Political Writings of John Dickinson*, 348; Baldwin, *Appendix*, 69, 73; Quincy, *Observations*, 48, 67, 68, 77; Bloch, *Visionary Republic*, 59.

15. Bloch, *Visionary Republic*, 56; Gruber, "American Revolution," 370.

16. Howe, "Republican Thought," 167, 150, 154; Hutson, "Origins of the Paranoid Style," in Hall, Murrin, and Tate, *Saints and Revolutionaries*, 336, 370–71.

17. For more on the Order of the Illuminati, see Chapter 2.

18. Camp, *Selling Fear*, 32.

19. Johnson, *Architects*, 61.

20. Stauffer, *New England*, 11, 144, 207–8, 229 (quotation), 230, 232, 246.

21. "Alien Act," and "Sedition Act," in Commager, *Documents*, 1: 1, 176, 177–78.

22. Schlesinger, *Imperial Presidency*, 255.

23. Goodman, *Toward a Christian Republic*, 24.

24. Bernard, *Light on Masonry*, 430.

25. Goodman, *Toward a Christian Republic*, vii, 3–6, 8, 29, 57 (quotation), 234. See also, Davis, "Some Themes of Counter Subversion."

26. Arrington and Bitton, *Mormon Experience*, 44.

27. Strong, *Our Country*, 113.

28. Arrington and Bitton, *Mormon Experience*, 44–64.

29. Morse, *Foreign Conspiracy*, 89.

30. Billington, *Protestant Crusade*, 33; McPherson, *Battle Cry of Freedom*, 131; Lyman Beecher, *Plea for the West*, 54; Beecher, *Papal Conspiracy*, 411.

31. Billington, *Protestant Crusade*, 53; McPherson, *Battle Cry of Freedom*, 137; Beecher, *Papal Conspiracy*, 418.

32. Davis, *Slave Power Conspiracy*, 7.

33. Nye, "Slave Power," in Curry and Brown, *Conspiracy*, 80.

34. Goodwill, *Slavery and Anti-Slavery*, 408; Julian, *Strength and Weakness*, 68, 70, 71, 73; Foner, *Free Soil*, 90, 99–101; Davis, *Slave Power Conspiracy*, 11, 18, 59, 72, 85; Davis, *Fear of Conspiracy*, 103–4, 362; Gienapp, *Origins*, 358–59, 362 (quotation).

35. Foner, *Free Soil*, 87–88, 94; Cairnes, *Slave Power*, 119; Davis, *Fear of Conspiracy*, 104.

36. Cash, *Mind of the South*, 92.

37. Freehling, *Prelude to Civil War*, 54–65.

38. See Trelease, *White Terror*.

39. Donnerly, *Caesar's Column*, 45, 124.

40. "Populist Party Platform," July 4, 1892, in Commager, *Documents*, 2: 143.

41. Farmer, *Conspiracy Against Silver*, 5–6, 99; Young, "Silver," 244, 252, 254–55.

42. Smoak, "Ghost Dances and Identity," 322, 337; *New York Times*, November 11, 1999, D3; Strong, *Our Country*, 55, 79; Higham, *Strangers*, 81. See also Kinzer, *Episode*.

43. Ostrander, *Prohibition Movement*, 66.

44. Goldberg, *Grassroots Resistance*, 21–30.

45. See Chalmers, *Social and Political Ideas of the Muckrakers*.

46. Roosevelt, *Foes*, 293–94.

47. "Industrial Workers Who Won't Work," *Literary Digest* 55 (July 28, 1917): 20.

48. Goldberg, *Grassroots Resistance*, 60–62.

49. Palmer, "Case," 174, 175, 180.

50. Murray, *Red Scare*, 192–94, 196, 210–11, 213–17, 219 (quotation), 235.

51. *Rocky Mountain American*, February 13, April 3, 1925.

52. White, *Ku Klux Klan*, 26.

53. *Good Citizen*, February, 1924.

54. White, *Heroes*, 34.

55. *Rocky Mountain American*, January 31, 1925; Evans, *Attitude*, 4; White, *Heroes*, 10–11; White, *Ku Klux Klan*, 50–53.

56. Lee, *Henry Ford*, 13.

57. *Aspects of Jewish Power*, 4: 3, 237; *Jewish Influence in American Life*, 4; Lee, *Henry Ford and the Jews*, 14–15, 30; Wik, *Henry Ford*, 178; Dinnerstein, *Antisemitism*, 80–83; Ribuffo, *Old Christian Right*, 11, 59.

58. Means, *Strange Death; Winter Catalogue, 1998–1999*, American Opinion Book Services, 5.

59. Kazan, *Populist Persuasion*, 119.

60. Ribuffo, *Old Christian Right*, xii, 58, 106; Brinkley, *Voices*, 150; Warren, *Radio Priest*, 137–38.

61. Cole, *Senator*, 91, 94, 96; Doenecke, *In Danger*, 37–38, 392–93.

62. Beard, *President Roosevelt*, 566.

63. Toland, *Infamy*, 321.

64. Theobald, *Final Secret*, 192–96, 201; Morgenstern, *Pearl Harbor*, ix, 327, 329; Prange, *Pearl Harbor*, 36–42; Toland, *Infamy*, 321; *New York Times*, May 26, 1999.

65. See Maurice Isserman, *Which Side?* and Harvey Klehr, *Heyday*.

66. Horowitz, *Beyond Left*, 185.

67. Ribuffo, *Old Christian Right*, 78–79, 127, 178, 184, 188–89, 193–96, 211, 215; Dennis, *Trial*, 14, 16, 71–73, 75–76.

68. Warren testimony, "National Defense Migrations," 11011–12, 11018.

Chapter 2. The Master Conspiracy

1. Donner, *Age*, 54; Theoharis, *Spying*, 66.

2. Latham, *Communist Controversy*, 373, 381; Donner, *Age*, 53–55, 132; Theoharis, *Spying*, 12, 66, 69, 73, 133, 158–59; O'Reilly, *Hoover*, 21–24.

3. Klehr, *Heyday*, 101, 190, 205–9, 222, 252–65, 309–17, 350–53, 365–66, 370; Weinstein, *Ambiguous Legacy*, 77–78; Latham, *Communist Controversy*, 102, 124, 150; Cochran, *Labor and Communism*, 95–98; Draper, *American Communism*, 185; Powers, *Not Without Honor*, 170.

4. Dilling, *Roosevelt's Red Record*, 3, 5.

5. Dilling, *Red Network*, 5.

6. Dies, *Trojan Horse*, 303.

7. Goodman, *Committee*, 21, 25, 87; Oshinsky, *Conspiracy*, 92–93; Dies, *Trojan Horse*, 33, 257, 297; Haynes, *Red Scare*, 69; O'Reilly, *Hoover*, 62–64; Theoharis, *Spying*, 196–97.

8. Caute, *Great Fear*, 26.

9. Chafe, *Unfinished Journey*, 98.

10. Griffith, *Politics of Fear*, 12.

11. Rogin, *Ronald Reagan*, 27.

12. Griffith, *Politics of Fear*, 48.

13. Miles, *Odyssey*, 210; Caute, *Great Fear*, 487–90, 500, 510–11, 515; Goodman, *Committee*, 207–22, 247, 254; Ceplaur and Englund, *Inquisition*, 258–324; Oshinsky, *Conspiracy*, 95–100; Latham, *Communist Controversy*, 211, 361–62. See also Weinstein, *Perjury*.

14. Fried, *Electoral Politics*, 194.

15. Weinstein, *Perjury*, 453.

16. Litchfield, *It's a Conspiracy*, 17.

17. Griffith, *Politics of Fear*, 11; Weinstein, *Perjury*, 451, 507.

18. Theoharis, *Seeds*, 31, 43; Oshinsky, *Conspiracy*, 95–97; "Truman Doctrine," March 12, 1947, in Commager, *Documents*, 2: 704–6.

19. "Truman Loyalty Order," March 22, 1947, in Commager, *Documents*, 2: 710.

20. Goldberg, *Grassroots Resistance*, 111.

21. Theoharis, *Seeds*, 136.

22. "McCarran Internal Security Act," September 23, 1950, in Commager, *Documents*, 2: 742.

23. Griffith, *Politics of Fear*, 34, 38; Theoharis, *Spying*, 44–55, 199, 202; Theoharis, *Seeds*, 101–3; Caute, *Great Fear*, 34, 39, 268–69, 272; Haynes, *Red Scare*, 163–64; Belknap, *Cold War*, 6–7, 47, 51–52, 79–81, 152–58; Tanner and Griffith, "Legislative Politics," 183–84 (quotation), 189.

24. Caute, *Great Fear*, 274; Theoharis, *Seeds*, 66, 101, 122.

25. Oshinsky, *Conspiracy*, 108–9.

26. Theoharis, *Seeds*, vii; Sayre, *Running Time*, 14; Miles, *Odyssey*, 131; Griffith, *Politics of Fear*, 49 (quotation); Rogin, *Intellectuals*, 228, 250, 253.

27. McCarthy, *America's Retreat*, 94–95.

28. Griffith, *Politics of Fear*, 89, 123.

29. Oshinsky, *Conspiracy*, 464; Gallup, *Gallup Poll, 1935–1971*, 2: 881, 934, 1201, 1237.

30. Horowitz, *Beyond Left*, 219.

31. Hoover, *Masters*, 297.

32. Radosh and Milton, *Rosenberg File*, 238.

33. Clark, *From the Danube*, 11.

34. *Communists Within the Government*, 6, 11, 24.

35. Whitfield, *Culture*, 81.

36. *Red Menace*.

37. Sayre, *Running Time*, 79–81; Whitfield, *Culture*, 133; Doherty, "Hollywood," 15–16.

38. Graham, *Deny*, 60; Sayre, *Running Time*, 25–26, 191, 196; Haslam, "Watch," 7, 10; Coombs, *American*, 48–49.

39. MacDonald, *Television*, vii, ix, 12, 102–3, 109–10, 146; Powers, *Not Without Honor*, 253; Whitfield, *Culture*, 66.

40. Heale, *American*, 148–49; Caute, *Great Fear*, 70, 403, 418; Oshinsky, *Conspiracy*, 140.

41. Executive Order 10450, April 27, 1953, in Commager, *Documents*, 2: 781.

42. Powers, *Not Without Honor*, 265–66, 273–74; Gallup, *Gallup Poll, 1935–1971*, 2: 1225, 1300; Davis, *Assault*, 5–7; Theoharis, *Spying*, 136–38, 234.

43. Latham, *Communist*, 369; Haynes, *Red Scare*, 170; Whitfield, *Culture*, 24.

44. Griffen, *Life*, 67–68, 99, 132, 135.

45. Broyles, *John Birch Society*, 28; Griffen, *Life*, 28–29, 35, 44, 62–63, 105–6, 111–12; Welch, *Blue Book*, unpaged; "Welch," FBI File.

46. Griffen, *Life*, 147–52, 164; Welch, *Again*, 5, 9, 12, 28, 40, 53, 61, 78, 187.

47. Welch, *Politician*, 6, 10, 13, 15, 16, 278, 279.

48. Welch, *Blue Book*, iii; Griffen, *Life*, 258.

49. Welch, *Blue Book*, 9, 19, 28, 29, 30, 33, 39, 52, 59, 93.

50. Welch, "Through All the Days to Be Delivered," in *New Americanism*, 63–64.

51. Griffen, *Life*, 4–6; Broyles, *John Birch Society*, 4, 27; Jasper, "Americanism's Standard Bearer," 32 (quotation).

52. Welch, *Blue Book*, iv, 116, 158–59; Broyles, *John Birch Society*, 46; Forster and Epstein, *Radical Right*, 140–41, 195; *New York Times*, March 7, 1965, 72, October 30, 1965, 23.

53. Welch, *Blue Book*, 76–94, 107–10, 167, 174; Broyles, *John Birch Society*, 103; Rohter, "Radical Rightists," 173; Forster and Epstein, *Danger*, 24–25; Toy, "Ideology and Conflict," 243.

54. Toy, "Ideology and Conflict," 248; Stone, "Birch Society of California," 54, 57, 58, 165; Grupp, "Social Correlates," 268, 224, 263, 294–95, 297–98; California Senate, *Report*, 12. For more on the social and economic characteristics of Birch Society members, see Berlet, "Trashing the Birchers," and Kraft, *Demographic Profile*.

55. Goldwater, *Conscience*, 22; Goldwater, *Why Not Victory*, 169.

56. Kolkey, *New Right*, 82.

57. Toy, "Ideology and Conflict," 238; Forster and Epstein, *Danger*, 47, 52, 132, 279; Kolkey, *New Right*, 77 (quotation).

58. Thomas M. Storke, "How Some Birchers Were Birched," *New York Times Magazine*, December 10, 1961, 102.

59. George Barrett, "Close-Up of the Birchers' 'Founder,'" *New York Times Magazine*, May 14, 1961, 92; Stanley Mosk and Howard Jewel, "The Birch Phenomenon Analyzed," *New York Times Magazine*, August 20, 1961, 12.

60. *Time* 77 (March 10, 1961): 22.

61. Quoted in *New York Times*, April 8, 1961, 13.

62. "Subversion of the Right," *Christian Century*, March 29, 1961, 379; Chester Morrison, "The Man Behind the John Birch Society," *Look*, September 26, 1961, 23–27; *Newsweek*, April 10, 1961, 38; Stephen M. Young, "Danger on the Right," *Saturday Evening Post*, January 13, 1962, 7; "The John Birch Society,"

America, April 15, 1961, 140–41; "The Question of Robert Welch," *National Review,* February 13, 1962, 84, 88.

63. *National Review,* February 27, 1962, 140.

64. Young, "Danger," 7.

65. Powers, *Not Without Honor,* 286; *New York Times,* March 9, 1961, 12, March 31, 1961, 10; Theoharis, *Spying,* 166, 169, 189; Gallup, *Gallup Poll, 1935–1971,* 3: 1715, 1756, 1896, 1977.

66. *The John Birch Society: Twenty-Five Years of Responsible Leadership,* 5, 7.

67. Robison, *Proof,* 52.

68. Griffen, *Life,* 246; Welch, "More Stately Mansions," in *New Americanism,* 135.

69. Welch, "Dissent," 56.

70. Webster, *Secret Societies,* passim; Webster, *World Revolution,* passim; Winrod, *Adam Weishaupt,* passim; Welch, "Truth in Time," 25–27; Welch, "If You Want It Straight," 1.

71. Welch, "Dissent," 53; Welch, "Truth in Time," 5–8; Welch, "In One Generation; Welch, "Touch of Sanity."

72. Welch, "Truth in Time," 21; Welch, "Touch of Sanity."

73. *American Opinion,* July–August, 1966, 76.

74. Welch, "Truth in Time," 4–6, 10, 11, 19, 21; Welch, "Two Revolutions," in *New Americanism,* 192; Welch, "In One Generation;" Welch, "Touch of Sanity," 157–58, 164, 171, 173; Gregg, "Legacy," 32.

75. Griffen, *Life,* 246.

76. Fletcher Knebel, "The GOP Attacks the John Birch Society," *Look,* 29, December 28, 1965, 74.

77. *New York Times,* December 8, 1968, 42.

78. Smoot, *Invisible Government,* 127.

79. Courtney and Courtney, *America's Unelected Rulers,* 4.

80. Schulzinger, *Wise Men,* passim.

81. Schlafly, *Choice,* 70, 102.

82. Allen, "C.F.R. Conspiracy," 49.

83. Allen, *None Dare,* 14, 18, 71, 88.

84. Allen, *Rockefeller File,* 170.

85. Skousen, *Naked Capitalist,* 4, 24, 39.

86. Griffin, *Fourth Reich,* 43, 75, 94, 120, 192; Epperson, *New World Order,* 144, 194, 196; Perloff, *Shadows,* 114; Epperson, *Unseen Hand,* 122, 155, 160, 205, 207.

87. McManus, *Insiders,* 25.

88. Ibid., passim.

89. Shoup and Minter, *Imperial Brain Trust,* vii, 85, 117.

90. Sklar, "Trilateralism: Managing Dependence and Democracy—An Overview," in *Trilateralism,* 8–9, 29, 35.

91. Sklar, "Trilateralism and the Management of Contradictions: Concluding Perspectives," in *Trilateralism,* 557.

92. U.S. Senate, 95th Congress, 2d sess., February 21, 1978, *Congressional Record,* 124: 3963.

93. Goldwater, *With No Apologies,* 277–87.

94. Stang, "It's Time," 26.

95. *New York Times,* February 8, 1980, 19.

96. McManus, *Insiders,* 36.

97. Goldberg, *Grassroots Resistance,* 139.

98. Perloff, *Shadow,* 180.

99. Stern, *Force,* 56.

100. Vankin and Whalen, *70 Greatest Conspiracies,* 27.

101. U.S. Senate, 100th Cong., 1st sess., December 15, 1987, *Congressional Record,* 133: 18146.

102. McManus, *Insiders,* 27–31.

103. "Conspiracy for Global Control: Special Report," *New American,* January 1997, 61.

104. Crawford, *Thunder on the Right,* 133; Armour, "Year-End Report," 3–4; *New York Times,* January 8, 1985, B6, September 1, 1986, 24; McManus, *Insiders,* 47–61; *Salt Lake Tribune,* February 16, 1992; Berlet, "Trashing the Birchers," 10; Kraft, *Demographic Profile,* 4.

105. Griffin, *Fourth Reich,* 112.

106. McManus, "Insiders Call the Shots," 44.

107. *New American,* July 6, 1998, 19.

108. Fenster, *Conspiracy Theories,* 85; McManus, *Insiders,* 75–85; Griffin, *Fourth Reich,* 112; Jaspar, "Soldiers," 17, 19; Keith, *Black Helicopters,* 147; Jaspar, "Mock-Up," 15–16; Ingraham, "Global Money Changers," 31–32; McManus, "Newt's Selective Rhetoric," 44.

109. *New York Times,* July 26, 1985, 9, October 25, 1989, 29; Pugmire, "FEMA Conspiracy," 3, 4, 13, 14, 17; Killebrew, "FEMA," 8, 12; Keith, *Black Helicopters,* 54, 56, 83, 110; Harry Martin, "FEMA: The Secret Government," February 12, 1999, www. sonic.net/sentiment/gucon.html (inactive); Velvet Hammer, "Executive Orders: Bonfire for the Constitution," January 9, 1998, www. thewinds.org/archive/government/fema/97.html; Geoff Metcalf, "Government Internment Camps," February 12, 1999, www.nebonet.com/headhome/ dadmisc/comps.htm.

110. Stern, *Force,* 19–39; *Salt Lake Tribune,* October 11, 1997.

111. Isikoff, "Waco Flame-Up," 30; Klaidman and Isikoff, "Fire That Won't Die," 27; Grigg, "Waco Deception," 12–15.

112. Berlet, "Violence," 283; Stern, *Force,* 35–36; Klasen, *White Man's Bible,* passim; Butler, *This Is Aryan Nations,* passim; Macdonald, *Turner Diaries,* passim.

113. Stern, *Force,* 13, 96–97; *Salt Lake Tribune,* July 14, 1996; *New York Times,* January 18, 1998, 16; Tharp and Holstein, "Mainstreaming," 26.

114. *Militia of Montana Preparedness Catalogue,* 1998.

115. *New York Times,* March 13, 1995, 8, April 24, 1995, 13; *CPA Book Publisher Catalogue,* 1997; Keith, *Black Helicopters,* 64–69; Stein, *Force,* 77–78, 223–24; *Christian Media,* winter 1999.

116. *Salt Lake Tribune,* March 30, 1997, October 18, 1998; Stern, *Force,* 225–29; Fenster, *Conspiracy Theories,* 180–81; Tharp and Holstein, "Mainstreaming," 27; alertsJBS.org. See also www.ufomind.com/para/conspire/; www.hevanet. com/; nitehawk/nwo.html (inactive); and www.parascope.com.

117. Keith, *Black Helicopters,* 68, 72, 76, 121, 143; Stern, *Force,* 142–44.

118. *Conspiracy Nation,* April 1996, 6.

119. Leiby, "Paranoia."

120. "A Question of Conspiracy," *Newsweek,* October 12, 1998, 48; Vankin and Whalen, *70 Greatest Conspiracies,* 70, 414; *New York Times,* June 3, 1997, 10; *Conspiracy Nation,* April 1996, June 1996; "Proof of Bombs and Cover-Up," *New American,* July 20, 1998, 10–15; "Has America Gone Conspiracy Crazy?" CNN, June 18, 1997; Marin and Gegax, "Conspiracy Mania," 66.

121. Ray, *Environmental Overkill,* 10.

122. www.eagleforum.org, February 2, 1999.

123. *New York Times,* July 6, 1995, 12.

124. Fenster, *Conspiracy Theories,* 34.

125. July 28–August 1, 1997.

126. *New York Times,* November 19, 1997, 26.

127. *Houston Chronicle,* April 18, 1997.

128. *New York Times,* August 26, 1999, 1.

129. *Salt Lake Tribune,* September 11, 1999.

130. *New York Times,* September 2, 1999, 12.

131. Klaidman and Isikoff, "Fire," 24; *Newsweek,* August 27, 1999, 18.

132. Key, "Waco," 5.

133. Phillips, "Conspiracy and the X-Files," 1, 4; Lowry, *Truth,* 27, 251.

134. Lavery, Hague, and Cartwright, *Deny All Knowledge,* 3.

135. "Erlenmeyer Flask," May 13, 1994.

136. "Patient X," March 1, 1998.

137. "Things Really Did Go Well in Dealey Plaza," November 17, 1996; "Just Down the Road a Ways from Graceland," November 24, 1996; "The Most Wonderful Time of the Year," December 1, 1996.

138. Fenster, *Conspiracy Theories,* 111, 113.

139. *Enemy of the State.*

140. Gregg, "Could It Happen in America?" 36, 38.

141. www.sjgames.com/Illuminati.

142. Hoisager, advertisement for "Insider Report."

143. *Salt Lake Tribune,* October 25, 1999.

144. Bonta, "New Age Roots," 26.

Chapter 3. The Rise of the Antichrist

1. Mather, *Wonders,* 34.

2. Revelation, 4:1, 12:3, 13:4, 13:16–18, 19:15, 21:1. All biblical citations are to the King James Version unless otherwise noted.

3. White, *Re-Entry,* 14; Daniel 7:24–25, Ezekiel, 38:2–3, Matthew 24:26–27, 34, 36.

4. Mather, *Mystery,* 38.

5. Wigglesworth, *Day of Doom,* verses v–vi.

6. Middlekauf, *Mathers,* 346–47.

7. Stein, "Transatlantic," in Patrides and Wittreich, *Apocalypse,* 266–71, 276; Fuller, *Naming the Anti-Christ,* 43, 49, 52, 64; Middlekauf, *Mathers,* 333, 335, 341, 349; Wojcik, *End,* 22; Mather, *Wonders,* 14–15; Miller, *Errand,* 59, 114 (quotation), 218.

8. Stein, "Transatlantic," 283, 287; Weber, *Apocalypses*, 171; Fuller, *Naming the Anti-Christ*, 66–67, 69; Boyer, *When Time Shall Be No More*, 226; Hatch, *Sacred Cause*, 39, 42.

9. Bloch, *Visionary Republic*, 53.

10. Tuveson, *Redeemer Nation*, 24.

11. Hatch, *Sacred Cause*, 17, 22–25, 52–53; Bloch, *Visionary Republic*, 53, 55–56, 75.

12. Stauffer, *New England*, 250.

13. Revelation, 17:5, 9.

14. Hatch, *Sacred Cause*, 155; Zamora, *Apocalyptic Vision*, 110; Wojcik, *End*, 21, 27; Weber, *Living*, 13–16; Weber, *Apocalypses*, 120; Tuveson, *Redeemer Nation*, 197–202.

15. 1 Thessalonians, 4:17.

16. Weber, *Living*, 16–24, 106; Johnson, *Architects*, 148–50; O'Leary, *Arguing*, 137–39, 158.

17. Weber, *Living*, 63–64.

18. Scofield, *Scofield Reference Bible*, 1.

19. O'Leary, *Arguing*, 137.

20. Scofield, *What Do the Prophets Say?* 9.

21. Ribuffo, *Old Christian Right*, 111.

22. Weber, *Living*, 109, 126, 129; Camp, *Selling Fear*, 78–79; Wojcik, *End*, 163; Smith, *Atomic Bomb*, 9; Thompson, *End*, 133–34.

23. Van Impe, *11:59*, 82.

24. Jeffrey, *Armageddon*, 199; O'Leary, *Arguing*, 141.

25. Matthew 24:24.

26. Wilkerson, *Vision*, 31, 43, 75; Falwell, "Last Days," *Jerry Falwell Teaches*; Hagee, *Beginning*, 85–100; Boyer, *When Time Shall Be No More*, 231–35.

27. Boyer, *When Time Shall Be No More*, 250–51, 263; Hadden and Swann, *Prime Time Preachers*, 56–60; Crawford, *Thunder*, 167.

28. Himmelstein, *To the Right*, 115, 117; Gallup and Castelli, *People's Religion*, 17; Weber, *Living*, 27; Hadden and Swann, *Prime Time Preachers*, 79–80; Fenster, *Conspiracy Theories*, 175; O'Leary, *Arguing*, 177–78.

29. Gallup and Castelli, *People's Religion*, 56, 57, 60.

30. Boyer, *When Time Shall Be No More*, 2–3, 55–56; Fuller, *Naming the Anti-Christ*, 18, 21; Wojcik, *End*, 143–45.

31. Boyer, *When Time Shall Be No More*, 305.

32. Lindsey, *Late Great Planet Earth*, 92.

33. Wojcik, *End*, 8; Weber, *Living*, 5; O'Leary, *Arguing*, 143–47; Lindsey, *Late Great Planet Earth*, 48, 81-83; Lindsey, *Apocalypse Code*, 31.

34. Lindsey, *Late Great Planet Earth*, 69–70, 139–40.

35. Ibid., 98–99, 101, 113, 140, 173, 164, 141–42, 151, 163, 166–67.

36. Lindsey, *1980s*, 128, 113, 123–24; Lindsey, *Apocalypse Code*, 104, 105.

37. Falwell, "Update on Prophecy, Part I," *Jerry Falwell Teaches*.

38. Van Impe, *11:59*, 106, 195, 206.

39. Van Impe, *Revelation Revealed*, 197.

40. Falwell, "Last Days," "Tribulation, First Half," "Update on Prophecy, Parts I and II," *Jerry Falwell Teaches*; Kirban, *Guide*, 290, 297.

41. Relfe, *New Money System*, 209, 51.

42. Fuller, *Naming the Anti-Christ*, 168, 181, 185; Relfe, *When Your Money Fails* and *New Money System*, passim; Lalonde, *Racing Toward*, 14; Yonge, "Skincode," 1.

43. Hadden and Shupe, *Televangelism*, 86.

44. Wojcik, *End*, 42.

45. Martin, "Waiting," 31; Fuller, *Naming the Anti-Christ*, 132; Wojcik, *End*, 30; Falwell, *Jerry Falwell Teaches*, vi; Gallup and Castelli, *People's Religion*, 148, 156; Wilcox, *God's Warriors*, 11; Hadden and Shupe, *Televangelism*, 292.

46. O'Leary and McFarland, "Political Use," 450.

47. *Los Angeles Times*, March 3, 1984.

48. Wills, *Under God*, 150.

49. Gallup and Castelli, *People's Religion*, 93; Wojcik, *End*, 8; Fineman, "God," 43; Dobson and Hindson, "Apocalypse Now?" 16

50. Robertson, *Shout*, 13, 14, 16.

51. Donovan, *Pat Robertson*, 4, 10–14, 13–15, 20, 27–30, 32–33; Harrell, *Pat Robertson*, 25, 29, 33–34; Robertson, *Shout*, 18

52. Robertson, *Shout*, 41.

53. Donovan, *Pat Robertson*, 45.

54. Robertson, *Shout*, 100, 231, 25, 27, 28, 31, 79–82; Donovan, *Pat Robertson*, 33–34, 37, 40, 52; Harrell, *Pat Robertson*, 45; Wills, *Under God*, 188–89.

55. Robertson, *Shout*, 177, 204, 226; Donovan, *Pat Robertson*, 61–65, 69, 71–72, 77; Robertson, *America's Dates*, 20.

56. Donovan, *Pat Robertson*, 100, 120; Foege, *Empire*, 99, 100; Harrell, *Pat Robertson*, 59–60, 62; Boyer, *When Time Shall Be No More*, 5; Bruce, *Pray TV*, 39, 102.

57. Donovan, *Pat Robertson*, 73; Harrell, *Pat Robertson*, 64, 67–68, 70, 77; King, "Record," 1; Hadden and Shupe, *Televangelism*, 94; Foege, *Empire*, 13; Robertson, *New Millennium*, 87; Gallup and Castelli, *People's Religion*, 152–53.

58. O'Leary and McFarland, "Political Use," 438–39.

59. Halsell, *Prophecy and Politics*, 10.

60. Robertson, *Answers*, 116, 155.

61. Robertson, *The Plan*, 61.

62. Robertson, *America's Dates*, 243.

63. Robertson, *The Plan*, 24, 27, 64, 66–67; O'Leary, *Arguing*, 186–87; Hertzke, *Echoes*, 85–86; *New York Times*, January 14, 1988.

64. Robertson, *America's Dates*, 11.

65. O'Leary, *Arguing*, 184–85, 186 (quotation), 187–89; O'Leary and McFarland, "Political Use," 441–48.

66. Hertzke, *Echoes*, 183 (quotation), 117, 136–37, 158, 179, 182, 231; Lienesch, *Redeeming America*, 17; Wilcox, *Onward*, 38–42, 62, 75; Foege, *Empire*, 131.

67. Robertson, *New Millennium*, 21, 69, 70, 71, 72, 74, 98, 99, 146, 152.

68. Robertson, *New World Order*, xvii, 9, 13.

69. Cantor, "Religious Right," 24; Robertson, *New World Order*, 181, 183.

70. Robertson, *New World Order*, 37, 65, 98, 256, 258.

71. LaHaye, *Beginning*, 76.

72. Zahner, *Secret Side*, 146.

73. Kah, *En Route*, 67, 69, 19.

74. McAlvany, *Toward a New World Order*, back cover.

75. Camp, *Selling*, 179.

76. Robertson, *End*, 29, 150.

77. LaHaye and Jenkins, *Left Behind*, 5, 114.

78. Gross, "Trial," 122; LaHaye and Jenkins, *Left Behind, Tribulation Force, Nicolae, Soul Harvest*.

79. Butler, *This Is Aryan Nations*, unpaged; Aho, *Politics*, 54, 101; Ridgeway, *Blood*, 53; Coates, *Armed and Dangerous*, 14–15, 82–83; Barkun, *Religion*, 49, 68.

80. Stern, *Force*, 30.

81. Barkun, "Racist Apocalypse," 127, 137; Barkun, *Religion*, 11, 51, 71, 78, 107, 111, 149–50, 162; Aho, *Politics*, 18–19, 53–55, 101–3, 265; Coates, *Armed and Dangerous*, 38, 86, 91; Klasen, *White Man's Bible*, passim.

82. Marrs, *Project L.U.C.I.D.*, 41, 25.

83. Marrs, *Dark Majesty*, ix, 18, 27, 33, 69, 113; Marrs, *Project L.U.C.I.D.*, ix–xii, 31, 126; Marrs, *Flashpoint* 98 (September 1997): 4, (April 1998): 5 (quotation), (June 1998): 2, (July 1998): 3; www.texemarrs.com, November 17, 1999.

84. Lind, *Up from Conservatism*, 115.

85. Radner, "New World Order," 848.

86. When critics confronted Robertson about his book, he declared: "My book . . . does not embrace a conspiracy theory of history and it certainly is not anti-Semitic." See Lind, "Rev. Robertson's Grand International Conspiracy Theory"; Podhoretz, "In the Matter of Pat Robertson"; Radner, "New World Order"; and Gustav Niebuhr, "Pat Robertson Says He Intended No Anti-Semitism in Book He Wrote Four Years Ago," *New York Times*, March 4, 1995.

87. Wojcik, *End*, 2, 98–99; Weber, *Apocalypses*, 201.

88. "Bad Moon Rising," written by John C. Fogerty. Used by permission of Jondora Music. All Rights reserved. *Green River*, 1969.

89. "War Pigs," words and music by Frank Iommi, John Osbourne, William Ward, and Terence Butler. Copyright © 1970 (Renewed) and 1974 Westminister Music Ltd., London, England. TRO—Essex Music International, Inc., New York, controls all publication rights for the U.S.A. and Canada. Used by permission.

90. "Abominations," *Blessed Are the Sick*, 1991.

91. Jackson Browne, "The Road in the Sky," *Late for the Sky*, 1974; Fuller, *Naming the Anti-Christ*, 223–34; Sex Pistols, "Anarchy in the UK," *Anarchy in the UK*, 1976; Iron Maiden, "Fates Warning," *No Prayer for the Dying*, 1990, "Sign of the Cross," *The X Factor*, 1995; Manowar, "Revelation (Death's Angel)," *Into Glory Ride*, 1983, "Bridge of Death," *Hail to England*, 1984; Judas Priest, "Pain Killer," *Pain Killer*, 1990; Danzig, "Long Way Back from Hell," "Snakes of Christ," "Devil's Plaything," *Lucifuge*, 1990, "Godless," "Heart of the Devil," "Left Hand Black," "Do You Wear the Mark?" *How the Gods Kill*, 1992; Blue Öyster Cult, "The Horsemen Arrive," *Bad Channels*, 1992; Morbid Angel, "Bleed for the Devil," "Damnation," *Altars of Madness*, 1989, "Fall from Grace," "Brainstorming," "Days of Suffering," *Blessed Are the Sick*, 1991, "Rapture," "Angel of Death," "Blood on My Hands," *Covenant*, 1993; *Antichrist Superstar*, 1996.

92. *X-Files*, "Duane Barry," October 14, 1994, "Terms of Endearment," January 3, 1999; *Millennium*, "Owls," March 6, 1998, "The Fourth Horseman," May 8, 1998, "The Time is Now," May 15, 1998; *Brimstone* pilot, October 23, 1998; *The Simpsons*, March 26, 1998, April 4, 1999.

93. Wojcik, *End*, 10; Wagar, *Terminal*, 24; Lamy, *Millennial Rage*, 26; Malone, *Movie Christs*, 122, 130.

94. *The Omen*, 1976.

95. *Damien: The Omen*, 1978.

96. *Omen III: The Final Conflict; Omen IV: The Awakening*, 1991.

97. December 16, 1997.

98. March 28, 2000.

99. December 15, 1998.

100. August 18, 1998.

101. March 24, 1998.

102. January 27, February 3, April 7, 14 (quotation), May 19, June 2, July 28, August 11, 18, 25, September 8, October 6, 1998, May 11, June 8, 1999.

103. Hagee, *Beginning*, 8.

104. Van Impe Ministries letter, July 13, 1998; Van Impe, "European," 4.

105. *Salt Lake Tribune*, June 13, 1998.

106. Dailey, *Millennial Deception*, 69.

107. *Salt Lake Tribune*, October 24, 1998, January 3, 1999; *Conspiracy Nation* newsletter 2 (April 1997): 1; http://www.the700club.org, February 18, 1998; *700 Club*, CBN, June 3, 1998; Fox, *Agenda*, 36, 57; Wojcik, *End*, 175, 185, 193; *New York Times*, January 27, 1999; Gallup, *Gallup Poll*, 1996, 204; Woodward, "Way," 68–69.

108. Woodward, "Way," 70; *Salt Lake Tribune*, October 25, 1997; Van Impe Ministries, *Perhaps Today* newsletter, November–December, 1999; Wojcik, *End*, 156. For examples, see, http://www.dccsa.com/greatjoy/anti.html, http://www.texemarrs.com/, and http://www.Bible-prophecy.com/index.htm.

109. Harrell, *Pat Robertson*, 218.

Chapter 4. The View from the Grassy Knoll

1. Weisberg, *Case Opened*, 176.

2. Guth and Wrone, *Assassination*, passim; Zelizer, *Covering the Body*, 34.

3. Holland, "Key," 52, 54.

4. Beschloss, "Johnson Tapes," 57.

5. *Newsweek* 134 (December 20, 1999): 68.

6. Litchfield, *It's a Conspiracy*, 227.

7. Holland, "Key," 52, 54; Thomas, "Real Cover-Up," 90; "Matter of Reasonable Doubt," 48.

8. Roberts, *Truth*, 40.

9. November 22, 1963.

10. November 23, 1963, 4; November 24, 1963, 2.

11. Zelizer, *Covering the Body*, 73, 75; Policoff, "Second Dallas Casualty," in Blumenthal and Yazijian, *Government by Gunplay*, 210; Payne, "Press Corps," 17, 27; William L. Rivers, "The Press and the Assassination," in Greenberg and Parker, *Kennedy Assassination*, 51–60; *New York Times*, November 23, 1963, 5; November 26, 1963, 14 (quotation).

12. McCauley and Jacques, "Popularity," 637, 644; Bob Herbert, "A Historian's View," *New York Times*, June 3, 1999, 25; Gallup, *Gallup Poll*, 1935–1971, 3: 1854; Paul B. Sheatsley and Jacob J. Feldman, "A National Survey on Public Reactions and Behavior," in Greenberg and Parker, *Kennedy Assassination*, 164.

13. Zelizer, *Covering the Body,* 66.

14. Mandel, "End," 52F.

15. *Washington Post,* December 18, 1963.

16. Dudman, "Uncertainties." See also Dudman, "Commentary," 18.

17. Minnis and Lynd, "Seeds of Doubt," 14, 16, 19; Meagher, *Accessories,* 460; Epstein, *Inquest,* 14, 174.

18. Joesten, *Oswald,* 138, 146, 151–52.

19. Oliver, "Marxmanship in Dallas," 1: 20, 21, 2: 73–74.

20. *Warren Commission Report,* 191, 22, 374, xii, xiii, 16–22, 50–56, 70–76, 96–111, 115–17, 119–22, 129, 195, 363–64, 637–68; Anson, *They've Killed the President,* 70.

21. September 28, 1964.

22. "The Warren Commission Report," *Time* 84 (October 2, 1964): 45.

23. Frewin, *Assassination,* 25; Anson, *They've Killed the President,* 138; Meagher, *Accessories,* 458; Ford, "Piecing Together," passim; Policoff, "Second Dallas Casualty," in Blumenthal and Yazijian, *Government by Gunplay,* 211–12 (quotation).

24. Epstein, *Inquest,* 30 (quotation); Posner, *Case Closed,* 408.

25. *Salt Lake Tribune,* August 12, 1997.

26. Posner, *Case Closed,* 408.

27. Epstein, *Inquest,* 122; Beschloss, "Johnson Tapes," 58; *Salt Lake Tribune,* October 6, 1997.

28. Thomas, "Real Cover-Up," 84.

29. O'Neill, *Man,* 178.

30. Holland, "Key," 57, 60; Posner, *Case Closed,* 81, 186–87, 210, 215–16, 406; Epstein, *Inquest,* 73–74; Thomas, "Real Cover-Up," 84; Donner, *Age,* 255.

31. Mailer, *Oswald's Tale,* 351.

32. Arthur Schlesinger, Jr., "*JFK*: Truth and Fiction," *Wall Street Journal,* January 10, 1992.

33. December 18, 1964.

34. Posner, *Case Closed,* 306; Hurt, *Reasonable Doubt,* 24, 432–33; Lifton, *Best Evidence,* 13.

35. Trillin, "The Buffs," 43, 45, 65–66, 68; Posner, *Case Closed,* 410–16; Epstein, "Who's Afraid," 204; Simon, *Dangerous Knowledge,* 21; Weisberg, *Case Opened,* 44; Guth and Wrone, *Assassination,* 11. Among the books appearing in 1965 and 1966 were Epstein, *Inquest;* Jones, *Forgive;* Lane, *Rush;* and Weisberg, *Whitewash.*

36. Lane, *Rush,* 90.

37. Epstein, *Inquest,* 56, 70, 110–11, 115–16, 119; Lane, *Rush,* 81–85, 90, 129, 172–73, 178, 180, 190, 324–42.

38. Weisberg, *Whitewash,* 76; Lane, *Rush,* 167; Posner, *Case Closed,* 174, 211–14, 343.

39. Anson, *They've Killed the President,* 80.

40. Lifton, *Best Evidence,* 81.

41. Anson, *They've Killed the President,* 80.

42. Epstein, *Inquest,* 49.

43. Lifton, *Best Evidence,* 81–82; Epstein, *Inquest,* 38, 92, 102; Lane, *Rush,* 66–68, 71–72, 76–78; Posner, *Case Closed,* 293; "Primer," 207.

44. Lundberg, "Closing the Case," 1736.

45. Breo, "JFK's Death," 2799.

46. Weisberg, *Whitewash*, 179; Lane, *Rush*, 64–66; Epstein, *Inquest*, 40–44, 93–95; Lifton, *Best Evidence*, 119–20, 154–56.

47. "Primer," 206; Simon, *Dangerous Knowledge*, 40; Lifton, *Best Evidence*, 58; Hennelly and Policoff, "JFK," in Stone and Sklar, *JFK*, 490.

48. Garson, *MacBird*, 48.

49. Lane, *Rush*, 279.

50. "Primer," 207; Meagher, *Accessories*, 384–86; Lane, *Rush*, 69, 248–49, 261, 274–75, 277, 324–25; Gates, "Bottom Line," 53.

51. Lane, *Plausible*, 361.

52. Solomon, "True Disbelievers," 96.

53. Lane, *Rush*, 25; Epstein, *Inquest*, iii; Anson, *They've Killed the President*, 74, 142; Zelizer, *Covering the Body*, 109; Moore, *Conspiracy*, 94; Simon, *Dangerous Knowledge*, 13.

54. Beschloss, "Johnson Tapes," 58; Thomas, "Real Cover-Up," 76; Anson, *They've Killed the President*, iii; Hersh, *Dark Side*, 450–51; *Salt Lake Tribune*, September 20, 1996.

55. *New York Times*, November 25, 1996, 36.

56. *Saturday Evening Post*, 240, December 2, 1967, 88.

57. Salisbury, *Time of Change*, 70–72; *Life*, 61, November 25, 1966; Hennelly and Policoff, "JFK," in Stone and Sklar, *JFK*, 490; Thompson, "Crossfire," passim.

58. Frewin, *Assassination*, 29–30; Hunt, *Dealey Plaza*, 47, 51, 53; Kurtz, *Crime*, xv; Zelizer, *Covering the Body*, 110; Hennelly and Policoff, "JFK," in Stone and Sklar, *JFK*, 485, 493; Gallup, *Gallup Poll, 1935–1971*, 3: 2044; Blumenthal and Yazijian, *Government*, ix; Simon, *Dangerous Knowledge*, 16.

59. Simon, *Dangerous Knowledge*, 21.

60. Thompson, *Six Seconds*, 25; Moore, *Conspiracy of One*, 29, 109; Anderson, "Kennedy Assassination," 1–4, 88; Posner, *Case Closed*, 202, 234 (quotation), 252.

61. Anderson, "Kennedy Assassination," 106–8; Hurt, *Reasonable Doubt*, 36. In the motion picture *Annie Hall* (1977), Woody Allen offered insight about the easy slip from common sense to farce:

> ALVIE: It's obsessing me. . . . So how is it possible for Oswald to have fired from two angles at once? It doesn't make sense. I'll tell you this: he was not marksman enough to hit a moving target at that range. But— if there was a second assassin—that's it! . . .
>
> ALLISON: Then everybody's in on the conspiracy: the FBI and the CIA and J. Edgar Hoover and the oil companies and the Pentagon and the men's room attendant at the White House?
>
> ALVIE: I would leave out the men's room attendant.

62. Garrison, *Heritage*, 75, 82, 38.

63. Hurt, *Reasonable Doubt*, 265.

64. Garrison, *Heritage*, 102 (quotation), 64, 83, 107, 156, 160, 162–63, 170, 176, 209–10; Posner, *Case Closed*, 430, 446; Kurtz, *Crime*, xi, 158; Hurt, *Reasonable Doubt*, 268, 272; Anson, *They've Killed the President*, 214; Marrs, *Crossfire*, 495.

65. Garrison, *Trail*, 176; Posner, *Case Closed*, 141–42; Marrs, *Crossfire*, 507;

Hurt, *Reasonable Doubt*, 262, 278, 283; Scheim, *Contract*, 10; Anson, *They've Killed the President*, 15, 105, 112, 119, 125.

66. Simon, *Dangerous Knowledge*, 8.

67. Posner, *Case Closed*, 417–18; Simon, *Dangerous Knowledge*, 17; Hunt, *Dealey Plaza*, 56.

68. Ryan and Kellner, *Camera Politica*, 95, 98–99; Frewin, *Assassination*, 99, 102–3; Simon, *Dangerous Knowledge*, 174–80, 183–85.

69. Simon, *Dangerous Knowledge*, 18–19, 45; Moore, *Conspiracy of One*, 101.

70. Anson, *They've Killed the President*, 272, 327, 269, 67, 111, 246, 253, 266–69, 272, 277–78, 300–301, 317.

71. Johnson, *Season*, 49.

72. Hunt, *Dealey Plaza*, 47–48; Fonzi, *Last*, 30, 38, 41; Johnson, *Season*, 48–51, 126–28, 223–24; Schorr, "Assassins," 14, 16–17; Zelizer, *Covering the Body*, 113–14.

73. House Select Committee, *Final Report*, 3–4, 41–44, 46, 97, 164, 169, 173, 176; Zelizer, *Covering the Body*, 116–19; Anderson, "Kennedy Assassination," 105.

74. Fonzi, *Last*, 12.

75. Kurtz, *Crime*, 186.

76. Gallup, *Gallup Poll, 1972–1977*, 2: 930.

77. Hennelly and Policoff, "JFK," in Stone and Sklar, *JFK*, 496; Zelizer, *Covering the Body*, 120; Posner, *Case Closed*, 238–39; Gallup, *Gallup Poll, 1972–1977*, 2: 927–30.

78. Epstein, *Legend*, 3, 44, 104, 110, 122, 260, 294.

79. Lifton, *Best Evidence*, 336, 806, 202, 404, 302, 391, 239, 605, 675, 763, 773, 784, 790, 795; Hurt, *Reasonable Doubt*, 424.

80. Hurt, *Reasonable Doubt*, 7, 192, 193, 204, 212, 240, 302, 305, 346, 351.

81. Garrison, *On the Trail*, 264 (quotation), 81, 263–64, 328, 337.

82. DeLillo, *Libra*, 51, 386.

83. Scheim, *Contract*, 287, 284, 255, 19, 75, 80, 85–86, 89, 90, 203, 271, 300, 305; Mark North's *Act of Treason* accepted this interpretation and considered FBI Director J. Edgar Hoover's role. Hoover, North maintained, knew of the mob contract but remained silent. With Kennedy dead, the director did not have to worry that he would be replaced after the president's victory in the 1964 election.

84. Groden and Livingstone, *High Treason*, 421, 83, 281, 416, 9, 16–17, 25, 82, 215, 281, 309, 331, 404.

85. Marrs, *Crossfire*, 433, 300, 186, 431, 539, 546; *New York Times*, February 2, 1992, VII, 28.

86. Hurt, *Reasonable Doubt*, 45, 241, 513; Goertzel, "Belief," 731; Groden and Livingstone, *High Treason*, 164.

87. Kagan, *Cinema*, 13.

88. Breskin, "Oliver Stone," 9, 13.

89. Riordan, *Stone*, 27, 35.

90. Kagan, *Cinema*, 17.

91. Salewicz, *Oliver Stone*, 8, 19, 21, 23; Riordan, *Stone*, 3, 8, 10, 11, 21, 35, 40; Breskin, "Oliver Stone," 7; Kagan, *Cinema*, 13, 18; Beaver, *Oliver Stone*, 4.

92. Riordan, *Stone*, 84, 88, 531–32; Mackey-Kallis, *Oliver Stone*, 147–48.

93. Anson, "Shooting," in Stone and Sklar, *JFK*, 213.

94. Prouty, *JFK,* 43, 80, 11, 14, 141, 310, 127.

95. Mackey-Kallis, *Oliver Stone,* 27.

96. Prouty, *JFK,* xxii, xxxii–iii, 220, 256, 266–68, 287.

97. *New York Times,* November 24, 1963, 12.

98. Berlet, "Friendly Fascists," 18; Gelb, "Kennedy and Vietnam," in Stone and Sklar, *JFK,* 591–92; Moss, *Vietnam,* 130; Herring, *America's Longest War,* 107.

99. Simon, *Dangerous Knowledge,* 211.

100. Riordan, *Stone,* 408.

101. "Splinters to the Brain," 52.

102. Riordan, *Stone,* 368.

103. See also Stone and Sklar, *JFK.*

104. "Splinters to the Brain," 53.

105. Riordan, *Stone,* 398–99, 407; Solomon, "True Disbelievers," 96; *New York Times,* December 17, 1995, H41.

106. Achincloss, "Twisted History," 47.

107. "JFK: Paranoid History," *Washington Post,* December 26, 1991.

108. "JFK: A Lie, but Harmless," *Washington Post,* January 10, 1992.

109. Simon, *Dangerous Knowledge,* 205; Mankiewicz, "About the Debate," in Stone and Sklar, *JFK,* 187; Maslin, "Oliver Stone," 15; Safire, "The Way It Really Was," 13; *New York Times,* January 16, 1992, 22.

110. Stone, "Who Is Rewriting History?" 35.

111. Riordan, *Stone,* 416.

112. Raskin, "*JFK,*" 487.

113. Zelizer, *Covering the Body,* 202, 206–7; Rogin, "*JFK,*" 500–505; Riordan, *Stone,* 443; Kurtz, *Crime,* lvi; Prouty, *JFK,* 350.

114. Zelizer, *Covering the Body,* 209; Butler, et al., "Psychological Impact," 237, 245, 248.

115. Kurtz, *Crime,* li.

116. Livingstone, *Killing Kennedy,* xv, 26, 116, 119, 123, 360, 364, 367.

117. Kurtz, *Crime,* ix, xlvi–liii.

118. *Seinfeld,* "The Boy Friend, Part I," February 12, 1992.

119. *Ruby* (1992); Simon, *Dangerous Knowledge,* 228; Frewin, *Assassination,* 75–77; *Quantum Leap,* "Lee Harvey Oswald," September 22, 1992; *The X-Files,* "Things Really Did Go Well in Dealey Plaza," November 17, 1996, "Small Potatoes," March 22, 1998.

120. *Coast to Coast A.M. with Art Bell,* April 28, 1999.

121. Cooper, *Behold,* 215–16, 222; *Dark Skies,* September 28, 1996; Mike Foster, "JFK," *World Weekly News,* January 11, 2000.

122. *Flashpoint,* February 1998.

123. Epperson, *Driver; Washington Post,* August 21, 1997; Piper, *Final Judgment,* 1, 8, 49, 57, 298.

124. *Final Report of the Assassination Records Review Board,* xxiii, 2, xxiv–xxvii, 42, 49, 71–72, 175–76; *New York Times,* September 29, 1998, 17, November 10, 1998, 20; *Salt Lake Tribune,* July 2, 3, November 28, 1997, August 1, 14, 1998; Posner, "Cracks," 49; Carlin, "Kennedy's Death," 10.

125. *New York Times,* September 29, 1998, 17.

126. "JFK Resources Online," http://users.southeast.net/cheryl/JFK.html, October 21, 1999 (inactive); "JFK Assassination Collection," http://www.erols.

com/simoules/JFK.htm, October 17, 1999 (inactive); "The Kennedy Assassination for the Novice," http://pages.prodigy.net/ whiskey99/, May 16, 2000 (inactive); "John F. Kennedy Assassination Home Page," www.informatik.uni-rostock.de/ Kennedy/body.html, October 24, 1999.

127. CNN News, November 23, 1998.

128. April 1, 2000.

129. April 4, 2000, 40–41.

130. "Men Who Killed Kennedy," August 16–21, 1999, March 20–25, 2000; Pipes, *Conspiracy*, 16; *New York Times*, May 28, 1995, 14; *Salt Lake Tribune*, May 18, 1997; "Militias and Messiahs," *Economist* 343 (April 5, 1997): 58; KUTV News, July 24, 1998.

131. Riordan, *Stone*, 355.

Chapter 5. Jewish Devils and the War on Black America

1. Goertze, "Belief," 734; DeParle, "Talk," *New York Times*, October 29, 1990, B7. See also Turner, *I Heard It*.

2. Lincoln, *Black Muslims*, 10; Elijah Muhammad, *Message*, 16–17, 97, 103, 111–12, 114–17; Elijah Muhammad, *Supreme Wisdom*, 12; Clegg, *Original Man*, 41–58.

3. Jabril Muhammad, *Farrakhan*, iv; Elijah Muhammad, *Supreme Wisdom*, 24–25, 41; Clegg, *Original Man*, 63; Goldman, *Death*, 43; Elijah Muhammad, *Message*, 17–18.

4. Gardell, *In the Name*, 56.

5. Lincoln, *Black Muslims*, 77.

6. Gardell, *In the Name*, 55; Allen, "Minister Louis Farrakhan," in Alexander, *Farrakhan Factor*, 77; Elijah Muhammad, *Message*, 171, 290; Elijah Muhammad, *Mother Plane*, 16; Lincoln, *Black Muslims*, 79, 86; Kempton, "Fall," 55.

7. Gardell, *In the Name*, 73 (quotation), 53, 59, 69, 71–74; O'Reilly, *Racial Matters*, 13, 42; Carson, *Malcolm X*, 27, 30.

8. Allen, "Minister Louis Farrakhan," 62; Malcolm X, *Autobiography*, passim; Lincoln, *Black Muslims*, 4.

9. Malcolm X, *Autobiography*, 284, 286.

10. Clegg, *Original Man*, 195, 244, 129.

11. Malcolm X, "Black Man's History," *The End of World Supremacy*, 35.

12. Malcolm X, *Autobiography*, 289.

13. Malcolm X, *Playboy* interview with Alex Haley, reprinted in Gallen, *Malcolm X*, 113.

14. Weitz, "Black Attitudes," 129.

15. Lerner and West, *Jews and Blacks*, 1–2; Weitz, "Black Attitudes," 9; Jahannes, *Blacks and Jews*, 4; Friedman, *What Went Wrong?* 44–45, 58–60, 84; Pogrebin, *Deborah*, 294; Diner, *In the Almost Promised Land*, 35, 74, 119–20, 164–91; Lewis, "Parallels," 564.

16. Scheiner, *Negro Mecca*, 131.

17. Clark, "Candor," 8.

18. Baldwin, "Negroes Are Anti-Semitic," in Hentoff, *Black Anti-Semitism*, 3–4.

19. Perry, *Malcolm*, 196.

20. Weisbord and Stein, *Bittersweet Encounter*, 40, 42; Katz, *Negro and Jew*, 99, 102, 112, 124–25; Bloom, "Interactions," 17, 179, 187; Reddick, "Anti-Semitism," 116; Berson, *Negroes and Jews*, 176, 192, 217; Labovitz, *Attitudes*, 12–24; Dinnerstein, *Anti-Semitism*, 202–6; Baldwin, *Notes*, 59; Halpern, *Jews and Blacks*, 167.

21. Wright, *Black Boy*, 70.

22. Friedman, *What Happened*, 28.

23. Dinnerstein, *Anti-Semitism*, 197–98; Friedman, *What Went Wrong?* 28, 79, 93, 100, 103; Wright, *Black Boy*, 77.

24. Drake and Clayton, *Black Metropolis*, I, 448.

25. Bloom, "Interactions," 134–35, 141, 152; Price, "Black Response," 132–33, 135, 183, 208; McDowell, "Race and Ethnicity," 138–42; Stevenson, "Points of Departure," 93–94, 145, 486, 489; Greenberg, *Or Does It Explode?* 3–4, 114–39; Naison, *Communists*, 321, 326; Cruse, *Crisis*, 147, 150, 158, 167, 169, 484; Diner, *In the Almost Promised Land*, 79–80; Weisbord and Stein, *Bittersweet Encounter*, 44–48.

26. "The Black and the Jew: A Falling Out of Allies," *Time* 93 (January 31, 1969): 55.

27. Price, "Black Response," 288.

28. Bayton, "Racial Stereotypes," 98.

29. Bloom, "Interactions," 165, 171–72; Gurock, *When Harlem Was Jewish*, 139, 145–47; Glazer and Moynihan, *Beyond the Melting Pot*, 71–73; Bulkin, Pratt, and Smith, *Yours in Struggle*, 69.

30. Heller and Pinkney, "Attitudes," 365–69.

31. Berson, *Negroes and Jews*, 8–9.

32. King, "Negroes," 8.

33. Berson, *Negroes and Jews*, 329.

34. Lincoln, *Black Muslims*, 155.

35. Ellerin, "Black Muslims," 2.

36. Malcolm X, *Autobiography*, 36.

37. Goldman, *Death*, 15.

38. Clegg, *Original Man*, 152–54; Lincoln, *Black Muslims*, 147, 149; *New York Times*, January 31, 1972, 14; Malcolm X, "Black Man's History," in *End*, 33–34.

39. Gardell, *In the Name*, 74–76, 79–84, 89; McPhail, "Louis Abdul Farrakhan," 121; Magida, *Prophet of Rage*, 77, 82–82, 104; Donner, *Age*, 213, 271; Carson, *Malcolm X*, 30; O'Reilly, *Racial Matters*, 271, 278. See also Evanzz, *Judas Factor*.

40. "SNCC and the Jews," *Newsweek* 70 (August 28, 1967): 22.

41. Weisbord and Kazarian, *Israel*, 33.

42. Carmichael, *Stokely Speaks*, 136–38; Weitz, "Black Attitudes," 171, 287; Weisbord and Stein, *Bittersweet Encounter*, 72–73; Ellis, " . . . Semitism," January 1966, 7, February 1966, 14–15.

43. Weitz, "Black Attitudes," 180–276; Friedman, *What Went Wrong?* 213–15, 268; Kaufman, *Broken Alliance*, 141–57; Berson, *Negroes and Jews*, 418–21; Weisbord and Stein, *Bittersweet Encounter*, 139–41, 164, 169.

44. Goldberg, *Jewish Power*, 291–92, 299, 302, 317–19, passim; Dinnerstein, *Anti-Semitism*, 215–16; Salzman and West, *Struggles*, 296–99; Stevenson, "Points of Departure," 17–18; Kaufman, *Broken Alliance*, 222–23, 274; Friedman, *What Went Wrong?* 309–13, 320.

45. Weisbord and Kazarian, *Israel*, 125.

46. Goldberg, *Jewish Power*, 322.

47. Pogrebin, "Anti-Semitism," 74.

48. Weisbord and Kazarian, *Israel*, 93, 100, 122; Goldberg, *Jewish Power*, 4, 203, 322–24; *New York Times*, August 17, 1979, 1; Kaufman, *Broken Alliance*, 245–46; Miller, "Black Viewpoints," 37; Dinnerstein, *Anti-Semitism*, 217.

49. Goldberg, *Jewish Power*, 5; Evanier, "Louis Farrakhan," 6; Silberman, *Certain People*, 339; Kaufman, *Broken Alliance*, 229.

50. Forster and Epstein, *New Anti-Semitism*, 208; Allen, "Minister Louis Farrakhan," 70–72; Magida, *Prophet of Rage*, 117, 122.

51. Magida, *Prophet of Rage*, 119–24, 131.

52. Ibid., 20.

53. Farrakhan, "Stop the Killing;" Gardell, *In the Name*, 119–20; Magida, *Prophet of Rage*, xvi, 4, 9–29; Gates, "Charmer," 119; Marshall, *Louis Farrakhan*, 25–26.

54. Magida, *Prophet of Rage*, 31–32; Marshall, *Louis Farrakhan*, 28.

55. Kurlander and Salit, *Independent Black Leadership*, 27.

56. *Muhammad Speaks*, December 4, 1964.

57. Marshall, *Louis Farrakhan*, 73.

58. McPhail, "Louis Abdul Farrakhan," 121; Magida, *Prophet of Rage*, 77, 83; Marshall, *Louis Farrakhan*, 59, 80. In 1998 Louis Farrakhan appointed Muhammad Abdul Aziz, who had been imprisoned for his part in the assassination of Malcolm X, as chief of security for the Harlem mosque and chief of security and training for the East Coast Region of the Nation of Islam.

59. Farrakhan, *Seven Speeches*, 117, 44.

60. Forster and Epstein, *New Anti-Semitism*, 210; Marshall, *Louis Farrakhan*, 100.

61. Gardell, *In the Name*, 122; Magida, *Prophet of Rage*, 119.

62. Marshall, *Louis Farrakhan*, 109.

63. Magida, *Prophet of Rage*, 124.

64. Evanier, *Louis Farrakhan*, 19–20.

65. Farrakhan, "Warning to the Government."

66. Gardell, *In the Name*, 262; Copage, "Farrakhan," 51; Magida, *Prophet of Rage*, 130–36; Allen, "Minister Louis Farrakhan," 79.

67. Farrakhan, "What Is the Need for Black History?" 73.

68. Lee, *Nation*, 107.

69. "Jackson and the Jews," *New Republic* 190 (March 19, 1984): 9.

70. Goldberg, *Jewish Power*, 324.

71. Weisbord and Kazarian, *Israel*, 148.

72. Kaufman, *Broken Alliance*, 256.

73. *Blacks and Jews News*, Fall–Winter 1994, 1; Magida, *Prophet of Rage*, 144, 179; Gardell, *In the Name*, 250; Blitzer, *Between Washington and Jerusalem*, 185.

74. Marshall, *Louis Farrakhan*, 139, 140.

75. Farrakhan, "Rise of Jesse Jackson."

76. *Chicago Tribune*, April 15, 1984.

77. Evanier, *Louis Farrakhan*, 41.

78. Jabril Muhammad, *Special Spokesman*, 169, 171; Gardell, *In the Name*, 253–54; Barnes, "Farrakhan Frenzy," 13.

79. Marshall, *Louis Farrakhan*, 145.

80. Blitzer, *Between Washington and Jerusalem*, 186; Marshall, *Louis Farrakhan*, 140.

81. Farrakhan, "Power at Last . . . Forever!"

82. Marshall, *Louis Farrakhan*, 147, 151; Gardell, *In the Name*, 139; Haskins, *Louis Farrakhan*, 95–96; Singh, *Farrakhan Phenomenon*, 179.

83. *Washington Post*, March 1, 1990.

84. Kurapka, "Hate Story," 20. On Hollywood and race see Rogin, *Blackface*, and Diner, "Trading Faces."

85. *Chicago Sun Times*, May 10, 1988.

86. Henry, "Pride and Prejudice," 26; *Chicago Sun Times*, July 18, 1993; *Chicago Tribune*, May 2, 4, 1988; *Washington Post*, May 3, 1988; Farrakhan, "The 1980s."

87. *Secret Relationship*, passim.

88. Brackman, *Ministry of Lies*, 1: 8, 9, 11, 24–25, 30, 69; Caplan, *Jew-Hatred*, 15, 32; *Blacks and Jews News*, September 1994, 1–2, Spring 1995, 1–2; *Blacks and Jews*, http://www.blacksandjews.com, May 23, August 4, 1997 (as www.tiac.net:80/users/lhl). See also, Martin, *Jewish Onslaught*, passim.

89. Singh, *Farrakhan Phenomenon*, 159.

90. *Washington Post*, March 1, 1990.

91. Farrakhan, "Revealing the Conspiracy."

92. *Washington Post*, March 1, 1990.

93. Gardell, *In the Name*, 327.

94. *Final Call*, May 26, 1998.

95. Farrakhan, "Politics."

96. Farrakhan, *Seven Speeches*, 99–100; *Torchlight*, 42; "Separation and Reparations"; "Politics"; "Revealing the Conspiracy"; "Stop the Killing!"; "White Supremacy"; "Black Youth"; "In Christ."

97. Farrakhan, "Rise of Jesse Jackson."

98. *Final Call*, October 6, 1998.

99. Kimberly Jane Wilson, "The Big Lie," *Final Call*, September 14, 1999, December 8, 22, 1998, Abdul Alim Muhammad, "Life Abundantly," August 25, September 15, 1998.

100. Carson, *Malcolm X*, 17; Gibbs, *Race and Justice*, 235–37; Farrakhan, "Separation and Reparations."

101. Farrakhan, "Stop the Killing!"

102. Farrakhan, "White Supremacy."

103. McPhail, "Passionate Intensity," 5–21; Singh, *Farrakhan Phenomenon*, 25, 187.

104. Lena Williams, "Blacks, Jews, and 'This Thing That Is Suffocating Us,'" *New York Times*, July 29, 1990, 5.

105. *Chicago Sun Times*, July 18, 1993; *New York Times*, March 5, 1994, 1, 8; Gardell, *In the Name*, 305–6, 341; Singh, *Farrakhan Phenomenon*, 34–35; Evanier, *Anti-Semitism*, 9–12; Hentoff, "Legitimation," 7, 21; William Raspberry, "Standing Up to the Jews," *Washington Post*, October 30, 1989; Henry, "Pride and Prejudice," 22.

106. Clarence Page, "Heartbeat of the Black Movement Gets Stronger," *Salt Lake Tribune*, September 21, 1993.

107. Gardell, *In the Name,* 243, 265; Evanier, *Anti-Semitism,* 17; *Washington Post,* April 23, 1989; *Salt Lake Tribune,* September 21, 1993; *New York Times,* January 25, 1994, 12; Singh, *Farrakhan Phenomenon,* 218; Reed, "Rise," 1; Wright and Glick, "Farrakhan's Mission," 25; Smith, "Who's Afraid," in Alexander, *Farrakhan Factor,* 107.

108. Haskins, *Louis Farrakhan,* 132–39; *Final Call,* September 27, October 20, 1995; Sadler, *Atonement,* vii, 49, 71, 76; "Losing Ground," *Newsweek* 119 (April 6, 1992): 20; Singh, *Farrakhan Phenomenon,* 243; Magida, *Prophet of Rage,* 168, 186; Gallup, *Gallup Poll,* 1995, 163; Marshall, *Louis Farrakhan,* 240. The Million Man March later inspired the Million Woman March and the Million Youth March. See *Salt Lake Tribune,* October 26, 1997, August 29, 1998; *Final Call,* August 25, August 31, September 15, 1998; *New York Times,* September 9, 1998, 25.

109. Linzer, *Nation of Islam,* 7, 8–9.

110. Transcript of "Farrakhan on Meet the Press," *Final Call,* May 20, 1997.

111. *Ugly Truth,* 7, 104, 130.

112. *Final Call,* June 29, 1992, June 17, November 25, 1997, May 12, 1998, January 12, 1999.

113. Berman, *Blacks and Jews,* 1–2. Farrakhan later rebuked Muhammad for his "mockery" and his "repugnant, malicious, mean-spirited . . . manner" but defended his "truths." Farrakhan declared: "My brother Khalid, he's a warrior, he's a fighter for his people. He's not the most diplomatic brother, but he's a fighter." Magida, *Prophet of Rage,* 181; Marshall, *Louis Farrakhan,* 208.

114. Linzer, *Nation of Islam,* 13; *Washington Post,* April 20, 1994.

115. Khalid Abdul Muhammad speech at San Francisco State University, May 21, 1997, ADL mailing.

116. Goldberg, *Jewish Power,* 15; Lori Epstein, "Ex-Farrakhan Aide Urges Violence in S.F. State Speech, *Jewish Bulletin of Northern California,* May 30, 1997; *New York Times,* January 26, 1994, 13, March 4, 1994, 10; Ross, *Schooled in Hate,* 15–17; Caplan and Linzer, *Uncommon Ground,* 1–5, 9–10, 17; "Blacks and Jews News," August 4, 1997, http://www.blacksandjews.com; *Final Call,* June 17, 1997.

117. *Final Call,* June 9, 1996.

118. Ibid., January 31, 1987.

119. Farrakhan, "The 1980s"; Farrakhan, "In Christ"; *Washington Post,* October 26, 1989, March 1, 1990; Jabril Muhammad, "Coming to Grips"; Cannon, "The Final Call?" 36; Gardell, *In the Name,* 131–35; *Final Call,* October 16, 1996, May 27, August 19, 1997 (quotation), June 23, 1998, October 5, 1999, January 4, 2000.

120. *Chicago Defender,* September 20, 1999.

121. *Final Call,* December 7, 1999.

122. Mark Hosenball and Gregory Vistica, "The Life and Times of a Rumor," *Newsweek* 131 (January 19, 1998): 31.

123. *New York Times,* March 23, 2000, 14.

124. Goertzel, "Belief," 734; Gallup, *Gallup Poll, 1976–1977,* 2: 928, *1995,* 219; Evan Thomas, "Death of an Assassin," *Newsweek* 131 (May 5, 1998): 32, (May 10, 1999): 27 (quotation).

125. *Washington Post,* March 17, 1998.

126. Fletcher, "Conspiracy Theories."

127. Hentoff, "Who Will Speak the Truth?"

128. Bates, "Is It Genocide?" 76.

129. De Parle, "Talk."

130. "Losing Ground," 21.

131. Berlet, *Right Woos Left*, 43.

132. Zoglin, "Not-So-Hot Copy," 81; Goertzel, "Belief," 734; Kelly, "Road," 65; Fletcher, "Conspiracy Theories;" Turner, *I Heard It*, 137–38, 159, 180, 182; *New York Times*, May 6, 1992, 14; Caplan, *Jew-Hatred*, 45; Pogrebin, "Blacks and Jews," 332.

133. See also lyrics to "Miss Ghetto" on the *New World Order* album (1996). "I'm Comin' Again," written by Tony Depula and Timothy Grimes.

134. *Washington Post*, October 13, 1997; Gardell, *In the Name*, 295–96; Marshall, *Louis Farrakhan*, 39; Cooper and Ferguson, "Return of the Paranoid Style," 31. For Ice Cube, see also lyrics to "No Vaseline" on *Death Certificate* and "Enemy" on *Lethal Injection*. "When I Get to Heaven," by O'Shea Jackson and Brian Gallow © 1993 WB Music Company, Gangsta Boogie Music, Claramax Music, and Jobete Music Co., Inc. (Contains samples from "Inner City Blues" by Marvin Gaye and James Nyx), Jobete Music Co., Inc. All Rights on behalf of Gangsta Boogie Music administered by WB Music Corp. All Rights Reserved. Used by permission Warner Bros. Publications U.S. Inc., Miami, Fla., 33014.

135. *Meet the Press*, April 13, 1997, October 18, 1998.

136. *Final Call*, January 13, November 24, December 8, 1998.

137. *Salt Lake Tribune*, February 27, 2000; *New York Times*, March 3, 1997, 13; *Final Call*, May 20, 1997, January 6, 1998; www.radioislam.net/talmud/index.htm, November 17, 1999; www.blacksandjews.com, June 25, 1999, June 22, 2000,; www.noi.org, June 20, 2000.

138. *Salt Lake Tribune*, April 3, 1999.

139. *Final Call*, March 16, April 6, 1999.

140. Lisa Miller, "Black Muslims Flock to Moderate Cleric," *Wall Street Journal*, July 9, 1999; *N.Y. Times*, February 28, 2000, 8; *Salt Lake Tribune*, May 18, 2000.

141. www.noi.org, June 23, 2000.

142. *Salt Lake Tribune*, December 3, 1998.

143. Cose, "Good News," 33.

Chapter 6. The Roswell Incident

1. Press conference, July 4, 1997.

2. *Albuquerque Journal*, July 5, July 4, 1997.

3. Pflock, *Roswell in Perspective*, 2.

4. Bloecher, *Report*, 8–11, 14; Jacobs, *UFO Controversy*, 35–38; *Roswell Morning Dispatch*, July 6, 1947; *Roswell Daily Record*, July 7, 1947.

5. *Roswell Morning Dispatch*, July 9, 1947; *Roswell Daily Record*, July 9, 1947.

6. Loftin, *Identified Flying Saucers*, 21.

7. Jerome Clark, "Crashed Saucers of the 1950s," in Eberhardt, *Roswell Report*, 92; Edwards, *Flying Saucers*, 76; Scully, *Behind the Flying Saucers*, 128–33.

8. Berlitz and Moore, *Roswell Incident*, 72, 76.

9. Friedman interview.

10. Berliner and Friedman, "Crashed Flying Saucers;" Friedman and Berliner, *Crash at Corona*, xi; Friedman interview.

11. Hollywood bought the rights to the book, which became a film in 1984.

12. Blum, *Out There*, 222–23; Joe Nickell and John F. Fischer, "The Crashed-Saucer Forgeries," in Eberhardt, *Roswell Report*, 119; Moore, "Roswell Incident"; Moore interview; Stanton Friedman e-mail to the author, July 9, 2000.

13. Moore interview; Moore, "Roswell Incident."

14. Berlitz and Moore, *Roswell Incident*, 7, 18, 33, 47, 48, 78–79, 83, 85, 88, 94, 95. The book mentions Stanton Friedman only in the context of the interviews that he conducted. An authors' acknowledgment did not make the final draft of the book. Friedman did receive a portion of Moore's share of the royalties. Friedman email to the author, July 9, 2000.

15. Schmitt interview.

16. Randle interview; www.randlereport.com, July 5, 2000; Schmitt interview.

17. Randle and Schmitt, *UFO Crash*, 117, 5, 271.

18. Ibid., 37, 40, 41–44, 50, 51, 53, 79, 87, 91–92.

19. Ibid., 47, 63, 74–75, 82, 90, 93, 97; Saler, Ziegler, and Moore, *UFO Crash*, 64.

20. Friedman and Berliner, *Crash at Corona*, xii (quotation), 101, 129, 192.

21. Randle and Schmitt, *Truth*, 7, 10, 16, 28, 99, 169–75, 272.

22. Peebles, *Watch the Skies!* 248; Randle, *Roswell UFO Crash Update*, 123–36.

23. Schmitt interview.

24. Peebles, *Watch the Skies!*, 248; Saler, Ziegler, and Moore, *U.F.O. Crash*, 160.

25. Smith, *Little Gray Men*, 29.

26. Schmitt interview.

27. Randle, *Conspiracy of Silence*, 27.

28. Randle, *History*, 6.

29. Stacy, "Morass," 11; Krass, *UFOs: The Public Deceived*, 303–4; Krass, *Real Roswell*, 89, 145, 154, 157, 177, 191–92, 194; Korff, *Roswell UFO Crash*, 42–51, 53–54, 61–64, 89–91, 99; Brookesmith, *UFO*, 155–60.

30. Vallee, *Revelations*, 232.

31. Korff, *Roswell UFO Crash*, 110; letter to Art Bell, April 10, 1996, in the author's possession.

32. Brown, *Cosmic Voyage*, 14, 183.

33. Strieber, *Majestic*, 159.

34. Pflock, *Roswell*, 114–16; Keel, "Roswell Furor," 58; Sutherly, *Strange Encounter*, 54–55; Eberhardt, *Roswell Report*, 48–55; Brown, *Cosmic Voyage*, 183–85; Strieber, *Majestic*, 119–20.

35. Friedman and Berliner, *Crash at Corona*, 132–33.

36. Friedman interview.

37. Moore interview; Friedman and Berliner, *Crash at Corona*, 55–56, 64–66, 195–97, 199; Hesemann and Mantle, *Beyond Roswell*, 90; Friedman, *Final Report*, A1–8.

38. Friedman and Berliner, *Crash at Corona*, 58, 68–69; Friedman, *Final Report*, 2–3, A9; Friedman, "Update," 272; Friedman, *Top Secret/Majic*, passim; Friedman interview; Hesemann and Mantle, *Beyond Roswell*, 93–95.

39. Howe, *Alien Harvest*, 136, 135, 143–57, 255–57; Howe interview; Hesemann and Mantle, *Beyond Roswell*, 110–13.

40. Vallee, *Revelations,* 40.

41. Mark Rodegher, "Some Thoughts on MJ-12," in Eberhardt, *Roswell Report,* 130.

42. Randle, *History,* 146.

43. Randle, *Conspiracy,* 6.

44. Friedman, *Top Secret/Majic,* xii.

45. Brookesmith, *UFO,* 95; Shawcross, *Roswell File,* 127, 131, 134; Patton, *Dreamland,* 199; Randle, *History,* 122–26.

46. Cooper, *Behold,* 28, 85, 196–204, 207–15, 226.

47. Commander X, *Incredible Technologies,* 7, 8, 11, 12, 21, 22, 49, 76; Commander X, *Ultimate Deception,* 4, 26, 31, 34, 91, 115. See also Hamilton, *Cosmic Top Secret;* Hayakawa, *UFOs;* and Steiger, *Rainbow Conspiracy.*

48. Jacobs, *UFO Controversy,* 51, 54.

49. Blum, *Out There,* 62–68; Jacobs, *UFO Controversy,* 31–32, 44, 50–54, 56; Peebles, *Watch the Skies!* 17, 34, 43; Patton, *Dreamland,* 97, 105–6.

50. Good, *Above Top Secret,* 333.

51. Jacobs, *UFO Controversy,* 32–33, 63, 68, 82, 87–95; Good, *Above Top Secret,* 328–29.

52. Tacker, *Flying Saucers,* v.

53. Strentz, "Survey," 196.

54. Jacobs, *UFO Controversy,* 297–98; Brookesmith, *UFO,* 35, 47; Loftin, *Identified Flying Saucers,* 21–22; Strentz, "Survey," 149, 179–86, 216.

55. Keyhoe, *Flying Saucer Conspiracy,* 13, 38.

56. Randle, *Conspiracy,* 203.

57. Randle and Schmitt, *Truth,* 115.

58. Hynek, *UFO Experience,* 196–97, 205–6, 300; Condon, *Scientific Study,* 1, 5, 38.

59. Schmitt interview.

60. Fawcett and Greenwood, *Clear Intent,* iii–v, 47, 113, 147, 180–81, 189; Good, *Above Top Secret,* 253, 327, 416; Vallee, *Revelations,* 83–84; Brookesmith, *UFO,* 79–80, 165–66; Klass, *UFOs: The Public Deceived,* 8–14; *New York Times,* January 14, 1979, 23; Gerald Haines, "CIA's Role in the Study of UFOs, 1947–1990," August 4, 1997, http://www.odci.gov/csi/studies/97uncles/ufo.html (inactive); Patrick Huyghe, "U.F.O. Files: The Untold Story," *New York Times Magazine,* October 14, 1979, 107.

61. Friedman, *Top Secret/Majic,* 107.

62. Hesemann and Mantle, *Beyond Roswell,* 108.

63. Randle and Schmitt, *UFO Crash,* 7.

64. Berliner and Friedman, "Crashed Flying Saucers;" Good, *Above Top Secret,* 416-18; Friedman, *Top Secret/Majic,* 74–77; Brookesmith, *UFO,* 80–81; Fawcett and Greenwood, *Clear Intent,* 187–89.

65. Eberhardt, *Roswell Report,* 31–33.

66. Good, *Above Top Secret,* 262; Moore, "Phil Krass," 19; Randle and Schmitt, *Truth,* 102–12 (quotation); Randle, *History,* 147–56; Allan, "Dubious Truth," 12.

67. Howe, *Alien Harvest,* 138; Howe interview; Good, *Alien Contact,* 111–12; Vallee, *Revelations,* 40–42 (quotation).

68. Blum, *Out There,* 226.

69. Moore interview; Moore letter to the author, June 18, 1999.

70. Good, *Above Top Secret*, 57, 117–18, 127; Friedman interview; Schmitt interview; Fawcett and Greenwood, *Clear Intent*, 225–28; Blum, *Out There*, 226–29, 232–34; Moore, "Roswell Incident"; Peebles, *Watch the Skies!* 256–59, 268–69; Brookesmith, *UFO*, 109–15; Korff, *Roswell UFO Crash*. 176–81; Patton, *Dreamland*, 203–5.

71. "G.A.O. Report on Roswell Released to the Public," *UFO Magazine*, September–October, 1995, 9.

72. *Washington Post*, January 14, 1994; *Salt Lake Tribune*, July 30, 1995; Berliner, "Rebuttal," 2; www.webcom.com/conspire, May 18, 1997 (inactive); Friedman, *Top Secret/Majic*, 109, 112, 116–17 (quotation). Don Schmitt has hinted that Steven Schiff's death at fifty-one years of age is suspicious and may have been effected because of these efforts. Schmitt interview.

73. *New York Times*, September 18, 1994, 1.

74. Weaver, *Report*, passim; Berliner, "Rebuttal," 2–8; Rodegher and Chesney, "Air Force Report," 3, 20–23.

75. Friedman interview.

76. Hickman, McConkey, and Barrett, "Fewer Sightings," 215, 219, 220; Strentz, "Survey," 47, 50, 55, 186, 300–303; McCartney, "Media," 20; Gallup, *Gallup Poll*, *1978*, 161, *1987*, 52, *1996*, 207.

77. *Weekly World News*, November 19, 1996, June 16, February 10, 1998.

78. Warren, *Keep Watching*, xv; Lucanio, *Them*, 1.

79. Good, *Alien Contact*, 131.

80. Janet Maslin, "The Blob, Modernized," *New York Times*, August 8, 1988, C6.

81. Klass, *Real Roswell*, 222; *Larry King Live*, October 7, 1994.

82. Vankin and Whalen, *70 Greatest Conspiracies*, 117–20; Friedman, *Top Secret/Majic*, 195, 203–4; Ecker, "Footage Update," 12; Brookesmith, *UFO*, 153; Mantle, "Santilli Alien Autopsy Film," 14–16; www.socorg/alienautopsy.html, June 16, 1998 (inactive).

83. January 23, 1997.

84. September 28, 1996.

85. "Mystery Ranch," April 29, 1997.

86. October 27, 2000.

87. "Fallen Angel," November 19, 1993; "Requiem," May 21, 2000; "Deep Throat," September 17, 1993; "Two Fathers," February 7, 1999; "The Unnatural," April 25, 1999.

88. "Anasazi," May 19, 1995; "Blessing Way," September 22, 1995; "Paper Clip," September 29, 1995.

89. Thieme, "How to Build," 36, 38–39.

90. www.uhaul.com/supergraphics/roswell/menu.html, August 2, 2000; *New York Times*, July 2, 1997, C5.

91. *UFO Magazine*, September–October, 1997, 15.

92. Handy, "Roswell or Bust," 65.

93. Gallup, *Gallup Poll*, *1935–1971*, 2: 2004, *1972–1977*, 1: 214, *1978*, 161–62, *1987*, 52–53, *1996*, 207, *1997*, 238; www.uhaul.com/supergraphics/roswell/menu.html, August 2, 2000; Klass, *Real Roswell Crashed Saucer*, 224–25; Handy, "Roswell or Bust," 64; Crews, "Mindsnatchers," 14; Spanos, et al., "Close Encounters," 629; *Weekly World News*, March 24, 1998, May 18, 1999.

94. June, 1997, 71.

95. *New York Times*, June 14, 1997, 1, 6.

96. Corso, *Day*, passim; *Weekly World News*, September 15, 1998.

97. Jordan, "Day," 29.

98. Leach, "Technology," 28.

99. Moore interview.

100. Schmitt interview.

101. Karl Pflock, "The Day After Roswell," *Mufon UFO Journal* 351 (July 1997): 16–19, 356 (December 1997): 6.

102. McAndrew, *Roswell Report*, passim; *New York Times*, June 25, 1997, 1, 15; Friedman interview.

103. August 3, 1997.

104. David Wise, "Big Lies and Little Green Men," *New York Times*, August 8, 1997, 21.

105. *New York Times*, August 3, 1997, 10; *Salt Lake Tribune*, August 4, 1997.

106. *World's Greatest Hoaxes*, December 28, 1998; *History's Mysteries*, April 17, 2000.

107. *Confirmation*, February 17, 1999.

108. Jedd, "Ufologists," 15.

109. "MJ-12: New Documents Rouse Old Dispute," *UFO* 14 (July 1999): 14–15.

110. George Filer, "Work Continues on Message That Gen. Ramey Holds in Hand," *Mufon UFO Magazine* 367 (November 1998): 15; Burleson, "Update," 17; Pawson, "Interpretation," 19; Connelly, "Ramey Letter," 18.

111. *Coast to Coast AM with Art Bell*, April 28, 1999; Martin, "MAJESTIC," 22; Schmitt interview; Jeffrey, "Roswell," 16.

112. Fox, *Agenda*, 36; Thomas, *Omega Conspiracy*, 171.

113. Wojcik, *End*, 175, 185, 202; Lindsey, *1980s*, 33; Goetz, *UFOs*, 75, 148–50; Bay, "Anti-Christ," http://www.cuttingedge.org/ce1030.html, June 16, 1999.

114. *Mufon UFO Journal* 364 (August 1998): 13; Carey and Schmitt, "Roswell 1999," 13.

Chapter 7. Mainstreaming Conspiracism

1. Stone, "Our Counterfeit History," 102.

2. Goodnight and Poulakos, "Conspiracy Rhetoric," 300; *Salt Lake Tribune*, March 21, 1997, August 9, 2000; *New York Times*, July 8, 1999, 1; Vankin and Whalen, *70 Greatest Conspiracies*, 100; Alter, "Age," 47.

3. Baty, *American Monroe*, 130–32; Siska, "Death," 5–6, 19, 22; Watson, "Calling," 40.

4. Litchfield, *It's a Conspiracy!* 174–77; *New York Times*, February 28, 1997, 1, 10, April 17, 1997, 1, April 3, 1998, 12, December 1, 1999, 15, December 9, 1999, 23; *Salt Lake Tribune*, December 1, 1999; Redman, "Conspiracy Decade," 5; Vankin and Whalen, *70 Greatest Conspiracies*, 233–34, 368. On the King assassination, see also Posner, *Killing the Dream*.

5. Guarino, *Murder*, 7.

6. *Today*, January 27, 1998.

7. Redman, "Conspiracy Decade," 7; Kenn Thomas, "Clinton Era Conspiracies," *Washington Post*, January 16, 1994; Frank Rich, "Why Foster Lives," *New York Times*, October 11, 1995, 13; *New York Times*, January 10, 1997, 19, January 28, 1998; Fabiani, "Communication Stream," 1–3.

8. Sanders, *Downing*, passim; *Salt Lake Tribune*, September 11, 1999, April 24, 2000.

9. *Salt Lake Tribune*, July 15, 2000.

10. Thieme, "How to Build," 38.

11. Blackmore, *Meme Machine*, 4, 6, 7, 14, 22; Lynch, *Thought Contagion*, 2–3. See also Brodie, *Virus of the Mind*; "Has America Gone Conspiracy Crazy?" *The American Edge*, CNN, June 18, 1997; "Conspiracy for Global Control: Special Report," *New American*, January 1997, 68.

12. Hester, "Patriots," 6, 8.

13. Thoreau, *Walden and Civil Disobedience*, 238.

14. Goldwater, *Conscience*, 17.

15. January 11, 1989.

16. Lee, "Summary," 54.

17. Peter Knight, "A Plague of Paranoia: Theories of Conspiracy Theory Since the 1960s," in Schultz, *Fear Itself*, 26; Melley, *Empire*, vii, 8; Kelly, "Road to Paranoia," 63–64; Dickensheets, "Something's Coming," 11; *New York Times*, February 20, 1997, 14.

18. "Dreamland," December 6, 1998.

19. "Patient X," March 1, 1998.

20. "All Lies Lead to the Truth," November 2, 1997.

21. "Sleepless," October 7, 1994; "Travelers," March 29, 1998. During the week of January 17–20, 2000, the History Channel offered "Conspiracy Theories" on *History's Mysteries* and featured the assassination of Robert Kennedy, the Odessa File, the Karen Silkwood story, and Roswell.

22. LaFave and Scott, *Criminal Law*, 526.

23. Abrams and Beale, *Federal Criminal Law*, 406–8, 411; LaFave and Scott, *Criminal Law*, 526–30; Ribuffo, *Old Christian Right*, 194.

24. Raines, *Conspiracy*, 9–12, 18; Epstein, *Great Conspiracy Trial*, 85–87, 89–92.

25. Moise, *Tonkin Gulf*, 99.

26. Wise, *Politics of Lying*, 14, 44–47; Moise, *Tonkin Gulf*, 86, 104, 204, 255; Warner, "Constructing the Credibility Gap," 1, 5–6, 16, 19–20; Goulden, *Truth*, 239–42; Goodwin, "President Lyndon Johnson," 42.

27. Kutler, *Abuse of Power*, 8.

28. Schlesinger, *Imperial Presidency*, 448; Marin and Gegax, "Conspiracy Mania," 71.

29. Johnson, *America's Secret Power*, 3, 27; Johnson, *Secret Agencies*, 5–7; Johnson, *Season*, 48–50, 223–24; Marks, *Search*, 58–59, 217; Lee and Shlain, *Acid Dreams*, xxiv, 3–12, 19, 27–28, 39.

30. Johnson, *Season*, 126–28; O'Reilly, *Hoover*, 346, 350; Theoharis, *Spying*, 156, 166, 181.

31. Schlesinger, *Imperial Presidency*, 345.

32. Griffin, *Chorus*, 16.

33. Blanton, "Rant!" 70; Richard Gid Powers, Introduction to Moynihan,

Secrecy, 2, 18, 58; Teff, *Secrecy,* 7; Wills, *Necessary Evil,* 310, 314–16; Bok, *Secrets,* 25, 106, 202; Will, "Secrecy and Stupidity," 94; *Salt Lake Tribune,* May 18, 1997.

34. Herring, "My Years," 5; *New York Times,* May 20, 1997, 10.

35. Blanton, "Rant!" 70; *New York Times,* May 29, 1997, 11; *Salt Lake Tribune,* December 7, 1999.

36. Lipset and Schneider, *Confidence Gap,* 1, 3, 15–16, 18, 46, 332, 399–400; Hunter and Bowman, *State of Disunion,* 15–19, 29, 69–71, 76; Nye and Zelikow, "Reflections," 273; Orren, "Fall," 81.

37. Blendon, Benson, Morin, et al., "Changing Attitudes," 211; Baughman, *Republic,* 174, 214; Katz, *Virtuous Reality,* 10–11, 55; McCormick, Miller, and Peraino, "Death Penalty," 26–28; *New York Times,* February 17, 2000, 12; *Salt Lake Tribune,* May 29, 2000; Hunter and Bowman, *State of Disunion,* 4.

Bibliography

Interviews

Stanton Friedman, Roswell, New Mexico, July 5, 1997.
Linda Howe, telephone interview, May 11, 1999.
William Moore, Los Angeles, June 4, 1999.
Kevin Randal, telephone interview, June 11, 1999.
Donald Schmitt, telephone interview, October 7, 1999.

Newspapers, Newsletters, and Magazines

In addition to the mass-circulation periodicals cited in the notes, the following have provided coverage of issues related to conspiracy thinking.

American Opinion.
Blacks and Jews News.
Bulletin of the John Birch Society.
Cherith Chronicle.
Conspiracy Nation.
Deep Politics Quarterly.
Fair Play.
Final Call.
Flashpoint.
Fourth Decade.
Good Citizen.
Insider Report.
International UFO Reporter.
Mufon UFO Journal.
New American.
Perhaps Today.
Rocky Mountain American.

Roswell Update.
UFO Magazine.
UFO Universe.

Film

Absolute Power (1996).
Air Force One (1997).
Alien (1979).
Aliens (1986).
All the President's Men (1976).
Apocalypse (1997).
Apocalypse II: Revelation (1998).
Apocalypse III: Tribulation (1999).
Arlington Road (1999).
The Arrival (1996).
Attack (1956).

Bad Day at Black Rock (1954).
Betrayed (1988).
Big Heat (1953).
Big Jim McClain (1953).
Birth of a Nation (1915).
The Blob (1958).
The Blob (1988).
Blow Out (1981).
Blow-Up (1966).
Boyz N the Hood (1991).
Capricorn One (1978).
Chain Reaction (1996).
Chicago Syndicate (1955).
Child of Darkness, Child of Light (1991).
China Syndrome (1979).
Close Encounters of the Third Kind
    (1977).
Conspiracy Theory (1997).
The Conspirator (1949).
Contact (1997).
The Conversation (1974).
Damien: Omen 2 (1978).
Dave (1993).
Devil's Advocate (1997).
Devil's Daughter (1991).
Devil Within Her (1975).
Eagle Has Landed (1977).
Earth vs. the Flying Saucers (1956).
Easy Rider (1969).
End of Days (1999).
Eraser (1996).
Erin Brockovich (2000).
E.T.: The Extra Terrestrial (1982).
Executive Action (1973).
Exorcist (1973).
Exorcist II: The Heretic (1977).
Exorcist III (1990).
The Faculty (1998).
First Blood (1982).
Forbidden Planet (1956).
From Russia With Love (1963).
General's Daughter (1998).
Get on the Bus (1996).
Godfather (1972).
Goldfinger (1964).
High Plains Drifter (1972).
Holocaust 2000 (1978).

Hoodlum (1997).
Insider (1999).
In the Line of Fire (1993).
Invaders from Mars (1953).
Invasion of the Body Snatchers (1956).
Invasion USA (1952).
Invisible Invaders (1959).
Jacob's Ladder (1990).
Jaws (1975).
JFK (1991).
Kansas City Confidential (1952).
Las Vegas Story (1952).
Logan's Run (1976).
Malcolm X (1992).
The Manchurian Candidate (1962).
The Man Who Knew Too Much (1954).
Marathon Man (1976).
Meet John Doe (1941).
Missing (1981).
Missing in Action (1984).
Missing in Action 2: The Beginning (1985).
Mr. Smith Goes to Washington (1939).
Mo' Better Blues (1990).
Murder at 1600 (1997).
My Son John (1952).
Network (1976).
New York Confidential (1955).
Night Moves (1982).
The Ninth Gate (2000).
Nixon (1995).
North by Northwest (1959).
Omega Code (1999).
The Omen (1976).
Omen III: Final Conflict (1981).
Omen IV: The Awakening (1991).
Outlaw Josey Wales (1976).
The Package (1989).
Parallax View (1974).
Pelican Brief (1993).
Philadelphia Experiment (1984).
Pickup on South Street (1953).
President's Analyst (1967).
Prince of Darkness (1987).
The Prophecy (1995).
Raiders of the Lost Ark (1981).
Rambo: First Blood, Part II (1985).
Rambo III (1988).

Rapture (1991).
Red Menace (1949).
Rollover (1981).
Rosemary's Baby (1968).
Roswell: The Aliens Attack (1999).
Ruby (1992).
The Sentinel (1977).
Serpico (1973).
Servants of Twilight (1991).
Seven Days in May (1964).
The Seventh Sign (1988).
Shadow Conspiracy (1996).
Siege (1998).
Silkwood (1983).
Silverado (1985).
The Skulls (1999).
Sleepy Hollow (1999).
Spawn (1997).
The Stand (1994).
Star Trek: Generations (1994).
Star Trek: Insurrection (1998).

Star Wars, Episode I: The Phantom Menace
    (1999).
Stepford Wives (1974).
Taken for a Ride (1996).
Target Earth (1954).
They Died with Their Boots On (1941).
Three Days of the Condor (1975).
The Truman Show (1998).
Twilight's Last Gleaming (1977).
The UFO Incident (1975).
The Unholy (1988).
The Untouchables (1987).
Wag the Dog (1997).
Warlock (1989).
Warlock: Armageddon (1993).
War of the Worlds (1953).
Who Framed Roger Rabbit (1988).
Witchcraft (1988).
Witchcraft II: The Temptress (1990).
Witness (1985).
The X-Files Movie (1998).

Television and Radio

"Alien Autopsy: Fact or Fiction?" FOX special, August 28, 1995.
"Apocalypse: How the Book of Revelation Has Affected Western Thought on
    the Apocalypse." Frontline, November 22, 1999.
"Confirmation: The Hard Evidence of Aliens Among Us?" NBC special Febru-
    ary 17, 1999.
"Conspiracies." A&E special, June 29, 1997.
"Conspiracy Theories." History's Mysteries, January 17–20, 2000.
"Deep Secrets." Travel Channel special, July 23, 2000.
"Has America Gone Conspiracy Crazy?" The American Edge, June 18, 1997.
"Men Who Killed Kennedy." History Alive, March 20–25, 2000.
"Mystery Ranch." News 4 Utah, April 29, 1997.
"Nazi America: A Secret History." History Channel special, January 17,
    2000.
"Reason to Believe." Travel Channel special, July 23, 2000.
"Roswell: Secrets Unveiled." History's Mysteries, April 17, 2000.
"The Roswell Incident." Discovery Channel special, May 26, 1996.
"The Rumor Mill." Sixty Minutes, March 2, 1997.
"Talk of the Nation." NPR, July 2, 1997.
"UFO Cover-Up? Live!" CBS special, October 14, 1988.
"UFOs: The First Encounters." A&E special, January 2, 1997.
"UFOs vs. the Government." The Unexplained, January 2, 1997.

"The Warren Report." CBS special, June 25–28, 1967.
"World's Greatest Hoaxes: Secrets Finally Revealed." FOX special, December 28, 1998.

Internet Websites

http://www.700club.org
http://www.artbell.com
http://www.Bible-prophecy.com/index.htm
http://www.blacksandjews.com
http://www.conspire.com
http://www.dccsa.com/greatjoy/
http://www.jvim.com
http://www.noi.org
http://parascope.com
http://www.radioislam.net/talmud/index.htm
http://www.randlereport.com
http://www.texemarrs.com
http://www.ufomind.com

Books, Articles, Videos, and Government Documents
General Conspiracy

Abrams, Norman, and Sara Sue Beale. *Federal Criminal Law and Its Enforcement.* 2d ed. St. Paul, Minn.: West, 1993.

Abramson, Jeffrey B., Christopher F. Arterion, and Gary R. Orren. *The Electronic Commonwealth: The Impact of New Media Technologies on Democratic Politics.* New York: Basic, 1988.

Altemeyer, Bob. *The Authoritarian Specter.* Cambridge: Harvard University Press, 1996.

Alter, Jonathan. "The Age of Conspiracism." *Newsweek* 130 (March 24, 1997): 47.

Andersen, Kurt. "The Age of Unreason." *New Yorker* 72 (February 3, 1997): 40–43.

Arrington, Leonard J., and Davis Bitton. *The Mormon Experience: A History of the Latter-Day Saints.* New York: Knopf, 1979.

Aspects of Jewish Power in the United States: The International Jew. Dearborn, Mich.: Dearborn, 1922.

Bailyn, Bernard. *The Ideological Origins of the American Revolution.* Cambridge: Harvard University Press, 1967.

——. *The Origins of American Politics.* New York: Vintage, 1968.

——, ed. *Pamphlets of the American Revolution, 1750–1765.* Vol. 1. Cambridge: Harvard University Press, 1965.

Baldwin, Ebenezer. *An Appendix Stating the Heavy Grievances the Colonies Labour Under from Several Late Acts of the British Parliament.* New Haven: T. and S. Green, 1774.

Barkun, Michael. *Disaster and the Millennium*. New Haven: Yale University Press, 1974.

Baty, S. Paige. *American Monroe: The Making of a Body Politic*. Berkeley: University of California Press, 1995.

Baughman, James L. *The Republic of Mass Culture: Journalism, Film Making, and Broadcasting in America Since 1941*. 2d ed. Baltimore: Johns Hopkins University Press, 1997.

Baum, Will C. "The Conspiracy Theory of Politics of the Radical Right in the United States." Ph.D. diss., University of Iowa, 1960.

Beard, Charles. *President Roosevelt and the Coming of War, 1941: A Study in Appearances and Realities*. New Haven: Yale University Press, 1948.

Beecher, Edward. *The Papal Conspiracy Exposed, and Protestantism Defended*. New York: M. W. Dodd, 1855.

Beecher, Lyman. *Plea for the West*. New York: Truman and Smith, 1835.

Berkhofer, Robert. *The White Man's Indian*. New York: Vintage, 1979.

Berlet, Chip. "Friendly Fascists: The Far Right Tries to Move in on the Left." *Progressive* 56 (June 1992): 16–20.

——. *Right Woos Left*. Somerville, Mass.: Political Research Associates, 1994.

——. "The Violence of Right-Wing Populism." *Peace Review* 7 (1995): 283–88.

Bernard, David. *Light on Masonry*. Utica, N.Y.: William Williams, 1829.

Billig, Michael. "Rhetoric of the Conspiracy Theory: Arguments in National Front Propaganda." *Patterns of Prejudice* 22 (1988): 23–34.

Billings, Kurt. "Mind Control and the New Millennium." *Preparedness Journal* 7 (January–February 1999): 17–18, 20–21.

Billington, Ray. *Protestant Crusade, 1800–1860: A Study of the Origins of American Nativism*. New York: Macmillan, 1938.

Blackmore, Susan, and Richard Dawkins. *The Meme Machine*. New York: Oxford University Press, 1999.

Blackstock, Nelson. *COINTELPRO: The FBI's Secret War on Political Freedom*. New York: Pathfinder, 1975.

Blanton, Tom. "Rant!" *George* 3 (October 1998): 70.

Blendon, Robert J., John M. Benson, Richard Morin, et al. "Changing Attitudes in America." In Nye, Zelikow, and King, *Why People Don't Trust Government*, 205–16.

Bok, Sissela. *Secrets: On the Ethics of Concealment and Revelation*. New York: Pantheon, 1982.

The Book of Mormon. Salt Lake City: Church of Jesus Christ of Latter-Day Saints, 1981; originally pub. 1830.

Boyd, Julian P., ed. *The Papers of Thomas Jefferson*, vol. 1, 1760–1776. Princeton: Princeton University Press, 1950.

Boyer, Paul, and Stephen Nissenbaum. *Salem Possessed: The Social Origins of Witchcraft*. Cambridge: Harvard University Press, 1974.

Breen, T. H. *Tobacco Culture: The Mentality of the Great Tidewater Planters on the Eve of the Revolution*. Princeton: Princeton University Press, 1985.

Briley, Richard, III. *Death of the Kingfish! Who Did Kill Huey Long?* Dallas: Triangle, 1960.

Brinkley, Alan. *Voices of Protest: Huey Long, Father Coughlin, and the Great Depression*. New York: Vintage, 1983.

Brock, David. "Private Lies." *George* 3 (October 1998): 120–24, 133.

Brodie, Richard. *Virus of the Mind: The New Science of the Meme.* Seattle: Integral, 1996.

Cairnes, John Elliot. *The Slave Power: Its Character, Career, and Probable Designs.* New York: Carleton, 1862.

Camp, Gregory S. *Selling Fear: Conspiracy Theories and End-Times Paranoia.* Grand Rapids, Mich.: Baker, 1997.

Cash, W. J. *The Mind of the South.* New York: Vintage, 1941.

Chalmers, David M. *The Social and Political Ideas of the Muckrakers.* New York: Citadel, 1964.

Cherry, Conrad. *God's New Israel: Religious Interpretations of American Destiny.* Englewood Cliffs, N.J.: Prentice Hall, 1971.

Churchill, Ward, and Jim Vander Wall. *Agents of Repression: The FBI's Secret Wars Against the Black Panther Party and the American Indian Movement.* Boston: South End, 1990.

Cohen, Jacob. "Conspiracy Fever." *Commentary* 60 (October 1975): 33–42.

Cole, Wayne S. *Senator Gerald P. Nye and American Foreign Relations.* Minneapolis: University of Minnesota Press, 1962.

Coleman, John. *Conspirators' Hierarchy: The Story of the Committee of 300.* Carson City, Nev.: American West, 1992.

Collett, John. "Funerary Pyres and Cheap Sarcophagi." Seminar paper, University of Utah, 1998.

Congressional Record.

Coombs, James. *American Political Movies: An Annotated Filmography of Featured Films.* New York: Garland, 1990.

Cooper, Matthew, and Greg Ferguson. "The Return of the Paranoid Style in American Politics." *U.S. News and World Report* 108 (March 12, 1990): 30–31.

Corliss, Richard. "The X Phones." *Time* 154 (August 9, 1999): 64–65.

CPA Catalogue. N.p.: CPA Book Publishers, 1997.

Crews, Frederick. "The Mindsnatchers." *New York Review of Books* 45 (June 25, 1998): 14–19.

Curry, Richard O., and Thomas M. Brown, eds. *Conspiracy: The Fear of Subversion in American History.* New York: Holt, Rinehart, and Winston, 1972.

Davidson, Philip. *Propaganda and the American Revolution, 1763–1783.* Chapel Hill: University of North Carolina Press, 1941.

Davis, David Brion, *The Slave Power Conspiracy and the Paranoid Style.* Baton Rouge: Louisiana State University Press, 1969.

———. "Some Themes of Counter-Subversion: An Analysis of Anti-Masonic, Anti-Catholic, and Anti-Mormon Literature." *Mississippi Valley Historical Review* 47 (September 1960): 205–24.

———, ed. *The Fear of Conspiracy: Images of Un-American Subversion from the Revolution to the Present.* Ithaca, N.Y.: Cornell University Press, 1971.

Davis, James. *Assault on the Left: The FBI and the Sixties Anti-War Movement.* Westport, Conn.: Praeger, 1996.

"Decoding the X-Files." *Newsweek* 131 (June 22, 1998): 70–76.

Demos, John Putnam. *Entertaining Satan: Witchcraft and the Culture of Early New England.* New York: Oxford University Press, 1982.

Dennis, Lawrence, and Maximilian St. George. *A Trial on Trial: The Great Sedition Trial of 1944*. New York: National Civil Rights Congress, 1945.

Diagnostic and Statistical Manual of Mental Disorders. 4th ed. Washington, D.C.: American Psychiatric Association, 1994.

Dickensheets, Scott. "Something's Coming!" *Edging West* 12 (Summer 1997): 10–13.

Dickstein, Morris. *Gates of Eden: American Culture in the Sixties*. Cambridge: Harvard University Press, 1997.

Doenecke, Justin D., ed. *In Danger Undaunted: The Anti-Intervention Movement of 1940–1941 as Revealed in the Papers of the America First Committee*. Stanford: Hoover Institution Press, 1990.

Donnelly, Ignatius. *Caesar's Column: A Story of the Twentieth Century*. Cambridge: Harvard University Press, 1960.

Donner, Frank J. *The Age of Surveillance*. New York: Knopf, 1980.

Dorfman, Richard. "Conspiracy City." *Journal of Popular Film and Television* 7 (1980): 434–56.

Dwyer, Jim, Peter Neufeld, and Barry Scheck. "When Justice Lets Us Down." *Newsweek* 135 (February 14, 2000): 59.

Dyson, Michael Eric. *Between God and Gangsta Rap: Bearing Witness to Black Culture*. New York: Oxford University Press, 1996.

Eatwell, Roger, and Noel O'Sullivan, eds. *The Nature of the Right: American and European Politics and Political Thought Since 1789*. Boston: Twayne, 1989.

Edwards, Paul N. *The Closed World: Computers and the Politics of Discourse in Cold War America*. Cambridge: MIT Press, 1996.

Emerson, Steven. "Ross Perot's Conspiracy Fever and Ours." *Wall Street Journal*, October 28, 1992.

Epstein, Jason. *The Great Conspiracy Trial: An Essay on Law, Liberty, and the Constitution*. New York: Random House, 1970.

Eringer, Robert. *The Conspiracy Peddlers: A Review of the Conspiracy Media in the United States*. Mason, Mich.: Loompanics Unlimited, 1981.

Esson, Dylan. "Mushrooming Conspiracies: The Legacy of Government Cover-Ups with the Downwinders of Southern Utah." Honors thesis, University of Utah, 1999.

Evans, Hiram Wesley. *The Attitude of the Ku Klux Klan Toward the Jew*. Atlanta: American Printing and Manufacturing Company, 1923.

Fabiani, Mark. "Communication Stream of Conspiracy Commerce." www.parascope.com/articles/0197/media.htm (July 1995).

Fallows, James. *Breaking the News: How the Media Undermine American Democracy*. New York: Pantheon, 1996.

Farmer, E. J. *The Conspiracy Against Silver, or A Plea for Bi-Metalism in the United States*. N.p: Hiles and Caggshall, 1886.

Fenster, Mark. *Conspiracy Theories: Secrecy and Power in American Culture*. Minneapolis: University of Minnesota Press, 1999.

Fischer, David Hackett. *Historians' Fallacies: Toward a Logic of Historical Thought*. New York: Harper and Row, 1976.

Foner, Eric. *Free Soil, Free Labor, Free Men: The Ideology of the Republican Party Before the Civil War*. New York: Oxford University Press, 1970.

Foner, Philip S., ed. *The Complete Writings of Tom Paine*. New York: Citadel, 1945.

Ford, Paul, ed. *The Political Writings of John Dickinson, 1764–1774.* New York: Da Capo, 1970.

Freehling, William W. *Prelude to Civil War: The Nullification Controversy in South Carolina, 1816–1836.* New York: Torch, 1965.

Freund, Charles Paul. "If History Is a Lie." *Washington Post,* January 19, 1992.

Gallup, George. *The Gallup Poll: Public Opinion, 1935–1971.* 3 vols. New York: Random House, 1972.

——. *The Gallup Poll: Public Opinion, 1972–1977.* 2 vols. Wilmington, Del.: Scholarly Resources, 1978.

——. *The Gallup Poll: Public Opinion, 1978–1998.* Yearly volumes. Wilmington, Del.: Scholarly Resources, 1979–1998.

Gara, Larry. "Slavery and the Slave Power: A Crucial Distinction." *Civil War History* 15 (March 1969): 5–18.

George, Harrison. *The I.W.W. Trial.* New York: Arno, 1969.

Gienapp, William. *The Origins of the Republican Party, 1852–1856.* New York: Oxford University Press, 1987.

Gilovich, Thomas. *How We Know What Isn't So: The Fallibility of Human Reason in Everyday Life.* New York: Free Press, 1991.

Glass, J. M. "Notes on the Paranoid Factor in Political Philosophy: Fear, Anxiety, and Domination." *Political Psychology* 9 (June 1988): 209–28.

Glick, Brian. *War at Home: Covert Action Against U.S. Activists and What We Can Do About It.* Boston: South End, 1989.

Goertzel, Ted. "Belief in Conspiracy Theories." *Political Psychology* 15 (December 1994): 731–42.

Goldberg, Robert Alan. *Grassroots Resistance: Social Movements in Twentieth Century America.* Prospect Heights, Ill.: Waveland, 1996.

Goldberg, Robert Alan, Eric Hinderaker, and Dean May. *American Views.* New York: Simon and Schuster, 1998.

Goldzwig, Steven R. "A Social Movement Perspective on Demagoguery: Achieving Symbolic Realignment." *Communication Studies* 40 (1989): 202–28.

Goodell, William. *Slavery and Anti-Slavery: A History of the Great Struggle in Both Hemispheres; with a View of the Slavery Question in the United States.* New York: William Harned, 1852.

Goodman, Paul. *Toward a Christian Republic: Anti-Masonry and the Great Transition in New England, 1826–1836.* New York: Oxford University Press, 1988.

Goodnight, G. Thomas, and John Poulakos. "Conspiracy Rhetoric: From Pragmatism to Fantasy in Public Discourse." *Western Journal of Speech Communication* 45 (Fall 1981): 299–316.

Goodwin, Richard. "President Lyndon Johnson: The War Within." *New York Times Magazine,* August 21, 1988, 35–38, 42, 48.

Goulden, James. *Truth Is the First Casualty: The Gulf of Tonkin Affair, Illusion and Reality.* Chicago: Rand McNally, 1969.

Graumann, Carl F., and Serge Moscovici, eds. *Changing Conceptions of Conspiracy.* New York: Springer, 1987.

Griffin, Susan. *A Chorus of Stones: The Private Life of War.* New York: Anchor, 1992.

Gruber, Ira D. "The American Revolution as a Conspiracy: The British View." *William and Mary Quarterly* 26 (July 1969): 360–72.

Guarino, Nicholas. *Murder in the First Degree.* Burnsville, Minn.: Wall Street Underground, 1996.

Hall, David D. "Middle Ground on the Witch-Hunt Debate." *Reviews in American History* 26 (June 1998): 345–52.

Halpin, Mikki. "Attack of the Killer Net Movies!" *Web Magazine* 1 (September 1997): 26–32.

Herring, George C. "My Years with the CIA." *OAH Newsletter* 25 (May 1997): 5–6.

Higham, John. "The Mind of a Nativist: Henry F. Bowers and the A.P.A." *American Quarterly* 4 (Spring 1952): 16–24.

——. *Strangers in the Land: Patterns of American Nativism, 1860–1925.* New York: Atheneum, 1970.

Hoffer, Peter Charles. *The Salem Witchcraft Trials: A Legal History.* Lawrence: University Press of Kansas, 1997.

Hofstadter, Richard. *The Paranoid Style of American Politics and Other Essays.* New York: Vintage, 1967.

Hofstadter, Richard, and Michael Wallace, eds. *American Violence: A Documentary History.* New York: Vintage, 1971.

Hosenball, Mark, and Gregory L. Vistica. "The Life and Times of a Rumor." *Newsweek* 131 (January 19, 1998): 31.

Hougan, Jim. *Secret Agenda: Watergate, Deep Throat, and the CIA.* New York: Random House, 1984.

Howard, Michael. *The Occult Conspiracy: Secret Societies, Their Influence and Power in World History.* Rochester, Vt.: Destiny, 1989.

Howe, John R. "Republican Thought and the Political Violence of the 1790s." *American Quarterly* 19 (Summer 1967): 147–65.

Hunter, James D., and Carl Bowman. *The State of Disunion: 1996 Survey of American Political Culture.* Vols. 1–2. Charlottesville, Va.: Post-Modernity Project, 1996.

Hutson, James. "The Origins of the Paranoid Style in American Politics: Public Jealousy from the Age of Walpole to the Age of Jackson." In David D. Hall, John M. Murrin, and Thad W. Tate, eds. *Saints and Revolutionaries: Essays on Early American History,* 332–72. New York: Norton, 1984.

"Industrial Workers of the World Who Won't Work." *Literary Digest* 55 (July 28, 1917): 20.

Isenberg, Barbara. "The G-Man as the Fall Guy." *Los Angeles Times,* August 27, 1988.

Isikoff, Michael. "The Waco Flame-Up." *Newsweek* 134 (September 6, 1999): 30.

Isserman, Maurice. *Which Side Were You On?: The American Communist Party During the Second World War.* Middletown, Conn.: Wesleyan University Press, 1982.

Ivins, Molly. "Guns and Virtual Cults May Create Deadly Mix." *Salt Lake Tribune,* April 25, 1999.

Jensen, Paul. "The Return of Dr. Caligari." *Film Comment* 7 (Winter 1971–72): 36–45.

Johnson, Diane. "What Do Women Want?" *New York Review of Books* 43 (November 28, 1996): 22–28.

Johnson, George. *Architects of Fear: Conspiracy Theories and Paranoia in American Politics.* Boston: Houghton Mifflin, 1983.

Johnson, Loch K. *America's Secret Power: The CIA in a Democratic Society.* New York: Oxford University Press, 1989.

———. *A Season of Inquiry: The Senate Intelligence Investigation.* Lexington: University of Kentucky Press, 1985.

———. *Secret Agencies: U.S. Intelligence in a Hostile World.* New Haven: Yale University Press, 1996.

Julian, George W. "The Strength and Weakness of the Slave Power: The Duty of Anti-Slavery Men." In *Speeches on Political Questions,* 67–82. New York: Hurd and Houghton, 1872.

Kakutani, Michiko. "Bound by Suspicion." *New York Times Magazine,* January 19, 1997, 16.

Karlsen, Carol F. *The Devil in the Shape of a Woman: Witchcraft in Colonial New England.* New York: Norton, 1987.

Katz, Jon. *Virtuous Reality.* New York: Random House, 1997.

Kaul, Donald. "Government, Politics, Internet, Sports All Indicate Paranoid Age." *Salt Lake Tribune,* May 22, 1997.

Kazin, Michael. *The Populist Persuasion: An American History.* New York: Basic, 1995.

Kelley, Tina. "Internet's Chain of Foolery." *New York Times,* July 1, 1999, D1.

Kelly, Michael. "The Road to Paranoia." *New Yorker* 71 (June 19, 1995): 60–64, 66–70, 72–75.

Kennedy, Robert F. *The Enemy Within.* New York: Harper Brothers, 1960.

Kick, Russ. *Outposts: A Catalogue of Rare and Disturbing Alternative Information.* New York: Carroll and Graf, 1995.

Kinzer, Donald L. *An Episode in Anti-Catholicism: The American Protective Association.* Seattle: University of Washington Press, 1964.

Kirn, Walter. "Conspiracy, U.S.A." *Time* 150 (July 7, 1997): 89–91.

Klaidman, Daniel, and Michael Isikoff. "A Fire That Won't Die." *Newsweek* 134 (September 20, 1999): 24–27.

Klehr, Harvey. *The Heyday of American Communism: The Depression Decade.* New York: Basic, 1984.

Knight, Peter. "A Plague of Paranoia: Theories of Conspiracy Theory Since the 1960s." In Schultz, *Fear Itself,* 23–50.

Knox, J. Wendell. *Conspiracy in American Politics, 1787–1815.* New York: Arno, 1972.

Kutler, Stanley, ed. *Abuse of Power: The New Nixon Tapes.* New York: Free Press, 1997.

LaFave, Wayne R., and Austin W. Scott, Jr. *Criminal Law.* 2d ed. St. Paul: West, 1986.

Lasch, Christopher. *The Culture of Narcissism: American Life in an Age of Diminishing Expectation.* New York: Norton, 1979.

Lavery, David, Angela Hague, and Marta Cartwright, eds. *Deny All Knowledge: Reading the X Files.* New York: Syracuse University Press, 1996.

Lavine, Harold. *5th Column in America.* New York: Doubleday, Doran, 1940.

Lease, Mary Ellen. *The Problem of Civilization Solved.* Chicago: Laird and Lee, 1895.

Lee, Albert. *Henry Ford and the Jews.* New York: Stein and Day, 1980.

Lee, Martin, and Bruce Shlain. *Acid Dreams: The Complete Social History of LSD: The CIA, the Sixties, and Beyond.* New York: Grove, 1985.

Lee, Robert W. "A Summary of Key Books on Conspiracy." *American Opinion* 24 (November 1981): 35–54.

Leiby, Richard. "Paranoia: Fear on the Left, Fear on the Right. Whoever They Are, They're Closing in." *Washington Post,* May 8, 1995.

Lepore, Jill. *The Name of War: King Philip's War and the Origins of American Identity.* New York: Vintage, 1999.

Levine, Robert S. *Conspiracy and Romance: Studies in Brockden Brown, Cooper, Hawthorne, and Melville.* Cambridge: Cambridge University Press, 1989.

Lipset, Seymour Martin. *American Exceptionalism: A Double-Edged Sword.* New York: Norton, 1996.

Lipset, Seymour Martin, and William Schneider. *The Confidence Gap: Business, Labor, and Government in the Public Mind.* New York: Free Press, 1983.

Litchfield, Michael. *It's a Conspiracy!* Berkeley: Earth Works, 1992.

Lowry, Brian. *The Truth Is Out There: The Official Guide to the X-Files.* New York: Harper Prism, 1995.

Ludlow, Peter, ed. *High Noon on the Electronic Frontier: Conceptual Issues in Cyberspace.* Cambridge: MIT Press, 1996.

Lynch, Aaron. *Thought Contagion.* New York: Basic, 1996.

Mackenzie, Angus. *Secrets: The CIA's War at Home.* Berkeley: University of California Press, 1997.

Marcus, George E., ed. *Paranoia Within Reason: A Casebook on Conspiracy as Explanation.* Chicago: University of Chicago Press, 1998.

Marin, Rick, and T. Trent Gegax. "Conspiracy Mania Feeds Our Growing National Paranoia." *Newsweek* 128 (December 30, 1996): 64–66, 71.

Marks, John. *The Search for the "Manchurian Candidate": The CIA and Mind Control.* New York: Norton, 1991.

Mayhew, Jonathan. *The Snare Broken.* Boston: R. and S. Draper, 1766.

McArthur, Benjamin. "They're Out to Get Us: Another Look at the Paranoid Tradition." *History Teacher* 29 (November 1995): 37–49.

McCormick, John, Mark Miller, and Kevin Peraino. "The Death Penalty on Trial." *Newsweek* 135 (June 12, 2000): 24–34.

McGlone, Robert E. "Rescripting a Troubled Past: John Brown's Family and the Harper's Ferry Conspiracy." *Journal of American History* 75 (March 1989): 1179–1200.

McPherson, James M. *Battle Cry of Freedom: The Civil War Era.* New York: Oxford University Press, 1988.

Means, Gaston B. *The Strange Death of President Harding.* New York: Guild, 1930.

Melanson, Philip H. *The Murkin Conspiracy: An Investigation into the Assassination of Dr. Martin Luther King, Jr.* New York: Praeger, 1989.

Melley, Timothy. *Empire of Conspiracy: The Culture of Paranoia in Postwar America.* Ithaca, N.Y.: Cornell University Press, 2000.

Miller, Arthur. *The Crucible.* New York: Penguin, 1952.

Moench, Doug. *The Big Book of Conspiracies.* New York: Paradox, 1995.

Moise, Edwin E. *Tonkin Gulf and the Escalation of the Vietnam War.* Chapel Hill: University of North Carolina Press, 1996.

Morgenstern, George. *Pearl Harbor: The Story of the Secret War.* New York: Devin-Adair, 1947.

Morse, Samuel F. B. *Foreign Conspiracy Against the Liberties of the United States.* New York: Leavitt, Lord, 1835.

Moynihan, Daniel Patrick. *Secrecy: The American Experience.* New Haven: Yale University Press, 1998.

Murray, Robert K. *Red Scare: A Study in National Hysteria, 1919–1920.* Minneapolis: University of Minnesota Press, 1955.

Nye, Joseph S., Jr., and Philip D. Zelikow. "Reflections, Conjectures, and Puzzles." In Nye, Zelikow, and King, *Why People Don't Trust Government,* 253–81.

Nye, Joseph S., Jr., Philip D. Zelikow, and David C. King, eds. *Why People Don't Trust Government.* Cambridge: Harvard University Press, 1997.

Olmsted, Kathryn. *Challenging the Secret Government: The Post-Watergate Investigations of the CIA and FBI.* Chapel Hill: University of North Carolina, 1996.

Orren, Gary. "Fall from Grace: The Public's Loss of Faith in Government." In Nye, Zelikow, and King, *Why People Don't Trust Government,* 77–107.

Oshinsky, David. "Enemies Right, Left, Everywhere." *New York Times,* February 12, 1998, 31.

Ostrander, Gilman M. *The Prohibition Movement in California, 1848–1933.* Berkeley: University of California Press, 1957.

Page, Clarence. "The Truth Is Out . . . Where?" *Chicago Tribune,* February 17, 1997.

Palmer, A. Mitchell. "The Case Against the Reds." *Forum* 63 (February 1920): 173–85.

Parker, Theodore. "The Nebraska Question: Some Thoughts on the New Assault upon Freedom in America and the General State of the Country in Relation Thereon." In John L. Thomas, ed. *Slavery Attacked: The Abolitionist Crusade,* 148–52. Englewood Cliffs, N.J.: 1965. Originally pub. 1854.

——. *The Slave Power.* Boston: American Unitarian Association, 1907.

Phillips, Amberlee. "Conspiracy and *The X-Files.*" Honors paper, University of Utah, 1998.

Phillips, Kevin. *The Cousins' Wars: Religion, Politics, and the Triumph of Anglo America.* New York: Basic, 1999.

Pipes, Daniel. *Conspiracy: How the Paranoid Style Flourishes and Where it Comes From.* New York: Free Press, 1997.

——. *The Hidden Hand: Middle East Fears of Conspiracy.* New York: St. Martin's, 1996.

Posner, Gerald. *Killing the Dream: James Earl Ray and the Assassination of Martin Luther King, Jr.* New York: Random House, 1998.

——. "The Truth About Memphis." *Newsweek* 131 (April 6, 1998): 54–56.

Powers, Richard Gid. *G-Men: Hoover's FBI in American Popular Culture.* Carbondale: Southern Illinois Press, 1983.

Prados, John. *Presidents' Secret Wars: CIA and Pentagon Covert Operations from World War II Through the Persian Gulf.* Chicago: Dee, 1996.

Prange, Gordon W. *Pearl Harbor: The Verdict of History.* New York: McGraw-Hill, 1986.

Quincy, Josiah, Jr. *Observations on the Act of Parliament, Commonly Called the Boston Port-Bill; with Thoughts on Civil Societies and Standing Armies.* Boston: Edes and Gill, 1774.

Raines, John C. *Conspiracy: The Implications of the Harrisburg Trial for the Democratic Tradition.* New York: Harper and Row, 1975.

Redman, Brian. "The Conspiracist Decade." *Conspiracy Nation* 3 (September 1997): 1–8.

Remington, R. A. "The Function of Conspiracy Theory in American Intellectual History." Ph.D. diss., St. Louis University, 1965.

Rheingold, Howard. *The Virtual Community.* New York: Simon and Schuster, 1991.

Ribuffo, Leo P. *The Old Christian Right: The Protestant Far Right from the Depression to the Cold War.* Philadelphia: Temple University Press, 1983.

Roberts, Cokie, and Steve Roberts. "Widespread Internet Access Points to Major Shift in Political Culture." *Salt Lake Tribune,* December 4, 1999.

Robins, Robert S., and Jerold M. Post. *Political Paranoia: The Psychopolitics of Hatred.* New Haven: Yale University Press, 1997.

Rogin, Michael. *Ronald Reagan, the Movie.* Berkeley: University of California Press, 1987.

Roosevelt, Theodore. *The Foes of Our Own Household.* New York: George H. Doran Company, 1917.

Rosen, James. "Conspiracy Theorists: Do They Know Something You Don't?" *Salt Lake Tribune,* August 24, 1997.

Rosen, Ruth. "The Sinister Images of 'X-Files.' " *Chronicle of Higher Education* 43 (July 11, 1997): 7.

Rosenthal, Bernard. *Salem Story: Reading the Witch Trials of 1692.* New York: Cambridge University Press, 1993.

Rusbridger, James, and Eric Nave. *Betrayal at Pearl Harbor: How Churchill Lured Roosevelt into World War II.* New York: Summit, 1991.

Ryan, Michael, and Douglas Kellner. *Camera Politica: The Politics and Ideology of Contemporary Hollywood Film.* Bloomington: Indiana University Press, 1988.

Safire, William. "Conspiracy Theory." *New York Times Magazine,* November 5, 1995, 24.

Sanders, James. *The Downing of TWA Flight 800.* New York: Zebra, 1997.

Sardar, Ziauddin, and Jerome R. Ravetz, eds. *Cyberfutures: Culture and Politics on the Information Superhighway.* New York: New York University Press, 1996.

Sargent, Lyman Tower, ed. *Extremism in America: A Reader.* New York: New York University Press, 1995.

Schlesinger, Arthur, Jr. *The Imperial Presidency.* New York: Popular Library, 1974.

Schrag, Peter. *Test of Loyalty: Daniel Ellsberg and the Rituals of Secret Government.* New York: Simon and Schuster, 1974.

Schulte, Brigid. "Conspiracy Sells." *Wisconsin State Journal,* July 13, 1997.

Schultz, Nancy Lusignan, ed. *Fear Itself: Enemies Real and Imagined in American Culture.* West Lafayette, Ind.: Purdue University Press, 1999.

Sciolino, Elaine. "Scrutiny for Spies." *New York Times,* September 7, 1991, 10.

Sebelius, Steve. "Conspiracy Nation." *Salt Lake City Weekly* 15 (August 20, 1998): 14–17.

Shapiro, David. *Neurotic Styles.* New York: Basic, 1965.

Sheehan, Neil, et al., eds. *The Pentagon Papers.* New York: Bantam, 1971.

Shermer, Michael. *Why People Believe Weird Things.* New York: Freeman, 1997.

Shills, Edward. *The Torment of Secrecy: The Background and Consequences of America Security Politics.* Glencoe, Ill.: Free Press, 1956.

Showalter, Elaine. *Hystorics: Hysterical Epidemics and Modern Culture.* New York: Columbia University Press, 1997.

Siska, Sean. "The Death or Murder of a Princess." Honors paper, University of Utah, 1998.

Slouka, Mark. *War of the Worlds: Cyberspace and the High-Tech Assault on Reality.* New York: Basic, 1995.

Smoak, Gregory. "Ghost Dances and Identity: Ethnogenesis and Racial Identity Among Shoshones and Bannocks in the Nineteenth Century." Ph.D. diss., University of Utah, 1999.

Spicer, Robert. *Conspiracy: Law and Class and Society.* London: Laurence and Wishart, 1981.

Stauffer, Vernon. *New England and the Bavarian Illuminati.* New York: Columbia University Press, 1918.

Stephanopoulos, George. "White House Confidential." *Newsweek* 130 (May 5, 1997): 34.

Strong, Josiah. *Our Country: Its Possible Future and Its Present Crisis.* New York: Baker and Taylor, 1885.

Sturken, Marita. *Tangled Memories: The Vietnam War, the AIDS Epidemic, and the Politics of Remembering.* Berkeley: University of California Press, 1997.

Tackett, Timothy. "Conspiracy Obsession in a Time of Revolution: French Elites and the Origins of the Terror, 1789–1792." *American Historical Review* 105 (June 2000): 691–713.

Tefft, Stanton K. *Secrecy: A Cross-Cultural Perspective.* New York: Human Sciences Press, 1980.

Tharp, Mike, and William Holstein. "Mainstreaming the Militia." *U.S. News and World Report* 122 (April 21, 1997): 24–37.

Theobald, Robert A. *The Final Secret of Pearl Harbor: The Washington Contribution to the Japanese Attack.* Greenwich, Conn.: Devin-Adair, 1954.

Theoharis, Athan G., ed. *A Culture of Secrecy: The Government Versus the People's Right to Know.* Lawrence: University Press of Kansas, 1998.

Theurer, Jesse S. "The Mormon Conspiracy." Honors paper, University of Utah, 1998.

Thoreau, Henry David. *Walden and Civil Disobedience.* Boston: Houghton Mifflin Co., 1960.

Toland, John. *Infamy: Pearl Harbor and Its Aftermath.* Garden City, N.Y.: Doubleday, 1982.

Trelease, Allen W. *White Terror: The Ku Klux Klan Conspiracy and Southern Reconstruction.* Baton Rouge: Louisiana State University Press, 1995.

U.S. House of Representatives. Select Committee Investigating National Defense Migration Hearings: Part 29, 77th Cong., 2d sess., 1942.

Vankin, Jonathan. *Conspiracies, Cover-ups, and Crimes: Political Manipulation and Mind Control in America.* New York: Paragon House, 1991.

Vankin, Jonathan, and John Whalen. *70 Greatest Conspiracies of All Time.* New York: Citadel, 1998.

Victor, Orville J. *History of American Conspiracies: A Record of Treason, Insurrection, Rebellion in the United States.* New York: James D. Torrey, 1863.

Vidal, Gore. "Yes, Hillary, There Is a Corporate Conspiracy Against Bill." *Salt Lake Tribune,* August 16, 1998.

Walsh, Lawrence E. *Firewall: The Iran-Contra Conspiracy and Cover-Up.* New York: Norton, 1997.

Warner, Tiffany. "Constructing the Credibility Gap: The Gulf of Tonkin Incident and Its Influence on Conspiracy Thinking in U.S. History." Honors paper, University of Utah, 1999.

Warren, Donald. *Radio Priest: Charles Coughlin, the Father of Hate Radio.* New York: Free Press, 1996.

Watson, Russell, "Calling Oliver Stone." *Newsweek* 130 (October 27, 1997): 40.

Weber, Thomas E. "Who Uses the Internet?" *Wall Street Journal,* December 9, 1996.

White, Alma. *Heroes of the Fiery Cross.* Zarephath, N.J.: Good Citizen, 1928.

———. *The Ku Klux Klan in Prophecy.* Zarephath, N.J.: Good Citizen, 1925.

Wik, Reynold M. *Henry Ford and Grass-Roots America.* Ann Arbor: University of Michigan Press, 1973.

Will, George F. "Secrecy and Stupidity." *Newsweek* 132 (October 12, 1998): 94.

Wills, Garry. *A Necessary Evil: A History of American Distrust of Government.* New York: Simon and Schuster, 1999.

———. "The New Revolutionaries." *New York Review of Books* 42 (August 10, 1995): 50–55.

Wise, David. *The Politics of Lying: Government Deception, Secrecy, and Power.* New York: Random House, 1973.

Wood, Gordon S. "Conspiracy and the Paranoid Style: Causality and Deceit in the Eighteenth Century." *William and Mary Quarterly* 39 (July, 1982): 401–41.

———. *Creation of the American Republic, 1776–1787.* Chapel Hill: University of North Carolina Press, 1969.

Yemma, John. "Conspiracies Are Everywhere." *Wisconsin State Journal,* September 29, 1996.

Young, Bradley J. "Silver, Discontent, and Conspiracy: The Ideology of the Western Republican Revolt of 1890–1901." *Pacific Historical Review* 64 (May 1995): 243–65.

Chapter 2: The Master Conspiracy

Abraham, Larry. *Countdown to the New World Order.* Video, 1990.

Allen, Gary. "The C.F.R. Conspiracy to Rule the World." *American Opinion* 12 (April 1969): 49–68.

———. *None Dare Call It Conspiracy.* Rossmoor, Calif.: Concord, 1971.

———. *The Rockefeller File.* Seal Beach, Calif.: '76 Press, 1976.

———. *Say "No!" to the New World Order.* Seal Beach, Calif.: Concord, 1987.

———. "They Run America," part 1. *American Opinion* 21 (May 1978): 1–4, 71–88. Part 2. *American Opinion* 21 (June 1978): 33–56, 105–10.

Armour, Charles R. "Year-End Report to Our Membership." *Bulletin* 334 (February 1987): 1–30.

Banta, Steve. "New Age Roots: Dark Foundations of the New World Order." *New American* 15 (March 1, 1999): 23–28.

———. "Two Revolutions." *New American* 14 (October 12, 1998): 27–32.

Barrett, George. "Close-Up of the Birchers 'Founder.'" *New York Times Magazine*, May 14, 1961, 13, 89, 91–92.

Barrett, Todd. "Once a Red, Always a Red." *Newsweek* 122 (September 17, 1990): 36.

Belknap, Michael R. *Cold War Political Justice: The Smith Act, the Communist Party, and American Civil Liberties*. Westport, Conn.: Greenwood, 1977.

Bell, Daniel, ed. *The New American Right*. Garden City, N.Y.: Doubleday-Anchor, 1964.

Bentley, Eric. *Thirty Years of Treason: Excerpts from Hearings Before the House Committee on Un-American Activities, 1938–1968*. New York: Viking, 1971.

Berlet, Chip. "Trashing the Birchers: Secrets of the Paranoid Right." *Boston Phoenix*, July 14–20, 1989, 10–11.

Billington, James H. *Fire in the Mind of Men: Origins of the Revolutionary Faith*. New York: Basic, 1980.

Brown, Julia. *I Testify: My Years as an FBI Undercover Agent*. Belmont, Mass.: Western Islands, 1966.

Broyles, J. Allen. *The John Birch Society: Anatomy of a Protest*. Boston: Beacon, 1966.

California Senate. *Twelfth Report of the Senate Fact-Finding Subcommittee on Un-American Activities*. Sacramento, 1963.

Caute, David. *The Great Fear: The Anti-Communist Purge Under Truman and Eisenhower*. New York: Simon and Schuster, 1978.

Ceplauer, Larry, and Steven Englund. *The Inquisition in Hollywood: Politics in the Film Community, 1930–1960*. Berkeley: University of California Press, 1983.

Chafe, William H. *The Unfinished Journey: America Since World War II*. New York: Oxford University Press, 1986.

Clark, Mark. *From the Danube to the Yalu*. New York: Harper and Row, 1954.

Cochran, Bert. *Labor and Communism: The Conflict That Shaped American Unions*. Princeton: Princeton University Press, 1977.

Commager, Henry Steele, ed. *Documents of American History*. New York: Appleton Century Crofts, 1958.

"Communist Influence as Percentage." *American Opinion* 6 (July–August, 1967): S1–4.

Communists Within the Government: The Facts and a Program. Washington, D.C.: Chamber of Commerce of the United States, 1947.

"Conspiracy for Global Conflict: Special Report." *New American*, January, 1997.

Courtney, Kent, and Phoebe Courtney. *America's Unelected Rulers*. New Orleans: Conservative Society of America, 1962.

Crawford, Alan. *Thunder on the Right: The "New Right" and the Politics of Resentment*. New York: Pantheon, 1980.

Darsey, James. *The Prophetic Tradition and Radical Rhetoric in America*. New York: New York University Press, 1997.

Dees, Morris, with James Corcoran. *Gathering Storm: America's Militia Threat*. New York: HarperCollins, 1996.

Dies, Martin. *The Trojan Horse in America*. New York: Dodd, Mead, 1940.

Dilling, Elizabeth. *The Red Network: A "Who's Who" and Handbook of Radicalism for Patriots*. Chicago, self-published, 1934.

——. *Roosevelt's Red Record and Its Background*. Chicago, self-published, 1936.

Doherty, Thomas. "Hollywood Agit-Prop: The Anti-Communist Cycle, 1948–1954." *Journal of Film and Video* 40 (Fall 1988): 15–27.

Draper, Theodore. *American Communism and Soviet Russia: The Formative Period*. New York: Viking, 1960.

Draskovich, S. M. *The John Birch Society Is a Threat to Whom?* Belmont, Mass.: N.p., n.d.

Elliston, Jon. "FEMA's X-File." *UFO Magazine* 14 (December 1999): 49–51.

Epperson, A. Ralph. *The New World Order*. Tucson: Publius, 1990.

——. *The Unseen Hand: An Introduction to the Conspiratorial Point of View*. Tucson: Publius, 1985.

Evans, Medford. "Conspiracy: The New World Order Isn't New." *American Opinion* 17 (December 1974): 47–52, 105–10.

Federal Bureau of Investigation. "Robert H. W. Welch, Jr." File 62-HQ-104401.

Flynn, John T. *The Road Ahead: America's Creeping Revolution, 1949*. New York: Devin-Adair, 1949.

Forster, Arnold, and Benjamin Epstein. *Danger on the Right*. New York: Random House, 1965.

Fried, Richard M. "Electoral Politics and McCarthyism: The 1950 Campaign." In Theoharis and Griffith, *The Specter*, 190–222.

Frieden, Jeff. "The Trilateral Commission: Economics and Politics in the 1970s." In Sklar, *Trilateralism*, 61–75.

Gardner, Martin. "Giving God a Hand." *New York Review of Books*, August 13, 1987, 17–18, 20–23.

Goldwater, Barry. *The Conscience of a Conservative*. Shepherdsville, Ky.: Victor, 1960.

——. *Why Not Victory? A Fresh Look at American Foreign Policy*. New York: McGraw-Hill, 1962.

——. *With No Apologies*. New York: William Morrow, 1979.

Goodman, Walter. *The Committee: The Extraordinary Career of the House Committee on Un-American Activities*. New York: Farrar, Straus, and Giroux, 1969.

Griffin, Des. *Fourth Reich of the Rich*. Clackamos, Ore.: Emissary, 1976.

Griffin, G. Edward. *The Life and Words of Robert Welch, Founder of the John Birch Society*. Thousand Oaks, Calif.: American Media, 1975.

Griffith, Robert. *The Politics of Fear: Joseph R. McCarthy and the Senate*. Lexington: University of Kentucky Press, 1970.

Grigg, William Norman. "American Patriot: The Legacy of Robert Welch." *New American* 14 (December 7, 1998): 29–33.

——. "Could It Happen in America?" *New American* 14 (December 7, 1998): 36–38.

——. "NATO and the Global Advance." *New American* 15 (May 10, 1999): 17–18.

——. "Waco Deception Up in Smoke." *New American* 15 (September 27, 1999): 12–15.

——. "Why Kosovo?" *New American* 15 (May 10, 1999): 8–11.

Grove, Gene. *Inside the John Birch Society*. Greenwich, Conn.: Fawcett, 1961.

Harper, Alan. *The Politics of Loyalty: The White House and the Communist Issue, 1946–1952*. Westport, Conn.: Greenwood, 1969.

Haynes, John Earl. *Red Scare or Red Menace? American Communism and Anti-Communism in the Cold War Era*. Chicago: Dee, 1996.

Heale, M. J. *American Anti-Communism: Combating the Enemy Within, 1830–1970*. Baltimore: Johns Hopkins University Press, 1990.

Hester, Jan. " 'Patriots' Warn Against New World Order." *UFO Magazine* 13 (September 1998): 6–9, 51.

Hoar, William. "New World Order." *American Opinion* 20 (April 1977): 13–20, 99.

Hoover, J. Edgar. *Masters of Deceit: The Story of Communism in America and How to Fight It*. New York: Holt, Rinehart, and Winston, 1958.

Horowitz, David A. *Beyond Left and Right: Insurgency and the Establishment*. Urbana: University of Illinois Press, 1997.

Huck, Susan L. "The Council on Foreign Relations and the Senate." *American Opinion* 23 (November 1979): 13–18, 85–94.

———. "Gambling with Subversion." *American Opinion* 20 (May 1977): 9–14, 85–92.

Ingraham, Jane H. "Global Money Changers." *New American* 15 (January 4, 1999): 27–32.

Jasper, William F. "Americanism's Standard-Bearer." *New American* 15 (December 6, 1999): 31–38.

———. "The Convergence Connection." *New American* 15 (July 19, 1999): 15–18.

———. "Mock-Up for Martial Law." *New American* 15 (April 26, 1999): 15–16.

———. "Rubber Stamp Report on OKC." *New American* 15 (February 1, 1999): 21–23.

———. "Soldiers in Your Backyard." *New American* 15 (April 26, 1999): 17–22.

John Birch Society. Appleton, Wis.: N.p., 1998.

Jones, Stephen, and Peter Israel. *Others Unknown: The Oklahoma City Bombing Case and Conspiracy*. New York: HarperCollins, 1998.

Keith, Jim. *Black Helicopters over America: Strikeforce for the New World Order*. Lilburn, Ga.: IllumiNet, 1994.

Key, Charles. "Waco and the OKC Bombing." *New American* 15 (October 11, 1999): 5.

Killebrew, Sara J. "FEMA: 'Shadow Government' for the New World Order." Honors paper, University of Utah, 1998.

Klehr, Harvey. *The Heyday of American Communism: The Depression Decade*. New York: Basic, 1984.

Knebel, Fletcher. "The GOP Attacks the John Birch Society." *Look* 29 (December 28, 1965): 74.

Kolkey, Jonathan Martin. *The New Right, 1960–1968, with Epilogue, 1969–1980*. Lanham, Md.: University Press of America, 1983.

Kovel, Joel. *Red Hunting in the Promised Land: Anti-Communism and the Making of America*. New York: Basic, 1994.

Kraft, Charles Jeffrey. *A Preliminary Socio-Economic and State Demographic Profile of the John Birch Society*. Somerville, Mass.: Political Research Associates, 1992.

Latham, Earl. *The Communist Controversy in Washington: From the New Deal to McCarthy*. Cambridge: Harvard University Press, 1966.

Lavine, Harold. *Fifth Column in America*. New York: Doubleday, Doran, 1940.

Leff, Laurel. "Whatever Happened to the John Birch Society?" *Wall Street Journal*, August 29, 1979.

Lipset, Seymour, and Earl Raab. *The Politics of Unreason: Right-Wing Extremism in America, 1790–1970.* New York: Harper and Row, 1970.

Macdonald, Andrew. *The Turner Diaries.* New York: Barricade, 1978.

MacDonald, J. Fred. *Television and the Red Menace: The Video Road to Vietnam.* New York: Praeger, 1985.

Mackenzie, Angus. *The CIA's War at Home.* Berkeley: University of California Press, 1997.

Matthews, J. B. *Odyssey of a Fellow Traveler.* New York: Mt. Vernon, 1938.

McCarthy, Joseph R. *America's Retreat from Victory: The Story of George Catlett Marshall.* New York: Devin-Adair, 1952.

——. "How Can We Account?" U.S. Senate. 82d Cong. 1st sess. June 14, 1951, *Congressional Record* 97: 6556–6603.

McManus, John F. *Changing Commands: The Betrayal of America's Military.* Appleton, Wis.: John Birch Society, 1995.

——. *The Insiders.* Appleton, Wis.: John Birch Society, 1996.

——. "Insiders Call the Shots." *New American* 14 (October 12, 1998): 44.

——. "Newt's Selective Rhetoric." *New American* 14 (June 8, 1998): 44.

——. *A Program for Responsible Citizenship.* Belmont, Mass.: Western Islands, 1986.

Miles, Michael. *The Odyssey of the American Right.* New York: Oxford University Press, 1980.

Militia of Montana Preparedness Catalogue. N.p., 1998.

Novak, Jeremiah. "The Trilateral Connection." *Atlantic* 240 (July 1977): 57–59.

Oliver, Revilo. "Review of Reviews." *American Opinion* 5 (June 1962): 31–37.

O'Reilly, Kenneth. *The FBI, HUAC, and the Red Menace.* New York: Associated Faculty Press, 1985.

Oshinsky, David M. *A Conspiracy So Immense: The World of Joe McCarthy.* New York: Free Press, 1983.

Peele, Gillian. *Revival and Reaction: The Right in Contemporary America.* New York: Oxford University Press, 1984.

Perloff, James. *The Shadows of Power: The Council on Foreign Relations and American Decline.* Belmont, Mass.: Western Islands, 1988.

Peters, Cynthia. *Collateral Damage: The New World Order at Home and Abroad.* Boston: South End, 1992.

Polsby, Nelson W. "Toward an Explanation of McCarthyism." *Political Studies* 8 (October 1960): 250–71.

Powers, Richard Gid. *Not Without Honor: The History of American Anti-Communism.* New York: Free Press, 1993.

Pugmire, Richard. "The FEMA Conspiracy: Creating the Image of an Un-American Agency." Honors paper, University of Utah, 1999.

Radosh, Ronald, and Joyce Milton. *The Rosenberg File: A Search for the Truth.* New York: Holt, Rinehart, and Winston, 1983.

Ray, Dixie Lee. *Environmental Overkill: Whatever Happened to Common Sense?* Washington, D.C.: Regnery Gateway, 1993.

Robison, John. *Proofs of a Conspiracy.* New York: George Forman, 1798.

Roddy, Dennis. "Trilateral Commission." *Deseret News,* May 19, 1996.

Rogin, Michael Paul. *The Intellectuals and McCarthy: The Radical Specter*. Cambridge: MIT Press, 1967.

Rohter, Ira. "Radical Rightists: An Empirical Study." Ph.D. diss., Michigan State University, 1967.

Saloma, John S. *Ominous Politics: The New Conservative Labyrinth*. New York: Hill and Wang, 1984.

Sayre, Nora. *Running Time: Films of the Cold War*. New York: Dial, 1982.

Schlafly, Phyllis. *A Choice Not an Echo*. Alton, Ill.: Pere Marquette, 1964.

Schrag, Peter. "America's Other Radicals." *Harper's Magazine* 241 (August 1970): 35–46.

Schomp, Gerald. *Birchism Was My Business*. New York: Macmillan, 1970.

Schrecker, Ellen W. *No Ivory Tower: McCarthyism in the Universities*. New York: Oxford University Press, 1986.

Schulzinger, Robert D. *The Wise Men of Foreign Affairs: The History of the Council on Foreign Relations*. New York: Columbia University Press, 1984.

"Scoreboard, 1980: Conspiracy Influence on May 1, 1980." *American Opinion* 23 (July–August, 1980): 79–104.

Sheerin, John B. "Catholic Right-Wing Extremists." *Catholic World* 194 (March 1962): 324–28.

Shoup, Laurence. "Jimmy Carter and the Trilateralists: Presidential Roots." In Sklar, *Trilateralism*, 199–211.

Shoup, Laurence, and William Minter. *Imperial Brain Trust: The Council on Foreign Relations and U.S. Foreign Policy*. New York: Monthly Review Press, 1977.

———. "Shaping a New World Order: The Council on Foreign Relations' Blueprint for World Hegemony." In Sklar, *Trilateralism*, 135–56.

Sklar, Holly. "Brave New World Order." In Peters, *Collateral Damage*, 3–46.

———. *Reagan, Trilateralism, and the Neoliberals: Containment and Intervention in the 1980s*. Boston: South End, 1986.

———, ed. *Trilateralism: The Trilateral Commission and Elite Planning for World Management*. Boston: South End, 1980.

Skousen, W. Cleon. *The Naked Capitalist*. Salt Lake City, self-published, 1970.

———. *The Naked Communist*. Salt Lake City: Ensign, 1961.

Smoot, Dan. *The Invisible Government*. Dallas: Dan Smoot Report, 1962.

Stang, Alan. "It's Time to Expose the Conspiracy." *American Opinion* 23 (December 1980): 25–29, 75–78.

———. *It's Very Simple: The True Story of Civil Rights*. Belmont, Mass.: Western Islands, 1965.

———. "The Reagan Administration and the C.F.R." *American Opinion* 25 (April 1982): 17–22, 77–84.

———. "Watergators." *American Opinion* 16 (September 1973): 1–16.

Steinberg, Peter L. *The Great "Red Menace:" United States Prosecution of American Communists, 1947–1952*. Westport, Conn.: Greenwood, 1985.

Steinfels, Peter. *The Neoconservatives: The Men Who Are Changing America's Politics*. New York: Simon and Schuster, 1979.

Stone, Barbara. "The John Birch Society of California." Ph.D. diss., University of Southern California, 1968.

Stormer, John A. *None Dare Call It Treason*. Florissant, Mo.: Liberty Bell, 1964.

Straus, Ira. "When Conspiracy Theory Replaces Thought." *Christian Science Monitor,* May 13, 1996.

Sutton, Anthony, and Patrick M. Wood. *Trilaterals Over Washington.* Scottsdale, Ariz.: August Corp., 1978.

Tanner, William R., and Robert Griffith. "Legislative Politics and 'McCarthyism': The Internal Security Act of 1950." In Theoharis and Griffith, *The Specter,* 172–89.

Theoharis, Athan G. *Seeds of Repression: Harry S. Truman and the Origins of McCarthyism.* Chicago: Quadrangle, 1971.

——. *Spying on Americans: Political Surveillance from Hoover to the Huston Plan.* Philadelphia: Temple University Press, 1978.

——, ed. *Beyond the Hiss Case: The FBI, Congress, and the Cold War.* Philadelphia: Temple University Press, 1982.

Theoharis, Athan G., and Robert Griffith, eds. *The Specter: Original Essays on the Cold War and the Origins of McCarthyism.* New York: Franklin Watts, 1974.

Thompson, Peter. "Bilderberg and the West." In Sklar, *Trilateralism,* 157–89.

Trow, Martin. "Small Businessmen, Political Tolerance, and Support for McCarthy." *American Journal of Sociology* 64 (November 1958): 270–81.

Vahan, Richard. *The Truth About the John Birch Society.* New York: Macfadden, 1962.

Warshaw, Robert. *The Immediate Experience: Movies, Comics, Theater, and Other Aspects of Popular Culture.* Garden City, N.Y.: Doubleday, 1962.

Webster, Nesta H. *Secret Societies and Subversive Movements.* New York: Christian Club of America, 1923.

——. *World Revolution.* London: Constable, 1921.

Weinstein, Allen. *Perjury: The Hiss-Chambers Case.* New York: Knopf, 1978.

Weinstein, James. *Ambiguous Legacy: The Left in American Politics.* New York: New Viewpoints, 1975.

Welch, Robert H. W., Jr. *Again, May God Forgive Us.* Chicago: Henry Regnery, 1952.

——. "Again, One Man's Opinion." *American Opinion* 24 (September 1981): 31–54.

——. *The Blue Book of the John Birch Society.* 9th printing. Belmont, Mass., self-published, 1961.

——. *A Brief Introduction to the John Birch Society.* Belmont, Mass.: Western Islands, 1962.

——. "Dissent." *American Opinion* 17 (December 1974): 53–56.

——. "If You Want It Straight." *American Opinion* 8 (December 1965): 1–8.

——. "In One Generation." R. Welch Presentations. Video, 1995.

——. "An Introduction to the John Birch Society." R. Welch Presentations. Video, 1995.

——. "An Invitation to Membership." R. Welch Presentations. Video, 1995.

——. *The Life of John Birch: In the Story of One American Boy, The Ordeal of His Age.* Chicago: Henry Regnery, 1954.

——. "Look at the Score." R. Welch Presentations. Video, 1995.

——. *The New Americanism and Other Speeches and Essays.* Boston: Western Islands, 1966.

——. *The Politician.* Belmont, Mass., self-published, 1963.

———. "A Touch of Sanity." R. Welch Productions. Video, 1965.

———. "The Truth in Time." *American Opinion* 9 (November 1966): 1–27.

———. "What Is the John Birch Society?" R. Welch Presentations. Video, 1995.

Westin, Alan F. "The Deadly Parallels: Radical Right and Radical Left." *Harper's Magazine* 224 (April 1962): 25–32.

———. "The John Birch Society: 'Radical Right' and 'Extreme Left' in the Political Context of Post World War II." In Bell, *New American Right*, 239–68.

Whitfield, Stephen. *The Culture of the Cold War*. Baltimore: Johns Hopkins Press, 1991.

Why Join the John Birch Society? Belmont, Mass.: N.p., 1961.

Winrod, Gerald B. *Adam Weishaupt: A Human Devil*. N.p., n.d.

Wolfe, Gary K. "Dr. Strangelove, Red Alert, and Patterns of Paranoia in the 1950s." *Journal of Popular Film* 5, no. 1 (1976): 57–67.

Chapter 3: The Rise of the Antichrist

Aho, James A. *The Politics of Righteousness: Idaho Christian Patriotism*. Seattle: University of Washington Press, 1990.

———. *The Thing of Darkness: A Sociology of the Enemy*. Seattle: University of Washington Press, 1994.

Barkun, Michael. "Divided Apocalypse: Thinking About the End in Contemporary America." *Soundings* 66 (Fall 1983): 257–80.

———. "Racist Apocalypse: Millennialism on the Far Right." *American Studies* 31 (Fall 1990): 121–40.

———. *Religion and the Racist Right: The Origins of the Christian Identity Movement*. Chapel Hill: University of North Carolina Press, 1994.

Bay, David. "Anti-Christ, Aliens, and UFO's." http://www.cuttingedge.org/ce1030.html (June 16, 1999).

The Bible. King James Version. New York: Ivy, 1991.

Block, Ruth. *Visionary Republic: Millennial Themes in American Thought, 1756–1800*. Cambridge: Cambridge University Press, 1985.

Boaz, David. "Pat Robertson's Crackpopulism." *Wall Street Journal*, February 10, 1988.

Boston, Robert. *The Most Dangerous Man in America? Pat Robertson and the Rise of the Christian Coalition*. Amherst, N.Y.: Prometheus, 1996.

Boyer, Paul S. *When Time Shall Be No More: Prophecy Belief in Modern American Culture*. Cambridge: Belknap, 1992.

Brookes, James H. *Maranatha, or, the Lord Cometh*. New York: Fleming H. Revell, 1870.

Bruce, Steve. *Pray TV: Televangelism in America*. London: Routledge, 1990.

Butler, Richard. *This Is Aryan Nations*. Hayden Lake, Idaho: Church of Jesus Christ Christian, 1980.

Cantor, David. *The Religious Right: The Assault on Tolerance and Pluralism in America*. New York: Anti-Defamation League, 1994.

Capps, Walter H. *The New Religious Right: Piety, Patriotism, and Politics*. Columbia: University of South Carolina Press, 1990.

Cassara, Ernest. "The Development of America's Sense of Mission." In Zamora, *Apocalyptic Vision*, 64–96.

Christian Underground Hotline Catalogue. N.p.: 1998.

Coates, James. *Armed and Dangerous: The Rise of the Survivalist Right.* New York: Hill and Wang, 1987.

Cook, Terry L. "Today's Technology Churns Toward the Mark of the Beast." In James, *Forewarning,* 89–116.

Corbett, Christopher. "Energy, Ecology, Economy: A Foreboding Forecast." In James, *Forewarning,* 271–90.

Dailey, Timothy J. *The Millennial Deception: Angels, Aliens, and the AntiChrist.* Grand Rapids, Mich.: Chosen, 1995.

DeLashmutt, Gary, Dennis McCallum, Jeff Gordon, and Doug Patch. "Covenantalism and Dispensationalism" and "Eschatology #3: End-Time Events." http://www.xenos.org (February 5, 1998).

Dobson, Ed, and Ed Hindson. "Apocalypse Now?" *Policy Review* 37 (Summer 1986): 16–22.

Donovan, John B. *Pat Robertson: The Authorized Biography.* New York: Macmillan, 1988.

Duck, Daymond R. "Harbingers of Humanism's Hurricane." In James, *Forewarning,* 67–87.

Eskelin, Neil. *Pat Robertson: A Biography.* Shreveport, La.: Huntington House, 1987.

Falwell, Jerry. *Armageddon and the Coming Wars with Russia.* Lynchburg, Va: Old-Time Gospel Hour, 1979.

———. *Dr. Jerry Falwell Teaches Bible Prophecy.* Old-Time Gospel Hour. Audio tape, 1979.

Fineman, Howard. "God and the Grass Roots." *Newsweek* 122 (November 8, 1993): 42–46.

Foege, Alec. *The Empire God Built: Inside Pat Robertson's Media Machine.* New York: Wiley, 1996.

Fox, B. *The Agenda: The Real Reason They're Here.* Kearney, Neb.: Morris, 1996.

Fuller, Robert. *Naming the Anti-Christ: The History of an American Obsession.* New York: Oxford University Press, 1995.

Gallup, George, and Jim Castelli. *The People's Religion: American Faith in the '90s.* New York: Macmillan, 1989.

Goetz, William R. *Apocalypse Next: The End of Civilization as We Know It?* Camp Hill, Pa.: Horizon, 1996.

———. *UFOs: Friend, Foe, or Fantasy? A Biblical Perspective on the Phenomenon of the Century.* Camp Hill, Pa.: Horizon, 1997.

Gow, Andrew. "Jerry Falwell Stumbles Badly in Adhering to the Terrible Myth of the Antichrist." *Salt Lake Tribune,* February 14, 1999.

Graham, Billy. *Approaching Hoofbeats: The Four Horsemen of the Apocalypse.* New York: Avon, 1983.

Green, John, and James L. Guth. "The Christian Right in the Republican Party: The Case of Pat Robertson's Contributors." *Journal of Politics* 50 (February 1988): 150–65.

Gross, Michael Joseph. "The Trials of the Tribulation." *Atlantic Monthly* 285 (January 2000): 122–28.

Hadden, Jeffrey K., and Anson Shupe. *Televangelism: Power and Politics on God's Frontier.* New York: Holt, 1988.

Hadden, Jeffrey K., and Charles Swann. *Prime Time Preachers: The Rising Power of Televangelism*. Reading, Mass.: Addison-Wesley, 1981.

Hagee, John. *Beginning of the End: The Assassination of Yitzhak Rabin and the Coming Antichrist*. Nashville: Thomas Nelson, 1996.

Halsell, Grace. *Prophecy and Politics: The Secret Alliance Between Israel and the U.S. Christian Right*. Chicago: Lawrence Hill, 1986.

Harrell, David Edwin, Jr. *Pat Robertson*. San Francisco: Harper and Row, 1987.

Hatch, Nathan O. *The Sacred Cause of Liberty: Republican Thought and the Millennium in Revolutionary New England*. New Haven: Yale University Press, 1977.

Heilbrunn, Jacob. "On Pat Robertson: His Anti-Semitic Sources." *New York Review of Books* 42 (April 20, 1995): 68–71.

Hertzke, Allen D. *Echoes of Discontent: Jesse Jackson, Pat Robertson, and the Resurgence of Populism*. Washington, D.C.: CQ, 1993.

Himmelstein, Jerome L. *To the Right: The Transformation of American Conservatism*. Berkeley: University of California Press, 1990.

Horwitz, Tony. "Rebel Voices: The Face of Extremism Wears Many Guises—Most of Them Ordinary." *Wall Street Journal*, April 28, 1995.

James, William T. "Earth's Stormy Horizon." In James, *Forewarning*, 7–23.

———. "New Europe's Eye of the Tornado." In James, *Forewarning*, 165–98.

———, ed. *Forewarning: Approaching the Final Battle Between Heaven and Hell*. Eugene, Ore.: Harvest House, 1998.

Jeffrey, Grant R. *Armageddon: Appointment with Destiny*. New York: Bantam, 1990.

Johnsen, Dale. "Christ Permits Antichrist to Emerge." http://www.nwinfo.net/~dmjohnsen/16Antichrist.html (February 18, 1998).

Kah, Gary H. *The Demonic Roots of Globalism: En Route to Spiritual Deception*. Lafayette, La.: Huntington House, 1995.

———. *En Route to Global Occupation*. Lafayette, La.: Huntington House, 1991.

Kermode, Mark. *The Exorcist*. London: BFI, 1997.

King, Wayne. "The Record of Pat Robertson on Religion and Government." *New York Times*, December 27, 1987, 1, 30.

Kirban, Salem. *Guide to Survival: How the World Will End!* Huntington Valley, Pa.: AMG, 1991.

Klassen, Ben. *The White Man's Bible*. Milwaukee: Milwaukee Church of the Creator, 1981.

Lacayo, Richard. "The End of the World as We Know It." *Time* 153 (January 18, 1999): 60–64, 67–68, 70.

LaHaye, Tim. *The Beginning of the End*. Wheaton, Il.: Tyndale House, 1991.

LaHaye, Tim, and Jerry B. Jenkins. *Left Behind: A Novel of the Earth's Last Days*. Wheaton, Ill.: Tyndale House, 1995.

———. *Nicolae: The Rise of the Antichrist*. Wheaton, Ill.: Tyndale House, 1997.

———. *Soul Harvest: The World Takes Sides*. Wheaton, Ill.: Tyndale House, 1998.

———. *Tribulation Force: The Continuing Saga of Those Left Behind*. Wheaton, Ill.: Tyndale House, 1996.

Lalonde, Peter, and Paul Lalonde. *Racing Toward . . . The Mark of the Beast*. Eugene, Ore.: Harvest House, 1994.

Lamy, Philip. *Millennial Rage: Survivalists, White Supremacists, and the Doomsday Prophecy*. New York: Plenum, 1996.

Lewis, David Allen. *Dark Angels of Light*. Green Forest, Ala.: New Leaf, 1985.

Lienesch, Michael. *Redeeming America: Piety and Politics in the New Christian Right*. Chapel Hill: University of North Carolina Press, 1993.

Lind, Michael. "Reverend Pat Robertson's Grand International Conspiracy Theory." *New York Review of Books* 42 (February 2, 1995): 21–25.

——. *Up From Conservatism: Why the Right Is Wrong for America*. New York: Free Press, 1996.

Lindsey, Hal. *Apocalypse Code*. Palos Verdes, Calif.: Western Front LTD, 1997.

——. *The Late Great Planet Earth*. Grand Rapids, Mich.: Zondervan, 1970.

——. *The 1980s: Countdown to Armageddon*. New York: Bantam, 1980.

——. *The Terminal Generation*. Old Tappan, N.J.: Revell, 1976.

Lloyd, James. "Portals, UFOs, and Planet X: The Return of the Rephaim." *Christian Media*, Second Quarter, 1999, 1–18.

Malone, Peter. *Movie Christs and Anti-Christs*. New York: Crossroads, 1990.

Marcussen, A. Jan. *National Sunday Law*. Thompsonville, Ill.: Amazing Truth, 1983.

Marrs, Texe. *Dark Majesty*. Austin: Living Truth, 1992.

——. *Project L.U.C.I.D.: The Beast 666 Universal Human Control System*. Austin; Living Truth, 1996.

Martin, William. "Waiting for the End." *Atlantic Monthly* 249 (June 1982): 31–37.

Mather, Cotton. *The Wonders of the Invisible World*. New York: Bell, n.d. Originally pub. 1692.

Mather, Increase. *The Mystery of Israel's Salvation*. New York: AMS, 1983. Originally pub. 1669.

McAlvaney, Donald S. *Toward a New World Order: The Countdown To Armageddon*. Phoenix: Western Pacific, 1992.

McCall, Thomas, and Zola Levitt. *Israel and Tomorrow's Temple*. Chicago: Moody, 1973.

McGinn, Bernard. "Portraying the AntiChrist in the Middle Ages." In Werner Verbeke, Daniel Verhelst, and Andries Welkenhuysen, eds., *The Use and Abuse of Eschatology in the Middle Ages*, 1–48. Leuven, Belgium: Leuven University Press, 1988.

Middlekauf, Robert. *The Mathers: Three Generations of Puritan Intellectuals, 1596–1728*. New York: Oxford University Press, 1971.

Miller, Perry. *Errand into the Wilderness*. New York: Harper Torchbooks, 1956.

Moody, Dwight. *The Second Coming of Christ*. Chicago: Moody, n.d.

Moore, Marvin. *The Antichrist and the New World Order*. Boise: Pacific, 1993.

Nelson, John Wiley. "The Apocalyptic Vision in American Popular Culture." In Zamora, *Apocalyptic Vision*, 154–82.

Niebuhr, Gustav. "Pat Robertson Says He Intended No Anti-Semitism in Book He Wrote Four Years Ago." *New York Times*, March 4, 1995.

O'Leary, Stephen D. *Arguing the Apocalypse: A Theory of Millennial Rhetoric*. New York: Oxford University Press, 1994.

O'Leary, Stephen D., and Michael McFarland. "The Political Use of Mythic Discourse: Prophetic Interpretation in Pat Robertson's Presidential Campaign." *Quarterly Journal of Speech* 75 (November 1989): 433–52.

Podhoretz, Norman. "In the Matter of Pat Robertson." *Commentary* 100 (August 1995): 27–32.

Queenan, Joe. "New World Order Nut." *Wall Street Journal*, December 31, 1991.

Radner, Ephraim. "New World Order, Old World Anti-Semitism." *Christian Century* 112 (September 13–20, 1995): 844–49.

Relfe, Mary Stewart. *The New Money System 666.* Montgomery, Ala.: Ministries, 1982.

———. *When Your Money Fails.* Montgomery, Ala.: League of Prayer, 1981.

Rich, Frank. "New World Terror." *New York Times*, April 27, 1995, 25.

Ridgeway, James. *Blood in the Face: The Ku Klux Klan, Aryan Nations, Nazi Skinheads, and the Rise of a New White Culture.* New York: Thunder Mouth's, 1990.

Rimer, Sara. "New Medium for the Far Right." *New York Times*, April 27, 1995, 1, 22.

Robertson, DeDe. *My God Will Supply.* Lincoln, Va.: Chosen, 1979.

Robertson, Pat. *America's Dates with Destiny.* Nashville: Thomas Nelson, 1986.

———. *Answers to 200 of Life's Most Probing Questions.* Nashville: Thomas Nelson, 1984.

———. *Beyond Reason: How Miracles Can Change Your Life.* New York: William Morrow, 1985.

———. *The End of the Age: A Novel.* Dallas: Word, 1995.

———. *New Millennium: Ten Trends That Will Impact You and Your Family by the Year 2000.* Nashville: Word, 1990.

———. *The New World Order.* Nashville: Word, 1991.

———. *The Plan.* Nashville: Thomas Nelson, 1989.

———. *The Secret Kingdom.* Dallas: Word, 1992.

———. *The Turning Tide.* Dallas: Word, 1993.

Robertson, Pat, and Jamie Buckingham. *Shout It from the Housetops.* South Plainfield, N.J.: Bridge, 1972.

Rosen, Moishe. *Y'Shua: The Jewish Way to Say Jesus.* Chicago: Moody, 1982.

Scofield, Cyrus I. *Scofield Reference Bible.* New York; Oxford University Press, 1917.

———. *What Do the Prophets Say?* Philadelphia: Sunday School Times, 1916.

Searcy, Jim. "The New World Order Religious System of the AntiChrist Is the Global Ethic." http://www.dccsa.com (February 9, 1998).

———. " 'Oblation' Says Who Is God." Audiotape, n.d.

Sheler, Jeffrey. "The Christian Covenant." *U.S. News and World Report* 117 (December 19, 1994): 62–71.

Smith, Chuck. *What the World Is Coming To.* Costa Mesa, Calif.: The Word for Today, 1977.

Smith, Wilbur M. *The Atomic Bomb and the Word of God.* Chicago: Moody, 1945.

———. *Before I Forget.* Chicago: Moody, 1971.

Stein, Stephen J. "Transatlantic Extensions: Apocalyptic in Early New England." In C. A. Patrides and Joseph Wittreich, eds., *Apocalypse in English Renaissance Thought and Literature,* 266–98. Ithaca, N.Y.: Cornell University Press, 1984.

Stern, Kenneth S. *A Force upon the Plain: The American Militia Movement and the Politics of Hate.* New York: Simon and Schuster, 1996.

Strozier, Charles B. *Apocalypse: On the Psychology of Fundamentalism in America.* Boston: Beacon, 1994.

Taylor, John. "Pat Robertson's God, Inc." *Esquire* 122 (November 1994): 77–83.

Thomas, I. D. E. *The Omega Conspiracy: Satan's Last Assault on God's Kingdom.* Oklahoma City: Hearthstone, 1986.

Thompson, Damian. *The End of Time: Faith and Fear in the Shadow of the Millennium.* Hanover, N.H.: University Press of New England, 1996.

Tuveson, Ernest Lee. *Redeemer Nation: The Idea of America's Millennial Role.* Chicago: University of Chicago Press, 1968.

Van Impe, Jack. *11:59 . . . and Counting!* Troy, Mich.: Jack Van Impe Ministries, 1983.

——. "The European Superstate and the Coming New World Order." http://www.jvim.com/PerhapsToday/SeptOct1995/NewWorldOrder.html (February 5, 1998).

——. *Revelation Revealed: Verse by Verse.* Troy, Mich.: Jack Van Impe Ministries, 1982.

Wager, W. Warren. *Terminal Visions: The Literature of the Last Things.* Bloomington: Indiana University Press, 1982.

Weber, Eugen. *Apocalypses: Prophecies, Cults, and Millennial Beliefs Through the Ages.* Cambridge: Harvard University Press, 1999.

Weber, Timothy. *Living in the Shadows of the Second Coming: American Premillennialism, 1875–1982.* Chicago: University of Chicago Press, 1987.

White, John Wesley. *Re-Entry!* Grand Rapids, Mich.: Zondervan, 1974.

Wigglesworth, Michael. *The Day of Doom; or, a Political Description of the Great and Last Judgment.* New York: American News, 1867.

Wilcox, Clyde. *God's Warriors: The Christian Right in Twentieth Century America.* Baltimore: Johns Hopkins University Press, 1992.

——. *Onward Christian Soldiers? The Religious Right in American Politics.* Boulder, Colo.: Westview, 1996.

Wilkerson, David. *The Vision.* Grand Rapids, Mich.: Spire, 1974.

Wills, Garry. "The Born-Again Republicans." *New York Review of Books* 39 (September 24, 1992): 9–14.

——. *Under God: Religion and American Politics.* New York: Simon and Schuster, 1990.

Wojcik, Daniel. *The End of the World as We Know It: Faith, Fatalism, and Apocalypse in America.* New York: New York University Press, 1997.

Woodward, Kenneth. "The Way the World Ends." *Newsweek* 134 (November 1, 1999): 66–74.

Zahner, Dee. *The Secret Side of History: Mystery Babylon and the New World Order.* Hesperia, Calif.: LTAA Communications, 1994.

Zamora, Lois Parkinson, ed. *The Apocalyptic Vision in America: Interdisciplinary Essays on Myth and Culture.* Bowling Green, Ohio: Bowling Green University Popular Press, 1982.

Chapter 4: The View from the Grassy Knoll

Achincloss, Kenneth. "Twisted History." *Newsweek* 123 (December 23, 1991): 46–49.

Albert, Michael. "Conspiracy? . . . Not!" In Stone and Sklar, *JFK,* 358–64.

Ambrose, Stephen E. "Writers on the Grassy Knoll: A Readers' Guide." *New York Times,* February 2, 1992, 1, 23–24.

Anderson, Stephan V. "Kennedy Assassination Study Guide." Unpublished, in the author's possession.

Ansen, David. "A Troublemaker for our Times." *Newsweek* 123 (December 23, 1991): 50.

———. "What Does Oliver Stone Owe History?" *Newsweek* 123 (December 23, 1991): 49.

Anson, Robert Sam. "The Shooting of JFK." In Stone and Sklar, *JFK,* 208–29.

———. *"They've Killed the President!" The Search for the Murderers of John F. Kennedy.* New York: Bantam, 1975.

"Assassination: The Trail to a Verdict." *Life* 57 (October 2, 1964): 40–41, 43–46, 48, 50B.

Assassination Records Review Board. *Final Report.* Washington, D.C.: 1998.

Beaver, Frank Eugene. *Oliver Stone: Wake-Up Cinema.* New York: Twayne, 1994.

Benson, Michael. *Who's Who in the JFK Assassination: An A to Z Encyclopedia.* New York: Carol, 1993.

Beschloss, Michael R. "An Assassination Diary." *Newsweek* 132 (November 23, 1998): 42–43.

———. "The Day That Changed America." *Newsweek* 122 (November 23, 1993): 61–62.

———. "The Johnson Tapes." *Newsweek* 130 (October 13, 1997): 56–62.

Blumenthal, Sid. "The Rockefeller Commission." In Blumenthal and Yazijian, *Government by Gunplay,* 243–49.

Blumenthal, Sid, and Harvey Yazijian, eds. *Government by Gunplay: Assassination Conspiracy Theories from Dallas to Today.* New York: Signet, 1976.

Breo, Dennis L. "JFK's Death: The Plain Truth from the MDs who did the Autopsy." *JAMA* 267 (May 27, 1992): 2794–2803.

———. "JFK's Death," part 2, "Dallas MDs Recall Their Memories." *JAMA* 267 (May 27, 1992): 2804–7.

Breskin, David. "Oliver Stone: An Interview with the Director." In Kunz, *The Films of Oliver Stone,* 3–64.

Buchanan, Thomas G. *Who Killed Kennedy?* New York: Putnam, 1964.

Butler, Lisa, Cheryl Koopman, and Philip Zimbardo. "The Psychological Impact of Viewing the Film *JFK*: Emotions, Beliefs, and Political Behavioral Intentions." *Political Psychology* 16 (June 1995): 237–58.

Carlin, John. "Kennedy's Death, Nazi Gold: Research Resources Grow at the National Archives." *OAH Newsletter* 27 (February 1999): 10.

CIA Critic Fletcher Prouty, Willis Carto's Liberty Lobby Network, JFK Conspiracy Theories, Lyndon LaRouche. Cambridge: Political Research Associates, 1992.

Crowdus, Gary. "Clarifying the Conspiracy: An Interview with Oliver Stone." *Cineaste* 19 (1992): 25–27.

DeLillo, Don. *Libra.* New York: Penguin, 1988.

Dowell, Pat. "Last Year at Nuremberg." *Cineaste* 19 (1992): 8–11.

Dudman, Richard. "Commentary of an Eyewitness." *Commentary* 149 (December 21, 1963): 18.

———. "Uncertainties Remain Despite Police View of Kennedy Death." *St. Louis Post Dispatch,* December 1, 1963.

Epperson, Ralph. *The Driver Shot President Kennedy!* Publius Press. Video, 1992.

Epstein, Edward Jay. *Inquest: The Warren Commission and the Establishment of Truth.* New York: Bantam, 1966.

——. *Legend: The Secret World of Lee Harvey Oswald.* New York: McGraw-Hill, 1978.

——. "Who's Afraid of the Warren Report?" *Esquire* 66 (December 1966): 204, 330–334.

Feshbach, Norma, and Seymour Feshbach. "Personality and Political Values: A Study of Reactions to Two Accused Assassins." In Greenberg and Parker, *Kennedy Assassination,* 289–304.

Fonzi, Gaeton. *The Last Investigation.* New York: Thunder's Mouth, 1993.

Ford, Gerald R. "Piecing Together the Evidence." *Life* 57 (October 2, 1964): 42, 47–50A.

Ford, Gerald R., and David W. Belin. "Kennedy Assassination: How About the Truth?" *Washington Post,* December 17, 1991.

Foster, Mike. "JFK Was Shot to Prevent Him from Revealing Truth about UFOs!" *Weekly World News,* January 11, 2000.

Frank, Jeffrey. "Who Shot JFK? The 30-Year Mystery." *Washington Post Book World,* October 31, 1993.

Frewin, Anthony. *The Assassination of John F. Kennedy: An Annotated Film, TV, and Videography, 1963–1992.* Westport, Conn.: Greenwood, 1993.

Garrison, Jim. *A Heritage of Stone.* New York: Putnam, 1970.

——. *On the Trail of Assassins.* New York: Warner, 1988.

Garson, Barbara. *MacBird!* New York: Grove, 1966.

Gates, David. "Bottom Line: How Crazy Is It?" *Newsweek* 123 (December 23, 1991): 52–54.

Gelb, Leslie H. "Kennedy and Vietnam." In Stone and Sklar, *JFK,* 391–92.

Gitlin, Todd. "The Stoning of Oliver Stone." In Stone and Sklar, *JFK,* 454–58.

Goldman, Peter. "Dallas: New Questions and Answers." *Newsweek* 85 (April 28, 1975): 36–38.

Greenberg, Bradley S., and Edwin B. Parker, eds. *The Kennedy Assassination and the American Public.* Stanford: Stanford University Press, 1965.

Grenier, Richard. "On the Trail of America's Paranoid Class: Oliver Stone's *JFK*." *National Interest* 27 (Spring 1992): 76–84.

Groden, Robert J., and Harrison Edward Livingstone. *High Treason: The Assassination of President John F. Kennedy and the New Evidence of Conspiracy.* New York: Berkeley, 1989.

Guth, DeLloyd, and David Wrone. *The Assassination of John F. Kennedy: A Comprehensive Historical and Legal Bibliography, 1963–1979.* Westport, Conn.: Greenwood, 1980.

Hamburg, Eric., ed. *Nixon: An Oliver Stone Film.* New York: Hyperion, 1995.

Hennelly, Robert, and Jerry Policoff. "JFK: How the Media Assassinated the Real Story." In Stone and Sklar, *JFK,* 484–99.

Herbert, Bob. "A Historians' View." *New York Times,* June 3, 1999, 25.

Herring, George C. *America's Longest War: The United States and Vietnam, 1950–1975.* New York: Wiley, 1979.

Hersh, Seymour M. *The Dark Side of Camelot.* Boston: Little, Brown, 1977.

Holland, Max. "The Key to the Warren Report." *American Heritage* 46 (September 1995): 50–64.

Hunt, Conover. *Dealey Plaza National Historical Landmark*. Dallas: Sixth Floor Museum, 1997.

Hurt, Henry. *Reasonable Doubt: An Investigation into the Assassination of John F. Kennedy*. New York: Henry Holt, 1985.

JFK: The Story That Won't Go Away. Los Angeles: Warner Brothers, 1991.

Joesten, Joachim. *Oswald: Assassin or Fall Guy?* New York: Marzani and Munsell, 1964.

Jones, Penn. *Forgive My Grief*. Midlothian: Midlothian Texas Mirror, 1966.

Kagan, Norman. *The Cinema of Oliver Stone*. New York: Continuum, 1995.

Kaplan, John. "The Case of the Grassy Knoll: The Romance of Conspiracy." In Winks, Robin, ed. *Historian as Detective: Essays on Evidence*. New York: Harper and Row, 1968.

Kovaleff, Theodore P. "JFK Assassination Books." *Presidential Studies Quarterly* 24 (Fall 1994): 901–9.

Krauss, Clifford. "28 Years After Kennedy's Assassination, Conspiracy Theories Refuse to Die." *New York Times*, January 5, 1992, 18.

Krauthammer, Charles. " 'JFK': A Lie, But Harmless." *Washington Post*, January 10, 1992.

Kunz, Don, ed. *The Films of Oliver Stone*. Lanham, Md.: Scarecrow, 1997.

Kurtz, Michael L. *Crime of the Century: The Kennedy Assassination from a Historical Perspective*. Knoxville: University of Tennessee Press, 1993.

Kwitny, Jonathan. "A Better Conspiracy Theory Than Oliver Stone's." *Wall Street Journal*, December 19, 1991.

Lacayo, Richard. "Smashing Camelot." *Time* 150 (November 17, 1997): 40–49.

Lane, Mark. *Plausible Denial: Was the CIA Involved in the Assassination of JFK?* New York: Thunder's Mouth, 1991.

——. *Rush to Judgment*. New York: Holt, Rinehart, and Winston, 1966.

Lardner, George, Jr. "On the Set: Dallas in Wonderland." *Washington Post*, May 19, 1991.

Lasch, Christopher. "The Life of Kennedy's Death." *Harper's* 267 (October 1983): 32–40.

Lewis, Anthony. "J.F.K." *New York Times*, January 9, 1992, 23.

Lifton, David S. *Best Evidence: Disguise and Deception in the Assassination of John F. Kennedy*. New York: Signet, 1980.

Livingstone, Harrison Edward. *High Treason 2, the Great Cover-Up: The Assassination of John F. Kennedy*. New York: Carroll and Graf, 1993.

——. *Killing Kennedy and the Hoax of the Century*. New York: Carroll and Graf, 1995.

Lundberg, George D. "Closing the Case in JAMA on the John F. Kennedy Autopsy." *JAMA* 268 (October 7, 1992): 1736–38.

MacDonald, Dwight. "A Critique of the Warren Report." *Esquire* 63 (March 1965): 59–63, 127–37.

Mackey-Kallis, Susan. *Oliver Stone's America: "Dreaming the Myth Outward."* Boulder, Colo.: Westview, 1996.

Mailer, Norman. "Footfalls in the Crypt." In Stone and Sklar, *JFK*, 438–48.

——. *Oswald's Tale: An American Mystery*. New York: Random House, 1995.

Manchester, William. *The Death of a President, November 1963*. New York: Harper and Row, 1967.

Mandel, Paul. "End to Nagging Rumors: The Six Critical Seconds." *Life* 55 (December 6, 1963): 52F.

Mankiewicz, Frank. "About the Debate." In Stone and Sklar, *JFK*, 187–89.

Margolis, Jon. "*JFK* Movie and Book Attempt to Rewrite History." *Dallas Morning News*, May 14, 1991.

Marrs, Jim. *Crossfire: The Plot That Killed Kennedy*. New York: Carroll and Graf, 1989.

Maslin, Janet. "Oliver Stone Manipulates His Puppet." *New York Times*, January 5, 1992, II, 15.

"A Matter of Reasonable Doubt." *Life* 61 (November 11, 1966): 138–50, 153.

McCauley, C., and S. Jacques. "The Popularity of Conspiracy Theories of Presidential Assassination: A Bayesian Analysis." *Journal of Personality and Social Psychology* 37 (May 1979): 637–44.

Meagher, Sylvia. *Accessories After the Fact: The Warren Commission, The Authorities and the Report*. Indianapolis: Bobbs-Merrill, 1967.

———. "Notes for a New Investigation." *Esquire* 66 (December 1966): 211, 335–36.

Medhurst, Martin J. "The Rhetorical Structure of Oliver Stone's *JFK*." In Kunz, *Films of Oliver Stone*, 207–26.

Minnis, Jack, and Staughton Lynd. "Seeds of Doubt: Some Questions About the Assassination." *New Republic* 149 (December 21, 1963): 14–20.

Mintz, Frank P. *The Liberty Lobby and the American Right*. Westport, Conn.: Greenwood, 1985.

Moore, Jim. *Conspiracy of One: The Definitive Book on the Kennedy Assassination*. Fort Worth: Summit Group, 1991.

Morley, Jefferson. "The Political Rorschach Test." *Los Angeles Times*, December 8, 1991.

Moss, George Donelson. *Vietnam: An American Ordeal*. Englewood Cliffs, N.J.: Prentice Hall, 1990.

Moynihan, Daniel Patrick. "The Paranoid Style." *Washington Post*, December 29, 1991.

Nelson, Anna Kasten. "The John F. Kennedy Assassination Records Review Board." In Athan G. Theoharis, ed., *A Culture of Secrecy: The Government Versus the People's Right to Know*, 211–31. Lawrence: University Press of Kansas, 1998.

North, Mark. *Act of Treason: The Role of J. Edgar Hoover in the Assassination of President Kennedy*. New York: Carroll and Graf, 1991.

O'Hehir, Andrew. "JFK: Tragedy into Farce." In Stone and Sklar, *JFK*, 269–73.

Olgesby, Carl. "The Conspiracy That Won't Go Away." In Stone and Sklar, *JFK*, 425–37.

———. "Presidential Assassinations and the Closing of the Frontier." In Blumenthal and Yazijian, *Government by Gunplay*, 188–207.

———. *Who Killed JFK?* Berkeley: Odonian, 1992.

Oliver, Revilo P. "Marxmanship in Dallas," part 1. *American Opinion* 7 (February 1964): 13–28.

———. "Marxmanship in Dallas," part 2. *American Opinion* 7 (March 1964): 65–78.

O'Neill, Tip. *Man of the House: The Life and Political Memoirs of Speaker Tip O'Neill*. New York: Random House, 1987.

Parshall, Gerald. "The Man with the Deadly Smile." *U.S. News and World Report* 115 (August 30, 1993): 62–72.

Payne, Darwin. *The Press Corps and the Kennedy Assassination*. Lexington, Ky.: Association for Education in Journalism, 1970.

Piper, Michael. *Final Judgment: The Missing Link in the JFK Assassination Conspiracy*. Washington, D.C.: Wolfe, 1995.

Policoff, Jerry. "The Media and the Murder of President Kennedy." *New Times* 5 (August 8, 1975): 28–36.

———. "The Second Dallas Casualty: The Media and the Assassination of Truth." In Blumenthal and Yazijian, *Government by Gunplay*, 208–30.

Posner, Gerald. *Case Closed: Lee Harvey Oswald and the Assassination of JFK*. New York: Anchor, 1993.

———. "Cracks in the Wall of Silence." *Newsweek* 132 (October 12, 1998): 49.

"A Primer of Assassination Theories." *Esquire* 66 (December 1966): 205–10, 334.

Prouty, L. Fletcher. *JFK: The CIA, Vietnam, and the Plot to Assassinate John F. Kennedy*. New York: Citadel, 1996.

Raskin, Marcus. "*JFK* and the Culture of Violence." *American Historical Review* 97 (April 1992): 487–99.

Richter, Mordecai. "It's a Plot." *Playboy* 22 (May 1975): 132–33, 179–85, 188–90.

Riordan, James. *Stone: The Controversies, Excesses, and Exploits of a Radical Filmmaker*. New York: Hyperion, 1995.

Rivers, William L. "The Press and the Assassination." In Greenberg and Parker, *Kennedy Assassination*, 51–60.

Roberts, Charles. *The Truth About the Assassination*. New York: Grosset and Dunlap, 1967.

Robins, Robert S., and Jerrold M. Post. "Political Paranoia as Cinematic Motif: Stone's 'JFK.'" http://mcadams.posc.mu.edu/robins.htm (January 10, 1998).

Rogin, Michael. "*JFK*: The Movie." *American Historical Review* 97 (April 1992): 500–505.

Rosenbaum, Ron. "Taking a Darker View." In Stone and Sklar, *JFK*, 396–401.

Rosenstone, Robert A. "*JFK*: Historical Fact/Historical Film." *American Historical Review* 97 (April 1992): 506–11.

Safire, William. "The Way It Really Was Not." *New York Times*, November 27, 1995, 13.

Salewicz, Chris. *Oliver Stone: Close Up*. New York: Thunder Mouth's, 1998.

Salisbury, Harrison E. "The Editor's View in New York." In Greenberg and Parker, *Kennedy Assassination*, 37–45.

———. *A Time of Change: A Reporter's Tale of our Time*. New York: Harper and Row, 1988.

Scheim, David E. *Contract on America: The Mafia Murder of President John F. Kennedy*. New York: Zebra, 1988.

Schlesinger, Arthur, Jr. "*JFK*: Truth and Fiction." *Wall Street Journal*, January 10, 1992.

Schorr, Daniel. "The Assassins." *New York Review of Books* 24 (October 3, 1977): 14–22.

Schramm, Wilbur. "Communication in Crisis." In Greenberg and Parker, *Kennedy Assassination*, 1–25.

Scott, Peter Dale. *Deep Politics and the Death of JFK*. Berkeley: University of California Press, 1993.

Sheatsley, Paul B., and Jacob J. Feldman. "A National Survey on Public Reactions and Behavior." In Greenberg and Parker, *Kennedy Assassination*, 149–77.

Simon, Art. *Dangerous Knowledge: The JFK Assassination in Art and Film*. Philadelphia: Temple University Press, 1996.

——. "The Making of Alert Viewers: The Mixing of Fact and Fiction in *JFK*. *Cineaste* 19 (1992): 14–15.

Solomon, Jole. "True Believers." *Newsweek* 122 (November 22, 1993): 96.

"Splinters to the Brain." *New Perspectives Quarterly* 9 (Spring 1992): 51–53.

Stang, Alan. "They Killed the President." *American Opinion* 19 (February 1976): 1–8, 59–72.

Stone, Oliver. "Address to the National Press Club." In Prouty, *JFK*, xiii–xxi.

——. "In Filming History: Question, Disbelieve, Defy." *Chronicle of Higher Education* 47 (July 14, 2000): 9–10.

——. "Our Counterfeit History." *George* 3 (October 1998): 102–5.

——. "The Secret History of the United States, 1943–1990." In Prouty, *JFK*, vii–xiii.

——. "Stone Shoots Back." In Stone and Sklar, *JFK*, 229–30.

——. "Stone's JFK: A Higher Trust." In Stone and Sklar, *JFK*, 198–202.

——. "Who Is Rewriting History?" *New York Times*, December 20, 1991, 35.

Stone, Oliver, and Zachary Sklar, eds. *JFK: The Book of the Film*. New York: Applause, 1992.

Summers, Anthony. *Conspiracy*. Norfork, England: Victor Gollancz, 1980.

Tannenbaum, Robert K. *Corruption of Blood*. New York: Signet, 1995.

Thomas, Evan. "The Real Cover-Up." *Newsweek* 122 (November 22, 1993): 66–95.

Thompson, Josiah. "The Crossfire That Killed Kennedy." *Saturday Evening Post* 240 (December 21, 1967): 27–31, 46, 50–55.

——. *Six Seconds in Dallas: A Micro-Study of the Kennedy Assassination*. New York: Bernard Geis Associates, 1967.

Toscano, Vincent L. *Since Dallas: Images of John F. Kennedy in Popular and Scholarly Literature*. San Francisco: R and E Research Associates, 1978.

Trillin, Calvin. "The Buffs." *New Yorker* 43 (June 10, 1967): 41–71.

Turner, William T. "The Shooting of George Wallace." In Blumenthal and Yazijian, *Government by Gunplay*, 57–67.

U.S. House of Representatives. Select Committee on Assassinations. *Final Report*, 95th Cong., 2d sess., 1979.

——. Select Committee on Assassinations. *Investigation of the Assassination of John F. Kennedy*. 95th Cong., 2d sess., 1979, 7 vols.

Wainwright, Loudon. "The Warren Report Is Not Enough." *Life* 61 (October 7, 1966): 38.

"Warren Commission Report." *Time* 84 (October 2, 1964): 45–55.

The Warren Commission Report: The President's Commission on the Assassination of President Kennedy. New York: Barnes and Noble, 1964.

Weisberg, Harold. *Case Open: The Omissions, Distortions, and Falsifications of Case Closed*. New York: Carroll and Graf, 1994.

——. *White Wash: The Report on the Warren Report.* Hyattstown, Md., self-published, 1965.

Welsh, Jim. "*JFK*: The Lesson and Legacy of Vietnam." In Kunz, *Films of Oliver Stone,* 227–37.

Wicker, Tom. "Does *JFK* Conspire Against Reason?" In Stone and Sklar, *JFK,* 241–46.

——. "The Right of Appeal for Lee Oswald." *New York Times,* September 25, 1966, E10.

Will, George. "*JFK*: Paranoid History." *Washington Post,* December 26, 1991.

Zelizer, Barbie. *Covering the Body: The Kennedy Assassination, the Media, and the Shaping of Collective Memory.* Chicago: University of Chicago Press, 1992.

Chapter 5: Jewish Devils and the War on Black America

Alexander, Amy, ed. *The Farrakhan Factor: African-American Writers on Leadership, Nationhood, and Minister Louis Farrakhan.* New York: Grove, 1998.

——. "Our Brother, the Other: Farrakhan and a Vigil for New Black Leadership." In Alexander, *Farrakhan Factor,* 1–17.

Alford, C. Fred. "If I Am You, Then You Are . . . False." In Helmreich and Marcus, *Blacks and Jews,* 51–63.

Allen, Ernest, Jr. "Minister Louis Farrakhan and the Continuing Evolution of the Nation of Islam." In Alexander, *Farrakhan Factor,* 52–102.

Baldwin, James. *Blacks and Jews.* Amherst: W. E. B. Dubois Department of Afro-American Studies, University of Massachusetts, 1988.

——. *The Fire Next Time.* New York: Dell, 1964.

——. "The Harlem Ghetto: Winter, 1948." *Commentary* 5 (February 1948): 165–70.

——. "Negroes Are Anti-Semitic Because They're Anti-White." In Hentoff, *Black Anti-Semitism,* 3–12.

——. *Notes of a Native Son.* New York: Dial, 1963.

Ball, George, and Douglas Ball. *The Passionate Attachment: America's Involvement with Israel, 1947 to the Present.* New York: Norton, 1992.

Baraka, Imamu. *Raise, Race, Rays, Raze: Essays Since 1965.* New York: Random House, 1969.

Barboza, Steven. *American Jihad: Islam After Malcolm X.* New York: Doubleday, 1993.

Bates, Karen Grisby. "Is it Genocide?" *Essence* 21 (September 1990): 76–82.

Bayton, James A. "The Racial Stereotyping of Negro College Students." *Journal of Abnormal and Social Psychology* 36 (January 1941): 97–102.

Bell, Derrick. "Farrakhan Fever: Defining the Divide Between Blacks and Jews." In Alexander, *Farrakhan Factor,* 211–27.

Bender, Eugene. "Reflections on Negro-Jewish Relationships: The Historical Dimension." *Phylon* 30 (Spring 1969): 56–65.

Berman, Paul, ed. *Blacks and Jews: Alliances and Arguments.* New York: Delacorte, 1994.

Berson, Lenora E. *The Negroes and the Jews.* New York: Random House, 1971.

"The B.E. Survey." *Black Enterprise* 20 (August 1990): 85–94.

"The Black and the Jew: A Falling Out of Allies." *Time* 93 (January 31, 1969): 55–59.

Blitzer, Wolf. *Between Washington and Jerusalem: A Reporter's Notebook.* New York: Oxford University Press, 1985.

Bloom, Steven. "Interactions Between Blacks and Jews in New York City, 1900–1930 as Reflected in the Black Press." Ph.D. diss., New York University, 1973.

Brackman, Harold. "The Ebb and Flow of Conflict: A History of Black-Jewish Relations Through 1900." Ph.D. diss., University of California, Los Angeles, 1977.

——. *Farrakhan's Reign of Historical Error: The Truth Behind the Secret Relationship Between Blacks and Jews.* Los Angeles: Simon Wiesenthal Center, 1992.

——. *Ministry of Lies: The Truth Behind the Nation of Islam's "The Secret Relationship Between Blacks and Jews."* New York: Anti-Defamation League, 1994.

Breitman, George, ed. *Malcolm X Speaks: Selected Speeches and Statements.* New York: Grove Weidenfeld, 1965.

Breitman, George, and Herman Porter. *The Assassination of Malcolm X.* New York: Pathfinder, 1969.

Bulkin, Elly, Minnie Bruce Pratt, and Barbara Smith. *Yours in Struggle: Three Feminist Perspectives on Anti-Semitism and Racism.* Ithaca, N.Y.: Firebrand, 1984.

Burdick, Emily. *Blacks and Jews in Literary Conversation.* New York: Cambridge University Press, 1998.

Cannon, Joseph. "The Final Call? An Exclusive Interview with Louis Farrakhan." *Utah Business,* July 1996, 29–40.

Caplan, Marc. *Academic Bigotry: Professor Tony Martin's Anti-Jewish Onslaught.* New York: Anti-Defamation League, 1995.

——. *Jew-Hatred as History: The Nation of Islam's "Secret Relationship."* New York: Anti-Defamation League, 1993.

Caplan, Marc, and Lori Linzer. *Uncommon Ground: The Black African Holocaust Council and Other Links Between Black and White Extremists.* New York: Anti-Defamation League, 1994.

Carmichael, Stokely. *Stokely Speaks: Black Power to Pan-Africanism.* New York: Random House, 1971.

Carmines, E. G., and J. A. Stimson. *Issue Evolution: Race and the Transformation of American Politics.* Princeton: Princeton University Press, 1989.

Carson, Clayborne. "Black-Jewish Universalism in the Era of Identity Politics." In Salzman and West, *Struggles in the Promised Land,* 177–96.

——. "Blacks and Jews in the Civil Rights Movement." In Washington, *Jews in Black Perspectives,* 113–31.

——. *Malcolm X: The FBI File.* New York: Carroll and Graf, 1991.

Cary, Lorene. "Why It's Not Just Paranoia." *Newsweek* 119 (April 6, 1992): 23.

Clark, Kenneth. "Candor on Negro-Jewish Relations." *Commentary* 1 (February 1946): 8–14.

Clarke, John H., ed. *Malcolm X: The Man and His Times.* New York: Collier, 1969.

——, ed. *Marcus Garvey and the Vision of Africa.* New York: Random House, 1974.

Clegg, Claude Andrew, III. *An Original Man: The Life and Times of Elijah Muhammad.* New York: St. Martin's, 1997.

Cohn, Norman. *Warrant for Genocide: The Myth of the Jewish World-Conspiracy and the Protocols of the Elders of Zion*. New York: Harper and Row, 1966.

Copage, Eric. "Farrakhan: On the Road with the Fiery Black Muslim Leader." *Life* 7 (August 1984): 51–54.

Cose, Ellis. "The Good News About Black America." *Newsweek* 133 (June 7, 1999): 28–40.

Crouch, Stanley. "Farrakhan, 1985–1996: The Consistency of Calypso Louis." In Alexander, *Farrakhan Factor*, 251–69.

Cruse, Harold. *The Crisis of the Black Intellectual*. New York: William Morrow, 1967.

Curry, George E. "Farrakhan, Jesse, and Jews." *Emerge*, July–August, 1994, 28–41.

Curtis, John S. *An Appraisal of the Protocols of Zion*. New York: Cambridge University Press, 1942.

Daniels, Ron. "The Farrakhan Phenomenon." *Z Magazine* 7 (June 1994): 16–18.

Davis, David Brion. "The Slave Trade and the Jews." *New York Review of Books* 41 (December 22, 1994): 14–16.

Davis, Lenwood G. *Black-Jewish Relations in the United States, 1752–1984: A Selected Bibliography*. Westport, Conn.: Greenwood, 1984.

De Parle, Jason. "Talk of Government Being Out to Get Blacks Falls on More Attentive Ears." *New York Times*, October 29, 1990, B7.

Diner, Hasia. *In the Almost Promised Land: American Jews and Blacks, 1915–1935*. Westport, Conn.: Greenwood, 1977.

———. "Trading Faces." *Commonquest* 2 (Summer 1997): 40–44.

Dinnerstein, Leonard. *Anti-Semitism in America*. New York: Oxford University Press, 1994.

———. "The Origins of Black Anti-Semitism in America." *American Jewish Archives* 38 (November 1986): 113–22.

Drake, St. Clair, and Horace R. Clayton. *Black Metropolis: A Study of Negro Life in a Northern City*. 2 vols. New York: Harcourt, Brace, 1945.

Dubois, W. E. B. *The Souls of Black Folk*. New York: Penguin, 1989. Originally pub. 1903.

Dyson, Michael Eric. *Making Malcolm: The Myth and Meaning of Malcolm X*. New York: Oxford University Press, 1995.

Edwards, Audrey. "A View of the Past, A Look to the Future." *Black Enterprise* 21 (August 1990): 77–82.

Ellerin, Milton. "Black Muslims: Source of Anti-Semitic Infection." *Currents* 2 (February 1972): 1–3.

Ellis, Eddie. ". . . Semitism in the Black Ghetto." *Liberator* 6 (January 1966): 6–7, (February 1966): 14–15, (April 1966): 14–16.

Eure, Joseph D., and Richard M. Jerome, eds. *Back Where We Belong: Selected Speeches by Minister Louis Farrakhan*. Philadelphia: PC International, 1989.

Evanier, David. *The Anti-Semitism of Black Demagogues and Extremists*. New York: Anti-Defamation League, 1992.

———. *Louis Farrakhan: The Campaign to Manipulate Public Opinion*. New York: Anti-Defamation League, 1990.

Evanzz, Karl. *The Judas Factor: The Plot to Kill Malcolm X*. New York: Thunder's Mouth, 1991.

"Excerpts of Interview with Louis Farrakhan." *Washington Post,* March 1, 1990.

Farrakhan, Louis. "Are Black People the Future World Rulers?" In Eure and Jerome, *Back Where We Belong,* 224–55.

——. "The Black Man Must Do for Self or Suffer the Consequences!" Audiotape, October 7, 1991.

——. "Black Youth: What Must Be Done." Audiotape, September 30, 1992.

——. "Black Youth Organize and Defend Your Community." *Final Call,* December 14, 1992.

——. "Christ's Imminent Return: He Makes All Things New!" Audiotape, May 21, 1983.

——. "Crisis in Black Leadership." *Essence* 15 (June 1984): 87–88, 146–48.

——. "District of Columbia's Financial Condition." CSpan, August 22, 1997.

——. "Exodus Politics: Organizing the Third Power." Audiotape, October 18, 1995.

——. "Farrakhan Delivers the Black Agenda." Audiotape, July 17, 1988.

——. "How to Give Birth to a God." In Eure and Jerome, *Back Where We Belong,* 83–113.

——. "In Christ All Things Are Possible." Audiotape, October 3, 1981.

——. "Interview with Tim Russert." *Meet the Press,* October 18, 1998.

——. "Malcolm: Hypocrite." *Muhammad Speaks,* December 4, 1964.

——. "Minister Farrakhan Speaks at Morgan State University." In Eure and Jerome, *Back Where We Belong,* 114–42.

——. "The 1980s: A Countdown to Armageddon!" Audiotape, October 5, 1980.

——. "Politics Without Economics Is Symbol Without Substance." In Eure and Jerome, *Back Where We Belong,* 200–223.

——. "P.O.W.E.R. at Last and Forever." Audiotape, October 7, 1985.

——. "Revealing the Conspiracy: Youth Gangs, Violence, and Drugs." Audiotape, June 25, 1989.

——. "The Rise of Jesse Jackson: His Impact on Black America." Audiotape, March 5, 1984.

——. "Self Improvement: The Basis for Community Development." In Eure and Jerome, *Back Where We Belong,* 168–99.

——. "Separation and Reparations: The Just Solution to the Black/White Problem." Audiotape, April 14, 1990.

——. *Seven Speeches.* Chicago: Final Call, 1992.

——. "Stop the Killing! The Respect and Protection of the Black Woman." Audiotape, June 5, 1990.

——. *A Torchlight for America.* Chicago: FCN, 1993.

——. *Warning to the Government of America.* Chicago: Elijah Muhammad Educational Foundation, 1983.

——. "What Is the Need for Black History?" In Eure and Jerome, *Back Where We Belong,* 47–79.

——. "White Supremacy and the Solution to the Problem of Race." Audiotape, April 21, 1990.

——. "Your Hand Must Produce the Kingdom!" Audiotape, November 18, 1984.

Farrakhan's Unchanged: The Continuing Message of Hate. New York: Anti-Defamation League, 1994.

Federal Funds for NOI Security Firms: Financing Farrakhan's Ministry of Hate. New York: Anti-Defamation League, 1995.

Findley, Paul. *They Dare to Speak Out: People and Institutions Confront Israel's Lobby.* Chicago: Lawrence Hill, 1989.

Fineman, Howard, and Vern E. Smith. "An Angry Charmer." *Newsweek* 126 (October 30, 1995): 32–38.

Fletcher, Michael. "Conspiracy Theories Can Often Ring True: History Feeds Black Mistrust." *Washington Post*, October 4, 1996.

Forster, Arnold, and Benjamin Epstein. *The New Anti-Semitism.* New York: McGraw Hill, 1974.

Friedman, Murray. *What Went Wrong? The Creation and Collapse of the Black-Jewish Alliance.* New York: Maxwell Macmillan, 1995.

Gaber, Julia E. "Lamb of God or Demagogue? A Burkean Cluster Analysis of the Selected Speeches of Minister Louis Farrakhan." Ph.D. diss., Bowling Green State University, 1986.

Gallen, David, ed. *Malcolm X: As They Knew Him.* New York: Ballantine, 1992.

Gardell, Mattias. *In the Name of Elijah Muhammad: Louis Farrakhan and the Nation of Islam.* Durham: Duke University Press, 1996.

Gates, Henry Louis, Jr. "After the Revolution." *New Yorker* 72 (April 29–May 6, 1996): 59–61.

——. "The Charmer." *New Yorker* 72 (April 29–May 6, 1996): 116–31.

Geltman, Max. *The Confrontation: Black Power, Anti-Semitism, and the Myth of Integration.* Englewood Cliffs, N.J.: Prentice Hall, 1970.

Gerber, David A., ed. *Anti-Semitism in American History.* Urbana: University of Illinois Press, 1987.

Gibbs, Jewelle Taylor. *Race and Justice: Rodney King and O. J. Simpson in a House Divided.* San Francisco: Jossey-Bass, 1996.

Glazer, Nathan. "Jews and Blacks: What Happened to the Grand Alliance?" In Washington, *Jews in Black Perspective*, 105–12.

Glazer, Nathan, and Daniel Patrick Moynihan. *Beyond the Melting Pot: The Negroes, Puerto Ricans, Jews, Italians, and Irish of New York City.* Cambridge: Harvard University Press, 1963.

Goldberg, J. J. *Jewish Power: Inside the American Jewish Establishment.* Reading, Mass.: Addison-Wesley, 1996.

Goldman, Peter. *The Death and Life of Malcolm X.* Urbana: University of Illinois Press, 1979.

Greenberg, Cheryl. *Or Does It Explode? Black Harlem in the Great Depression.* New York: Oxford University Press, 1991.

Gurock, Jeffrey S. *When Harlem Was Jewish, 1870–1930.* New York: Columbia University Press, 1979.

Halpern, Ben. *Jews and Blacks: The Classic American Minorities.* New York: Herder and Herder, 1971.

"Has Farrakhan Changed?" *Frontline*, November–December 1993.

Haskin, Jim. *Louis Farrakhan and the Nation of Islam.* New York: Walker, 1996.

Heller, Celia Stopnicka, and Alphonso Pinkney. "The Attitudes of Negroes Toward Jews." *Social Forces* 43 (March 1965): 364–69.

Helmreich, Alan, and Paul Marcus, eds. *Blacks and Jews on the Couch: Psychoanalytical Reflections on Black-Jewish Conflict.* Westport, Conn.: Praeger, 1998.

Hendrickson, Stephen, ed. *Understanding the New Black Poetry*. New York: William Morrow, 1973.

Henry, William, III. "Pride and Prejudice." *Time* 143 (February 28, 1994): 22–27.

Hentoff, Nat. "The Legitimation of Farrakhan." *Intermountain Jewish News*, August 31, 1990.

——. "Who Will Speak the Truth to Spike Lee?" *Washington Post*, December 19, 1992.

——, ed. *Black Anti-Semitism and Jewish Racism*. New York: Bacon, 1969.

Hitchens, C. H. "The False Messiah Who Hates the Jews." *The Spectator* 256 (January 25, 1986): 12, 14.

Holmes, Steven. "Ministry of Hope, Message of Hate." *New York Times*, March 4, 1994, 1, 10.

Hume, Ellen. "Blacks and Jews Find Confrontation Rising Over Jesse Jackson." *Wall Street Journal*, May 29, 1984.

Interview with Malcolm X. *Playboy Magazine* 10 (May 1963): 53–54, 56–62.

"Jackson and the Jews." *New Republic* 190 (March 19, 1984): 9–10.

Jacobson, Kenneth. *The Protocols: Myth and History*. New York: Anti-Defamation League, 1981.

Jahannes, James A. *Blacks and Jews: A New Dialogue*. Savannah, Ga.: State College Press, 1983.

Johnson, Mary A. "I Will Never Bow Down: But Farrakhan Says He Seeks Dialogue." *Chicago Sun Times*, July 18, 1993.

Jones, James H. *Bad Blood: The Tuskegee Syphilis Experiment*. New York: Free Press, 1993.

Katz, Shlomo, ed. *Negro and Jew: An Encounter in America, a Symposium Compiled by Midstream Magazine*. New York: Macmillan, 1967.

Kaufman, Jonathan. *Broken Alliance: The Turbulent Times Between Blacks and Jews in America*. New York: Scribner, 1988.

Kennedy, John. "One in a Million." *George* 2 (October 1996): 106–10, 143–44.

King, Martin Luther, Jr. "Negroes, Jews, Israel, and Anti-Semitism." *Jewish Currents* 22 (January 1968): 7–9.

Kousser, J. Morgan, and James M. McPherson, eds. *Religion, Race, and Reconstruction*. New York: Oxford University Press, 1982.

Kramer, Michael. "Loud and Clear: Farrakhan's Anti-Semitism." *New York* 18 (October 21, 1985): 22–23.

Kunjufu, Jawanza. *Countering the Conspiracy to Destroy Black Boys*. N.p.: African-American Images, 1985.

Kurapka, David. "Hate Story." *New Republic* 198 (May 30, 1988): 19–20.

Kurlander, Gabrielle, and Jacqueline Salit, eds. *Independent Black Leadership in America*. New York: Castillo International, 1990.

Labovitz, Sherman. *Attitudes Toward Blacks Among Jews: Historical Antecedents and Current Concern*. San Francisco: R & E Associates, 1975.

Laufer, Leo. "Anti-Semitism Among Negroes." *The Reconstructionist* 14 (October 29, 1948): 10–17.

Lee, Martha F. *The Nation of Islam: An American Millenarian Movement*. Lewiston, Maine: Edwin Mellen, 1988.

Leo, John. "Black Anti-Semitism." *Commonweal* 89 (February 14, 1969): 618–20.

Lerner, Michael, and Cornel West. *Jews and Blacks: A Dialogue on Race, Religion, and Culture in America*. New York: Plume, 1996.

Lester, Julius. "The Time Has Come." *New Republic* 193 (October 28, 1985): 11–12.

Levine, Lawrence W. *Black Culture and Black Consciousness*. New York: Oxford University Press, 1977.

Levinsohn, Florence Hamlish. *Looking for Farrakhan*. Chicago: Dee, 1997.

Lewis, David Levering. "Parallels and Divergences: Assimilationist Strategies of Afro-American and Jewish Elites from 1910 to the Early 1930s." *Journal of American History* 71 (December 1984): 543–64.

Lewis, David Levering, and David Brion Davis. "Jews and Blacks in America: An Exchange." *New York Review of Books* 47 (March 9, 2000): 53.

Lincoln, C. Eric. *The Black Muslims in America*. Boston: Beacon, 1961.

Linzer, Lori. *The Nation of Islam: The Relentless Record of Hate*. New York: Anti-Defamation League, 1995.

Locke, Hubert G. *The Black Anti-Semitism Controversy: Protestant Views and Perspectives*. Selinsgrove, Pa.: Susquehanna University Press, 1994.

Lomax, Louis. *When the Word Is Given*. Cleveland: World, 1963.

"Losing Ground." *Newsweek* 119 (April 6, 1992): 20–22.

Magida, Arthur S. *Prophet of Rage: A Life of Louis Farrakhan and His Nation*. New York: Basic, 1996.

Malcolm X. *By Any Means Necessary*. New York: Pathfinder, 1970.

———. *The End of White World Supremacy: Four Speeches*. New York: Little, Brown, 1971.

———. *On Afro-American History*. New York: Pathfinder, 1967.

Malcolm X., as told to Alex Haley. *Autobiography of Malcolm X*. New York: Ballantine, 1965.

Marcus, Laurence R. *Fighting Words: The Politics of Hateful Speech*. Westport, Conn.: Praeger, 1996.

Marriott, Michael. "Ministry of Hope, Message of Hate." *New York Times*, March 5, 1994, 1, 8.

Marsh, Clifton E. *From Black Muslims to Muslims: The Transition from Separatism to Islam, 1930–1980*. Metuchen, N.J.: Scarecrow, 1984.

Marshall, A. *Louis Farrakhan: Made in America*. N.p.: BSB, 1996.

Martin, Tony. *The Ideological and Organizational Struggles of Marcus Garvey and the Universal Negro Improvement Association*. Dover, Mass.: Majority, 1976.

———. *The Jewish Onslaught: Dispatches from the Wellesley Battlefield*. Dover, Mass.: Majority, 1993.

Marx, Gary T. *Protest and Prejudice: A Study of Beliefs in the Black Community*. New York: Harper and Row, 1967.

McCloud, Aminah Beverly. *African-American Islam*. New York: Routledge, 1995.

McDowell, Winston. "Race and Ethnicity During the Harlem Jobs Campaign." *Journal of Negro History* 69 (Fall 1984): 134–46.

McPhail, Mark Lawrence. "Louis Abdul Farrakhan, Religious Leader." In Richard W. Leeman, ed., *African-American Orators: A Bio-Critical Sourcebook*, 120–33. Westport, Conn.: Greenwood, 1996.

———. "Passionate Intensity: Louis Farrakhan and the Fallacies of Racial Reasoning." *Quarterly Journal of Speech* 84 (November 1998): 416–29.

Melnick, Jeffrey. *A Right to Sing the Blues: African-Americans, Jews, and American Popular Song*. Cambridge: Harvard University Press, 1999.

Miller, Alan. "The Protocols of the Learned Elders of Zion." Independent Study Project, University of California, Berkeley, 1997.

Miller, Jack C. "Black Viewpoints on the Mid-East Conflict." *Journal of Palestine Studies* 10 (Winter 1981): 37–49.

Muhammad, Elijah. *The Fall of America*. Chicago: Muhammad's Temple of Islam #2, 1973.

———. *Message to the Blackman in America*. Chicago: Muhammad's Mosque of Islam #2, 1965.

———. *The Mother Plane*. Atlanta: Secretarius Memps, 1992.

———. *Our Savior Has Arrived*. Chicago: Muhammad's Temple of Islam #2, 1974.

———. *The Supreme Wisdom: Solution to the So-Called Negroes' Problem*. Chicago: University of Islam, 1957.

Muhammad, Jabril. "Coming to Grips with Min. Farrakhan's Vision and What It Means to the World." *Final Call*, October 12, 1999.

———. *Farrakhan: The Traveler*. Phoenix: Phnx SN, 1985.

———. *A Special Spokesman*. Phoenix: Phnx SN, 1984.

Muhammad, Simeon. "Myth or Reality? The Camp Van Dorn Massacre." *Final Call*, January 4, 2000.

Naison, Mark. *Communists in Harlem During the Depression*. New York: Grove, 1983.

O'Reilly, Kenneth. *"Racial Matters": The FBI's Secret File on Black America, 1960–1972*. New York: Free Press, 1989.

Ostow, Mortimer. "Black Myths and Black Madness: Is Black Anti-Semitism Different?" In Helmreich and Marcus, *Blacks and Jews*, 85–102.

Page, Clarence. "Heartbeat of Black Movement Gets Stronger." *Salt Lake Tribune*, September 21, 1993.

———. "Maybe Paranoia Makes Sense in Dealing with Abusive FBI." *Salt Lake Tribune*, September 20, 1997.

Perry, Bruce. *Malcolm: The Life of a Man Who Changed Black America*. Barrytown, N.Y.: Stanton Hill, 1991.

Pogrebin, Letty Cottin. "Anti-Semitism in the Women's Movement." *Ms* 10 (June 1982): 45–49, 62, 65–66, 69–74.

———. "Blacks and Jews: Different Kinds of Survival." *Nation* 252 (September 23, 1991): 332–35.

———. *Deborah, Golda, and Me: Being Female and Jewish in America*. New York: Crown, 1991.

Porter, Jack. "John Henry and Mr. Goldberg: The Relationship Between Blacks and Jews." *Journal of Ethnic Studies* 7 (Fall 1979): 73–86.

Price, Isabel. "Black Response to Anti-Semitism: Negroes and Jews in New York, 1880 to World War II." Ph.D. diss., University of New Mexico, 1973.

Quinley, Harold, and Charles Y. Glock. *Anti-Semitism in America*. New York: Free Press, 1979.

Raspberry, William. "Standing Up to the Jews." *Washington Post*, October 30, 1989.

Reddick, L. D. "Anti-Semitism Among Negroes." *Negro Quarterly* 1 (Summer 1942): 112–22.

Reed, Adolph, Jr. "All for One and None for All." *Nation* 252 (January 28, 1991): 86–92.

——. "The Rise of Louis Farrakhan." *Nation* 252 (January 21, 1991): 1, 51–56.

Reyes, Daniel Díaz. "The 1935 Riot: Historical Analysis of Black-Jewish Relations." History project, University of Utah, 1997.

Rich, Frank. "Jew World Order." *New York Times,* March 9, 1995, 15.

"The Rift Between Blacks and Jews." *Time* 143 (February 28, 1994): 218–34.

Ringle, Ken. "Farrakhan's Figures: Did He Count the Crowd from a UFO?" *Washington Post,* October 22, 1995.

Rogin, Michael. *Blackface, White Noise: Jewish Immigrants in the Hollywood Melting Pot.* Berkeley: University of California Press, 1996.

Rose, Peter I. "Blacks and Jews: The Stained Alliance." *Annals of the American Academy of Political and Social Science* 454 (March 1981): 55–69.

Rosenblatt, Roger. "The Demagogue in the Crowd." *Time* 126 (October 21, 1985): 102.

Ross, Jeffrey, ed. *Schooled in Hate: Anti-Semitism on Campus.* Washington, D.C.: Anti-Defamation League, 1997.

Sadler, Kim, ed. *Atonement: The Million Man March.* Cleveland: Pilgrim, 1996.

Salzman, Jack, and Cornel West, eds. *Struggles in the Promised Land: Toward a History of Black-Jewish Relations in the United States.* New York: Oxford University Press, 1997.

Schappes, Morris U. "LeRoi Jones and Anti-Semitism." *Jewish Currents* 22 (May 1968): 20–25.

Scheiner, Seth. *Negro Mecca: A History of the Negro in New York City, 1865–1920.* New York: New York University Press, 1965.

Schlesinger, Arthur M., Jr. *The Disuniting of America: Reflections on a Multicultural Society.* New York: Norton, 1998.

The Secret Relationship Between Blacks and Jews. Boston: Historical Research Department of the Nation of Islam, 1991.

Shankman, Arnold. *Ambivalent Friends: Afro-Americans View the Immigrant.* Westport, Conn.: Greenwood, 1982.

Sheppard, Harold J. "The Negro Merchant: A Study of Negro Anti-Semitism." *American Journal of Sociology* 53 (September 1947): 96–99.

Silberman, Charles. *A Certain People: American Jews and Their Lives Today.* New York: Summit, 1985.

Singh, Robert. *The Farrakhan Phenomenon: Race, Reaction, and the Paranoid Style in American Politics.* Washington, D.C.: Georgetown University Press, 1997.

Smith, Anna Deavere. *Fires in the Mirror: Crown Heights, Brooklyn, and Other Identities.* New York: Anchor, 1993.

Smith, Erna. "Who's Afraid of Louis Farrakhan? The Media and Race Relations Coverage." In Alexander, *Farrakhan Factor,* 103–17.

Smith, Robert. "Black Power and the Transformation from Protest to Politics." *Political Science Quarterly* 96 (Fall 1981): 431–43.

Smith, Robert C. *We Have No Leaders: African Americans in the Post–Civil Rights Era.* Albany: State University of New York Press, 1996.

Spear, Alan. *Black Chicago: The Making of a Negro Ghetto.* Chicago: University of Chicago Press, 1967.

Stern, Kenneth S. *Holocaust Denial*. New York: American Jewish Committee, 1993.

Stevenson, Marshall Field, Jr. "Points of Departure, Acts of Resolve: Black-Jewish Relations in Detroit, 1937–1962." Ph.D. diss., University of Michigan, 1988.

Thomas, Evan. "Death of an Assassin." *Newsweek* 131 (May 5, 1998): 32–33.

Tivan, Edward. *The Lobby: Jewish Political Power and American Foreign Policy*. New York: Simon and Schuster, 1987.

Tsukashima, Ronnie Tadao. "The Social and Psychological Correlates of Anti-Semitism in the Black Community." Ph.D. diss., University of California, Los Angeles, 1973.

Turner, Patricia A. *I Heard It Through the Grapevine: Rumor in African-American Culture*. Berkeley: University of California Press, 1993.

Turner, Richard Brent. *Islam in the African-American Experience*. Bloomington: Indiana University Press, 1997.

The Ugly Truth About the Anti-Defamation League. Washington, D.C.: Executive Intelligence Review, 1992.

Valentin, Hugo. *Anti-Semitism, Historically and Critically Examined*. New York: Viking, 1936.

Van Biema, David. "Marching to Farrakhan's Tune." *Time* 146 (October 16, 1995): 74–75.

Washington, Joseph R., Jr., ed. *Jews in Black Perspectives: A Dialogue*. Rutherford, N.J.: Fairleigh Dickinson University Press, 1984.

Weisbord, Robert G., and Richard J. Kazarian. *Israel in the Black-American Perspective*. Westport, Conn.: Greenwood, 1985.

Weisbord, Robert G., and Robert Stein. *Bittersweet Encounter: The Afro-American and the American Jew*. Westport, Conn.: Negro Universities Press, 1970.

Weitz, Marvin. "Black Attitudes to Jews in the United States from World War II to 1976." Ph.D. diss., Yeshiva University, 1977.

West, Cornel. "Black Anti-Semitism and the Rhetoric of Resentment." *Tikkun* 7 (January–February, 1992): 15–16.

Whitfield, Stephen. "A Critique of Leonard Dinnerstein's 'The Origins of Black Anti-Semitism in America.'" *American Jewish Archives* 39 (November 1987): 193–202.

"Who Speaks for Black America." *Black America* 21 (August 1990): 82.

Williams, Lena. "Blacks, Jews, and 'This Thing That Is Suffocating Us.'" *New York Times,* July 29, 1990, E5.

Wills, Garry. "A Tale of Three Leaders." *New York Review of Books* 43 (September 19, 1996): 61–74.

Wolfenstein, E. Victor. "Black Liberation and the Jewish Question." In Helmreich and Marcus, *Blacks and Jews*, 67–84.

Wright, Lynda, and Daniel Glick. "Farrakhan's Mission." *Newsweek* 115 (March 19, 1990): 25.

Wright, Richard. *Black Boy: A Record of Childhood and Youth*. Cleveland: World, 1937.

Zoglin, Richard. "Not-So-Hot Copy in San Jose." *Time* 149 (May 26, 1997): 81–82.

Allan, Christopher D. "Dubious Truth About the Roswell Crash." *International UFO Reporter* 19 (May–June 1994): 12–14.

Allan, Christopher D., and Kevin D. Randle. "Jesse Marcel and the Roswell Incident: An Exchange." *International UFO Reporter* 18 (May–June, 1993): 13–14, 21.

Beck, Chip. "Requiem for a Fighter." *UFO Magazine* 13 (October 1998): 10–11.

Beckley, Timothy Green. *The UFO Silencers*. New Brunswick, N.J.: Inner Light, 1990.

Berliner, Don. *A Rebuttal of the Air Force Project Mogul Explanation for the 1947 Roswell, New Mexico, UFO Crash*. Mount Rainier, Md.: Fund for UFO Research, 1995.

Berliner, Don, and Stanton Friedman. "Crashed Flying Saucers in New Mexico." Audiotape, October, 1991.

Berlitz, Charles. *The Bermuda Triangle: An Incredible Saga of Unexplained Disappearances*. Garden City: N.Y.: Doubleday, 1974.

Berlitz, Charles, and William Moore. *The Roswell Incident*. New York: Grosset and Dunlap, 1980.

Birnes, William J. "Children of Roswell." *UFO Magazine* 13 (November 1998): 14–23.

———. "The CIA Report on UFOs," part 1. *UFO Magazine* 14 (November 1999): 16–21.

Bishop, Gregory. "They Paid Me to Say This! Bill Moore Explains Himself." *Excluded Middle* 1, no. 2 (1993): 12–17.

Bloecher, Ted. *Report on the UFO Wave of 1947*. Washington, D.C., self published, 1967.

Blum, Howard. *Out There: The Government's Secret Quest for Extraterrestrials*. New York: Simon and Schuster, 1990.

Bourdais, Gildas. "American Documents: What Do They Reveal/Hide?" *Mufon UFO Journal* 357 (January 1998): 17–19.

Brookesmith, Peter. *UFO: The Government Files*. New York: Barnes and Noble, 1996.

Brown, Courtney. *Cosmic Voyage: A Scientific Discovery of Extraterrestrials Visiting Earth*. New York: Dutton, 1996.

Bryan, C. D. B. *Close Encounters of the Fourth Kind: Alien Abductions, UFOs, and the Conference at M.I.T.* New York: Knopf, 1995.

Bullard, Thomas. "Mysteries in the Eye of the Beholder: UFOs and Their Correlates as a Folkloric Theme Past and Present." Ph.D. diss., Indiana University, 1982.

Burleson, Donald R. *Flute Song*. Merrimack, N.H.: Black Mesa, 1996.

———. "Update on Deciphering General Ramey Letter." *Mufon UFO Journal* 371 (March 1999): 17.

Carey, Thomas J. "The Continuing Search for the Roswell Archaeologists: Closing the Circle." *International UFO Reporter* 19 (January–February, 1994): 4–12.

Carey, Thomas J., and Donald R. Schmitt. "Roswell 1999: What's New?" *Mufon UFO Journal* 373 (May 1999): 13–15.

——. "Roswell 1999: What's New?" part 2, "Deathbed Confessions." *Mufon UFO Journal* 374 (June 1999): 11–13.

Commander X. "The Commander X Files." *UFO Universe* 7 (Spring 1997): 42–53.

——. *Incredible Technologies of the New World Order: UFOs—Tesla—Area 51.* New Brunswick, N.J.: Abelard Productions, 1997.

——. *The Ultimate Deception.* New Brunswick, N.J.: Abelard Productions, 1990.

Condon, Edward. *The Scientific Study of Unidentified Flying Objects.* New York: Dutton, 1969.

Cooper, Milton William. *Behold a Pale Horse.* Sedona, Ariz.: Light Technology, 1991.

Corso, Philip J., with William J. Birnes. *The Day After Roswell.* New York: Simon and Schuster, 1997.

Davids, Paul. "The UFO Coverup Continues . . ." part 1, "Down in Roswell," part 2, "Reply to the Air Force Report on the Roswell Incident." Kozy Images, video, 1994.

——. "Waiting on Roswell Revelations," part 3. *UFO Magazine* 14 (June 1999): 16–22.

Dean, Jodi. *Aliens in America: Conspiracy Cultures from Outerspace to Cyberspace.* Ithaca, N.Y.: Cornell University Press, 1998.

Dennett, Preston E. "The Intimidation and Murder of UFO Witnesses." *UFO Universe* 6 (Winter 1996): 53–60.

Deuley, Tom. "The Other Side of MJ-12." *Mufon UFO Journal* 373 (May 1999): 10–12.

——. "The Other Side of MJ-12," part 2. *Mufon UFO Journal* 374 (June 1999): 5–9.

Dowdy, Andrew. *The Films of the Fifties.* New York: Morrow, 1973.

Eberhardt, George, ed. *The Plains of San Agustin Controversy, July 1947.* N.p.: Fund for UFO Research, 1992.

——. *The Roswell Report: An Historical Perspective.* Chicago: Center for UFO Studies, 1991.

Edwards, Frank. *Flying Saucers, Serious Business.* New York: Lyle Stuart, 1966.

Fawcett, Lawrence, and Barry J. Greenwood. *Clear Intent: The Government Coverup of the UFO Experience.* Englewood Cliffs, N.J.: Prentice Hall, 1984.

Finlinson, Richard M. "Secrecy and the Birth of MJ-12." Honors paper, University of Utah, 1998.

Flaherty, Robert. "Flying Saucers and the New Angelology: Mythic Projection of the Cold War and the Convergence of Opposites." Ph.D. diss., University of California, Los Angeles, 1990.

Fox, Cynthia. *The Search for Extraterrestrial Life. Life,* March 2000, 46–56.

Friedman, Stanton. "Crash at Corona: The Latest on the Roswell Incident and MJ-12." Audiotape, October, 1990.

——. "Crashed Saucers, Majestic-12, and the Debunkers." Paper delivered at the 23d Annual Mufon symposium, Albuquerque, New Mexico, July, 1992.

——. *Final Report on Operation Majestic 12.* Mt. Rainier, Md.: Fund for UFO Research, 1990.

——. "Flying Saucers Are Real!" J. C. Curley, Video, 1996.

——. "The Roswell Incident: The USAF and the *New York Times*." Unpublished, 1994.

——. *Top Secret/Majic*. New York: Marlowe, 1996.

Friedman, Stanton, and Don Berliner. *Crash at Corona: The U.S. Military Retrieval and Cover-Up of a UFO*. New York: Marlowe, 1992.

Genge, N. E. *The Unofficial X-Files Companion*. New York: Crown, 1995.

——. *The Unofficial X-Files Companion II*. New York: Avon, 1996.

Good, Timothy. *Above Top Secret: The Worldwide U.F.O. Cover-Up*. New York: Morrow, 1988.

——. *Alien Contact: Top-Secret UFO Files Revealed*. New York: Morrow, 1993.

Grant, Judith. "Trust No One: Paranoia, Conspiracy Theories, and Alien Invasions (Earth, 1947–Present)." Paper presented to the American Political Science Association Meeting. Washington, D.C. (August 1997).

Hamilton, William F. *Cosmic Top Secret: America's Secret UFO Program*. New Brunswick, N.J.: Inner Light, 1991.

Handy, Bruce. "Roswell or Bust." *Time* 149 (June 23, 1997): 62–67.

Haslam, Mara. "'Watch the Skies': Conspiratorial Themes in Science-Fiction Movies of the 1950s." Honors paper, University of Utah, 1999.

Hayakawa, Norio F. *UFOs: The Great Deception and the Coming New World Order*. New Brunswick, N.J.: Inner Light, 1993.

Hesemann, Michael, and Philip Mantle. *Beyond Roswell: The Alien Autopsy Film, Area 51, and the U.S. Government Coverup of UFOs*. New York: Marlowe, 1997.

Hickman, John, E. Dale McConkey, III, and Matthew Barrett. "Fewer Sightings in the National Press: A Content Analysis of UFO News Coverage, the *New York Times*, 1947–1995," *Journal of UFO Studies* 6 (1995–96): 213–25.

Howe, Linda Moulton. *An Alien Harvest: Further Evidence Linking Animal Mutilations and Human Abductions to Alien Life Forms*. Cheyenne: Pioneer, 1989.

——. *Glimpses of Other Realities*. New Orleans: Paper Chase, 1998.

Hynek, J. Allen. *The UFO Experience: A Scientific Inquiry*. New York: Ballantine, 1972.

Jacobs, David M. *Secret Life: Firsthand Accounts of UFO Abductions*. New York: Simon and Schuster, 1992.

——. *The UFO Controversy in America*. Bloomington: Indiana University Press, 1975.

James, Caryn. "TV Nourishes the Appetite of Conspiracy Enthusiasts." *New York Times*, February 26, 1996, B1–2.

Jaroff, Leon. "Did Aliens Really Land?" *Time* 149 (June 23, 1997): 68–71.

Jedd, Marcia. "Ufologists Mull Government's Involvement." *UFO Magazine* 12 (January–February, 1997): 13–14, 16.

Jeffrey, Kurt. "Roswell: Anatomy of a Myth." *Mufon UFO Journal* 350 (June 1997): 3–17.

Jensen, Paul. "The Return of Dr. Caligari: Paranoia in Hollywood." *Film Comment* 7 (Winter 1971–72): 36–45.

Keyhoe, Donald. *The Flying Saucer Conspiracy*. New York: Henry Holt, 1955.

——. *Flying Saucers: Top Secret*. New York: Putnam, 1960.

——. *Flying Saucers Are Real*. New York: Fawcett, 1950.

Klass, Philip J. "Crash of the Crashed Saucer Claim." *Skeptical Inquirer* 10 (Spring 1986): 234–41.

———. "The MJ-12 Crashed-Saucer Documents' Parts 1 and 2." *Skeptical Inquirer* 11 (Winter 1987–88): 137–46.

———. *The Real Roswell Crashed-Saucer Coverup*. New York: Prometheus, 1997.

———. *UFOs: The Public Deceived*. Buffalo, N.Y.: Prometheus, 1983.

———. *UFOs Explained*. New York: Random House, 1974.

———. *UFOs Identified*. New York: Random House, 1968.

Korff, Kal K. *The Roswell UFO Crash: What They Didn't Want You to Know*. New York: Prometheus, 1997.

Krauss, Laurence M. "Stop the Flying Saucer, I Want to Get Off." *New York Times,* February 22, 1999, 21.

Laura, Ernesto G. "Invasion of the Body Snatchers." In Guy Johnson, ed., *Focus on the Science Fiction Film*, 71–73. Englewood Cliffs, N.J.: Prentice Hall, 1972.

Leach, Robert T. "Roswell, 50 Years Later: What Do We Know?" *UFO Magazine* 12 (May–June 1997): 18–21.

Lear, John. "The Disputed CIA Documents on UFOs." *Saturday Review* 49 (September 3, 1966): 45–50.

Loftin, Robert. *Identified Flying Saucers*. New York: David McKay, 1968.

Lowry, Brian. *Trust No One: The Official Third Season Guide to the X-Files*. New York: Harper Prism, 1996.

———. *The Truth Is Out There: The Official Guide to the X-Files*. New York: Harper Prism, 1995.

Lucanio, Patrick. *Them or Us: Archetypal Interpretations of Fifties Alien Invasion Films*. Bloomington: Indiana University Press, 1987.

Maccabee, Bruce. "CIA's UFO Explanation Is Preposterous." *Mufon UFO Journal* 354 (October 1997): 3–6.

Martin, Robert Scott. "MAJESTIC Leak Grows into Paper Flood." *UFO Magazine* 14 (December 1999): 22–23.

Maslin, Janet. "The Blob as Social Barometer." *New York Times,* August 5, 1988, B19.

———. "The Blob, Modernized." *New York Times,* August 5, 1988, C6.

McAndrew, James. *The Roswell Report*. Washington, D.C.: Headquarters, United States Air Force, 1997.

"MJ-12: New Documents Rouse Old Dispute." *UFO Magazine* 14 (July 1999): 14–15.

Moore, William L. "New Evidence of Crashed Saucers." *Frontiers of Science* 3 (January–February 1982): 24–27.

———. "Phil Klass and the Roswell Incident: The Skeptics Deceived." *International UFO Reporter* 11 (July–August 1986): 15–22.

———. "The Roswell Incident and MJ-12: UFO Coverup." Audiotape, 1989.

———. "The Roswell Investigation: New Evidence, New Conclusions." *Frontiers of Science* 3 (July–August 1981): 22–25.

Moore, William L., and Charles Berlitz. *The Philadelphia Experiment: Project Invisibility*. New York: Fawcett, 1979.

Mullins, John F. "Fate Puts FEMA in Charge." *UFO Magazine* 14 (December 1999): 40–48.

Murphy, Brian. "Monster Movies: They Came from Beneath the 50s." *Journal of Popular Film* 1 (Winter 1972): 31–44.

Nintzel, Jim, and Hector Acua. "Space Case: Roswell, New Mexico, Capitalizes on UFO Controversy with a Flying Saucer Jamboree." *Private Eye Weekly* 12 (August 17, 1997): 11–14.

Patton, Phil. *Dreamland: Travels Inside the Secret World of Roswell and Area 51.* New York: Villard, 1998.

Pawson, John. "An Interpretation of the Ramey Letter." *Mufon UFO Journal* 376 (August 1999): 19.

Peebles, Curtis. *Watch the Skies! A Chronicle of the Flying Saucer Myth.* Washington, D.C.: Smithsonian Institution Press, 1994.

Peyser, Marc. "Roswell: The Sequel." *Newsweek* 130 (July 7, 1997): 65.

Pflock, Karl T. "The Day After Roswell." *Mufon UFO Journal* 351 (July 1997): 16–20.

——. *Roswell in Perspective.* Washington, D.C.: Fund for UFO Research, 1994.

——. "Roswell, the Air Force, and Us." *International UFO Reporter* 19 (November–December 1994): 3–5, 24.

Polan, Dana. *Power and Paranoia: History, Narrative and the American Cinema.* New York: Columbia University Press, 1986.

Randle, Kevin D. *Conspiracy of Silence.* New York; Avon, 1997.

——. *A History of UFO Crashes.* New York: Avon, 1995.

——. "The Project Mogul Flights and Roswell." *International UFO Reporter* 19 (November–December 1994): 6–7, 23.

——. "Randle Responds to Jeffrey on Roswell." *Mufon UFO Journal* 351 (July 1997): 7–10.

——. *Roswell UFO Crash Update: Exposing the Military Cover-Up of the Century.* New Brunswick, N.J.: Global Communications, 1995.

——. *The UFO Casebook.* New York: Warner, 1989.

Randle, Kevin D., and Schmitt, Donald R. *The Truth About the UFO Crash at Roswell.* New York: Avon, 1994.

——. *UFO Crash at Roswell.* New York: Avon, 1991.

Randles, Jenny. *The UFO Conspiracy: The First Forty Years.* New York: Barnes and Noble, 1987.

——. *UFO Retrievals: The Recovery of Alien Spacecraft.* London: Blandford, 1995.

Recollections of Roswell. Parts 1 and 2, video. Mt. Rainier, Md.: Fund for UFO Research, n.d.

Rodeghier, Mark, and Mark Chesney. "The Air Force Report on Roswell: An Absence of Evidence." *International UFO Reporter* 19 (September–October 1994): 3, 20–24.

Roswell: The UFO Coverup. Video, Free Spirit Productions, 1998.

Sagan, Carl. *The Demon-Haunted World: Science as a Candle in the Dark.* New York: Random House, 1995.

Salch, Dennis. *Science Fiction Gold: Film Classics of the Fifties.* New York: McGraw-Hill, 1979.

Saler, Benson, Charles A. Ziegler, and Charles B. Moore. *U.F.O. Crash at Roswell.* Washington D.C.: Smithsonian Institution Press, 1997.

Samuels, Stuart. "The Age of Conspiracy and Conformity: Invasion of the Body Snatchers." In John E. O'Connor and Martin A. Jackson, eds., *American History American Film: Interpreting the Hollywood Image.* New York: Continuum, 1988.

Scully, Frank. *Behind the Flying Saucers.* New York: Henry Holt, 1950.

Shawcross, Tim. *The Roswell File.* Osceola, Wis.: Motorbooks International, 1997.

Sheffield, Derek. *UFO: A Deadly Concealment.* London: Blandford, 1996.

Shirkey, Robert J. *Roswell 1947: "I Was There."* Roswell: Movin' On, 1999.

Smith, Toby. *Little Gray Men: Roswell and the Rise of Popular Culture.* Albuquerque: University of New Mexico Press, 2000.

Spanos, Nicholas, Patricia Cross, Kerby Dickson, and Susan DuBreuil. "Close Encounters: An Examination of UFO Experiences." *Journal of Abnormal Psychology* 102 (November 1993): 624–32.

Stacy, Dennis. "The Morass That Is Roswell." *UFO Magazine* 13 (November 1998): 11.

Steiger, Brad, ed. *Project Blue Book: The Top Secret UFO Findings Revealed.* New York: Ballantine, 1976.

Steiger, Brad, and Sherry Hansen Steiger. *The Rainbow Conspiracy.* New York: Pinnacle, 1994.

Stockstill, Bill. "Is It Time to Move on?" *UFO Magazine* 15 (July–August 2000): 20–23.

Strentz, Herbert Joseph. "A Survey of Press Coverage of Unidentified Flying Objects, 1947–1966." Ph.D. diss., Northwestern University, 1970.

Strieber, Whitley. *Majestic.* New York: Berkeley, 1989.

Sutherly, Curt. *Strange Encounters: UFOs, Aliens, and Monsters Among Us.* St. Paul: Llewellyn, 1996.

Tacker, Lawrence. *Flying Saucers and the U.S. Air Force.* Princeton: Van Nostrand, 1960.

Thieme, Richard. "How to Build a UFO . . . Story." *Internet Underground* 1 (November 1996): 36–41.

Vallee, Jacques. *Revelations: Alien Contact and Human Deception.* New York: Ballantine, 1991.

Warren, Bill. *Keep Watching the Skies! American Science Fiction Movies of the Fifties, 1950–1957.* Jefferson, N.C.: McFarland, 1982.

Weaver, Richard, and James McAndrew. *The Roswell Report: Fact Vs. Fiction in the New Mexico Desert.* Washington, D.C.: Headquarters, United States Air Force, 1995.

Weist, Cathy. "Area 51: The Evolution of a Conspiracy Theory." Honors paper, University of Utah, 1998.

Wilkins, Harold T. *Flying Saucers on the Attack.* New York: Citadel, 1954.

Wilson, Jim. "Roswell Plus 50." *Popular Mechanics* 174 (July 1997): 48–53.

Wise, David. "Big Lies and Little Green Men." *New York Times,* August 8, 1997, 21.

Index

Cambodia, 50, 87
Capehart, Homer, 28
Capra, Frank, 139, 246
Carmichael, Stokely, 176
Carnegie Foundation, 48
Carr, Waggoner, 110
Carter, Chris, 62, 98, 254
Carter, Jimmy, 51, 52, 54, 55, 91, 163, 235
CASE (Committee Against Summit Entanglements), 42
Casey, William, 53
Castellano, Lillian, 114
Castro, Fidel: Kennedy's policy on, 110, 127, 133; assassination attempts against, 113, 121, 128, 143, 146
Catholic Church: portrayed as conspirator, 5, 8–9, 12–13, 15, 22, 71; and Jews, 16, 95; and John Birch Society, 44; pope as Antichrist, 70; and Protestantism, 71, 153; and apocalypticism, 79, 80, 93, 102; and African Americans, 160
Central Intelligence Agency: and dissidents, 36; covert operations of, 52; and Kennedy assassination, 52, 110, 127–28, 129, 132, 133, 137, 145, 146; portrayed as conspirator, 110, 137, 146, 150, 255, 257; and Oswald, 111, 124, 135; and Castro, 113; and Warren Report opponents, 120; and Garrison, 125; and Stone, 142; UFO files of, 145; and Freedom of Information Act, 147; and Nation of Islam, 161; and African Americans, 182; Robertson Panel, 209; and UFO sightings, 211, 228; and U.S. Air Force, 213; and Roswell incident, 214, 228; and Clinton, 235; and motion picture industry, 249
Charles, Prince of Wales, 93
Charles, Robert, 61
Chavis, Benjamin, 178, 186
Chiang Kai-shek, 39
Chicago Seven, 253
China: and Communist Party, 26, 38; and Eisenhower, 39; and Reagan, 53; and apocalypticism, 75, 78, 79, 91; and Kennedy assassination, 107
Christian Broadcast Network, 86
Christian Coalition, 76

Christian Crusade, 89
Christian Identity movement, 53, 56, 94–96, 173
Christianity: and conspiracy thinking, 65, 67; and Second Coming, 66, 74, 76; growth of evangelical churches, 76–77, 80, 81–82, 84, 92, 96, 103, 104; and Republican Party, 76, 89; and ecumenicalism, 81; and African Americans, 152, 153. See also Apocalypticism; Bible
Church, Frank, 44
Churchill, Winston, 137
CIO (Congress of Industrial Organizations), 24
Civil Rights Act, 188
Civil rights groups: and Communist Party, 22, 24, 37; purging of, 35; and segregation, 43; portrayed as conspirators, 47; and Kennedy assassination, 110, 126; and Nation of Islam, 155, 168; and Jews, 159–60, 162; and Federal Bureau of Investigation, 162, 255; and Farrakhan, 186; and conspiracy thinking, 238
Civil War, 9–11, 71–72
Clark, Kemp, 108
Clark, Kenneth B., 157, 163
Clark, Mae, 165
Clark, Mark, 32
Clark, Ramsey, 121
Clark, Vernon, 190
Clinton, Bill: portrayed as conspirator, 54–55, 63, 235–37, 256; as Antichrist, 93; and Christian Identity movement, 96; and Jews, 186; and Roswell incident, 225; and conspiracy thinking, 257
Clinton, Hillary, 96, 236, 256
Clyburn, James, 188
Coalition on Political Assassinations, 147
Coercive Acts, 5
COINTELPRO. See Counter Intelligence Program
Cold War: and Roosevelt, 18; and conspiracy thinking, 27, 251, 256; and Truman Doctrine, 28; and Birch, 41; and Council on Foreign Relations, 48, 52; and apocalypticism, 91; and Kennedy assassination, 107, 112, 124, 137, 138, 139; and UFO sightings,

Diana, Princess of Wales, x, 234
Díaz-Balart, Lincoln, 236
Didion, Joan, 243
Diem, Ngo Dinh, 138
Dies, Martin, 25, 40
Dies Committee, 25, 27, 33
Dilling, Elizabeth, 19, 24–25, 40
DNA testing, 259
Dodd, Thomas, 44
Domhoff, G. William, 51
Donnerly, Ignatius, 12
Doty, Richard, 206, 213
Doyle, Clive, 237
Dred Scott decision, 10
DuBose, Thomas, 196
Dudman, Richard, 109
Dulles, Allen, 109, 113
Dwight, Timothy, 71
Dymally, Mervyn, 182

Eagle Forum, 60
Eastern Europe, 26, 40, 91
Ebert, Roger, 142
Ebola viruses, 95
Edwards, Frank, 193
Edwards, Jonathan, 1–2, 70
Eisenhower, Dwight D.: and conspiracy
    thinking, 35–36, 37, 53; and Mar-
    shall, 39; portrayed as conspirator,
    39, 42, 44, 47, 146; and Robertson,
    91; and Stone, 139; and Roswell inci-
    dent, 200, 205; and Majestic Twelve,
    207; and aliens, 208; and UFO re-
    search community, 214
Embro, Stephen, 9
Emenegger, Robert, 213
Emmons, Nathaniel, 7
Entertainment industry, 67. See also Mo-
    tion picture industry; Music industry;
    Popular culture; Radio; Television
Epperson, A. Ralph, 49, 146
Epstein, Edward, 114, 120, 123, 130–31, 132
Equal Rights Amendment, 76
Erlichman, John, 170
Espy, Mike, 182
European Common Market, 78
European Union, 80, 90, 102, 104
Extraterrestrials: and internet websites,
    ix, 222; and surveys, x; and Kennedy
    assassination, 145, 208; and Majestic
    Twelve, 145, 205, 206, 207–8; and Ros-
    well incident, 189, 190, 201, 203; and

conspiracy thinking, 193, 233, 244,
    256; and Order of the Illuminati,
    208, 230–31; and U.S. government,
    211, 220–21; and newspapers, 216;
    and motion picture industry, 216–18,
    219, 228–29, 246; and television,
    218–20, 229–30; and merchandisers,
    222–23. See also Roswell incident

Falwell, Jerry, 80, 82, 85, 95, 96, 103
Fard, Wallace D., 151–53, 154, 156, 160, 169
Farrakhan, Louis: and Nation of Islam,
    151, 165, 166, 168, 169–70, 177, 186;
    and Jews, 168, 171, 172–74, 180, 184,
    186, 237; and Jackson, 170, 171; and
    politics, 170–72, 187; and conspiracy
    thinking, 174–77, 181–82, 183, 188,
    237, 239, 242; and black establish-
    ment, 178; and Million Man March,
    178–79, 237; and apocalypticism,
    181; and motion picture industry,
    183–85; and music industry, 185–86;
    health issues, 187
Fascism, 19, 23, 24
FBI. See Federal Bureau of Investigation
Federal Bureau of Investigation (FBI): for-
    mation of, 14; and conspiracy think-
    ing, 19; and Roosevelt, 19, 23; and loy-
    alty of federal employees, 29; and
    television, 35, 63, 221; Counter Intelli-
    gence Program, 36; covert operations
    of, 52, 128; and Kennedy assassination,
    52, 107, 109, 110, 115, 123, 129, 143,
    146; and Communist Party, 56, 255;
    and Ruby Ridge, 56–57; portrayed as
    conspirator, 61, 110, 169, 179, 255;
    and Oswald, 111, 124, 132–33; and
    Kennedy autopsy report, 112, 119, 122;
    and Warren Commission, 113; and
    Lane, 120; and Freedom of Information
    Act, 147; and Nation of Islam, 153–54,
    161–62, 169, 255; and African Ameri-
    cans, 175–76, 182; and UFO sightings,
    210, 211; and motion picture industry,
    229
Federal Emergency Management
    Agency (FEMA), 53, 55, 59, 96
Federal Reserve Act, 179
Federal Reserve System, 46, 88, 95
FEMA (Federal Emergency Management
    Agency), 53, 55, 59, 96
Fenster, Mark, xii

Louis X. *See* Farrakhan, Louis
Louis XVI (king of France), 46
Lowery, Joseph, 178
Ludlum, Robert, 243
Lusitania, 46
Lynd, Staughton, 109

MacArthur, Douglas, 38, 39
Mafia, 121, 125, 127, 128, 129–30, 133, 139, 143, 146
Magrath, J. Howard, 29
Mailer, Norman, 114, 120, 243
Majestic Twelve (MJ-12), 145, 205–7, 214, 221, 223, 226, 229, 230
Malcolm X: and conspiracy thinking, x; and Ku Klux Klan, 154, 160; and Nation of Islam, 154–56; and Jews, 155–56, 158; assassination of, 161, 174; and Elijah Muhammad, 161; and Farrakhan, 165, 166, 168, 169; and Federal Bureau of Investigation, 176, 182
Maltais, Jean, 194
Maltais, Vern, 194
Mandela, Nelson, 177
Manhattan Project, 198
Mansfield, Mike, 44
Mao Tse-Tung, 88
Marcel, Jesse, 192, 194, 196, 198, 215, 219, 220
Marcello, Carlos, 125, 133
March on Washington (*1963*), 155, 170
Marrs, Jim, 135, 137, 145
Marrs, Texe, 95, 146, 179
Marshall, George C., 30–31, 38, 39
Marshall, Thurgood, 155
Martin, Joseph, 27
Martin, Shirley, 114
Marx, Karl, 24, 46, 91, 179
Masons. *See* Freemasons; Order of the Illuminati
Mather, Cotton, 3, 67, 69–70
Mather, Increase, 69
Mayhew, Jonathan, 5
McAlvany, Donald, 92
McBoyle, Johnny, 193–94
McCarran Internal Security Act, 29
McCarthy, Joseph, 30–31, 36, 37, 38, 39, 244
McCarthyism, 4, 30
McCartney, Paul, 234
McCloy, John, 109, 112
McCone, John, 107
McDonald, Larry, 54, 92

McManus, John, 53
McNamara, Robert, 253–54
McVeigh, Timothy, 60, 238
Meagher, Sylvia, 114, 119, 239
Means, Gaston, 16
Media: and conspiracy thinking, ix–x, xii, 108, 232, 240, 243, 251, 257, 260; and Roosevelt, 23; and John Birch Society, 45; and Insiders, 48; portrayed as conspirators, 49; and Trilateral Commission, 52; and Clinton, 54; and New World Order, 54; and Ruby Ridge, 56; and militia movement, 58; and evangelical Christians, 77; and Robertson, 84, 93; and apocalypticism, 88; and Kennedy assassination, 107–8, 111, 117, 146; and Nation of Islam, 155, 156; and Jews, 162; and Farrakhan, 169, 178; and African Americans, 174–75; and Roswell incident, 190, 192, 231; and extraterrestrials, 206; and UFO research community, 215; and UFO phenomena, 229. *See also* Motion picture industry; Newspapers; Radio; Television
Medical experiments, 175
Metzger, Thomas, 94, 172
Middle East, 26, 50, 74, 80, 88, 100, 151, 163
Militia movement, 58–60, 253
Millennialism. *See* Apocalypticism
Miller, Arthur, 3–4
Miller, Perry, 70
Miller, William, 71
Million Family March, 187
Million Man March, 178–79, 184, 237
Minnis, Jack, 109
Minter, William, 51
Missouri Compromise, 10
Mogul Project, 215
Mohammed, Imam W. Deen, 187
Mondale, Walter, 51
Monk, Maria, 8
Monroe, Marilyn, x, 234
Moon, Sun Myung, 101
Moore, William: and Roswell incident, 195–96, 197, 205–6, 207, 212, 213–14; on Corso, 227; and conspiracy thinking, 239, 242
Morality, 40, 76, 102
Moral Majority, 76, 80
Morgan, J. P., 49, 52
Mormons, 7–8, 9, 12, 71, 93

67; and apocalypticism, 84, 89, 91, 92, 94, 103; and Kennedy assassination, 137; and Farrakhan, 179; and Majestic Twelve, 207

New York Times, 61, 108, 111, 121, 141, 142, 215, 223, 228

Ngo Dinh Diem, 138

NICAP (National Investigations Committee on Aerial Phenomena), 195

Nixon, Richard: and Communist party, 28; and John Birch Society, 44; portrayed as conspirator, 49, 51, 134–35, 140, 254; resignation of, 145; and Jackson, 170; and Wallace, 235; and conspiracy thinking, 253

North, Oliver, 142

North American Free Trade Agreement (NAFTA), 54, 80

North Atlantic Treaty Organization (NATO), 47

North Korea, 26

Novels, 93–94, 133, 243, 251

NRA (National Rifle Association), 61

NSA (National Security Agency), 63, 211

NSC (National Security Council), 210, 214

Nuclear Test-Ban Treaty of *1963,* 124

Nye, Gerald, 17

O'Donnell, Kenneth, 113

Oklahoma City bombing, 60, 61, 102, 234, 238

Oliver, Revilo, 110

Oppenheimer, Robert, 256

Order of the Illuminati: and conspiracy thinking, 6, 45–46, 47, 49; board game, 63–64; and apocalypticism, 71, 91, 92, 94, 103; and Jews, 95, 96, 146; and Kennedy assassination, 146; and Majestic Twelve, 207; and aliens, 208, 230–31

Oswald, Lee Harvey: McVeigh compared to, 60; and Kennedy assassination, 105, 110, 113, 115, 116, 120, 123–25, 126, 127, 128, 139; Ruby's killing of, 105–6, 108, 116, 124, 140, 145; portrayed as conspirator, 107, 108–9, 110, 119, 121, 129, 130–33, 135; and Central Intelligence Agency, 111, 124, 135; and Soviet Union, 132, 148; and Anti-Defamation League, 146; innocence of, 238

Oswald, Marina, 134

Paganism, 65

Palestine Liberation Organization, 163, 170

Palmer, A. Mitchell, 14–15

Panama Canal, 52

Paranoid style, and conspiracy thinking, xi–xii, 21, 151, 188, 232, 234, 239

Parks, Rosa, 178

Parris, Samuel, 3

Pearl Harbor, 18, 34

Pelley, William, 17, 19

Pentagon Papers, 254

Perloff, James, 49, 53

Perry, Malcolm, 107, 108

Pew, J. Howard, 43

Pflock, Karl, 203

Phillips, Wendell, 9

Piper, Michael, 146

Pipes, Daniel, xi

Poland, 53

Politics: and conspiracy thinking, xi, 6, 13, 20, 26, 38, 43, 45, 234, 251; and Mormons, 8; and Order of the Illuminati, 46; and Council on Foreign Relations, 48; and apocalypticism, 75, 76–77, 79, 84–85, 96; and Robertson, 88–90; and Kennedy assassination, 110; and Farrakhan, 170–72, 187; and African Americans, 181

Polygamy, 7–8

Poole, Elijah. *See* Muhammad, Elijah

Popular culture, xii, 101–2, 143, 215, 251. *See also* Media

Populist Party, 12

Porter, Robert, 196

Posner, Gerald, 141–42

Post, Jerold, xii

Powell, Adam Clayton, Jr., 159, 174

Presley, Elvis, 234

Progressive Era, 13, 46

Project Blue Book, 209–11, 216, 228, 256

Project Grudge, 209, 212

Project Sign, 209, 212

Protestantism: and conspiracy thinking, 2, 5, 8–9, 12–13, 20, 22; and Ku Klux Klan, 15; and Jews, 16, 22; and Catholic Church, 71, 153. *See also* Christianity

Protocols of the Elders of Zion, The, 16, 17, 74, 94, 172, 174

Prouty, Fletcher, 137, 138, 139, 142

Public Health Service, U.S., 175, 255
Pynchon, Thomas, 243

Quintanilla, Hector, 210
Qur'an, 176, 242

Rabin, Yitzhak, 102
Racism, 57, 165, 177
Radio: and Lindbergh, 17; and Jews, 18,
168; and Communist Party, 27, 43;
and Council on Foreign Relations, 53;
and New World Order, 58; and apocalypticism, 80, 82, 86; and Kennedy assassination, 145; and Roswell incident, 193, 198; and conspiracy
thinking, 243
Ramey, Roger, 192, 194, 196, 199, 204–
5, 214, 230
Randle, Kevin, 197–200, 202–3, 207,
210–11, 212, 219
Rangel, Charles, 171
Rapture: and apocalypticism, 72, 73, 74,
77, 79, 80, 83, 84, 89, 94, 99, 101,
103, 104; and Christian Identity
movement, 95; and conspiracy thinking, 237
Rather, Dan, 141
Ray, Dixie Lee, 60
Ray, James Earl, 235
Reagan, Ronald: and Communist Party,
27; and John Birch Society, 43–44,
48, 53; and Trilateral Commission,
52; and conspiracy thinking, 53–54,
235, 241, 259; portrayed as conspirator, 53, 256; and Federal Emergency
Management Agency, 55; and apoca-
lypticism, 82, 84; and Robertson, 89;
and Christian Identity movement, 96;
assassination attempt on, 137
Red Scare, 14, 22–23, 30, 34
Reform Party, 64
Regan, Donald, 53
Relfe, Mary, 81, 239
Religion, 7–9, 12, 20, 65, 70, 71, 75, 93.
See also Apocalypticism; Bible; Catholic Church; Christianity; Nation of Islam; Protestantism
Reno, Janet, 61–62
Republican Party: and Civil War, 10, 11;
and conspiracy thinking, 26–28, 30,
36, 38; and Welch, 38–39; and
Schlafly, 48; and Council on Foreign
Relations, 55; and Christianity, 76,

89; and Robertson, 88–89; and Afri-
can Americans, 184
Rhodes, Cecil, 49
Ribuffo, Leo, xii
Rivera, Geraldo, 127
Roberts, Oral, 82
Robertson, Pat: and conspiracy think-
ing, 67, 239, 241; and apocalypticism,
82, 84–92, 93, 102, 103; as Antichrist,
93; and Christian Identity movement,
95; and anti-Semitism, 96
Robertson Panel, 209–10, 212
Robeson, Paul, 174
Robins, Robert, xii
Robison, James, 96
Robison, John, 45
Rockefeller, David, 52, 235
Rockefeller, Nelson, 49, 207–8, 235
Rockefeller Commission, 128, 146
Rockefeller family, 49, 52, 235
Rockefeller Foundation, 48, 91
Rockwell, George Lincoln, 160
Rodeghier, Mark, 206–7
Rogin, Michael, xii
Roosevelt, Eleanor, 255
Roosevelt, Franklin D.: portrayed as con-
spirator, 17, 18, 25, 47, 137; and con-
spiracy thinking, 19, 23; and Japa-
nese Americans, 19–20; and
American Communists, 24; and
Marshall, 39; and apocalypticism,
88; and Jews, 186. See also New Deal
Roosevelt, Theodore, 13
Root, E. Merrill, 41
Roper, Hugh Trevor, 120
Rosenberg, Ethel, 30, 31, 37, 253
Rosenberg, Julius, 30, 31, 37, 253
Roswell incident: and conspiracy thinking, x, xii, 190, 204, 205–9, 212, 214–
15, 231, 237; anniversary of, 189,
225–26, 237; and motion picture industry, 190, 218, 228–29; and television, 190, 219–21, 222, 226, 229; history of, 192–204; and UFO research
community, 220, 227; and internet
websites, 222; and merchandisers,
222–23, 224
Rothschild family, 16, 52, 91, 160, 162,
179
Rovere, Richard, 120
Ruby, Jack: killing of Oswald, 105–6,
108, 116, 124, 140, 145; relationship
with Oswald, 111; and Weisberg, 119;